Lebanon County Pennsylvania

United States Direct Tax of 1798

for

Bethel Township, East Hanover Township,
Heidelberg Township, Lebanon Township,
Londonderry Township

Gladys Bucher Sowers

HERITAGE BOOKS
2006

HERITAGE BOOKS
AN IMPRINT OF HERITAGE BOOKS, INC.

Books, CDs, and more—Worldwide

For our listing of thousands of titles see our website
at
www.HeritageBooks.com

Published 2006 by
HERITAGE BOOKS, INC.
Publishing Division
65 East Main Street
Westminster, Maryland 21157-5026

Copyright © 2004 Gladys Bucher Sowers

All rights reserved. No part of this book may be reproduced or transmitted in any form or by any means, electronic or mechanical, including photocopying, recording or by any information storage and retrieval system without written permission from the author, except for the inclusion of brief quotations in a review.

International Standard Book Number: 978-1-58549-821-1

Table of Contents

	Page
Introduction	1
Historic Setting of Lebanon County	1
History of the Direct Tax of 1798	1
Property Owners	2
Assessment Forms Used	2
The Assessors	3
Information from the Assessments	4
House Summary	4
Barn Summary	5
Trades	6
Slave Owners	7
Comments/Conclusions	8
Map showing Lebanon County	10
Direct Tax of 1798 – Bethel Township	11
Direct Tax of 1798 – East Hanover Township	39
Direct Tax of 1798 – Heidelberg Township	54
Direct Tax of 1798 – Lebanon Township	88
Direct Tax of 1798 – Londonderry Township	142
Index	165

Lebanon County – Direct Tax of 1798

Introduction

The 1798 Direct Tax is an important resource tool for historians and researchers. It provides a one-time snapshot of every property in the country in 1798, including the name of the property owner, houses and their dimensions, barns and their dimensions, and all buildings, such as outhouses, kitchens, and shops, located on the property. It lists the name of tenants, acreages, and land values, slaves owned, and in most cases, it provides the name of at least one adjoining property owner. Finally, it provides an assessed value of the property listed. It is a unique tax listing that gives detailed information concerning the residents of 1798.

Historic Setting of Lebanon County

The Province of Pennsylvania originally had three counties: Chester, Bucks, and Philadelphia. On 10 May 1729 Lancaster County was formed from Chester County, and on 4 March 1785, Dauphin County was formed from Lancaster County. The townships included in this study include those Dauphin County townships which presently form Lebanon County. They are:

> Bethel Township – established 1739
> East Hanover Township – established 1785
> Heidelberg Township – established 1757
> Lebanon Township – established 1729
> Londonderry Township – established 1768

For purposes of this tax assessment, Pennsylvania was divided into divisions. The five townships listed above are included in the Fourth Division.

History of the Direct Tax of 1798

The Revolutionary War was over. George Washington had served as President of the United States from 1789 to 1797 after which he determined to retire to his Mount Vernon home. John Adams became the candidate for the Federalist Party; he opposed Thomas Jefferson of the Democratic-Republican Party. Adams won the election by 71 votes and Thomas Jefferson became the Vice-President. The inauguration of Adams took place on March 4, 1797.

During the Revolutionary War, France served as a close ally to the Colonies, but following the Revolutionary conflict, France became disillusioned with the United States. The French government believed that the Americans should help them with their quarrel with England. When help from the Americans did not come, France adopted trade regulations against this country. American vessels were captured by the French and France demanded large sums of money before negotiations could begin. The American Army, Navy and Marines were reactivated. President Adams and the Congress believed that a war with France was imminent. Money was needed.

On July 9, 1798 Congress passed an act providing "for the valuation of lands and dwelling houses and the enumeration of slaves within the United States," followed, on July 14, 1798, by the passage of "An Act to lay and collect a direct tax within the United States." The passage of this Act was intended to raise $1,000,000 to be used to increase the armed forces for the pending war with France. Congress determined that Pennsylvania's portion was to be $237,177.72. The Direct Tax of 1798 involved, as part of the assessment, counting the number of "windows" and "lights;" the tax became known as the "Window Tax." Other names became the "Glass Tax," and in some parts of the state, the "Hot Water Tax," because housewives sometimes poured hot water from the second floor window on the assessor when he came to their door.

The Tax was opposed in the form of loud protests. In Bucks County, Pennsylvania, John Fries, a farmer who had served in the Revolutionary War, gathered a force of approximately 60 men to oppose the tax. Arrests were made, the Federal Marshal arrested Fries for treason and sentenced him to death. Fries was later pardoned by President Adams after the storm of war between France and America was averted. In 1799 a treaty of peace was signed by the United States and the new leader of France, Napoleon Bonaparte.

Property Owners

A summary of the properties assessed includes:

Bethel Township	263
East Hanover Township	147
Heidelberg Township	302
Lebanon Township	501
Londonderry Township	192
Total:	1405

Assessment Forms Used

The assessment for the Townships in this study was taken by using six forms:

A - lists information on Dwelling houses and outhouses, dimensions, stories, acres, building materials, adjoining proprietors, and value (as determined by the Assistant Assessor).

B - lists Lands, Lots, Buildings, and Wharves, owned, possessed, or occupied within the specific Division. Included is the name of the owner/occupant, the barns, and other buildings (such as Smith shops, outhouses, etc., the adjoining proprietors, and valuation of the various buildings).

D - lists the valuation of the dwelling.

E - lists the valuation of the barn and outhouses.

I - provides a consolidation of information previously provided on Form A.

II -   provides a consolidation of information previously provided on Form B.

The Assessors

The Principal Assessor for all the Townships was John Thome. Assistant Assessors were as follows:

Bethel Township:	Henry Snebely
	Michael Stroh
East Hanover Township:	William Campbell
Heidelberg Township:	Mathias Bitner
	Henry Weiss
Lebanon Township:	Abraham Doebler
	Christopher Uhler
Londonderry Township:	William Hay
	Patrick Hay

Following all the assessments for a township, the Assistant Assessor/Assessors signed a statement as follows:

We the Assistant Assessor(s) of the Township of _____ in the County of Dauphin within the 4th division of the State of Pennsylvania do Certify that the foregoing List and Valuation are Just and true according to the best of my/our knowledge and belief. Witness our hands this ___ day of August 1799.

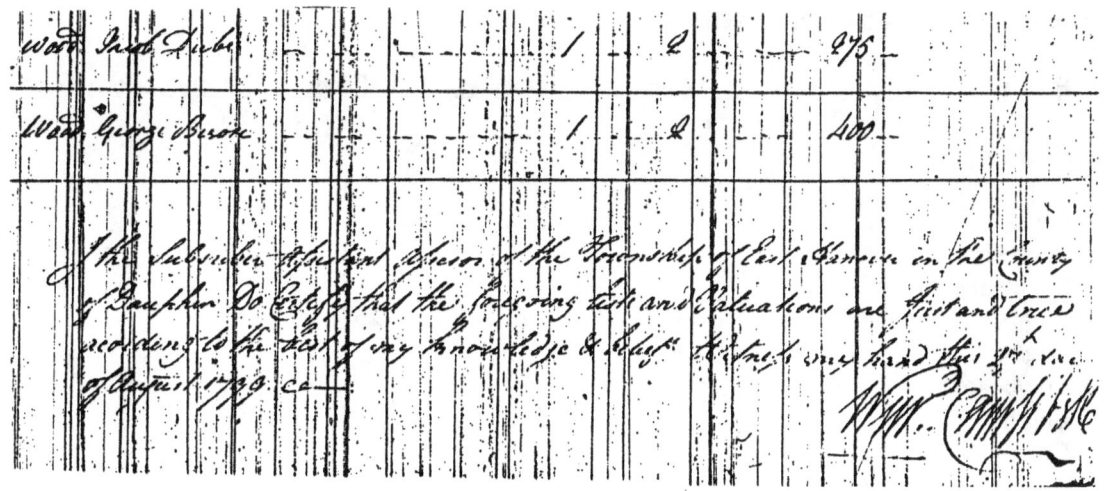

This statement was followed by the verification of John Thome, the Principal Assessor:

I do hereby Certify that on Examination of the foregoing lists and Valuations as represented by the Assistant Assessors and myself appear to me to be Justly and truly stated.

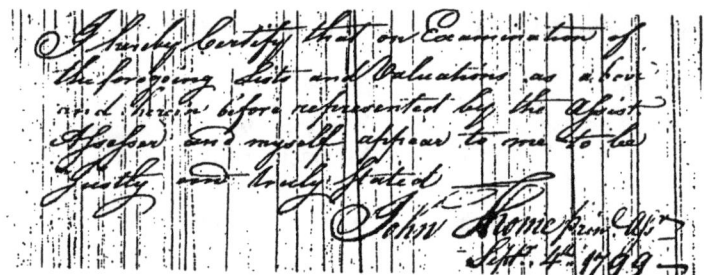

Information from the Assessments

A review of the assessment information indicates that most of the structures were built of log. Assessors used differing terminology: log, round log, square log, hewn log, log/bark, log/wood, and log/stone. Stone was also used, but was not as prevalent.

House Summary:

Total Number of houses in each Township:

Bethel: Township	332
East Hanover Township	191
Heidelberg Township	350
Lebanon Township	687
Londonderry Township	241

The assessors stated that the houses were constructed of:

House	Bethel	E. Hanover	Heidelberg	Lebanon	Londonderry
Boarded			2		
Brick			1	5	
Frame	2		2	5	
Frame/brk.			5	2	
Limestone			48	5	
Log	105	18	11	267	
Log/bark			1		
Log/board			9		
Log/hewn			233	5	
Log/rd.	2		5	1	
Log/sq.	173			73	
Log/stone			5	11	

House	Bethel	E. Hanover	Heidelberg	Lebanon	Londonderry
Log/wood	3				
Ruffstone	2				
Sandstone			2		
Stone	7	8	7	110	49
Stone/brk.			1		
Stone/wd.		3	2	10	3
Wood	8	123		149	172
Wood/brk.	1			2	
Matl. not listed	29	39	16	42	17
Total:	332	191	350	687	241

Barn Summary:

Total number of barns and bank barns in each Township:

	Barns	Bank Barns	Total
Bethel Township	105	77	182
East Hanover Township	107	23	130
Heidelberg Township	218*	--	218
Lebanon Township	340*	--	340
Londonderry Township	161*	--	161

* The assessors did not distinguish between barns and bank barns in these townships.

The barns were constructed of:

	Bethel	E. Hanover	Heidelberg	Lebanon	Londonderry
Frame				1	
Limestone			3		
Log	92	103*	77	166	
Log, bark			1		
Log, hewn			32		
Log, rd.	1	1	21		
Log, sq.	4			1	
Log/ stone	1				
Stone		7	23	80	
Stone, log			46	56	
Stone, part		16			
Wood		1		2	
Wood/stone	1			16	
Matl. not listed	83	2	15	18	161
Total:	182	130	218	340	161

*Three barns are listed as double barns.

Information on the tax records includes the condition of the buildings, frequently stating that the building was "old," "new," or "unfinished."

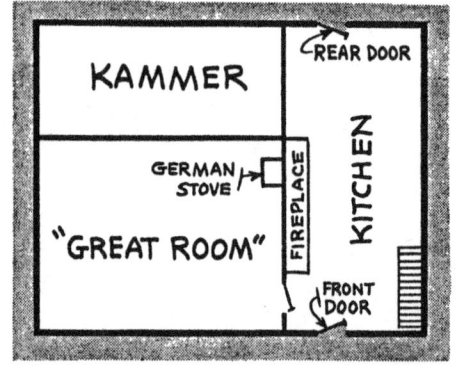

A typical first floor in a log house
(Kammer: chamber/first floor sleeping room)

A Pennsylvania bank barn with forebay

Trades

The list of shops listed by the Assessors indicates that this was an agricultural area which created a demand for many types of services in each Township. Specific shops listed are as follows:

Shop	Bethel	E. Hanover	Heidelberg	Lebanon	Londonderry
Bait House		1			
Boring Mill			2		
Brewhouse			1	1	
Brick Yard	1				
Butcher Shop				1	
Carpenter Shop				1	
Coal House		1		3	
Cooper Shop	1		1		
Coppersmith Shop				1	
Currier Shop	4				
Doctor Shop				1	
Deyer Shop				1	
Dyeing Shop				1	
Fulling Mill	1	1	1	1	
Grist/saw mill	6	3	9	20	7
Hatter Shop	3		2	9	
Hemp Mill				1	2
Joiner Shop	5		2	5	
Mill House	1	1		1	
Nailor Shop				1	

Shop	Bethel	E. Hanover	Heidelberg	Lebanon	Londonderry
Oil Mill	2			3	
Paper Mill				1	
Potter Shop	1			1	
School House	2				
Shoemaker Shop				1	
Smith Shop	21	6	9	32	9
Still House	22	5	8	22	4
Tanyard		3	2	7	2
Tanyard/Barkhouse		1			
Turner Shop			1		
Wagonmaker shop	2	2	2	6	
Weaver Shop	7	1	4	3	6
Wood Shop	1				

Some of the trades are well known; others may be forgotten. A few of the industries listed above may require explanation:

Fulling Mill – "Fulling" is the process whereby wool is scoured, beaten, and cleansed of the lanolin grease with which sheep make themselves warm and waterproof.[1]

Tanyard, Tanyard/Barkhouse – A place where hides are tanned, i.e., converted into leather by steeping them in an infusion of oak or some other bark, by which they are impregnated with tannin or tannic acid. The tanner prepared leather for harnesses, collars for horses, aprons, belts, leather for shoes; he sold hair to felt makers, plasterers and brick makers; he sold hoofs and horns to glue makers, and fat to soap and candle makers.[2]

Still House – Many types of beverages were produced in the Still house. Distilling spirits was an integral part of life in colonial times; spirits were used for medicinal purposes and were sold to local taverns by independent farmers. In addition to rye whiskey, corn whiskey, and applejack, distilleries were also used to produce birch, sassafras and wintergreen drinks.

Slave Owners

The assessors recorded eight land owners who had a total of 14 slaves. Tax records for 1798 provide the following information:

Township	Owner	Whole No. of Slaves of All Ages	No. of Slaves Exempted from Taxation by Law or Disability	No. of Slaves above 12 and under 50 years of age subject to taxation
Bethel	--	--	--	--

---

[1] Simon Winchester. The Map that Changed the World – William Smith and the Birth of Modern Geology. (New York: HarperCollins Publishers, Inc., 2002), p. 104.
[2] Carter W. Craigie. "Tanning in Chester County, Pennsylvania 1711 – 1850." Pennsylvania Folklife. Vol. XVIII, No. 1, pp. 2-15. Autumn 1968.

Township	Owner	Whole No. of Slaves of All Ages	No. of Slaves Exempted from Taxation by Law or Disability	No. of Slaves above 12 and under 50 years of age subject to taxation
E. Hanover	Boal, Robert	1	--	1
	Bradley, Dan'l.	1	--	1
Heidelberg		--	--	--
Lebanon	Coleman, Robt.	5	2	3
	Buehlor, Henry	1	--	1
	Ulrich, Martin	1	--	1
Londonderry	Hays, Patrick	3	--	3
	Hays, Robert	1	1	--
	Kelly, James	1	1	--

Comments/Conclusions:

It should be noted that sometimes individual property identification numbers on the tax assessor's lists (e.g., B29, B88, B126, etc.) were erroneously duplicated by the assessors. Numbers are not always written in consecutive order and some lists have only portions of the properties numbered. Numbers presented in this study are those listed by the tax assessors.

The assessors listed the names of the property owners alphabetically by the first letter of the last name only. The names have here been alphabetized for each township and numbers for each property (1, 2, 3, etc.) have been added.

Each property lists the name of the owner in bold print. If a tenant is listed for the property, his/her name appears in lighter print below the name of the owner.

Assessors sometimes listed the name as they heard it. Examples include Lightner, Leightner and Littner; Mayer, Moyer, and Meyer, and Saybold, Seybold, and Sebolt. In this volume, all variations of names appear as written in the assessments. The index includes all names as entered by the assessors.

The numbers appearing below the name of the owner and occupant (A10 B10 D10 E10 I- II-) are reference numbers. They indicate the forms used by the assessor and the numbers assigned to the property by the assessor. They are provided for those who wish to refer to the original microfilm. The assessor did not number the names on Forms I and II, thus the designation I- and II- are noted.

The column labeled "Adjoining" lists the name of the adjoining property owner which the assessor listed on his forms. These names should be helpful to those who wish to reconstruct the area in which a 1798 resident lived.

While Bethel Township and East Hanover Township assessors provided "window" and "light" information for a few properties, Londonderry Township assessors collected this information on many of the houses, kitchens, and spring houses.

The amount of property owned was listed by acres and perches; one acre of land equals 160 perches. Assessors noted any structure which was not completed by 1 October 1798. Assessment was not made on these properties.

The Index located at the end of this book shows all names listed throughout the assessments. Each listing includes the page on which the name appears as well as the township where the property was located.

The Pennsylvania Direct Tax lists are contained in National Archives Record Group M-372. Every effort has been made to accurately list the material provided in this document. The text has been checked several times, however, errors may still exist.

The size of houses listed herein seems quite small compared to the homes of today. An entire log home might fit into a present day family room. Researchers may obtain further information on the families who lived in these houses by searching the 1800 Census records.

Assessors sometimes listed more than requested information. For example, the assessor wrote that Henry Landis, of Londonderry Township, used the upper story of his home for a Meeting House; John Reily (Heidelberg Township) claimed himself "exempted from paying tax by reason of a wound received during the American Revolution," and Casper Brensencober (Bethel Township) was "an old blind poor man." Jacob Keller (Lebanon Township) "acknowledges to have 14 acres more. Has made a fraudulent return," and John Stoever (Lebanon Township) "has not made a return of all his lands – fraudulent."

Assessors described the quality of the land. Many farms in Bethel Township had "gravel land." East Hanover Township had mainly "gravel land" and "clay land;" while Heidelberg Township had many properties with "oak land" or "limestone land." Descriptions of land in Lebanon and Londonderry Township land varied; but assessors listed many properties with "limestone land."

Although not assessed as such, the owners of Taverns and Public Houses are sometimes indicated. Tavern owners include Christopher Capp (Bethel); Frederick Bullman, John Kapp, Godfry Kiener, Peter Leiss, John Meisser, Samuel Rex, and Henry Shaefer, Esq. (Heidelberg). Public Houses are listed only in Lebanon Township and include William Bergenhoff, Christian Casel, Anthony Doebler, John Dubs, Philip Fisher, and John Stoever.

Those who are descendants of persons listed in these pages can find evidence of the size, condition, and value of their ancestral homes. Names and measurements listed on the assessments may be compared to old deeds and records of original family homesteads. Neighbors listed on these assessments sometimes hold the key to family marriages. The search for information on "family history" is important. The information listed in this tax assessment helps to provide a glimpse of the kind of houses in which our ancestors lived, the trades with which they were associated, and the properties they held.

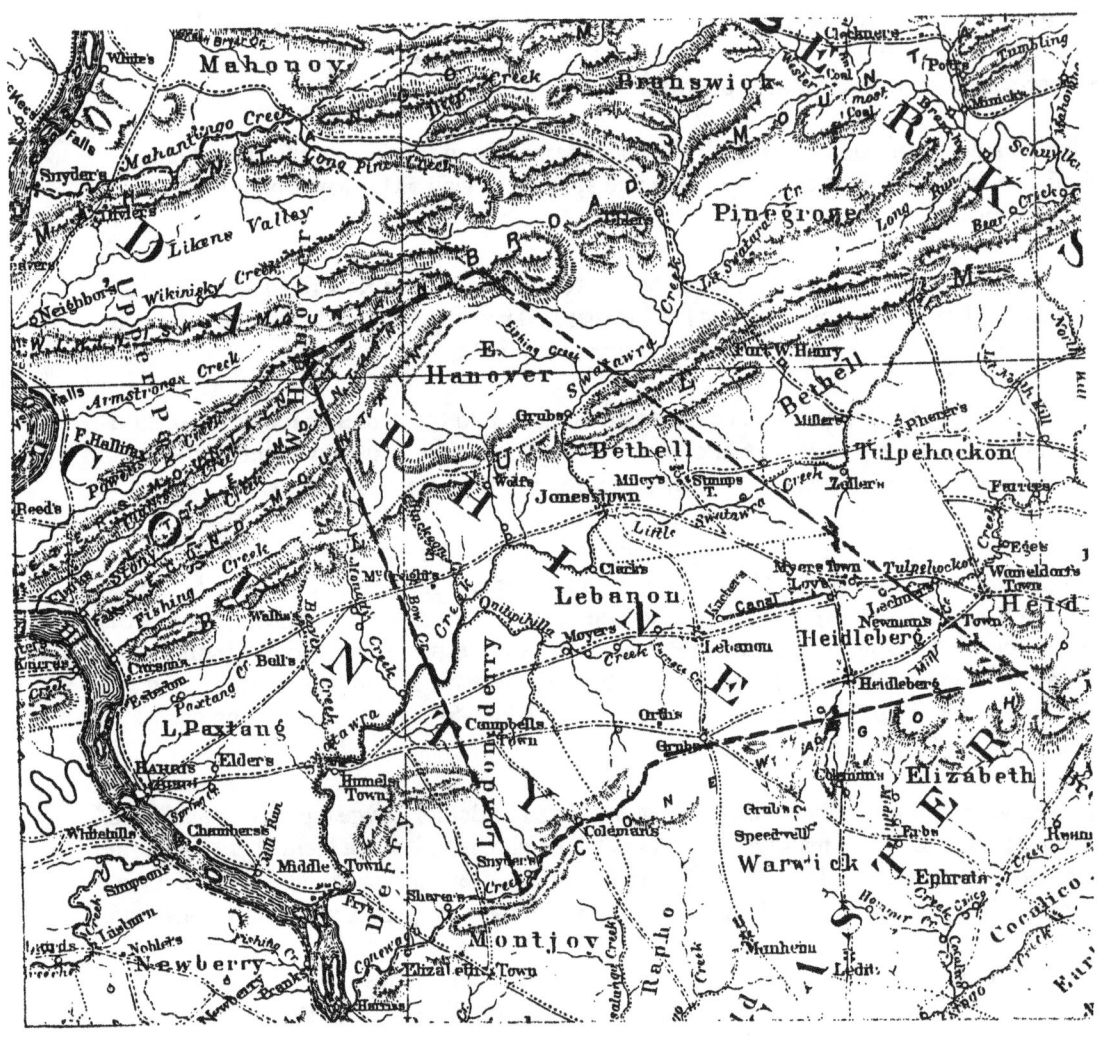

1792 map of Dauphin County indicating the area which later became Lebanon County. This area includes the following Townships: Bethel, East Hanover, Heidelberg, Lebanon and Londonderry.

Direct Tax of 1798 - Bethel Township

No.	Owner/Occupant/Ref.	Adjoining	Building	Dimen.	Matls.	Stories	Acres Perch	Assmt.	Valuation
1	**Ache, John** A3 B3 D3 E3 I-3 II-	Woolf, John	House Stable	20 x 20 12 x 12	sq. log rd. log	2	24P	150	187.50
			In Jones Town. New building but indifferently finished.						
			Lot in Jonestown.				48P		10
2	**Albert, Nicholas** A1 B1 D1 E1 I-1 II-	Shuy, Martin	House Spring house	35 x 30 20 x 18	ruffstone stone/log	2	2A	880	1100
			House good and well finished.						
			Barn	99 x 25	stone/wd.		210A		3465
			Good land.						
3	**Anderson, James** Lynch, James I-	Stoner, Jacob	House	40 x 20	wood		1A		
			6 windows, 52 lights.						
4	**Artz, John** A2 B2 D2 E2 I-2 II-	Litener, Jacob	House	28 x 26	sq. log	2	2A	150	187.50
			New house upper story unfinished since October last.						
			Stable Smith shop	24 x 18 20 x 15	log log		38A		228
			Poor gravel.						
5	**Bacastose, Henry** A25 B22 D25 E22 I-29 II-	Bacastose, Jacob	House Barn	25 x 16 55 x 20	sq. log log	1	2A 94A	150	187.50 564
			Gravel land and no timber on it.						
6	**Bacastose, Jacob** A17 B16 D17 E16 I-19 II-	Walborn, Martin	House Stable	28 x 25 39 x 15	sq. log log	1	2A 94A	175	218.75 564
			New house. Poor gravel land.						
7	**Batteicher, Saml.** A24 D24 I-28	Kitler, Jacob	House Shop Stable	30 x 20 20 x 15 15 x 12	sq. log sq. log log	2 1	40P	175	218.75
			Wagon maker shop. Stumpstown. Midling good house.						
8	**Battelgor, Casper** **Batteicher, Casper** A10 B9 D10 E9 I-11 II-	Meily, Jacob	House Spring house Barn	28 x 25 20 x 18 51 x 21	sq. log sq. log log	2 1	2A 128A	225	281.25 1280
			Gravel land. House not well finished.						
			Mountain land on south side of Little Mountain (wood land).				30A		8
9	**Batz, John** B5 E5 II-	Beny, Melchr.	House	20 x 18	log		100A		400
10	**Beck, Michael** A18 B17 D18 E17 I-20 II-	King, Peter	House Stable	18 x 15 20 x 18	sq. log log	1	2A 1A 120P	100	125 17.50
			Old house put back over road.						

Direct Tax of 1798 - Bethel Township

No.	Owner/Occupant/Ref.	Adjoining	Building	Dimen.	Matls.	Stories	Acres Perch.	Assmt.	Valuation
	A4 B4 D4 E4 I-4 II-		Old house, but good, well finished.						
			Barn	54 x 24	log		153A		1530
			Still house	30 x 37					
			Smith shop	18 x 46					
			Stony land.						
12	Becker, Jacob B28 E28 II-	Hunsecker, Rudy	House (poor) Stable	13 x 18			16A 109P		85
13	Becker, John A19 B18 D19 E18 I-21 II-	Seltzer, John	House Kitchen Stable, old	22 x 19 22 x 10 18 x 12	sq. log sq. log sq. log	1	48P	100	125
		Heilman, George	Lot in Jonestown. Old house. Poor man. Has been "exemtet" from tax this several years past. All the buildings old.				1A 32P		25
14	Bender, Adam B27 E27 II-	Leamy, Jacob	Land				48A		10
15	Bene, Henry Ben, Henry Been, Henry A26 B23 D26 E23 I-30 II-	Bene, Jacob Ben, Jacob	House (old) House Barn New house upper story not finished. Stony gravel land.	35 x 30 20 x 18 24 x 18	stone log	2 1	2A 142A	500	625 1136
16	Beny, Melchior Beny, John Glesmer, Abm. Gebhart, Nicolas A9 B7 B8 D9 E7 E8 I-9 I-10 II-	Beshor, John Glinfelter, Albert	House (good) House Midling good log house. Barn House Barn Stable	28 x 25 25 x 22 30 x 20 18 x 15 65 x 24 18 x 15	sq. log sq. log log log stone/log	1 1	2A 2A 150A 260A	250 160	312.50 200 600 2730
		Weaver, Philip	House Poor gravel land. Old House.	22 x 18			48P		65
17	Beshor, Elisabh. A28 B25 D28 E25 I-32 II-	Rudy, Jonas	House Barn Old house. Old barn. Gravel land.	20 x 17 57 x 24	sq. log log	1	2A 173A	100	125 1730
18	Beshor, John A8 B8 D8 E8 I-8 II-	Satezan, Adam	House Spring house Bank barn Old. But good house. Partly new. Good gravel land.	28 x 21 18 x 15 55 x 25	sq. log log/stone	2 1	2A 148A	360 1776	450
19	Beshor, John Wetzel, Wm. A13 B12 D13 E12 I-14 I-15 II-	Long, Isral Capp, Jacob	House House (old) Stable Good well finished house. Near "Swetara."	30 x 28 24 x 20 30 x 18	sq. log sq. log sq. log	2 1	2A 2A	610	762.50
		Title, Henry	House Stable Good house, old Stable.	24 x 20 15 x 12	sq. log log	2	2A 48P	310	387.50
		Graybill, Israel	Bank barn Loam bottom. Good gravel land. Good meadow.	50 x 24			198A		2970

Direct Tax of 1798 - Bethel Township

No.	Owner/Occupant/Ref.	Adjoining	Building	Dimen.	Matls.	Stories	Acres Perch.	Assmt.	Valuation
		Krider, Lewis	Meadow lot in Jonestown.				1A 140P		45
20	**Beshor, Peter**	Capp, Jacob	House	27 x 22	sq. log	2	2A	330	412.50
	Beshor, John		Spring house	12 x 12	sq. log				
	A21 B20 D21 E20 I-24 I-25 II-		Stable	20 x 16	log				
			Good finished house. Spring house old.						
		Wirt, Conrat	House	18 x 15	sq. log	1	2A	100	125
			Bank barn	77 x 28			138A		1242
			Stable	15 x 15			48P		288
			Old house. Gravel and loam bottom land.						
21	**Bickle, John**		House	32 x 28	sq. log	2	40P	1300	1625
	Bickle, John Jr.		Kitchen	14 x 12	sq. log	1			
	A5 D5 I-5		Stable	18 x 20	sq. log				
			House	33 x 28	sq. log	2			
			Wash house	28 x 10	frame	1			
			Corner Lot, Jonestown; occupied by the owner. The first three buildings and the other by his son. The houses are finished and in good order.						
22	**Bickel, John Esq.**		House	37 x 24	sq. log	2	40P	860	1075
	Boyer, John		Kitchen	12 x 10	sq. log	1			
	Herman, Dan'l.		Stable	30 x 12	sq. log				
	A6 B6 D6 E6 I-6 II-	Huby, Fred	House	30 x 26	sq. log	2			
			Old house. Corner lot in Jonestown on Market Square adjoining Fred Huby's new house. Houses both on one lot, they are well finished, good order, The last is only built and finished since last October.						
		Herman, George	Lot in Jones Town.				1A 142P		30
		Beshor, John	Lot in Jones Town.				60P		50
		Martin, King	Lot in Jones Town.				144P		30
23	**Bixler, Joseph**	Holdeman, John	House	30 x 25	log				300
	B29 E29 I-35 II-		Spring house	20 x 18	log				
			Barn	57 x 27			150A		1950
			Good gravel land.						
24	**Brado, Kitty**	Snebly, Henry	House	24 x 20	sq. log	2	96P	125	156.25
	A23 D23 I-27		Stable	15 x 12	rd. log				
			Poor widow. Stumpstown. Old Stable.						
25	**Brand, Adam**	Spitler, John	House	18 x 15	log	1	2A	100	125
	A27 B24 D27 E24 I-31 II-		Lot				116A		1392
			Old house. Good gravel land.						
26	**Brecht, John**	Houtz, John	House	18 x 18	rd. log	2	48P	150	187.50
	Harman, John		Kitchen	18 x 7	rd. log	1			
	A20 B19 D20 E19 I-22 I-23 II-		Stable, old	18 x 12	rd. log				
			All small buildings of old logs. Jonestown, back street.						
		Shindle, Peter	House	27 x 22	wood	2	96P	300	375
		(in Stumpstown)	Store Kitchen	27 x 12	wood	1			
			Stable	20 x 16	wood				

Direct Tax of 1798 - Bethel Township

No.	Owner/Occupant/Ref.	Adjoining	Building	Dimen.	Matls.	Stories	Acres Perch.	Assmt.	Valu-ation
		Campbell, John	Lot in Jonestown.				1A 46P		64
		Kittle, Jacob	Lot in Stumpstown.				96P		15
			Good houses in Stumpstown.						
27	**Brensencober, Casp.**	Wengert, John	House	20 x 15	log	1	2A	100	125
	Brensenkobr, Casp.	Straw, Michl.	Stable	18 x 15			5A		60
	A-29 B-26 D-29 E26 I-34 II-		Old house. The man is an old blind poor man.						
			Midling good land.						
28	**Brichbill, John**	Shewey, Martin	House	30 x 28	sq. log	1	2A	182	227.50
	A14 B13 D14 E13 I-16 II-		House	18 x 15	wood				
			Bank barn	65 x 24			158A		2680
			Midling good house. 18 x 15 house is old.						
			Good land, barn good.						
29	**Brown, David**	Brown, Jacob	House	28 x 25	sq. log	1	2A	100	125
	A16 B15 D16 E15 I-18 II-		Barn	42 x 25	log		106A		1272
			Old house. Good land, old barn.						
30	**Brown, Jacob**	Brown, David	House	30 x 26	sq. log	2	2A	425	531.25
	A15 B14 D15 E14 I-17 II-		Barn	60 x 28	log		106A		1272
			Good land. New, well finished house.						
31	**Bruner, Daniel**	Beck, Philip	House	24 x 20	sq. log	2	2A	200	250
	A7 B7 D7 E7 I-7 II-	Faver, Philip	Barn	20 x 15	sq. log		18A		144
			New house, upper story not finished. Poor land.						
32	**Bucher, Peter**	Fetterhoff, Balzar	House (old)	21 x 18	sq. log	1	2A	100	125
	A12 B10 D12 E10 I-13 II-		Barn	30 x 15	log		11A		66
			Stony gravel land.						
33	**Buchmyer, John**	Rudy, Jonas	House	33 x 30	sq. log	1	2A	275	343.75
	BuchMeier, John		Spring house	24 x 20	log/stone	1			
	A11 B11 D11 E11 I-12 II-		Barn	56 x 28	log		113A		1130
			Old. House well finished. Gravel land.						
34	**Bun, Jacob**	Bun, Henry	House	30 x 20	sq. log	1	2A	175	218.75
	A22 B21 D22 E21 I-26 II-		Barn	40 x 20	log		137A		1370
			Stony gravel land.						
35	**Capp, Christopher**	Ranck, John	House	51 x 30	sq. log	2	48P	1200	1500
	Capp, Christn.		Kitchen	27 x 15	sq. log	1			
	A32 B32 D32 E32 I-39 II-		Stable	30 x 14	log				
			Shed	30 x 12	frame				
			Shed	25 x 12	frame				
			Two Lots in Jonestown.				96P		18
			Well finished house. Good stand for Tavern.						
36	**Capp, Jacob**	Wilhelm, Henry	House	30 x 20	sq. log	2	40P	800	1000
	Haffa, John	(Jonestown -	Kitchen	12 x 10	sq. log	1			
	Capp, Christian	corner House)	Shed	27 x 12	frame				
	A30 B30 D30 E30 I-36 I-37 II-		Stable	30 x 15	log				

Direct Tax of 1798 - Bethel Township

No.	Owner/Occupant/Ref.	Adjoining	Building	Dimen.	Matls.	Stories	Acres Perch.	Assmt.	Valuation
			Good house, well finished.						
		Beshor, Peter	House (new)	27 x 24	sq. log	2	1A	350	437.50
			House	30 x 24	sq. log	1	1A	275	343.75
			Old, good house.					25	
			Spring house	15 x 12	sq. log				
		Beshor, John	Barn	72 x 26	log		156A		2184
			Barn	49 x 20	log				
			Still house	24 x 20					
			Bark barn	20 x 18					
			Loam bottom and good gravel land. Meadows good.						
37	Clark, Thomas B29 E29 II-	Knegey, Jacob	Bank barn	25 x 20			52A		416
			Grist/sawmill	70 x 28					1800
			Spring house						
		Steckpeck, Michl.	Lot - Stony woodland.				11A		44
			Gravel land.						
38	Conrad, Jacob A31 B31 D31 E31 I-38 II-	Herner, Michael	House (old)	40 x 18	sq. log	2	2A	100	125
			Barn	50 x 24	log		100A		600
			Poor gravel land.						
39	Daub, John A36 B35 D36 E35 I-43 II-	Ditzler, Casper	House (good)	27 x 21	sq. log	2	2A	350	437.50
			Bank barn	48 x 21			110A		660
			Gravel land, no timber.						
40	Derr, Rudolph Brown, Philip A41 D41 I-49	Hauty, John	House	28 x 27	sq. log	2	96P	300	375
			Kitchen	28 x 12	sq. log	1			
			Stable	20 x 12	log				
			Old house, old buildings.						
41	Desh, John Dixler, Abraham A33 D33 I-40	Strohm, Abraham	House	28 x 24	sq. log	2	2A	325	406.25
			Good new house.						
			House (old)	18 x 15	sq. log	1			
	Desh, John A34 B33 D35 E33 I-41 II-	Beny, Melchor	House	30 x 27	sq. log	1	2A	225	281.25
			Good old house.						
			Spring house	18 x 16	stone/wd.	1			
			Bank barn	63 x 26			128A		1280
			Good barn, gravel land.						
			Mountain land				30A		30
			Bank barn	70 x 24			102A		1020
			Barn good, gravel land.						
			Mountain land.				15A		15
42	Desh, Margaret Walborn, Andw. B39 E39 II-	Wagoner, John	House	27 x 20	log		48P		70
			In Stumps Town.						
		Overholser, Christn.	Stable	15 x 10			2A		32
			Meadow lot.						
43	Dice, David Deiss, David	Fisher, Jacob	House	30 x 25	sq. log	2	2A	650	812.50
			Spring house	22 x 19	sq. log	2			

Direct Tax of 1798 - Bethel Township

No.	Owner/Occupant/Ref.	Adjoining	Building	Dimen.	Matls.	Stories	Acres Perch.	Assmt.	Valu-ation
	A38 B37 D38 E37 I-45 II-		Good new house and Spring house.						
			Old house	20 x 13					
			Bank barn	60 x 25			270A		2430
			Stable	15 x 12					
			Stable	30 x 15					
			Stable	18 x 15					
			Stony and gravel land.						
44	Dice, John	Wolf, Christian	House (good)	30 x 27	sq. log	1	2A	200	250
	Deiss, John		Barn	40 x 20	log		200A		1800
	Everhard, John		Gravel land, good timber.						
	A37 B36 D37 E36 I-44 II-								
45	Dixler, Casper	Lightner, Jacob	House (good)	32 x 28	sq. log	2	2A		520
	Ditzler, Casper		House (old)	18 x 16	sq. log	1			
	A35 B34 D35 E34 I-42 II-		Spring house	15 x 12	sq. log	1			
			Bank barn	60 x 25			203A		1624
			Old house not finished. Spring House is old.						
			Barn good, gravel land.						
46	Dubbs, Henry	Zering, Jacob	House	30 x 26	sq. log	1	2A	210	262.50
	Ludwig, Casper	Zearing, Jacob	Spring house	10 x 8	stone	1			
	A39 B38 D39 E38 I-46 I-47 II-		Barn	90 x 21	log		186A		2883
			Still house	20 x 18					
			Good gravel land and good meadow.						
		Wilt, Jacob	House	36 x 28	log	1	2A	160	200
			Spring house	10 x 8	stone				10
			Barn	70 x 26	log		115A		1380
			Old houses. Good gravel land and good meadow.						
47	Dubbs, John	Ranck, Peter	House	28 x 24	sq. log	2	48P	250	312.50
	Leamy, Christian		Smith shop	22 x 10	log				
	A40 D40 I-48		John Dups, deceased. Old house, old shop.						
48	Egler, Jacob	Hower, Fred	House (old)	24 x 18	sq. log	1	96P	100	125
	A45 D45 I-53		Stable (old)	15 x 12					
49	Eller, Michael	Seltzer, John	House (old)	28 x 22	sq. log	2	48P	200	250
	A44 B42 D44 E42 I-52 II-		Stable	18 x 12	log				
		Grumbine, Jacob	Lot in Jonestown				96P		18
50	Emrich, Widow	Isenhawer, John	House (old)	27 x 16	sq. log	1	2A	125	156.25
	Bader, Geo.	Esinhower, John	Barn	57 x 24	log		110A		880
	A43 B41 D43 E41 I-51 II-		Gravel land.						
51	Esinhower, John	Fetterhoff, Baltzer	House	25 x 24	sq. log	2	2A	320	400
	Eysenhouer, John		Spring house	20 x 15	stone				
	A42 B40 D42 E40 I-50 II-		Bank barn	50 x 21			122A		976
			Upper story of house unfinished. Gravel land.						
52	Faber, Jacob (heirs)	Beany, Melchor	House (old)	33 x 18	sq. log	1	2A	125	156.25

Direct Tax of 1798 - Bethel Township

No.	Owner/Occupant/Ref.	Adjoining	Building	Dimen.	Matls.	Stories	Acres Perch.	Assmt.	Valuation
	Fisher, Michael A48 B45 D48 E45 I-56 II-		Barn Still house	40 x 18	log		80A		640
			Mountain land - adjoining Little Mtn. Stony and gravel land. Stony wood land.				16A		16
53	Faber, Margaret A49 B46 D49 E46 I-57 II-	Beany, Melchor	House Wagonmaker shop	24 x 15 18 x 16	sq. log	1	2A	125	156.25
			Barn Midling good house. Gravel land.	48 x 20	log		73A		584
54	Faber, Philip A51 B48 D51 E48 I-59 II-	Wendelblech, Adam	House (good) Bank barn Oil mill Smith shop Gravel land.	32 x 28 60 x 24 24 x 18	sq. log	2	2A 220A	475	593.75 2310
55	Feehman, Leonard Fehman, Leond. A46 B43 D46 E43 I-54 II-	Hautz, John	House Barn Old house out of repair. Gravel land.	40 x 24 50 x 24	sq. log log	1	2A 198A	150	187.50 1980
56	Feeman, George Fihman, George Niss, Jacob	Wengart, John	House Spring house	28 x 22 26 x 20	sq. log sq. log	2 2	2A	450	562.50
	Neise, Jacob Ness, Jacob A66 B58 D66 E58 I-75 I-76 II-	Besore, Peter	House midling good. Spring House not finished. House (old) Bank barn	24 x 20 80 x 20	sq. log	1	2A 188A	150	187.50 2256
			Gravel land, good meadow. Stable Poor gravel past bottom.	20 x 20	sq. log		138A		1104
57	Feeser, Peter Firrer, Petter A63 D63 I-72	Miley, Jacob	House (old) Kitchen Barn	26 x 16 26 x 10 27 x 18	sq. log sq. log sq. log	2 1	1A 32P	225	281.25
58	Feeser, Peter Jackey, Lorentz A53 B50 D53 E50 I-61	Shewey, Martin Shewey, Mart.	House (old) Out house	30 x 30 30 x 20	sq. log stone	1 1	2A	400	500
			30 x 20 house joins the old house. Out house Bank barn Good limestone land. Still house House Barn Mountain land - stony.	24 x 18 110 x 26 35 x 18 20 x 18 30 x 20	sq. log log	1	168A 220A		3348 440
59	Feesich, George Foessig, George A65 D65 I-74	Eller, Michl.	House (old) Kitchen Hatter shop	20 x 18 20 x 9 20 x 10	rd. log frame rd. log	1	48P	100	125
60	Felker, Henry A56 B53 D56 E53 I-64 II-	Shally, John	House (good) Barn	26 x 24 40 x 18	stone log	1	2A 77A	350	437.50 462

Direct Tax of 1798 - Bethel Township

No.	Owner/Occupant/Ref.	Adjoining	Building	Dimen.	Matls.	Stories	Acres Perch.	Assmt.	Valuation
			Smith shop	20 x 15					
			Stony land.						
61	**Felty, Sebastian**	Saylor, Peter	House (old)	35 x 24	sq. log	1	2A	200	250
	Yeakly, Henry		House	20 x 17		1			
	A62 B57 D62 E57 I-71 II-		Barn	45 x 22			200A		1400
			Stable	20 x 20					
			Stony land.						
62	**Felty, Ulrich**	Homan, Fred	House (old)	19 x 15	sq. log	1	144P	120	150
	A59 D59 I-68		Stable (good)	20 x 20	log				
63	**Fetterer, Stephen**	Hiller, George	House (good)	20 x 16	sq. log	1	48P	100	125
	Fitterrn, Stephen		Stable	15 x 12	rd. log				
	A57 D57 I-65								
64	**Fetterhof, Balzer**	Isenhawer, John	House	28 x 26	sq. log	2	2A	250	312.50
	A47 B44 D47 E44 I-55 II-	Esinhower, John	Barn	55 x 16	log		160A		720
			House new but not finished. Stony and gravel land.						
65	**Fiegart, William**	Lidig, Kitty	House (good)	25 x 20	sq. log	2	48P	200	250
	Figart, William		Stable	16 x 12					
	A61 D61 I-70								
66	**Figart, Hannah**	Figart, Wm.	House	12 x 11		1	48P		25
	B56 E56 II-		Poor lot in Jonestown.						
67	**Fisher, Jacob**	Miller, Henry	House (old)	24 x 20	sq. log	1	2A	200	250
	Fetterhof, Jacob		Spring house	20 x 18	sq. log	1			
	A54 B51 D54 E51 I-62 II-		Bank barn	70 x 22			260A		2080
			Stable	18 x 12					
			Still house	20 x 18					
			Stony land.						
68	**Fisher, Vendel**	Clinefelter, Abm.	House (new)	27 x 24	sq. log	2	2A	200	250
	Fisher, Wendel	Kleinfelter, Albt.	House (old)	20 x 18	sq. log	1			
	A52 B49 D52 E49 I-60 II-		Barn	36 x 16	log		148A		962
			Stable	15 x 12					
			Poor gravel land.						
			Lot - Stony mountain land.				60A		120
69	**Fogel, Andrew**	Young, Jacob	House	24 x 20	sq. log	2	48P	200	250
	A64 D64 I-73		Smith shop	20 x 15	log/wood				
			Stable	18 x 10	rd. log				
			Buildings midling good.						
70	**Fox, Henry**	Yechly, Rudy	House (good)	28 x 26	sq. log	2	2A	450	562.50
	Fuchs, Henry	Yeakly, Rudy	Bank barn	60 x 24			148A		1480
	A55 B52 D55 E52 I-63 II-		Weaver shop	18 x 12					
			Gravel land.						

Direct Tax of 1798 - Bethel Township

No.	Owner/Occupant/Ref.	Adjoining	Building	Dimen.	Matls.	Stories	Acres Perch.	Assmt.	Valuation
71	Frank, Barbara Franck, Barbara Spitler, Jacob A50 B47 D50 E47 I-58 I-59 II-	Spitler, John	House Spring house Midling good House. House (old) Bank barn Good gravel land. Barn Stony and gravel land.	30 x 30 18 x 15 40 x 18 60 x 24 24 x 15	sq. log log sq. log log	2 1 1	2A 2A 134A 28A	480 125	600 156.25 2010 168
72	Frelinghausen, Peter A60 D60 I-69	Fetterer, Stephen	House Stable Good house. The lot good.	24 x 18 20 x 12	sq. log rd. log	2	80P	250	312.50
73	Fuchs, Barbara B54 E54 II-	Volkmartz, Fred Waldemartz, F.	House (old) In Stumbstown.	20 x 16	log		48P		25
74	Fulk, Christn. Fulck, Christian A58 B55 D58 E55 I-67 II-	Rancke, John	House Kitchen House Shed Stable School House in Jonestown. Old house out of repair. Shed & Stable good. Corner lot in Jonestown.	28 x 22 28 x 10 12 x 10 35 x 15 24 x 12	sq. log sq. log sq. log frame log	2 1 1	48P 48P	600	750 7
75	Gassert, Jacob Est. A77 B67 D77 E67 I-86 II-	Felty, Sebastian	House Kitchen House Bank barn New house, good finish. Stone and gravel land.	36 x 27 15 x 12 27 x 21 80 x 30	sq. log	2 1	2A 170A	520	650 1360
76	Geesy, George B59 E59	Overholser, Christn.	House (old) Stable	30 x 20 18 x 15	log		48P		50
77	Gembill, John Gembell, John A67 D67 I-77	Bright, John	House Stable Old house, upper story unfinished. Old stable.	26 x 22 15 x 10	sq. log log	2	144P	225	281.25
78	George, Henry A69 D69 I-79	Lauch, John	House (good)	24 x 20	log	2	72P	300	375
79	Gettle, Jacob Gettel, Jacob A80 B70 D80 E70 I-89 II-	Botiger, Saml. Bright, John Overholser, Christn.	House Kitchen Barn Corner house in Stumps Town. Three lots in Stumtstown. Meadow lot in Stumtstown.	30 x 26 30 x 12 30 x 18	sq. log sq. log sq. log	2 1	80P 144P 2A	600	750 18 25
80	Gilbert, Samuel A73 B63 D73 E63 I-82 II-	Lantz, Abraham Overholser, Christ.	House (old) Stable Currier shop Beam house	21 x 17 30 x 15 20 x 15	sq. log	1	50P 2A 50P 48P 1A 128P	100	125 200 60 60

Direct Tax of 1798 - Bethel Township

No.	Owner/Occupant/Ref.	Adjoining	Building	Dimen.	Matls.	Stories	Acres Perch.	Assmt.	Valuation
			60 acres meadow lot.						
81	**Gneagy, Jacob** Gneagey, Jacob A78 B68 D78 E68 I-87 II-	Leamy, Tobias Light, Henry	House (old) Bank barn Mountain land Gravel land.	36 x 26 55 x 25	sq. log	1	2A 125A 50A	200	250 1063 150
82	**Greechbam, Wm.** Grichbam, Wm. Grigbaum, Wilm. Zander, Michl. A76 B66 D76 E66 I-84 II-	Hochlander, Geo.	House Bank barn Stony and gravel land.	30 x 26 48 x 24	sq. log	1	2A 128A	200	250 896
83	**Groh, John** A72 B62 D72 E62 I-81 II-	Hunsecker, Saml.	House Spring house Bank barn Mountain land Old house out of repair. Farm has good gravel land.	50 x 25 20 x 18 80 x 30	sq. log sq. log	1 1	2A 136A 25A	150	187.50 2040 50
84	**Groh, Peter** A75 B65 D75 E65 I-84 II-	Miley, Henry Meily, Henry	House (old) Barn Weaver shop Mountain land Good gravel land. Mountain land is woodland.	30 x 28 45 x 22 24 x 20	sq. log sq. log	1 1	2A 80A 25A	275	343.75 1200 50
85	**Grove, Jacob** A79 B69 D79 E69 I-88 II-	Witt, Jacob	House Barn Good gravel land. House is old.	33 x 26 77 x 26	sq. log log	2	2A 143A	500	625 2002
86	**Grove, Peter** Groff, Peter A74 B64 D74 E64 I-83 II-	Overholser, Jacob Meily, Henry	House Spring house Bank barn The house midling. Good gravel land.	30 x 28 20 x 16 63 x 22	sq. log	2 1	2A 125A	360	450 1875
87	**Grumbine, Jacob** A68 D68 I-78	Pickel, John	House Built since 1st of October. Not finished.	30 x 26	sq. log	2	48P		400
88	**Heckendorn, Erhart** Hecktorn, Ernst Short, David A90 B80 D90 E80 I-102 II-	Stineman, Jacob	House (old) House Barn Still house Gravel land.	28 x 23 18 x 13 18 x 15	sq. log log log	2	2A 48P 171A	175	218.75 1593
89	**Hecketsweler, Geo.** Hickesweller, Geo. A91 B81 D91 E81 I-103 II-	Fesich, Geo. Dollinger, Georg	House (old) Stable Lot in Jonestown.	24 x 18 18 x 16	sq. log sq. log	1	48P 144P	100	125 21
90	**Hele, John** A94 D94 I-106	Hinckel, Henry	House (old) Stable	26 x 20 18 x 15	sq. log sq. log	2	2A	150	187.50
91	**Herner, Michl.** A86 B76 D86 E76 I-96 II-	Ditzler, Casper Conrad, Jacob	House Bank barn	29 x 25 50 x 24	sq. log	2	2A 126A	250	312.50 756

Direct Tax of 1798 - Bethel Township

No.	Owner/Occupant/Ref.	Adjoining	Building	Dimen.	Matls.	Stories	Acres Perch.	Assmt.	Valuation
			House is midling. Gravel land.						
92	Hersberger, Abm. A89 B79 D89 E79 I-101 II-	Hunsecker, Rud. Dice, David	House (old) Spring house Barn Stable Gravel and stone.	28 x 24 18 x 15 55 x 22 18 x 18	sq. log sq. log	1 1	2A 200A	150	187.50 1400
93	Hess, John A95 B84 D95 E84 I-107 II-	Saybolt, Abm. Rank, Peter	House Stable Lot near Jonestown. Midling good house. Old stable.	24 x 13 20 x 10	sq. log sq. log	2	48P 2A	150	187.50 25
94	Hileman, George Heilman, George A93 B83 D93 E83 I-105 II-	Jones Town	House (old) House (new) Bank barn In Jonestown. Good gravel land.	27 x 18 18 x 12 57 x 28	sq. log stone	1 2	1A 1A 98A	200 250	250 1470
95	Hiller, George B85 E-85 II-	Fetterer, Stephen Jonestown	House (old)	18 x 17		1	48P		75
96	Hinckel, Henry Hinkel, Henry A92 B82 D92 E82 I-104 II-	Shead, Charles Rank, John	House Kitchen Weaver shop Stable Good house. In Jonestown. Meadow lot in Jonestown.	30 x 21 30 x 12 18 x 15 20 x 15	sq. log sq. log sq. log	2 1 1	48P 1A 40P	500	625 45
97	Hochlander, George B87 E87 II-	Miller, Christn.	Stable Grist/saw mill Stony gravel land.	18 x 16 36 x 30		2	11A		44 900
98	Hoeman, Fredk. A97 D97 I-109	Saybold, Abm.	House Hatter shop New house not finished.	22 x 21 21 x 12	sq. log sq. log	2 1	48P	150	187.50
99	Hoffer, John Haffe, John A96 D96 I-108	Lutheran Church	House Smith shop Stable House not finished.	24 x 20 20 x 12 13 x 11	sq. log sq. log sq. log	2	48P	200	250
100	Hofman, Michl. A82 B72 D82 E72 I-92 II-	Steever, Casper	House (new) Barn Good land.	30 x 28 56 x 20	sq. log log	1	2A 48P	200	250 720
101	Holdeman, John A101 B88 D101 E88 I-111 II-	Bixler, Joseph	House Spring house Bank barn Good gravel land.	30 x 30 21 x 10 65 x 24	log log	1 1	2A 150A	300	375 1950
102	Hoober, Fredk. A100 D100 I-111	Bickel, John	House Built since 1st of October last.	26 x 22	log	2	30P		600

Direct Tax of 1798 - Bethel Township

No.	Owner/Occupant/Ref.	Adjoining	Building	Dimen.	Matls.	Stories	Acres Perch.	Assmt.	Valuation
103	**Hoober, Henry** A98 B86 D98 E86 I-110 II-	Wengert, John	House (old) Bank barn Gravel land.	27 x 24 50 x 24	sq. log	2	1A 123A	150	187.50 1230
104	**Houtz, Christian** A85 B75 D85 E75 I-95 II-	Shewey, Christn.	House (old) Spring house Bank barn Good land.	27 x 26 15 x 12 87 x 33	sq. log sq. log	1 1	2A 200A	200	250 3000
105	**Houtz, Henry** Hautz, Henry A84 B73 D84 E73 I-94 II-	Moyer, Jacob Moyer & Feeser	House (good) Bank barn Midling good land.	45 x 28 96 x 30	sq. log	2	2A 198A	500	625 2970
106	**Houtz, John** Finkel, Widow A81 B71 D81 E71 I-90 I-91 II-	Smith, Peter Derr, Rudolph	House (old) House (old) Kitchen (old) Stable (old) Bank barn Good gravel land. Mountain land	28 x 27 30 x 27 15 x 12 20 x 18 72 x 24	log/wood sq. log sq. log sq. log	2 2 1	2A 96P 178A 100A	500 350	625 437.50 1958 200
107	**Hower, Fredk.** A99 D99 I-111	Rudy, Widow	House (old) Stable	49 x 17 14 x 12	log	1 1	96P	100	125
108	**Hunsecker, Christian** A87 B77 D87 E77 I-97 I-98 II-	Shirk, Casper	House Spring house House is midling good. Spring House is old.	28 x 24 20 x 18	sq. log sq. log	1 1	2A	250	312.50
		Dice, David Herner, Michl. Miller, David Herner, Unger	House (old) House (old) Bank barn Good gravel land. Bank barn Barn Stony land.	20 x 18 22 x 18 70 x 24 20 x 18 40 x 20	sq. log sq. log log log	1 1	2A 2A 168A 150A 109A	100 100	125 125 2016 900 763
109	**Hunsecker, Rudy** A88 B78 D88 E78 I-100 II-	Hershberger, Abm Dice, David	House (old) Barn Poor land.	39 x 20 40 x 20	sq. log	1	2A 80A	125	156.25 480
110	**Hunsecker, Saml.** A83 B74 D83 E74 I-93 II-	Lantz, John	House (good) Spring house Bank barn Good gravel land.	30 x 28 22 x 13 70 x 30	sq. log sq. log	2 1	2A 223A	450	562.50 3345
111	**Jones, William Est.** D- E-		House Land			2	100A		200 2400
112	**Keller, Jacob** A104 B91 D104 E91 I-115 II-	Light, Henry	House Spring house Bank barn Midling house and old Spring house. Poor gravel land.	31 x 30 18 x 16 64 x 24	sq. log sq. log	1 1	2A 130A	300	375 1170
113	**Kemp, John**	Young, Geo.	House	28 x 21	sq. log	2	48P	300	375

Direct Tax of 1798 - Bethel Township

No.	Owner/Occupant/Ref.	Adjoining	Building	Dimen.	Matls.	Stories	Acres Perch.	Assmt.	Valuation
	Kimp, John A107 B94 D107 E94 I-118 II-		Weaver shop Stable New house not finished.	26 x 14 20 x 12	sq. log rd. log	1			
		Meily, Martn.	Lot - Jonestown "out lot."				1A 40P		20
114	Kemp, Mathias A109 D109 I-120	Moyer, Christian	House (old) Stable	29 x 27 16 x 12	sq. log sq. log	2	48P	180	225
115	King, Peter Keeny, Peter Keney, Peter A106 B93 D106 E93 I-117 II-	Light, Henry	House Bank barn House is midling. Gravel and stone.	26 x 24 56 x 24	sq. log	1	2A 54A	200	250 459
116	Klick, John A103 B90 D103 E90 I-114 II-	Unger, Val Light, John	House Bank barn Old House out of repair. Poor gravel land.	34 x 20 76 x 30	log	1	2A 200A	100	125 1800
117	Klinefelter, Albert Jr. Gleinfelter Albt. Jr. A70 B60 D70 E60 II-	Fisher, Wendel	House (good) Bank barn Stony and gravel land.	30 x 28 60 x 24	sq. log	2	2A 150A	300	375 900
118	Klinefelter, Albert Sr. Gleinfelter, Albt. Sr. Glinefelter, Abraham A71 B61 D71 E61 I-80 II-	Wolf, Nicholas	House (old) Spring house Bank barn	21 x 18 20 x 18 54 x 15	sq. log sq. log	1 1	2A 50A	150	187.50 300
119	Kohr, John Kore, John Satizan, Michl. A110 B97 D110 E97 I-120 II-	Satazan, Adam	House House Barn Gravel land.	26 x 28 35 x 18 50 x 20	log log log	2 1	2A 2A 96A	450 150	562.50 187.50 864
120	Kore, John Kohr, John A102 B89 D102 E89 I-113 II-	Wolf, Christian Light, John	House (old) Bank barn Gravel and stone.	26 x 25 45 x 20	sq. log	1	2A 60A	150	187.50 390
121	Kore, Michael Kohr, Michl. Oyer, Rudy A105 B92 D105 E92 I-116 II-	Groh, Peter	House (old) Wash house House is frame filled with brick. House (new) Bank barn Smith shop Stable Grist/sawmill Good gravel land.	34 x 30 16 x 20 22 x 20 50 x 24 2 x 16 28 x 15 24 x 24	frame log sq. log	2 1 1	1A 1A 113A	520 120	650 150 1356 900
122	Krider, Lewis B96 E96 II-	Martin, John	House House is made of bark & beam. Meadow lot. Currier shop	90 x 16 12 x 10			1A 59P		400
123	Kriser, Godfried Keiser, Godfrid A101 B88 D101 E88 I-112 II-	Mease, Henry	House Old house Bank barn	20 x 16 12 x 16 40 x 24	sq. log sq. log	2 1	2A 98A	150	187.50 588

Direct Tax of 1798 - Bethel Township

No.	Owner/Occupant/Ref.	Adjoining	Building	Dimen.	Matls.	Stories	Acres Perch.	Assmt.	Valuation
			New house, old adjoining new house. Bottom and gravel land.						
124	**Kurtz, Widow** A108 B95 D108 E95 I-119 II-	Achey, John	House (old) Kitchen Stable	28 x 24 28 x 10 20 x 15	sq. log sq. log sq. log	2 1	72P	300	375
		Hess, John	Lot - Jonestown "out lot."				2A		30
125	**Lantz, Henry** A116 B104 D116 E104 I-127 II-	Light, Henry	House (good) barn Gravel land.	28 x 25 55 x 24	sq. log log	2	2A 130A	400	500 1170
126	**Lantz, Jacob** Lentz, Jacob A111 B97 D111 E97 I-121 II-	Shaeffer, Michl.	House (old) Spring house Bank barn Midling gravel land.	24 x 24 18 x 16 64 x 30	sq. log sq. log	1 1	2A 148A	200	250 1480
127	**Larick, Christoph** Lerch, Christoph A122 B110 D122 E110 I-133 II-	Stineman, Jacob	House (old) Barn Stony and gravel.	35 x 18 90 x 24	sq. log log	1	2A 206A	100	125 1648
128	**Larick, John** Lerch, John A127 B115 D127 E115 I-138 II-	George, Henry Jones, John Est. Camp, John	House Stable Currier shop Lot (out lot) House is midling good.	22 x 14 12 x 10 18 x 15	sq. log	2	72P 96A 1A 80P	200	250 150 30
129	**Leamy, Jacob** Lemy, Jacob Dewees, David A129 B116 D129 E116 I-140 II-	Walborn, Andrew	House Smith shop Stable House is midling good.	28 x 20 15 x 10 12 x 10	sq. log sq. log sq. log	2	48P	200	250
		Hess, John Sebolt, Abm. Saybold, Abm.	House Stable Lot (out lot) in Jonestown House is midling.	20 x 16 14 x 14	sq. log sq. log	2	48P 1A 80P	150	187.50 25
130	**Leamy, Tobias** A123 B111 D123 E111 I-134 II-	Sherk, Casper	House (old) Bank barn Good gravel land.	27 x 18 80 x 28	sq. log	1	2A 194A	120	150 2910
131	**Lentz, Abraham** A113 B100 D113 E100 I-124 II-	Gilbert, Saml. Haldeman, John	House Barn Old rotten house. Gravel land.	42 x 20 75 x 30	sq. log log	1	2A 138A	100	125 1197
132	**Lentz, John** A114 B102 D114 E102 I-125 II-	Hunsecker, Saml.	House Spring house Barn Stable Midling good house. Gravel land.	30 x 28 12 x 10 66 x 24 20 x 18	sq. log sq. log log	2 1	2A 98A	408	510 1470
133	**Lidig, Catherine** A128 D128 I-139	Figart, William	House House is midling.	24 x 20	sq. log	1	48P	100	125

Direct Tax of 1798 - Bethel Township

No.	Owner/Occupant/Ref.	Adjoining	Building	Dimen.	Matls.	Stories	Acres Perch.	Assmt.	Valuation
134	Light, Henry	Light, John	House	40 x 16	sq. log	2	2A	100	125
	Sebastian, Fred		Bank barn	76 x 28			190A		2280
	Sam, Jacob		Stable	16 x 12					
	Gnaus, Jacob		Old house out of repair. Gravel land.						
	A117 B105 D117 E-105	Miller, Christian	House	22 x 18	sq. log	1	2A	100	125
	I-128 II-	Light, John	House	20 x 18	sq. log	1	2A	100	125
			Used for School House.						
		Keeny, Peter	House (old)	22 x 18		1	2A	100	125
		King, Peter	Stable	20 x 16			140A		1260
			Gravel land.						
		Lantz, Henry	House	28 x 22	sq. log	1	2A	300	375
			Spring house	22 x 18	stone	1			
			Bank barn	52 x 24			100A		900
			House is midling good. Gravel land.						
135	Light, Henry	Felker, Henry	House (old)	28 x 27	sq. log	1	2A	200	250
	A121 B109 D121 E109 I-132 II-		Bank barn	70 x 24			150A		1500
			Fulling mill	26 x 18					
			Gravel land.						
136	Light, John Jr.	Light, Henry	House	34 x 25	sq. log	2	2A	400	500
	Light, John		Kitchen	12 x 10	sq. log	1			
	A119 B107 D119 E107 I-130 II-		Bank barn	60 x 25			200A		2600
			New house not finished. Gravel land.						
			House	30 x 26	sq. log	2	2A	350	437.50
			Barn	60 x 26	log				
			Grist/saw mill	40 x 26					1400
			New house not finished.						
		Miller, David	House (old)	30 x 24	sq. log	1	2A	200	250
			Smith shop				122A		1037
			Gravel land.						
137	Light, Peter	Snavely, Isaac	House	32 x 28	sq. log	1	2A	225	281.25
	A130 B117 D130		Spring house	26 x 19	sq. log				
	E117 I-141 II-		Barn	60 x 25	log		128A		1280
			House is midling good. Stony gravel land.						
138	Lightner, Jacob	Ardtz, John	House	30 x 28	sq. log	2	2A	400	500
	Leightner, Jacob		Spring house	20 x 18	sq. log	1			
	Littner, Jacob	Brown, Andrew	Barn	70 x 25	log		128A		960
	A115 B103 D115 E103 I-126 II-		House and Spring house are midling good. Gravel land.						
139	Long, Abm.	Long, Christian	House	35 x 25	sq. log	2	2A	360	450
	A124 B112 D124 E112		Spring house	15 x 12	sq. log	1			
	I-135 II-	Wert, Conrad	Out house	20 x 14			126A		1134
			Bank barn	62 x 25					
			House is midling good. Gravel land.						
140	Long, Christian	Long, Wm.	House	25 x 20	sq. log	2	2A	200	250
	Long, Israel	Spitler, John	House	21 x 18	sq. log	1	2A	100	125
	A112 B98 D112 E98	Long, Killian	Barn	40 x 20	log		96A		882
	I-122 II-		Cooper shop	30 x 18					

Direct Tax of 1798 - Bethel Township

No.	Owner/Occupant/Ref.	Adjoining	Building	Dimen.	Matls.	Stories	Acres Perch.	Assmt.	Valuation
			Stable	18 x 15					
			One house is new, the other midling good. Gravel land.						
141	**Long, Henry** B99 E99 I-123 II-	Long, Christn.	House (old) Barn Weaver shop Gravel land.	28 x 24 60 x 24	sq. log log	2	100A 98A		882
142	**Long, Israel** Loser, Jacob Spitler, Widow A126 B114 D126 E114 I-137 II-	Beck, Philip	House (old) Spring house House (new) Barn Swamp lands.	27 x 21 18 x 15 20 x 16 45 x 24	sq. log sq. lod sq. log log	1 1 1	2A 2A 280A	150 100	187.50 125 2520
143	**Long, Kilian** A125 B113 D125 E113 I-136 II-	Long, Abm. Dubs, Henry	House Barn House is not finished. Gravel land.	28 x 22 30 x 20	sq. log log	2	2A 90A	150	187.50 900
144	**Loose, Jacob** Lose, Jacob A120 B108 D120 E108 I-131 II-	Miller, Christian Dice, David	House (old) Bank barn Still house Smith shop Oil mill Gravel land.	26 x 24 40 x 16 16 x 14 15 x 12 20 x 16	sq. log	1	2A 56A	150	187.50 392
145	**Lutz, Philip** A118 B106 D118 E106 I-129 II-	Shellen, Jacob Keller, Jacob	House Barn Poor land.	30 x 15 45 x 16	log log	1	2A 70A	100	125 476
146	**Mark, Henry** Merck, Henry A141 B126 D141 E126 I-154 II-	Light, Peter	House Stable House is midling good. Gravel land.	30 x 28 18 x 18	sq. log	1	2A 18A	200	250 144
147	**Martin, John** Greenwalt, Leond. A146 B131 D146 E131 I- II-	Wilt, Dewalt Larick, John Seltzer, Christ	House (old) Stable Beam/Currier Shop in Jones Town.	30 x 26 20 x 24 60 x 20	log	2	96P 96P 1A 80P	200	250 75 250
148	**Mease, Henry** **Miss, Henry** Neyman, Wm. Nyman, Wm. A131 B118 D131 E118 I-143 II-	Mease, John	House (good) Kitchen Spring house Bank barn Part good land and part mountain. Stable Still house	39 x 30 18 x 16 20 x 18 70 x 24 20 x 18 18 x 15	stone stone stone/log	2 1 1	2A 148A	700	875 1148
		Blue Mtn.	House (old) Poor land.		log		80A		480
		Satazan, Jacob	House (old) Mountain land (good).		log		50A		400
149	**Mease, John** **Miss, John**	Mease, Henry	House Bank barn	31 x 24 70 x 24	sq. log	2	2A 106A	250	312.50 848

Direct Tax of 1798 - Bethel Township

No.	Owner/Occupant/Ref.	Adjoining	Building	Dimen.	Matls.	Stories	Acres Perch.	Assmt.	Valuation
	Sieffert, Peter		Smith shop	12 x 10					
	Pifer, Peter		House (old)	20 x 18	log		90A		720
	A132 B120 D132		Stable (old)	18 x 16					
	E120 I-144 II-		House is midling good. Land is midling good.						
150	Miley, Henry	Groh, Peter	House (good)	28 x 27	sq. log	2	2A	400	500
	Miley, John		Barn	60 x 20	log		98A		1470
	Moser, Geo.		Still house	20 x 18	log				
	A137 B125 D137 E125 I-150 II-		Smith shop	28 x 16	log				
			Good gravel land.						
			House (old)	24 x 18	sq. log	1	2A	125	156.25
			Barn		log				
		Kore, Michl.	House (old)	27 x 20	sq. log	1	2A	150	187.50
		Core, Michl.	Barn	60 x 20	log		131A		1310
			Gravel, midling good.						
		Botiger, Caspr.	House (old)	24 x 20	sq. log	2	2A	125	156.25
			Barn	30 x 16	log		18A		126
		Grow, Peter	Lot - mountain land.				25A		50
151	Miley, Jacob	Volever, Peter	House	30 x 30	stone	2	96P	1200	1500
	Meily, Jacob		Kitchen	30 x 20	stone	1			
	Geese, Henry		Kitchen	30 x 20	stone	1			
	A144 B127 D144		Barn	50 x 24	log				
	E127 I-157 II-		Stable	20 x 20	log				
			Corner in Stumpstown.						
		Botiger, Casper	House (old)	28 x 26	log	1	2A	125	156.25
			Barn	60 x 22	log		160A		1600
			Gravel land.						
			Lot in Stumpstown.				30A		450
			Gravel land (good).						
		Bean?, Jacob	Lot - woodland				15A		120
		Kneagey land	Mountain land				500A		250
152	Miley, Martin	Rank, Peter	House	31 x 27	sq. log	2	40P	900	1125
	Meily, Martin		Barn	32 x 16	rd. log				
	A142 B128 D142		Shed	20 x 12	frame				
	E128 I-155 II-		Corner lot in Jones Town Market square.						
		Fetterrer, Stephen	Lot in Jonestown.				48P		10
		Camp, John	Lot (out lot)				3A 80P		50
		Sheade, Chas.	Lot - meadow lot.				1A 48P		40
153	Miller, Christian	Loose, Jacob	House (old)	26 x 24	sq. log	1	2A	160	200
	Raybock, Peter	Light, Henry	Bank barn	55 x 25			164A		1230
	A139 B132 D139 E132		Stable	24 x 14					
	E152 II-		Smith shop	20 x 18					
			Gravel land.						
154	Miller, Conrad	Lot in Stumpstown	House	18 x 15	log		48P		25
	B129 E129 II-		Stable	15 x 12					
155	Miller, David	Light, John	House (new)	30 x 26	sq. log	1	2A	125	156.25
	A138 B124 D138 E124 I-151 II-		Barn	50 x 24	log		98A		784

Direct Tax of 1798 - Bethel Township

No.	Owner/Occupant/Ref.	Adjoining	Building	Dimen.	Matls.	Stories	Acres Perch.	Assmt.	Valuation
			Gravel land.						
156	**Miller, George**	Bucher, Peter	House	29 x 28	sq. log	2	2A	275	343.75
	Stump, Adam		Barn	45 x 24	log		170A		1190
	A133 B121 D133 E121 I-145 II-		House is midling good. Poor land.						
157	**Miller, Henry**	Saylor, Peter	House (new)	24 x 22	sq. log	1	2A	100	125
	A140 B126 D140		Barn	48 x 20	log		46A		368
	E126 I-153 II-		Stony land.						
158	**Mish, Jacob**	Martin, John	House (old)	30 x 18	log	1	136P	175	218.75
	A143 D143 I-156		Stable	18 x 15	log				
159	**Moyer, _____**	Wilhelm, Henry	House (poor)	24 x 20	log	2	20P	250	312.50
	Stine, George	Bickel, John	Lot in Jonestown.				48P		10
	A145 B130 D145 E130 I- II-								
160	**Moyer, Christian**	Lantz, Abm.	House (new)	21 x 22	sq. log	1	1A	150	187.50
	A136 D136 I-149		Stable	10 x 15	sq. log				
161	**Moyer, Christn.**	Camp, Mathias	House	20 x 18			48P		30
	B133 E133 II-		In Stumps Town.						
162	**Moyer, Frederick**	Mease, John	House (old)	25 x 14	sq. log	2	2A	100	125
	Strohm, Abm.		House (old)	15 x 12					
	A134 B119 D134		Bank barn	60 x 80			80A		480
	E119 I-146 II-		Smith shop	15 x 12					
			Poor land.						
163	**Moyer, Jacob**	Hofman, Michl.	House (old)	27 x 21	sq. log	1	2A	175	218.75
	Myer, Jacob	Houtz, Henry	Barn	60 x 22	log		82A		1353
	A135 B123 D135 E123 I-148 II-		Barn	45 x 23	log				
			Land is good part limestone.						
164	**Moyer, John**	Sherk, Casper	House (old)	28 x 24	sq. log	1	2A	175	218.75
	Myer, John	Shirk, Casper	Bank barn	55 x 25			138A		1794
	A147 B122 D147 E122 I-147 I- II-		Gravel land.						
165	**Neese, Henry**	Saybolt, Abm.	House (old)	31 x 18	log	1	48P	160	200
	Saybolt, Abm.		Stable	15 x 12					
	A149 D149 I-								
166	**Neycomer, Jacob**	Weller, Philip	House	27 x 18	log	1	1A	200	250
	Newcomer, Jacob	Weller, Philip	House	24 x 18	log	1	1A	150	187.50
	A150 B134 D150 E134 I- II-		Barn	50 x 24	log		150A		1350
			Gravel land.						
167	**Noll, John**	Ditzler, Casper	House	28 x 30	log	2	2A	400	500
	Brown, John		Bank barn	60 x 21			168A		1512
	A148 B134 D148 E134 I- II-		Gravel land.						
		Ditzler, Casper	House	26 x 28	log	1	2A	175	218.75
			Bank barn	55 x 24			197A		1379

Direct Tax of 1798 - Bethel Township

No.	Owner/Occupant/Ref.	Adjoining	Building	Dimen.	Matls.	Stories	Acres Perch.	Assmt.	Valuation
			Houses are midling good.						
168	**Orendorf, Christian** Worrel, Joseph A154 D154 I-	Gilbert, Saml.	House Corner lot, good house.	26 x 24	sq. log	2	48P	200	250
169	**Overholser, Christn.** Oberholzer, Christn. Fox, Charles A151 B135 D151 E135 I- II-	Stumps Town	House (old) Barn Gravel land. House Room Barn (old)	18 x 17 27 x 18 27 x 9 40 x 20	log log log log log	1 2 1	2A 148A 48P	175 200	218.75 2220 250
170	**Overholser, Jacob Jr.** A152 B136 D152 E136 I- II-	Overholser, Christn.	House (old) Spring house Barn Gravel land - good.	30 x 28 20 x 18 67 x 28	sq. log sq. log log	1	2A 167A	275	343.75 2505
171	**Overholser, Jacob Sr.** A153 B137 D153 E137 I- II-	Overholser, Christn.	House Barn Out Lot near Stumpstown Out Lot near Stumpstown Out Lot near Stumpstown (meadow)	28 x 18 40 x 20	sq. log log	1	48P 14A 144P 5A	125	156.25 121 30 100
172	**Pefley, John** A157 B140 D157 E140 I- II-	Sherk, Casper, Jr.	House (good) House (old) Bank barn Gravel land.	27 x 24 20 x 18 54 x 21	log	1	2A 150A	200	250 1350
173	**Pefly, David** A156 B139 D156 E139 I- II-	Shewey, Martin	House Midling good house. House (old) Barn Barn Good gravel land.	28 x 30 20 x 15 60 x 25 40 x 20	log log log	1	2A 150A	200	250 2100
174	**Pefly, Jacob** A155 B138 D155 E138 I- II-	Smith, Peter	House (old) Barn Gravel land.	24 x 18 51 x 21	log log	1	2A 56A	100	125 448
175	**Petrie, John** A158 D158 I-	Weaver, Adam	House (old) Stable	22 x 18 12 x 10	log	1	48P	100	125
176	**Ranck, Peter** Rank, Peter Ward, Samuel A160 B142 D160 E142 I- II-	Dubbs, John	House (old) Joiner shop Stable New house, Corner Lot, not finished.	35 x 30 17 x 17 40 x 16	log wood wood	2 1	48P	100	125
		Miley, Martin	House Joiner shop Stable	24 x 20 16 x 10 12 x 10	wood wood	2 1	40P	375	468.75
		Hess, John	Lot (out lot in Jonestown)				2A		35

Direct Tax of 1798 - Bethel Township

No.	Owner/Occupant/Ref.	Adjoining	Building	Dimen.	Matls.	Stories	Acres Perch.	Assmt.	Valuation
177	**Rank, John** Ranck, John A161 B143 D161 E143 I- II-	Capp, Christoph Ranck, Peter Selzer, Christn. Hinkel, Henry	House (good) Joiner shop Stable Lot (out lot) in Jonestown. Lot - meadow Lot - meadow	28 x 20 18 x 15 18 x 15	wood wood wood	2 1	48P 1A 120P 2A 1A	500	625 25 40 30
178	**Rauch, Jacob** Roush, Jacob A162 B144 D162 E144 I- II-	Shally, John Wagoner, Sebastn.	House (old) Spring house Barn Stony land.	30 x 16 16 x 20 40 x 20	sq. log log	1 1	2A 100A	200	250 900
179	**Riddle, Jacob** A159 B141 D159 E141 I- II-	Backenstose, Henry	House Barn House not finished. Gravel land (poor).	30 x 25 50 x 20	log log	2	2A 68A	250	312.50 476
180	**Rudy, Jacob** A163 D163 I-	Wengard, Joseph	House Currier shop Mill house Stable Corner lot in Stumbs Town. Gravel land.	20 x18 18 x12 18 x 18 15 x 18	wood/brk. frame frame frame	1	80P	275	343.75
181	**Rudy, Jonas** A164 B146 D164 E146 I- II-	Besore, Widow Weaver, Henry	House (good) Barn Still house	30 x 28 50 x 24	ruffstone log	2	2A 117A	500	625 1053
182	**Rudy, Widow** B145 E145 I- II-	Hoover, Fredk.	House (old) Stable Smith shop	19 x 16 15 x 18			 96P		 80
183	**Satazan, Adam** Satazan, Adam Jr. A168 B149 D168 E149 I- II- 	Besore, John Mease, Henry	House (old) Spring house Barn Good gravel land. Mountain land	32 x 18 18 x 12 61 x 20	log log	1	2A 48A 40A	150	187.50 576 320
184	**Satazan, Jacob** A167 B149 D167 E149 I- II-	Wendelblech, Geo.	House Barn Midling good House.	24 x 20 40 x 14	log log	1	2A 87A	200	250 783
185	**Saybold, Abm.** Seybolt, Abm. Sebolt, Abm. Colb, Philip A192 B173 D192 E173 I- II- Hess, John Kurtz, Widow	Ness, Henry Hess, John Kurtz, Widow	House Kitchen Shed Barn Good house in Jonestown. House (old) Kitchen Stable Lot (out lot)	26 x 24 21 x 16 20 x 10 30 x 16 24 x 20 20 x 11 16 x 12	sq. log log log log sq. log log log	2 1 2	96P 48P 5A	625 325	781.25 406.25 75
186	**Saylor, Peter** Seiler, Peter	Miller, Henry Light, Henry	House Barn	26 x 24 50 x 22	log log	1	2A 130A	200	250 1235

Direct Tax of 1798 - Bethel Township

No.	Owner/Occupant/Ref.	Adjoining	Building	Dimen.	Matls.	Stories	Acres Perch.	Assmt.	Valu- ation
	A180 B161 D180 E161 I- II-		Still house	20 x 18					
			Midling good house. Gravel land.						
187	Seltzer, Christian		House	30 x 20	wood	2	48P	500	625
	Dollinger, Geo.	Widele, Danl.	Kitchen	30 x 12	log	1			
	Regengast, Geo.		Shed	14 x 20	log				
	A190 B169 D190 E169 I- II-		Stable	12 x 14	log				
			New house built since 1st of October.						
		Widele, Danl.	House	30 x 36	wood	2	144P	100	125
			Kitchen	20 x 15	log	1			
		Hileman, Geo.	House (old)	20 x 16	wood	1	2A	325	406.25
			Stable	10 x 16					
		Uhler, Martin	House (good)	32 x 28	log	2	2A		
		Woods, James	Lot, meadow				1A 120P		50
		Martin, John	Lot, meadow				1A 120P		80
		Mily, Martin	Lot, meadow				144P		27
		Dubs, John	Barn	48 x 24	log		202A		3030
			Good gravel land.						
188	Seltzer, Henry	Miley, Jacob	Brick yard				72P		60
	B176 E176 II-								
189	Seltzer, John	Becker, John	House	28 x 24	log	2	96P	450	562.50
	A182 D182 I-		Joiner shop	12 x 16					
			Stable	12 x 17					
			Midling good house.						
190	Shaeffer, Michl.	Smith, Peter	House	28 x 27	log	2	2A	300	375
	A172 B153 D172 E153 I- II-		Barn	68 x 24	log		128A		1024
			Still house	24 x 20					
			Midling house. Gravel land.						
191	Shally, John	Rauch, Jacob	House	30 x 26	log	1	2A	150	187.50
	Gass, John	Snevely, John	House	24 x 20	log	1	2A	100	125
	A179 B160 D179 E160 I- II-	Miller, Henry	Barn	50 x 20	log		200A		1800
			30 x 26 is old poor house; 24 x 20 is midling house.						
			Stony gravel land.						
192	Shead, Charles	Hinckel, Henry	House (old)	22 x 18	sq. log	2	96P	400	500
	Shed, Charles		Kitchen	22 x 12	log				
	A194 B174 D194 E174 I- II-		Stable	24 x 12	log				
		Miley, Martn.	Lot, meadow				3A 80P		80
193	Shewey, Christn.	Martin, Shewey	House (old)	30 x 27	log	1	2A	250	312.50
	Shuey, Christn.		Bank barn	61 x 28			132A		1980
	A173 B154 D173 E154 I- II-		Gravel land.						
194	Shewey, Martin	Feeser, Peter	House (good)	45 x 25	log	2	2A	500	625
	Shuey, Martin		Bank barn	73 x 30			169A		2788
	Alwine, Werner		Good land.						
	Spitler, Henry		House (old)	23 x 20	log	1	2A	125	156.25
	A176 B158 D176 E158 I- II-	Holdeman, John	Barn	62 x 24	log		200A		3000

Direct Tax of 1798 - Bethel Township

No.	Owner/Occupant/Ref.	Adjoining	Building	Dimen.	Matls.	Stories	Acres Perch.	Assmt.	Valuation
			Good land.						
			House	24 x 28	log	1	1A	120	150
			Barn	70 x 25	log		143A		2073
			Good land.						
			House (good)	30 x 28	log	2	2A	400	500
			Stable	20 x 18					
195	**Shindle, Peter** Segar, Widow B170 E170 ll-	Brecht, John	House (old)	24 x 18			48P		50
196	**Shirk, Casper** A177 B159 D177 E159 l- ll-	Grove, Peter	House (old) Spring house Bank barn Still house Smith shop Gravel land - good.	30 x 30 18 x 15 99 x 24 20 x 20 18 x 15	log log	1 1	2A 2A 247A	250	312.50 3458
197	**Shirk, Casper, Jr.** A195 B165 D195 E165 l- ll-	Pefly, John	House (old) Bank barn Gravel land.	24 x 20 73 x 30	log	1	2A 118A	100	125 1062
198	**Smith, Peter Jr.** A170 B151 D170 E151 l- ll-	Houtz, John	House (old) Barn Gravel land.	25 x 24 57 x 22	log log	1	2A 100A	225	281.25 900
199	**Smith, Peter Sr.** A171 B152 D171 E152 l- ll-	Houtz, John Shuey, Christn.	House (new) Bank barn Still house Gravel land.	30 x 28 60 x 24 24 x 20	log	2	2A 198A	400	500 1980
200	**Snevely, Henry** A184 B166 D184 E166 l- ll-	Wagoner, Conrd. Stumpstown Mily, Jacob Mily, Jacob Dubs, John	House (old) Kitchen Barn Lot Lot, meadow Lot. meadow Lot Gravel land.	31 x 20 31 x 12 39 x 16	log	2	120P 5A 192P 192P 117A	400	500 75 30 25 1170
201	**Snevely, Isaac** Snebly, Isaac A181 B163 D181 E163 l- ll-	Light, Henry	House Out house Spring house Bank barn Still house House is midling good. Land is gravel and stone.	28 x 27 20 x 24 20 x 18 70 x 22 30 x 28	log log log	1	2A 228A	300	375 2508
202	**Snevely, John** Snebly, John A178 B162 D178 E150 l- ll-	Martin, Alexr.	House (old) Bank barn Still house Stony gravel land.	40 x 20 60 x 24 20 x 20	log	1	2A 216A	150	187.50 1944

Direct Tax of 1798 - Bethel Township

No.	Owner/Occupant/Ref.	Adjoining	Building	Dimen.	Matls.	Stories	Acres Perch.	Assmt.	Valuation
203	Speeker, Peter Spyker, Peter A185 B167 D185 E167 I- II-	Bickel, John	House (good) Kitchen Stable	20 x 21 10 x 12 12 x 10	sq. log	2	40P	400	500
		Wilhelm, Henry Woods, James	Lot (out lot) Lot, meadow				3A 106P 1A 40P		50 25
204	Spitler, John A174 B155 174 E155 I- II-	Besore, John	House (good) Bank barn Good gravel land.	29 x 25 32 x 24	log	2	2A 151A	475	593.75 2265
205	Statler, Michl. A193 D193 I-	Leaman, Jacob	House (old)	20 x 15	sq. log	1	48P	100	125
206	Staub, Margaret B175 E175 I- II-	Walborn, Jacob	House (poor) Stable	22 x 16 15 x 12			48P		60
		Overholser, Christ	Lot, meadow				2A		50
207	Stine, Abm. A191 D191 I-	Hoover, Fred	House (good) Kitchen Shed Barn	27 x 21 12 x 11 21 x 10 27 x 22	sq. log sq. log sq. log sq. log	2	50P	500	625
208	Stine, Elisabeth A187 B172 D187 E172 I- II-	Spiker, Peter	House (old) Kitchen Stable	28 x 24 28 x 15 20 x 18	sq. log	2	40P	525	656.25
		Spyker, Peter Sebolt, Abm.	Lot, meadow Lot (out lot)				4A 3A		64 40
209	Stine, George A188 D188 I-	Gilbert, Saml.	House New house not finished.	26 x 24	sq. log	2	48P	100	125
210	Stine, Henry A186 B168 D186 E168 I- II-	Fettle, Henry	House (good) Kitchen Stable Stable	32 x 30 20 x 16 40 x 16 12 x 20	sq. log	2	48P	1100	1375
		Hileman, Geo.	Lot				4A		60
211	Stineman, Jacob Snevely, John A183 B164 D183 E164 I- II-	Heckedom, Erhart Heckedom, Albert	House Spring house Midling good house. House (old) Barn Stable Gravel land.	30 x 28 15 x 12 24 x 18 39 x 26 16 x 12	log	2	2A 136A	400	500 1224
212	Stover, Casper Stower, Casper A175 B156, B157 D175 E156 I- II-	Hoffman, Michl. Houtz, Henry	House Bank barn Midling house. Grist/saw mill Land	48 x 25 37 x 25 Good gravel land. 30 x ?	log/wood	2	2A 174A 14A	400	500 2610 1100 126
213	Straw, Daniel	Peck, Philip	House (old)	40 x 20	log	2	2A	200	250

Direct Tax of 1798 - Bethel Township

No.	Owner/Occupant/Ref.	Adjoining	Building	Dimen.	Matls.	Stories	Acres Perch.	Assmt.	Valuation
	Stroh, Daniel A165 B147 D165 E147 I- II-		Bank barn Weaver shop Stony and gravel land.	60 x 24 18 x 15			88A		600
214	**Straw, Michael** **Stroh, Michael** A166 B148 D166 E148 I- II-	Peck, Philip	House Joiner shop Lot Midling house. Stony land.	24 x 20 24 x 10	log log	1	1A 2A	200	250 20
215	**Straw, Michl. Sr.** A189 B171 D189 E171 I- II-	Wenger, John Felty, Sebastian Potts, John	House (good) Spring house Bank barn Gravel land. House (old) Grist/saw mill Bank barn Stony mountain land. Mountain land	28 x 27 18 x 15 60 x 24 24 x 20 55 x 42 35 x 18	log/wood log/stone	2	2A 100A 128A 50A	500	625 1500 2500 768 200
216	**Strohm, Abm.** A169 B150 D169 E150 I- II-	Weaver, Henry	House (old) Out house Bank barn Gravel land.	30 x 25 20 x 18 60 x 20	log	1	2A 183A	250	312.50 1830
217	**Tittle, Henry** A196 D196 I-	Stine, Henry	House (good) Kitchen Stable	28 x 21 28 x 10 18 x 15	sq. log	2 1	48P	450	562.50
218	**Uhler, Martin** Uhler, John Waggoner, Michl. A199 B179 D199 E179 I- II-	Seltzer, Christian	House (old) Spring house House (old) Barn Stable Stable Still house Gravel land - good.	24 x 48 18 x 16 20 x 18 60 x 24 16 x 15 21 x 18 26 x 24	sq. log log log	1 1 1	1A 1A 199A	200 100	250 125 2786
219	**Unger, Valentine** A198 B178 D198 E178 I- II-	Backenstose, Henry	House (old) Barn Poor gravel land.	26 x 20 24 x 36	log log	1	2A 90A	100	125 450
220	**Urich, Henry** A197 B177 D197 E177 I- II-	Weaver, Henry	House (old) Gravel land. House (old) Barn	24 x 22 20 x 20 35 x 18	stone log	2	2A 108A	200	250 972
221	**Waggoner, Conrad** **Wagoner, Conrd.** A218 D218 I-	Snebely, Henry	House (old) Stable	26 x 20 16 x 10	log	2	48P	100	125
222	**Wagoner, John** A231 B211 D231 E211 I- II-	Desh, Margaret	House (good) Wood shop	24 x 20 18 x 15	log log	1	96P	150	187.50

Direct Tax of 1798 - Bethel Township

No.	Owner/Occupant/Ref.	Adjoining	Building	Dimen.	Matls.	Stories	Acres Perch.	Assmt.	Valuation
		Strohm, Abm.	Stable Lot, meadow	18 x 15	log		1A 18P		30
223	**Wagoner, Sebastn.** A228 B208 D228 E208 I- II-	Rauch, Jacob Round top	House Bank barn Still house Lot	20 x 18 60 x 24 16 x 15	log	1	2A 100A 30A	175	218.75 900 150
			Midling good House. Stony land.						
224	**Walborn, Andrew** A230 D230 I-	Layman, Jacob Leaman, Jacob	House House not finished.	18 x 16	log	2	48P	100	125
225	**Walborn, Christn.** B180 E180 II-	Walborn, Jacob	House Stable (small) Poor land.	18 x 15			31A		186
226	**Walborn, George** B210 E210 II-	Gissey, George	House Stable In Stumpstown.	30 x 15 20 x 12		1	48P		65
227	**Walborn, Jacob** B180 E180 II-	Moyer, Fred	House Stable	20 x 16 15 x 12			28A		168
228	**Walborn, Martin** A208 B190 D208 I- II-	Backenstose, Jacob	House (old) Barn Poor gravel land.	37 x 16 39 x 15	log log	1	2A 22A	100	125 131
229	**Walborn, Martin** B181 E181 E190 I- II-	Walborn, Christn.	House Stable (small)	18 x 12			28A		168
230	**Waldemartz, Fred** A216 D216 I-	Willy, August	House (old) Stable	35 x 19 12 x 10	log	1	144P	100	125
231	**Weaver, Adam** **Wever, Adam** A227 D227 I-	Petrie, John	House (old) Smith shop Stable	26 x 20 20 x 10 18 x 12	log log log	1	1A 128P	200	250
232	**Weaver, George** **Weber, George** A203 B185 D203 E185 I- II-	Uhler, Martin Snebely, Henry	House (old) Stable Smith shop Lot - gravel.	18 x 15 12 x 11 12 x 10	log	1	1A 120P 2A	100	125 20
233	**Weaver, Henry** **Weber, Henry** A204 B186 D204 E186 I- II-	Botiger, Casper Boticher, Casper	House (old) Barn Gravel land.	26 x 18 80 x 25	log log	1	2A 154A	150	187.50 1617
234	**Weaver, Philip** A219 B198 D219 E198 I- II-	Beany, Melchor Miley, Jacob	House (old) Shop Stable Lot, meadow	21 x 27 27 x 15 15 x 12	log log log	1 1 1	148P 2A	200	250 32
235	**Webbert, Andrew**	Henner, Michl.	House (old)	32 x 22	log	2	2A	200	250

Direct Tax of 1798 - Bethel Township

No.	Owner/Occupant/Ref.	Adjoining	Building	Dimen.	Matls.	Stories	Acres Perch.	Assmt.	Valuation
	A213 B195 D213 E195 I- II-	Hirner, Michl.	House (old) Bank barn Poor gravel land.	22 x 16 64 x 24	log	1	2A 126A	100	125 756
236	Weller, Philip A206 B188 D206 E188 I- II-	Isenhawer, John	House (good) Spring house Barn Gravel land.	30 x 28 18 x 15 60 x 24	log log	2	2A 115A	475	593.75 1150
237	Wendelblech, Adam A201 B183 D201 E183 I- II-	Faber, Philip	House Spring house Barn New good house. Gravel land.	32 x 28 15 x 12 74 x 22	log log	2	2A 98A	475	593.75 980
238	Wendelblech, Geo. A202 B184 D202 E184 I- II-	Wenddelblech, Adam Polk, John	House Barn Lot New house not finished. Gravel land and stone.	27 x 23 55 x 20	log log	2	2A 104A 54A	200	250 1040 108
239	Wenger, Jacob A207 B189 D207 E189 I- II-	Smith, Peter	House (old) Barn Smith shop Gravel land.	20 x 18 37 x 12 18 x 15	log log	1	2A 8A	125	156.25 80
240	Wenger, John Wengart, John A221 B202 D221 E202 I- II-	Straw, Michl.	House (old) Spring house Bank barn Out house (old) Good land.	30 x 28 12 x 10 60 x 26	log	1	2A 110A	300	375 1650
241	Wenger, Joseph Wengart, Joseph A222 B204 D222 E204 I- II-	Rudy, Jacob Moyer, Christn. Snavely, Henry	House (old) Smith shop Stable Lot Located in Stumpstown.	30 x 20 28 x 14 22 x 20	log	2	40P 48P 144P	175	218.75 45 30
242	Wenner, Jacob A205 B187 D205 E187 I II-	Weaver, Henry	House (old) Barn Poor gravel land.	30 x 18 40 x 18	log log	1	2A 48A	100	125 384
243	Wetzel, William B200 E200 II-	Worrel, Joseph	House Stable Land in lots.	20 x 24 15 x 12			144P		64
244	Widel, Danl. Widle, Danl. A224 B205 D224 E205 I- II-	Seltzer, Christian Meily, Martn.	House (old) Potter shop Stable Lot (out lot)	28 x 24 24 x 12 15 x 12	log log log	2	48P 2A 18P	500	625 30
245	Wilhelm, Henry A229 B209 D229 E109 I- II-	Capp, Jacob	House (old) Hatter shop Stable	27 x 23 16 x 9 26 x 18	log log log	2	60P	400	500

Direct Tax of 1798 - Bethel Township

No.	Owner/Occupant/Ref.	Adjoining	Building	Dimen.	Matls.	Stories	Acres Perch.	Assmt.	Valuation
		Widle, Daniel	Lot				3A		45
		Stryker, Peter	Lot in Jones Town.				4A 120P		60
246	Willy, Augustus A217 D217 I-	Waldemartz, Fred	House (good) Stable	31 x 18 19 x 15	log	1	1A 26P	175	218.75
247	Wilt, Dewald Est. A223 B199 D223 E199 I- II-	Martin, John Shead, Charles	House Stable Lot in Jones Town.	24 x 20 18 x 15	log	2	48P 144P	200	250 45
248	Wilt, Jacob Wolf, Paul A215 B197 D215 E197 I- II-	Dubs, Henry	House (old) House (old) Barn Barn Still house Good land.	26 x 22 28 x 15 66 x 30 54 x 25 15 x 20	log log log log	1 1	2A 2A 162A	200 100	250 125 2673
249	Wirt, Conrad A214 B196 D214 E196 I- II-	Long, Kilian Fechman, Geo.	House Barn Still house Midling good house. Gravel land.	22 x 16 40 x 18 16 x 18	log log	1	2A 8A	150	187.50 72
250	Wirt, Michael Wert, Michael A220 B201 D220 E201 II-	Kurtz, Widow Wolfe, John (lots)	House (old) Weaver shop Stable Lots	24 x 21 21 x 10 20 x 12	log log log	1	48P 144P	150	187.50 30
251	Wolever, Peter Stanz, Widow B203 E-203 II-	Miley, Jacob Willing, August	House (old) Stable	20 x 18 10 x 12			40P 2A 80P		65 36
252	Wolf, Christian A211 B193 D211 E193 I- II-	Glick, John	House (good) Barn Gravel land (poor).	26 x 28 60 x 20	log log	2	2A 108A	225	281.25 756
253	Wolf, Christian Jr. A210 B192 D210 E192 I- II-	Wolf, Christian Sr.	House (good) Bank barn Midling good land.	28 x 28 58 x 24	log	1	2A 120A	250	312.50 1200
254	Wolf, Christian Sr. A209 B191 D209 E191 I- II-	Hunsecker, Christian Miller, David	House (good) House (old) House Bank barn Stable Midling good land, stony.	30 x 30 24 x 20 20 x 16 100 x 32 15 x 16	log log	1 1	2A 2A 168A 98A	275 100	343.75 125 2352 490
255	Wolf, Nicholas A232 B211 D232 E211 I- II-	Desh, John	House Barn Stony land, poor.	40 x 19 30 x 20	log log	1	2A 45A	100	125 180
256	Wolf, Peter A200 B182 D200 E182 I- II-	Core, John	House (old) House	29 x 26 18 x 14	log	1	2A	135	168.75

Direct Tax of 1798 - Bethel Township

No.	Owner/Occupant/Ref.	Adjoining	Building	Dimen.	Matls.	Stories	Acres Perch.	Assmt.	Valuation
			Bank barn	36 x 24			98A		588
			Still house						
			Stony land.						
257	**Wolf, Widow**	Achey, John	House (good)	40 x 36	stone	2	48P	1400	1750
	A226 B207 D226 E207 I- II-		Kitchen	15 x 16	stone	1			
			Shed	40 x 12	stone				
			Stable	30 x 12	stone				
		Weaver, Wm.	Lot - in Jones Town.				96P		20
258	**Woods, James**	Rank, Peter	House (good)	30 x 26	log	2	48P	700	875
	A225 B206 D225 E206 I- II-		Stable	20 x 15					
		Stine, Henry	Lot (out lot) Jones Town.				4A		60
259	**Worrel, Joseph**	Strohm, Abm.	House (old)	26 x 24	log	1	2A	120	150
	A212 B194 D212 E194 I- II-		Stable	16 x 15			13A		135
			Gravel land.						
260	**Yeakly, Rudolph**	Fox, Henry	House	27 x 22	log	1	2A	200	250
	A234 B212 D234 E212 I- II-		Barn	50 x 20	log		127A		1270
			Midling good house. Gravel land.						
			House	20 x 16	log				
261	**Young, George**	Camp, John	House (old)	24 x 19	log	2	48P	200	250
	School, Francis		Kitchen	24 x 9	log				
	A235 D235 I-		Shop	12 x 18	log				
			Stable	22 x 12	log				
262	**Young, Jacob**	Bickel, John	House (old)	20 x 18	log	2	96P	200	250
	Grumbine, Jacob		Stable	14 x 12					
	A233 D233 I-								
263	**Zering, Jacob**	Dubs, Henry	House (old)	30 x 26	frame	1	2A	300	375
	A236 B213 D236 E213 I- II-		Spring house	20 x 18	log	1			
		Leamy, Tobias	Bank barn	70 x 24			128A		1664
			Gravel land.						

Direct Tax of 1798 - East Hanover Township

No.	Owner/Occupant/Ref.	Adjoining	Building	Dimen.	Matls.	Stories	Acres Perch.	Assmt.	Valuation
1	**Ainsworth, John** A3 B2 D3 E2 I- II-	Ramsey, James Ramsy, James	House W - 6 L - 72 Kitchen Barn House is midling good. Gravel land.	20 x 25 10 x 10	wood log log	1	2A 103A	450	495 1193
2	**Alberdal, Francis** Alberdal, John A5 B5 D5 E5 I- II-	Campbell, Wm. Alberdal, Nicholas	House W - 3 L - 44 - midling good House W - 14 L - 168 - new house Barn (double) Barn (double) Good land.	25 x 30 22 x 28	wood wood log log	1 2	2A 2A 112A 103A	400 500	440 550 1750 1595
3	**Alberdal, Nichlos** A4 B3 D4 E3 I- II-	Albright, John	Kitchen W - 4 L - 47 - good home House (old) Barn (double) Stable Good land.	26 x30 12 x 20	wood wood log	1	2A 133A	400	440 2100
4	**Albright, John** A2 B4 D2 E4 I- II-	Roads, John Rhoads, John	House (old) W - 2 L - 24 Barn Gravel land (poor).	33 x 15	wood log	1	2A 142A	130	143 1318
5	**Andrews, Hugh** Ainsworth, Widow A1 B1 D1 E1 I- II-	Dininger, John	House W -11 L-252 Outhouse W - 1 L - 6 House W - 3 L - 24 Poor house Barn (old) Barn (old) Good land.	30 x 32 16 x 16 26 x 24	stone wood wood log log	2 1	80P 2A 262A 80P	600 120	660 132 4017
6	**Backenstose, John Sr.** Backenstose, Jacob A7 B7 D7 E7 I- II- 	 Andrews, Hugh	House W - 5 L - 76 - good house Stable W - 4 L - 42 Barn Smith shop Gravel land. Mountain land	27 x 29 25 x 27 18 x 15	wood wood log	2 1	2A 2A 160A 200A	420 160	462 170 1810 200
7	**Bamgartner, Philip** A10 B10 D10 E10 I- II-	Lee, Andrew	House (poor) W - 2 L - 10 House	18 x 25 25 x 27	log log	1 2	2A	120	132

Direct Tax of 1798 - East Hanover Township

No.	Owner/Occupant/Ref.	Adjoining	Building	Dimen.	Matls.	Stories	Acres Perch.	Assmt.	Valuation
			Built since 1st of October. Slate land.						
			Barn		log		118A		1240
8	Barthmay, Adam B14 E14 II-	Pross, Peter	House (old) Stable Poor land.	30 x 18	log log		100A		440
9	Bartlemy, Vendle A9 B9 D9 E9 I- II-	Graham, Henry Esq.	House (good) W - 3 L - 36 Barn (old) Poor land.	22 x 40	log log	1	2A 118A	300	330 492
10	Bell, Robert A8 B8 D8 E8 I- II-	Stine, Philip	House W - 3 L - 26 Barn House is poor. Gravel land.	21 x 27	wood log	1	2A 54A	150	165 462
11	Besore, George Beashore, George A15 B16 D15 E16 I- II-	Core, Christian	House House (old) Bank barn Still house House is midling. Gravel land.	24 x 28 16 x 15 25 x 24	wood log pt. stone	2	2A 100A 98A	400	440 950 1473
12	Besore, Isaac A6 B6 D6 E6 I- II-	Swartz, John	House W - 14 L - 189 - midling good Outhouse Barn Slate land.	28 x 30 15 x 20	wood wood log	2 1	2A 118A	400	440 1102
13	Besore, Mathias Beashore, Mathias A17 B17 D17 E17 I- II-	Copenhever, Thos.	House (poor) Barn Gravel land.	22 x 25	wood log	1	2A 144A	250	275 1828
14	Bickel, John Esq. Fulmor, George Firbner, George A16 B19 D16 E19 I- II-	Prost, George Brost, George Pruss, George	House House (old) Barn Houses are midling poor. Poor land.	21 x 18 24 x 30	wood wood log	2 1	2A 199A	200	220 1413
15	Boal, Robert A11 B11 D11 E11 I- II-	Harper, John	House Springhouse Barn Good house. Limestone land. Owner of one slave. Between 12 and 50 yrs. subject to taxation.	20 x 40 12 x 15	wood stone log	2	2A 240A	550	605 3700
16	Bowan, James Winebecker, Henry A18 B18 D18 E18 I- II-	Weidman, John Widman, John	House (good) Barn Poor land.	26 x 30	wood log	2	2A 200A	400	440 1440
17	Bradly, Danl. Bradley, Danl. Esq. A14 B15 D14 E15 I- II-	Boal, Robt.	House Kitchen Bank barn House is midling good. Limestone land.	27 x 27 24 x 27	wood wood pt. stone	2 1	2A 133A	400	440 2295

Direct Tax of 1798 - East Hanover Township

No.	Owner/Occupant/Ref.	Adjoining	Building	Dimen.	Matls.	Stories	Acres Perch.	Assmt.	Valuation
			Owner of one slave. Between 12 and 50 yrs, subject to taxation.						
18	**Breckbill, John**	Harper, John	House	28 x 30	stone	2	1A	900	990
	Brightbill, John	Stine, Philip	House	28 x 30	wood	1	2A	300	330
	Breckbill, Henry		Barn		log		129A		1906
	Brekbill, John Jr.		Grist/sawmill						2000
	A12 B12 D12 E12 I- II-		Barn		log		98A		1060
			Good gravel land.						
			Mountain land				50A		50
			Houses are well finished and good.						
19	**Brekbill, Peter**	Brekbill, John	House	25 x 27	wood	1	2A	350	385
	Brightbill, Peter		Barn (old)		log		128A		1812
	A13 B13 D13 E13 I- II-		Mountain land				50A		50
			House is tolerable. Good gravel land.						
20	**Campbell, John**	Campbell, Wm.	House (old)	21 x 24	wood	1	2A	150	165
	Campbell, Margt.		Barn, (small)		log		24A		270
	A25 B26 D25 E26 I- II-		Gravel land.						
21	**Campbell, William**	Albertall, Frances	House	27 x 29	wood	2	2A	550	605
	A19 B20 D19 E20 I- II-		Kitchen	20 x 25	wood	1			
			Shed	14 x 30	wood				
			Barn		log		100A		1580
			Tanyard Shop	20 x 50					
			Bait house	12 x 14					
			Houses are tolerable good. Limestone land.						
22	**Clark, Benjamin Jr.**	Stine, Adam	House	16 x 20	wd/stone	1	2A	250	275
	Hersberger, Abm.	Stone, Adam	Barn		log		123A		1733
	A21 B22 D21 E22 I- II-		Stable				33A		413
			House is midling. Good gravel land.						
23	**Clark, Thomas Esq.**	Stine, Adam	House (old)	20 x 25	wood	1	1A	125	137.50
	Hedrick, Peter	Stone, Adam	House (old)	12 x 15	wood	1	1A	150	165
	A24 B25 D24 E25 I- II-	Young, Andrew	Barn (old)		log		334A		4706
			Very good gravel land.						
			Land				10A		150
			Bottom land on Swatara.						
24	**Copenhaver, Thos.**	Besore, Mathias	House	20 x 27	wood	1	2A	200	220
	Copinhaffer, Thos.		Barn		log		144A		1808
	A23 B24 D23 E24 I- II-		House is midling. Gravel land.						
25	**Cossart, Jacob**	Shead, Chas.	House	16 x 25	wood	1	1A	125	137.50
	A22 B23 D22 E23 I- II-		Stable		log		5A		50
			House is midling poor. Slate land.						
26	**Cossart, John**	Sheaffer, Geo.	House	24 x 28	wood	2	2A	400	440
	Goodman, Adam		Outhouse	12 x 15	wood	1			
	A20 B21 D20 E21 I- II-		Stable	12 x 12	wood	1			
			House	20 x 24		2	2A	100	110

Direct Tax of 1798 - East Hanover Township

No.	Owner/Occupant/Ref.	Adjoining	Building	Dimen.	Matls.	Stories	Acres Perch.	Assmt.	Valuation
			Barn		log		258A		2650
			Houses are midling good. Clay spoutie land.						
27	Darkis, John	Peifer, Henry	House (old)	22 x 26	wood	1	1A	100	110
	Darkis, Michael	Klick, Ludwig	House (old)	22 x 26	wood	1	2A	150	165
	A27 B28 D27 E28 I- II-		Stable, small				2A		30
			Stable				4A		42
			Gravel land.						
28	Deninger, John	Cossart, John	House (old)	21 x 21	wood	2	2A	150	165
	Dininger, John		Barn		log		156A		1756
	A26 B27 D26 E27 I- II-		Gravel land.						
29	Dubs, Jacob	Young, John	House	24 x 26	wood	2	2A	300	330
	A28 B29 D28 E29 I- II-	Yong, John	Barn, old		log		180A		3190
			House is midling. Gravel land.						
30	Elder & Kain Co.	Coleman, Robt. land	Mountain land				246A		246
	B32 E32 II-								
31	Emrich, John	Zimmerman, Michl.	House, old	25 x 16	log		5A		80
	B31 E31 II-		Stable and Potters Shop						
			Gravel land.						
32	Eyer, John	Mecklin, Philip	House	21 x 18			5A		125
	B30 E30 II-		Stable						
			Bottom land on Swetara.						
33	Farling, George	Simon, John	House	18 x 20			15A		205
	Ferling, George		Stable						
	B34 E34 II-		Gravel land.						
34	Favour, Adam	Rhoads, John	House	22 x 35					
	Faber, Adam		House	16 x 20					
	Painter, Jacob		Barn		log		87A		950
	B33 E33 II-		Slate land.						
35	Fecht, Peter		House						30
	D- E-		Outhouse						
			Land				150A		450
36	Fehler, Jacob		House						40
	D- E-		Outhouse						
			Land				300A		1640
37	Fox, Anthony	Mark, George	House	23 x 30	wood	1	2A	250	275
	A29 B35 D29 E35 I- II-		Barn		log		132A		784
			House is midling. Poor land.						
38	Garberik, Philip	Winter, Christian	House (good)	25 x 36	wood	1	2A	500	550
	Garbarich, Phillip	Winter, Stophel	Springhouse	8 x 11	pt. stone	1			
	A31 B38 D31 E38 I- II-		Barn		log		198A		2674

Direct Tax of 1798 - East Hanover Township

No.	Owner/Occupant/Ref.	Adjoining	Building	Dimen.	Matls.	Stories	Acres Perch.	Assmt.	Valuation
			Gravel land.						
39	Garbrick, Adam Garberich, Adam A32 B39 D32 E39 I- II-	Garbarick, Philip	House Barn House is midling. Gravel land.	25 x 26	wood log	1	2A 148A	250	275 1896
40	Garbrick, John A34 B36 D35 E36 I- II-	Stewart, William	House (poor) Springhouse Barn Gravel land.	18 x 28	wood log	1	2A 138A	200	220 1548
41	Gardner, Bernard Gardner, Barnhard Gardner, Martin Sheaffer, Margt. A33 B40 D34 E40 I- II-	Winter, Henry	House House Shop/Stable Barn Limestone land.	25 x 30 20 x 35 18 x 20	wood wood wood log	1 1 1	1A 1A 2A 158A	300 300 100	330 330 110 2470
42	Gartner, George Gardner, George A35 B41 D36 E41 I- II-	Garbrick, Adam Garbarich, Adam	House (poor) Wagoneer shop Barn Gravel land.	20 x 25 15 x 20	wood log	1	2A 76A	150	165 714
43	Graham, Henry Esq. Fox, John A30 B37 D30 E37 I- II-	Low, James	House House is tolerable good. House (old) Barn Barn (old) Clay spoutie land. Gravel.	26 x 26 18 x 30	wood wood log log	2 1	1A 2A 123A 106A	400 100	440 110 1393 1186
44	Graham, James (heirs) Kreamer, Andrew McKinney, John B42 E42 II-	Ainsworth, John	House (old) House (old) Barn (old) Stable (old) Gravel land.	18 x 20 16 x 18	 log log		 179A		 1840
45	Harper, Widow Harper, John Harper, Thom. A37 B45 D38 E45 I- II-	Boal, Robt.	House House is midling good. Stable Barn Mill house (old) Mill house is old, out of use. Limestone land.	25 x 48 11 x 18	wood wood log stone	1	2A 217A	550	605 3315 30
46	Harrison, Isaac Bigham, Joseph A36 B44 D37 E44 I- II-	 Graham, Henry Bell, Robert	House House is midling good. House (old) Bank barn Barn Fulling mill Clay spoutie land. Gravel.	22 x 26 15 x 20	stone log stone stone stone	1	2A 150A 93A	500	550 1450 764 1000
47	Hedrick, John A38 B46 D39 E46 I- II-	Brekbill, Peter Brightbill, Peter	House (old) Bank barn Gravel land.	26 x 28	wood pt. stone	1	2A 128A	250	275 1964

Direct Tax of 1798 - East Hanover Township

No.	Owner/Occupant/Ref.	Adjoining	Building	Dimen.	Matls.	Stories	Acres Perch.	Assmt.	Valuation
48	Helem, Conrad Helm, Conrad A39 B49 D40 E49 I- II-	Tittle, George	House (old) Barn (old) Midling gravel land.	24 x 26	wood log	1	2A 128A	200	220 946
49	Henning, Mathias Honning, Mathias A42 B50 D43 E50 I- II-	Walmer, Peter	House (good) House (old) Barn Gravel land.	28 x 30 15 x 20	wood log	2	2A 148A	450	495 1920
50	Hess, Henry Wagoner, John A41 B48 D42 E48 I- II-	Glick, Ludwig Glick, Ludwig Klick, Ludwig	House (old) House (old) Stable Barn (old) Gravel land.	14 x 24 18 x 20	wood log rd. log	1 1	2A 2A 148A	175 100	192.50 110 1658
51	Hess, Mathias A40 B47 D41 E47 I- II-	Hess, Henry	House Stable Land House is midling good. Gravel land.	20 x 20	wood	1	2A 7A	100	110 56
52	Hoofnagle, Felty Hoofnagel, Valentine B43 E43 II-	Straw, Michael	House Stable Gravel land.	16 x 20	log log		50A		602
53	Houtz, Jacob D- E-		House Outhouse Land				570A		150 3430
54	Hower, John D- E-		House Outhouse Land				80A		60 320
55	Kern, Nicholas Kairn, Nicholas A49 B57 D50 E57 I- II-	Bruner, Henry	House Bank barn Mountain land House is midling good. Gravel land.	20 x 40	wd/stone stone	1	2A 126A 311A	300	330 1434 311
56	Ketz, Nicholas Frantz, Jacob A43 B51 D44 E51 I- II-	Lutz, Henry	House (good) House (old) House (old) Barn Barn Sandy land.	24 x 30 18 x 21 18 x 21	wood log log log	1	2A 178A	400	440 2296
57	King, Widow Hershberger, Abm. A44 B52 D45 E52 I- II-	Myer, Jacob	House (good) Barn Poor land.	17 x 30	wood log	1	1A 45A	400	440 257
58	Kingrich, Peter A45 B53 D46 E53 I- II-	Clark, Thomas Seltzer, Michl.	House House is part old and part new. New part built since 1st of October.	26 x 46	wood	2	2A	200	220

Direct Tax of 1798 - East Hanover Township

No.	Owner/Occupant/Ref.	Adjoining	Building	Dimen.	Matls.	Stories	Acres Perch.	Assmt.	Valu-ation
			Weaver Shop						
			Barn		log		198A		2634
			Slate land.						
59	Klick, Ludwig	Besore, George	House	24 x 28	wood	1	2A	200	220
	Kleick, Ludwigh	Hess, Henry	Barn (old)		log		148A		1512
	A47 B55 D48 E55 I- II-		House is midling. Gravel land.						
60	Kneagy, Jost	Clark, Thomas Esq.	House	18 x 30	wood	1	2A	300	330
	A46 B54 D47 E54 I- II-		Bank barn		pt. stone		178A		2080
			Old house in midling repair. Gravel land						
61	Kolp, Philip						50A		50
	E-								
62	Kore, Christian	Besore, George	House (old)	20 x 25	wood	1	2A	150	165
	Kohr, Christian	Beshore, George	Bank barn		pt. stone		148A		1502
	A48 B56 D49 E56 I- II-		Smith shop	17 x 20					
			Gravel land.						
63	Lee, Andrew	Bombartner, Philip	House (old)	14 x 35	wood	1	2A	150	165
	Bomberger, Christly		Barn		log		158A		2578
	A53 B61 D54 E61 I- II-		Bottom land on Swetara.						
64	Leidig, Michl.	Straw, Michael	House	18 x 27	wood	1	2A	250	275
	A52 B60 D53 E60 I- II-		Still house (old)	16 x 22					
			Barn (old)		log		78A		810
			House is midling. Gravel land.						
65	Lose, Jacob		Land				150A		450
	E-								
66	Low, James	Cossert, John	House (old)	24 x 30	wood	1	2A	120	132
	A50 B58 D51 E58 I- II-		Barn		log		106A		1090
			Cold clay land.						
67	Lowmiller, John	Clark, Benjamin	House (old)	21 x 37	wood	1	2A	225	247.50
	A54 B62 D55 E62 I- II-		Barn		log		128A		1596
			Gravel land.						
68	Lutz, Henry	Ketz, Nichlos	House	25 x 32	wood	2	2A	350	385
	A51 B59 D52 E59 I- II-		Outhouse						
			Barn		log		165A		1855
			House is midling. Slate land.						
69	Mark, Adam	Seltzer, Michael	House (old)	17 x 38	wood	1	2A	150	165
	A61 B69 D62 E69 I- II-		Barn		log		135A		1670
			Gravel land.						
70	Mark, David	Besore, Isaac	House (old)	20 x 30	wood	1	2A	100	110
	A55 B63 D56 E63 I- II-		Stable		log		29A		268

Direct Tax of 1798 - East Hanover Township

No.	Owner/Occupant/Ref.	Adjoining	Building	Dimen.	Matls.	Stories	Acres Perch.	Assmt.	Valuation
			Still house	12 x 20					
			Sandy land.						
71	Martin, George	Fox, Anthony	House (good)	28 x 30	wood	2	2A	450	495
	Mark, George		Bank barn		pt. stone		128A		1182
	A63 B71 D64 E71 I- II-		Smith shop	12 x 12	log				
			Slate land.						
72	Martin, John	Harrison, Isaac	House	20 x 22	wood		656 sq.ft.	200	220
	A59 B67 D60 E67 I- II-		Kitchen	12 x 18	log	1			
			Tanner shop	22 x 22					50
			Tanyard/Barkhouse						
			House is part good.						
73	Mickling, Philip	Swartz, Henry	House	19 x 24	wood	1	2A	200	220
	Mecklin, Philip		Kitchen	19 x 21	log	1			
	A56 B64 D57 E64 I- II-		Barn (small)		log		28A		272
			House is midling. Slate land.						
74	Miller, Christian	Young, Andrew	House (good)	21 x 40	wd/stone	1	2A	500	550
	A60 D61 I-		Springhouse	15 x 15	stone	1			
75	Miller, Henry	Shirk, Abm.	House (good)	26 x 30	wood	2	2A	450	495
	Bumgartner, Henry	Shark, Abm.	Work Shop	12 x 26		1			
	A58 B66 D59 E66 I- II-	Albright, John	Barn		log		199A		1240
			Stable				117A		1190
			Gravel land.						
76	Miller, John	Young, Andrew	House (old)	18 x 20	log				
	Miller, Christr.	Mark, George	Bank barn				128A		1842
	Miller, Stophel		Good gravel land						
	B68 E68 II-		House (old)	18 x 20	log				
			Stable (small)				90A		680
			Stable (small)						
			Poor land.						
77	Minnick, John		House						60
	D- E-		Outhouse						
			Land				200A		800
			Land				200A		800
			Land				92A		368
			Land				100A		100
78	Mourer, Michael	Low, James	House (old)	22 x 28	wood	2	2A	220	242
	Mowra, Michael		Barn		log		100A		525
	A57 B65 D58 E65 I- II-		Poor land.						
79	Musser, Henry	Kern, Nicklos	House (old)	29 x 29	wood	1	2A	150	165
	A64 B72 D65 E72 I- II-	Besore, George	House (old)	24 x 26	wood	1	1A	150	165
		Kavin, Nichs.	Barn		log		97A		821
			Mountain land				30A		30
			Clay land.						

Direct Tax of 1798 - East Hanover Township

No.	Owner/Occupant/Ref.	Adjoining	Building	Dimen.	Matls.	Stories	Acres Perch.	Assmt.	Valuation
80	Myer, Jacob Mier, Jacob Moyer, Jacob A62 B70 D63 E70 I- II-	Stine, Abm. Stone, Adam Heron, Ned Kemple, Christn. Kingrich, Christn.	House Part built since 1st of October. Bank barn House (old) Still house House (old) Stable House (old) Stable Stable Gravel land.	24 x 33 16 x 16 18 x 20 16 x 16 16 x 20	wood pt. stone log log log	2	2A 200A	200	220 2465
81	Peck, Andrew A65 B73 D66 E73 I- II-	Sheaffer, George	House Stable Land House is midling. Poor land.	20 x 23	wood	1	2A 21A	130	143 84
82	Poor, Nicklos A66 B74 D67 E74 I- II-	Gingrich, Peter	House (poor) Wash house Barn Poor land.	20 x 24 12 x 16	wood log	1	2A 144A	280	308 1068
83	Pross, George Pruss, George A69 B78 D70 E78 I- II-	Sheade, Charles	House (old) Outhouse Barn (old) Gravel land.	20 x 24 12 x 15	 log	1 1	2A 192A	155	170.50 1940
84	Pross, Peter Pruss, Peter A67 B75 D68 E75 I- II-	Ramler, Leond.	House Outhouse Barn House is midling good. Poor land.	18 x 22	wood log	1	2A 86A	300	330 566
85	Pruner, Henry Prunner, Henry A68 B76 D69 E76 I- II-	Hess, Henry	House House is midling good. House (old) Bank barn Gravel land.	20 x 25 15 x 18	wood wood stone	1 1	1A 1A 198A	300 100	330 110 2075
86	Pruner, Henry Jr. Prunner, Henry Jr. B77 E77 II-	Woods, James (Col.)	Land Gravel land.				20A		180
87	Rambler, Leond. Raumler, Leonard A75 B86 D85 E86 I- II-	Harrison, Isaac	House (good) Bank barn Gravel land.	21 x 25	wood pt. stone	2	2A 178A	450	495 2158
88	Ramsey, James A72 B81 D82 E81 I- II-	Ainsworth, John	House Barn (old) House is midling. Gravel land.	18 x 21	wood log	1	2A 98A	250	275 1113
89	Rank, George Rauch, George Miller, Odelia	Cassart, John	House (old) Outhouse House (old)	21 x 42 16 x 21	log wood	1 1	1A 1A	150 100	165 110

Direct Tax of 1798 - East Hanover Township

No.	Owner/Occupant/Ref.	Adjoining	Building	Dimen.	Matls.	Stories	Acres Perch.	Assmt.	Valuation
	A71 B80 D81 E80 I- II-		Barn Clay land.		log		100A		1045
90	Rauck, Henry Rouch, Henry A74 B85 D84 E85 I- II-	Siderbricker, Philip	House (old) Barn Poor land.	18 x 20	wood log	1	2A 100A	150	165 630
91	Rhoad, John A70 B79 D80 E79 I- II-	Swartz, Henry	House (good) Outhouse House Barn Stable Gravel land.	28 x 32 13 x 17 16 x 20	wood wood log log	2	80P 175A	600	660 1973
92	Road, Conrad Rhoads, Conrad Wickart, Francis A73 B84 D83 E84 I- II-	Royer, Saml. Shuey, Henry	House House is midling good. Outhouse House (poor) House Bank barn Barn (old) Mountain land Poor clay land.	14 x 19 14 x 19 20 x 25 20 x 25	stone log wood wood pt. stone log	1 1 1 1	1A 1A 1A 50A 60A 50A	250 200 150	275 220 165 525 565 50
93	Royer, Saml. Ryer, Saml. A76 B87 D86 E87 I- II-	Road, Conrad Rhoads, Conrad	House Barn Mountain land House is midling.	24 x 28	wood log	1	2A 148A 100A	250	275 1382 100
94	Ruker, Christophr. Runker, Christr. B83 E83 II-	Ainsworth, John	House (old) Barn Poor land.	24 x 27	log log		135A		1010
95	Rumberger, George B82 E82 II-	Seigler, Henry	House (old) Barn Poor land.	18 x 24	log log		 45A		 395
96	Satezahn, Peter D- E		House Outhouse Land				 250A		60 1650
97	Seltzer, Christn. Selsir, Christian Spangler, Michl. A104 B116 D114 E116 I- II-	Wingert, Christn.	House (old) Barn Gravel land.	20 x 24	wood log	1	2A 174A	150	165 1760
98	Seltzer, Michael A86 B98 D96 E98 I- II-	Mark, Adam	House (old) Bank barn Gravel land.	16 x 20	wood stone	1	2A 138A	200	220 1936

Direct Tax of 1798 - East Hanover Township

No.	Owner/Occupant/Ref.	Adjoining	Building	Dimen.	Matls.	Stories	Acres Perch.	Assmt.	Valuation
99	Sering, Christian A100 B112 D110 E112 I- II-	Musser, Henry Walmer, Peter	House (old) Outhouse Barn Gravel land. House (old) Stable Most part mountain land.	26 x 28 15 x 15	wood log log	1	2A 171A 195A	200	220 1926 317
100	Sering, Henry (heirs) Sering, Ludwig Steger, Jacob Sagor, Jacob A103 B115 D113 E115 I- II-	Sering, Ludwig Seltzer, Christn. Shaufler, Christian	House (good) House House is midling. House (old) Bank barn Barn Tanyard (small) Gravel land.	27 x 29 27 x 29 14 x 16	stone wood pt. stone log	2 2	1A 2A 106A 100A	800 300	880 330 1260 1050
101	Sering, Ludwig Tibbins, John A102 B114 D112 E114 I- II-	Shaufler, Val. Tibbins, John	House House is midling House (good) Bank barn Barn Gravel land.	24 x 28 27 x 29	wood wood pt stone log	1 2	2A 2A 200A 105A	250 400	275 440 2175 1205
102	Shead, Charles A95 B107 D105 E107 I- II-	Pross, George Pruss, George	House Outhouse Barn House is midling. Gravel land.	24 x 27	wood log	2	2A 98A	300	330 1020
103	Sheaffer, George Shaffer, George A79 B90 D89 E90 I- II-	Cossart, John	House (old) Barn Poor land.	20 x 30	wood log	1	2A 75A	200	220 405
104	Shewey, Henry Jr. A88 B100 D98 E100 I- II-	Road, Conrad Rhoad, Conrad	House (poor) Barn Gravel land.	24 x 25	wood log	1	2A 70A	225	247.50 690
105	Shewy, Henry Shewy, Ludwig A101 B113 D111 E113 I- II-	Wolmer, John Garbarick, Adm.	House (good) House Stable Barn Gravel land. Barn Cold clay land.	28 x 30 20 x 24 20 x 24	wood wood wood log log	2 1 1	2A 2A 2A 246A 50A	500 200	550 220 2781 450
106	Shirk, Abraham Shark, Abraham A85 B97 D95 E97 I- II-	Miller, Henry	House Outhouse Bank barn House is midling. Gravel land.	27 x 28	wood pt. stone	2	2A 104A	400	440 1240
107	Shoufler, Christn. Shaufler, Christn. A98 B110 D108 E110 I- II-	Smith, Valentine Smith, Felty	House (old) Barn Gravel land.	28 x 30	wood log	1	2A 66A	150	165 680

Direct Tax of 1798 - East Hanover Township

No.	Owner/Occupant/Ref.	Adjoining	Building	Dimen.	Matls.	Stories	Acres Perch.	Assmt.	Valuation
108	**Shoufler, Valentine** Shaufler, Valentine A97 B109 D107 E109 I- II-	Sering, Ludwig Tibbins, John	House (good) House (old) Bank barn Barn Gravel land.	30 x 35 15 x 20	wood pt. stone log	2	1A 120A 175A	800	880 1495 1965
109	**Siderbriker, Philip** Sidestricker, Philip A93 B105 D103 E105 I- II-	Rauch, Henry	House (old) Barn (old) Poor land.	24 x 25	wood log	1	2A 198A	200	220 1328
110	**Siglar, Henry** Seigler, Henry A84 B96 D94 E96 I- II-	Miller, Henry	House Barn (old) House is midling. Gravel land.	27 x 29	wood log	2	2A 82A	450	495 860
111	**Simmerman, John** Smeltzer, Adam A83 B95 D93 E95 I- II-	Light, Henry Light, Henry Seigler, Henry	House (good) House (old) Stable Bank barn Smith shop Gravel land.	25 x 27 16 x 20	wood wood wood stone	2 1	2A 2A 146A	500 100	550 110 1760
112	**Simmerman, Michl.** A94 B106 D104 E106 I- II-	Emerick, John	House (poor) Stable (small) Slate land.	16 x 25	wood	1	2A 7A	100	110 80
113	**Simon, John** B91 E91 II-	Ainsworth, John	House (old) Barn Sandy soil.	35 x 20	log log		120A		1330
114	**Sloan, John** Rowan, Hugh A78 B89 D88 E89 I- II-	Dinninger, John	House (good) Kitchen House (old) Barn Gravel land.	25 x 30 16 x 16 12 x 16	stone stone log	2 1	80P 117A	600	660 1205
115	**Smith, Valentine** A99 B111 D109 E111 I- II-	Shoufler, Christian	House Barn House is midling good. Gravel land.	28 x 30	wood log	1	2A 100A	375	412.50 1050
116	**Stever, Adam** Steever, Adam A96 B108 D106 E108 I- II-	Tibbins, John	House (old) Springhouse Barn Gravel land.	24 x 27 12 x 16	wood wood log	1 1	2A 137A	275	302.50 1131
117	**Stewart, John** A91 B103 D101 E103 I- II-	Stewart, William	House (old) Barn (old) Good gravel land.	18 x 28	wood log	1	2A 104A	150	154 1376
118	**Stewart, William** Hamer, Peter A92 B104 D102 E104 I- II-	Stewart, John Ryer, Saml.	House (old) Barn Very good land. Mountain land	22 x 36	wood	1	2A 218A	175	192.50 3310 51

Direct Tax of 1798 - East Hanover Township

No.	Owner/Occupant/Ref.	Adjoining	Building	Dimen.	Matls.	Stories	Acres Perch.	Assmt.	Valuation
119	**Stine, Adam** Stone, Adam A89 B101 D99 E101 I- II-	Clark, Benjamin	House Springhouse Barn House is midling good. Slate land.	27 x 30 15 x 20	wood wood log	1 1	2A 123A	500	550 1396
120	**Stine, Adam Jr.** Stone, Adm. Jr. A87 B99 D97 E99 I- II-	Moyers, Jacob Myer, Jacob Mier, Jacob	House (good) Kitchen Barn Good gravel land.	16 x 18 16 x 18	wood wood log	2 1	2A 123A	450	495 1659
121	**Stine, Philip** A90 B102 D100 E102 I- II-	Boal, Robt. Bell, Robt.	House Springhouse Bank barn House is midling good. Gravel land.	25 x 30 10 x 15	wood stone stone	1 1	2A 148A	400	440 2016
122	**Straw, Michael** Rudy, Jacob Wolf, Jacob A82 B94 D92 E94 I- II-	Hoofnagel, Valn. Hoofnagel, Felty	 Barn Grist/sawmill House is midling. Gravel land.	20 x 22	stone log pt. stone	2	2A 188A	350	385 1950 1000
123	**Strohding, Andrew** D- E-		House Outhouse Land				 150A		20 450
124	**Swartz, George** A77 B88 D87 E88 I- II-	Albertall, Francis	House (good) Outhouse Barn Wagonmaker shop Slate land.	29 x 34 18 x 21 19 x 22	wood wood log	2 1	80P 135A	550	605 1560
125	**Swartz, Henry** A80 B92 D90 E92 I- II-	Rhoads, John Road, John	House (old) Barn Slate land.	24 x 30	wood log	1	2A 63A	160	176 670
126	**Swartz, John** Bolton, Valtn. Bolton, Felty A81 B93 D91 E93 I- II-	Besore, Isaac Alberdall, Nichlos	House Outhouse House not finished 1st of October last. House (poor) Barns (2) Smith shop Slate land.	27 x 31 13 x 15 22 x 26 17 x 18	wood wood wood log	2 1 1	2A 2A 126A	150 100	165 110 1446
127	**Thomas, Widow** B117 E117 II-	Lutz, Henry	House Stable Slate land.	20 x 24			10A		130
128	**Tibbins, John** A107 B120 D117 E120 I- II-	Stower, Adam	House (old) Barn Gravel land.	18 x 20	wood log	1	2A 73A	200	220 767
129	**Tittle, George** A106 B119 D116 E119 I- II-	Tittle, Jacob	House Barn	24 x 26	wood log	2	2A 78A	300	330 664

Direct Tax of 1798 - East Hanover Township

No.	Owner/Occupant/Ref.	Adjoining	Building	Dimen.	Matls.	Stories	Acres Perch.	Assmt.	Valuation
			House is midling good. Gravel land.						
130	Tittle, Jacob	Tittle, Geo.	House (old)	26 x 28	wood	1	1A	150	165
	A105 B118 D115 E118 I- II-		House (old)	17 x 20	wood	1	1A	150	165
			Barn		log		98A		814
			Gravel land.						
131	Uhland, George	Bradly, Danl. Esq.	House (old)	16 x 30	wood	1	2A	250	275
	A108 B121 D118 E121 I- II-		Barn		log		198A		2036
			Part slate, part bottom land.						
132	Vendling, Jacob	Albright, John	House (old)	20 x 34	wood	1	2A	200	220
	A109 B122 D119 E221 I- II-	Stone, Adam	Barn		log		91A		762
			Gravel land.						
133	Wagoner, Jacob	Albright, John	House (old)	17 x 34	wood	1	2A	150	165
	A110 B123 D120 E123 I- II-		Barn		log		32A		312
			Slate land.						
134	Wallace, John	Bowen, James	House (small)	12 x 15	log		50A		72
	B131 E131 II-		Stable (old)						
			Mountain land.						
135	Walmer, John	Shewy, Henry	House	26 x 28	wood	1	2A	400	440
	A115 B128 D125 E128 I- II-		Barn		log		180A		2040
			House is midling good. Gravel land.						
136	Wengart, Abram.		House						250
	D- E-		Outhouse						
			Land				140A		1680
137	Wideman, John Sr.	Bowen, James	House (old)	20 x 30	wood	2	2A	350	385
	Weidman, John Esq.		Kitchen	20 x 32					
	Union Forge	Woods, James	Barn	27 x 80	log		280A		2900
	Hammel, Isaac		Land				225A		60
	A118 B132 D128 E132 I- II-		Union Forge Coal House						3000
			Grist/sawmill						1500
	Fisher, John		House	17 x 20					20
	Angst, Nichls.		House	17 x 20					30
	Bowen, Jas.		House	17 x 20					60
	Shesler, John		House	17 x 20					20
	Large, Stephen		House	17 x 20					30
	McCady, Jeremiah		House	17 x 20					20
	Mease, Geo.		House	17 x 20					60
	Holsberger, ____		House	17 x 20					30
			All small houses belonging to the Forge for the use of the workmen.						
			Some midling land, some poor land, wood cut off.						
			Some mountain land.						
138	Wingart, Christn.	Seltzer, Christn.	House	24 x 28		2	2A	450	495
	A114 B127 D124 E127 I- II-		House is midling good.						

Direct Tax of 1798 - East Hanover Township

No.	Owner/Occupant/Ref.	Adjoining	Building	Dimen.	Matls.	Stories	Acres Perch.	Assmt.	Valuation
		Shead, Charles	House (old)	20 x 24		1	2A	150	165
			Bank barn		pt. stone		156A		1881
			Bank barn		pt. stone		123A		1355
			Gravel land.						
139	**Winter, Christn.**	Winter, Henry	House (good)	27 x 32	wood	2	1A	500	550
	Winter, Christopher		Barn		log		99A		1347
	A112 B125 D122 E125 I- II-		Gravel land.						
140	**Winter, Henry**	Boal, Robt.	House	17 x 30	wood	1	1A	275	302.50
	A111 B124 D121 E124 I- II-		House is midling good.						
			House (old)	16 x 21	wood	1	1A	150	165
			Bank barn		pt. stone		98A		1464
			Still house	15 x 20					
			Gravel land.						
141	**Wolf, Widow**	Clark, Thomas	House	14 x 18	stone	2	80P	400	440
	A113 B126 D123 E126 I- II-		Kitchen	8 x 18	stone	1			
			Stable (old)				20A		190
			House is midling good.						
			Slate land.						
142	**Wolmer, Peter**		House	20 x 33	wood	1	2A	375	412.50
	Walmer, Peter	Henning, Mathias	Springhouse	15 x 20	stone	1			
	A116 B129 D126 E129 I- II-		Barn		log		98A		1040
			House is midling good. Gravel land.						
143	**Woods, James Col.**	Bowen, James	House (old)	15 x 30	wood	1	2A	150	165
	Pointer, Adam	Weidman, John Esq.	Barn		log		178A		1108
	A117 B130 D127 E130 I- II-		Poor land.						
144	**Young, Andrew**	Miller, Christian	House (good)	28 x 30	stone	2	80P	750	825
	A119 B133 D129	Miller, John	Kitchen	12 x 16	stone	1			
	E133 I- II-		Barn		log		129A		1583
			Gravel land.						
145	**Young, James**	Miller, John	House (old)	16 x 24	wood	1	2A	150	165
	A120 B134 D130 E134 I- II-		Stable (small)				58A		474
			Gravel land.						
146	**Young, John**	Dubs, Jacob	House (old)	26 x 28		1	2A	275	302.50
	A121 B135 D131 E135 I- II-		Barn		log		157A		1291
			Smith shop (old)						
			Gravel and poor land.						
147	**Young, Widow**	Besore, George	House	27 x 29	wood	2	2A	400	440
	A122 B136 D132	Smith, Felty	Barn		log		198A		2020
	E136 I- II-		Land				100A		1000
			Midling good house. Gravel land.						

Direct Tax of 1798 - Heidelberg Township

No.	Owner/Occupant/Ref.	Adjoining	Building	Dimen.	Matls.	Stories	Acres Perch.	Assmt.	Valuation
1	Achenbach, Anthony B4 E4 II-	Pollem, John	Land				60A	240	288
			Mountain land, mostly cleared; 4 Dol./Acre.						
2	Achy, Henry A1 B1 D1 E1 I- II-	Kumler, Henry	House Barn	30 x 27 60 x 30	limestone rd. log	2	2A 150A	450 2400	562.50 2880
			House is midling old, not quite finished. Barn of midling quality; dry limestone land of a midling quality - a 16 Dol./Acre value.						
3	Achy, Samuel A2 B2 D2 E2 I- II-	Strack, Henry	House Barn	36 x 32 52 x 38	hewn log stone	2	2A 91A	400 1366	500 1639.20
			House is of hewn logs and weather boards, not quite finished. Barn new, not quite finished; limestone land, dry. Valued at 10 Dol./Acre.						
4	Albrecht, Martin A3 D3 I-	Sheferstown	House Barn (small)	26 x 22 20 x 25	frame log	1	2A 100P	200	250
			House is frame filled with bricks. Condition is bad, old. Barn is old. Lot adjoining the Market Square.						
5	Albrecht, Widow A6 D6 I-	Sheferstown	House	22 x 20	log/bd.	1	100P	150	187.50
			House is of hewn log and boards. In midling order.						
6	Armeshan, Mathias A4 B3 D4 E3 I- II-	Sheferstown Ream, Peter Sr.	House Stable Land	36 x 26	hewn log hewn log	2	100P 3A	300 48	375 57.60
			House is in midling order, only half finished. Limestone land. Valued at 10 Dol./Acre.						
7	Artz, Christn. A5 D5 I-	Myerstown	House Outhouse	24 x 22 21 x 12	hewn log hewn log	1	2A	150	187.50
			House is old, in bad order. Outhouse is not used.						
8	Baasler, Adam A38 B27 D38 E27 I- II-	Baasler, Simon	House Barn Grist mill Saw mill	30 x 20 50 x 28 30 x 40 12 x 40	limestone stone/log stone	1	2A 86A	400 1978 800 150	500 2373.60 960 100
			House is in midling order. Barn midling good. The land limestone of good first quality. Grist mill - part burrs, part country stones. Bad order, scarce in water. Saw mill - double geered; bad order and old.						
9	Baasler, Simon Basler, Simon A17 B15 D17 E15 I- II-	Moyer, John	House Springhouse Outhouse Barn	32 x 28 20 x 18 21 x 18 70 x 30	hewn log limestone limestone stone/log	2	2A 188A	300 4700	375 5640
			House is old and in bad order. Springhouse in midling order. Land first quality; barn new and finished. Value - 25 Dol./Acre.						

Direct Tax of 1798 - Heidelberg Township

No.	Owner/Occupant/Ref.	Adjoining	Building	Dimen.	Matls.	Stories	Acres Perch.	Assmt.	Valuation
10	Baasler, Simon, Exr. Hawkly, Henry A32 D32 I-	Myerstown	House Stable (small) House and stable are old and in bad order.	32 x 18	hewn log log	1		102	127.50
11	Badorff, John A16 B14 D16 E14 I- II-	Badorff, Peter	House Barn House well finished and good order. Good gravel land, part watered meadow. Value - 14 Dol./Acre.	36 x 28 70 x 22	limestone hewn log	2	2A 113A	600 1582	750 1898.40
12	Badorff, Peter A15 B13 D15 E13 I- II-	Shitz, Jacob	House Barn House nearly new, well finished. Barn in good order. Gravel land, part watered meadow. Value - 12 Dol./Acre.	30 x 24 60 x 28	hewn log stone/log	2	2A 158A	350 1896	437.50 2275.20
13	Becker, George Jr. Becker, Frederick A26 B23 D26 E23 I- II-	Hoffman, Jacob	House House Barn Barn One house is old, in good order. Other house is quite old and decayed. Good new barn; gravel land second quality. Old and decayed barn.	32 x 30 24 x 20 80 x 30 60 x 25	hewn log hewn log stone/log hewn log	2 1	2A 2A 120A 140A	400 150 2160 2240	500 187.50 2592 2688
14	Becker, George Sr. A8 B6 D8 E6 I- II-	Royer, John	House Barn Good house, well finished. All limestone land of the first quality; with fine watered down medow. Value - 24 Dol./Acre.	40 x 35 80 x 30	sandstone stone	2	2A 198A	1000 4752	1250 5702.40
15	Becker, John A7 B5 D7 E5 I II-	Hoffman, Jacob	House Barn Good house, well finished. An excellent fountain of spring water before the door. Good barn, in good order. Land part limestone, greater part gravel. Value - 18 Dol./Acre.	30 x 28 73 x 30	hewn log stone	2	2A 148A	550 2644	687.50 3172.80
16	Becker, Nichls. I-	Sheferstown	House 2 lots.	20 x 18	hewn log	1	1A 40P	150	
17	Beckly, Frederick A19 B16 D19 E16 I- II-	Focht, George	House House This house adjoins the first house. Barn House is of stone - new and well finished. The log in the old dwelling house adjacent is new. Indifferent barn; good dry land. Value - 18 Dol./Acre.	34 x 26 18 x 20 50 x 20	limestone hewn log log	2 1	2A 148A	600 2664	750 3196.80
18	Bee, John A31 D31 I-	Myerstown	House Stable (small) House and stable in midling order.	26 x 24 26 x 24	hewn log rd. log	2		175	218.75

Direct Tax of 1798 - Heidelberg Township

No.	Owner/Occupant/Ref.	Adjoining	Building	Dimen.	Matls.	Stories	Acres Perch.	Assmt.	Valu- ation
19	**Beiler, Christian** A12 B10 D12 E10 I- II-	Lantz, John Waggoner, George	House Barn	36 x 20 60 x 28	hewn log rd. log	1	2A 175A	200 2800	250 3360
			Old house, in indifferent order. Good dry limestone land. Barn midling. Value - 16 Dol./Acre.						
20	**Beiler, John** A13 B11 D13 E11 I- II-	Crill, John	House Barn	30 x 26 49 x 26	hewn log stone/log	2	2A 98A	300 1372	375 1646.40
			New and well finished. Dry, broken limestone land. Barn in good order, new. Value - 14 Dol./Acre.						
21	**Bennage, Henry** Fidler, Ludwig A34 D34 I-	Myerstown	House Outhouse Stable (small)	28 x 24 30 x 20	hewn log hewn log	1 1		200	250
			The lots in one fence. House and stable are in midling order.						
22	**Benner, Martin** A18 D18 I-	Uhrich, John	House	22 x 20	rd. log	1	2A	175	218.75
			Old and in indifferent order.						
23	**Bettz, Samuel** A35 D35 I-	Newmanstown	House Joiner shop Stable (small)	24 x 18 18 x 12 18 x 12	hewn log hewn log rd. log	2 1	1A	200	250
			Buildings in good order.						
24	**Bitner, Mathias** A10 B8 D10 E8 I- II-	Troutman, Jonas	House Springhouse Barn	26 x 28 8 x 10 45 x 24	hewn log hewn log rd. log	2	2A 170A	200 2210	250 2652
			House not finished, in bad order. Covered with straw, old and of little value. Part gravel, part limestone, more than half is gravel; not maybe meadow. An old barn in bad order. Value - 13 Dol./Acre.						
25	**Blecher, Jacob** A30 D30 I-	Myerstown	House Wagoner shop Stable (small)	30 x 26 30 x 20 30 x 20	log log log	2 1	2A	450	562.50
			Land in 5 contiguous lots in said Town; the house in good order. Shop is good. Stable in good order.						
26	**Blecher, Widow** A36 B26 D36 I- II-	Waggoner, Geo.	House Barn	20 x 18 30 x 18	hewn log rd. log	1	2A 36A	110 540	137.50 648
			House is in poor order. Barn midling order. The land limestone and dry.						
27	**Bob, Daniel** A11 B9 D11 E9 I- II-	Bitner, Mathias	House Springhouse Barn	24 x 24 10 x 12 30 x 20	hewn log hewn log rd. log	1	2A 80A	150 480	187.50 576
			An old house in bad order. A good spring, a little unhandy. Midling and indifferent. Poor gravel land. Value - 6 Dol./Acre.						
28	**Boeshore, Adam** A21 B18 D21 E18 I- II-	Braun, Michael	House Barn	21 x 15 40 x 18	hewn log rd. log	2	2A 78A	105 390	131.25 468

Direct Tax of 1798 - Heidelberg Township

No.	Owner/Occupant/Ref.	Adjoining	Building	Dimen.	Matls.	Stories	Acres Perch.	Assmt.	Valuation
			House is old and in bad order. Barn indifferent; land with ground oaks. Value - 5 Dol./Acre.						
29	**Boyer, Phillip** A24 B21 D24 E21 I- II-	Sheferstown Grum, John	House Barn Land	30 x 18 28 x 18	hewn log log	1	2A 2A	300 24	375 28.80
			House is old, in bad order. the land - 4 lots adjoining. Barn is in bad order. Gravel land.						
30	**Braun, George (heirs)** Seibert, Christian Jr. A27 B24 D27 E24 I- II-	Brown, Phillip	House Barn	32 x 28 40 x 20	limestone rd. log	2	2A 138A	700 3036	875 3643.20
			House is new, finished and in good order. Barn in bad order; good limestone land.						
31	**Braun, Michael** A20 B17 D20 E17 I- II-	Mosser, Michael	House Barn	28 x 23 35 x 20	hewn log log	1	2A 100A	175 500	218.75 600
			House is in midling order. Barn poor order; poor gravel land; in ground oaks. Value - 5 Dol./Acre.						
32	**Braun, Phillip** Brown, Widow A28 B25 D28 E25 E26 I- II-	Noll, George	House House Barn	30 x 28 20 x 18 70 x 30	limestone limestone stone	2 1	2A 138A	600 3174	750 3808.80
			House is old, in bad order. Second house is in midling order; the Widow is seat of second occupant. Barn midling good order; the land is good limestone bottom.						
33	**Brecht, Phillip** A23 B20 D23 E20 I- II-	Sheferstown Sheferstown	House Stable (small) Smith shop Land	22 x 20 18 x 12 18 x 12	hewn log rd. log rd. log	1	1A 40P 1A 40P	200 20	250 24
			Land is in two lots; house new, in midling order. Stable in good order, Smith shop is in midling order. Limestone land.						
34	**Brecht, Widow** A37 D37 I-	Sheferstown	House	20 x 18	hewn log	1	100P	105	131.25
			House is in midling order.						
35	**Breidenbach, Phillip** A14 B12 D14 E12 I- II-	Kuster, John	House Tanhouse Barn Land	26 x 24 20 x 18 30 x 20	hewn log hewn log hewn log	2 1	2A 60A	600 900	750 1080
			Buildings in midling order. Dry limestone land. Value - 15 Dol./Acre.						
36	**Brubaker, Daniel** A25 B22 D25 E22 I- II-	Shenk, John	House Springhouse Barn	36 x 33 40 x 20 60 x 30	limestone limestone stone	2 2	2A 212A	1000 4028	1250 4833.60
			New, finished and in good order. Part one story high, part two story. Midling old, bad order. A capital spring. Good barn, good limestone land, good meadows.						

Direct Tax of 1798 - Heidelberg Township

No.	Owner/Occupant/Ref.	Adjoining	Building	Dimen.	Matls.	Stories	Acres Perch.	Assmt.	Valuation
37	**Bullman, Fredk.** A33 D33 I-	Myerstown	House Stable/shed (small)	45 x 20	log/bd.	2	2A	500	625
			House is occupied as a Tavern and store and in good repair. Stable/shed in bad order.						
38	**Bullman, John** A9 B7 D9 E7 I- II-	Moore, John	House Springhouse Barn Smith shop	30 x 20 15 x 12 65 x 30 15 x 12	hewn log hewn log hewn log hewn log	2 2	2A 164A	500 3280	625 3936
			An old house, indifferent order. Middling good order. An excellent Spring. All limestone land; good quality. Barn midling good order, the Smith shop is only used for his own work. Value - 20 Dol./Acre.						
39	**Bunner, Henry Esq.** A29 D29 I-	Myerstown	House Stable (small) Buildings in good order.	26 x 24	hewn log log	2	2A	300	375
40	**Burky, Henry** A22 B19 D22 E19 I- II-	Sheferstown	House Barn (small)	26 x 20	hewn log rd. log	1	100P	125	156.25
		Moore, Peter	Land Land				2A 80P 2A 80P	38 38	45.60 45.60
		Sheferstown	Land				90P	8	9.60
		Swanger, Nicholas	Land				3A	48	57.60
			House is in indifferent order. Old, in bad repair. All limestone land.						
41	**Canal Company** Feuks, John Elleberger, John A40 B29 D40 E29 I- II-	Deckert, Jacob	House Barn Grist mill Land (Counting Canal)	28 x 22 50 x 20 45 x 24	hewn log hewn log limestone	2	2A 150A 33A	250 1950 825 800	312.50 2340 990 960
			House is in midling good order. Old barn in poor order. Good gravel land. Grist mill - part burrs, part country stones, midling good order, scarce of water.						
42	**Coleman, Robert Esq.** Shram, Henry A39 B28 D39 E28 I- II-	Becker, John	House Barn	25 x 21 30 x 20	log rd. log	1	2A 80A	105 480	131.25 576
			House is old, good for nothing. Old barn, in bad order. Poor gravel land.						
43	**Deckert, Jacob** Blecker, George A46 B34 D46 E34 I- II-	Eckert, Jonas	House Barn	30 x 28 60 x 28	hewn log hewn log	2	2A 131A	350 2358	437.50 2829.60
			House is in good order. Bad barn, good gravel land; good quality meadow.						
44	**Dengler, John** Newman, John Strickler, Peter A48 B38 D48 E38 I- II-	Newmanstown	House Barn (small) Stable (small) Stable (small)	24 x 28 24 x 20 25 x 21	hewn log hewn log hewn log	1 1 2	80P 1A 80P	200 105 300	250 131.25 375
		Saltzgeber, ___	Land Mountain land				9A 7A	135 42	162 50.40
			House is in midling good order. One stable is in bad order;						

Direct Tax of 1798 - Heidelberg Township

No.	Owner/Occupant/Ref.	Adjoining	Building	Dimen.	Matls.	Stories	Acres Perch.	Assmt.	Valuation
			one stable is new and in good order. Midling limestone land.						
45	Diel, Abram A47 B35 D47 E35 I- II-	Groh, Widow	House Barn House is in midling good order. Bad barn, ground oak land.	24 x 20 30 x 18	hewn log rd. log	1	2A 58A	150 348	187.50 417.60
46	Dierwechter, Ehrhart A42 B31 D42 E31 I- II-	Ditzler, Christian	House Barn House is old and in bad order. Barn in good order, dry limestone land.	40 x 22 60 x 28	hewn log stone/log	1	2A 148A	200 2516	250 3019.10
47	Diffebach, Widow Brown, Adam A44 B33 D44 E33 I- II-	Diffebach, Benj. Exr. of his Father's Estate	House House Barn House is in good order. Spring house under it in midling order. Barn midling order, good limestone land, good meadows.	32 x 16 30 x 22 80 x 20	limestone hewn log hewn log	2 1	2A 118A	500 2832	625 3398.40
48	Diffenbach, Benjm. A43 B32 D43 E32 I- II-	Diffebach, Peter	House Barn House is in good repair. Good limestone land. Barn in midling order.	46 x 25 23 x 18	log/bd. log	2	2A 18A	450 324	562.50 388.80
49	Dissinger, Geo. A51 B37 D51 E37 I- II-	Sheferstown Sheferstown	House Stable (small) Land (2 lots) House is old and in bad order.	26 x 20	hewn log	1	100P 1A 40P	105 20	131.25 24
50	Dissinger, John A52 B38 D52 E38 I-	Sheferstown Sheferstown	House Smith shop (small) Land (4 lots) Buildings are old and in bad order.	22 x 20		2 1	100P 2A 80P	150 40	187.50 48
51	Ditman, John A50 B36 D50 E36 I- II-	Sheferstown Sheferstown Kline, John	House Barn (small) Land (4 lots) Land House in good order; barn in midling order. Being 4 lots in Sheferstown, adjoining other near Sheferstown, adjoining John Kline. Limestone land.	26 x 20 30 x 16	log/bd. hewn log	1	100P 2A 64P 7A	250 34 112	312.50 40.80 134.40
52	Ditzler, Christ. Miller, David A45 D45 I-	Miller, Daniel	House House is old and in bad order.	30 x 23	hewn log	1	2A	105	131.25
53	Ditzler, Christian Miller, David A41 B30 D41 E30 I- II-	Gerret, George	House Barn Barn House is in midling good order. Dry limestone land. 15 x 18 barn on gravel land in ground oaks, poor barn.	30 x 26 50 x 24 15 x 18	hewn log rd. log rd. log	2	2A 75A 48A	300 1275 326	375 1530 391.10

Direct Tax of 1798 - Heidelberg Township

No.	Owner/Occupant/Ref.	Adjoining	Building	Dimen.	Matls.	Stories	Acres Perch.	Assmt.	Valuation
54	Dubler, Morris A278 I-	Newmanstown	House House is in midling order.	20 x 15	hewn log	1	1A	105	
55	Dubler, Widow A53 D53 I-	Sheferstown	House Lots (3) House is in bad order.	20 x 18	hewn log	1	1A 120P	105	131.25
56	Duncan, Ph. Matzenberger, John A49 D49 I-	Myerstown	House Stable (small) House is old and in bad order.	26 x 22	hewn log	1		180	225
57	Eckert, Jonas Eckhart, Jonas A55 B39 D55 E39 I- II-	Lehmy, Christian	House Springhouse (small) Barn	35 x 30 65 x 25	limestone limestone hewn log	2	2A 194A	600 4462	750 5354.40
			House and springhouse in midling order. Midling barn, good limestone land, large quantity of good meadows.						
58	Ege, George Esq. B43 E43 II-	Weick, Christian	Land Mountain land.				200A	600	720
59	Eichholtz, Jacob Gassert, Adam A54 D54 I-	Myerstown	House Stable (small) 1 1/2 lots contiguous. Buildings in midling order.	30 x 24	hewn log	1	1A	150	187.50
60	Eisseman, Widow A281 I-	Newmanstown	House Barn (small) House is in midling order.	20 x 18	hewn log	1	1A 80P	200	
61	Erpff, Phillip A56 B40 D56 E40 I- II-	Sheferstown	House Kitchen Barn	36 x 26 18 x 13 26 x 20	limestone limestone log	2 1	2A	700	875
		Shitz, Peter Unbehind, Jacob	Land Land				2A 2A	32 32	38.40 38.40
			House is good and well finished. Kitchen in midling order. Barn in bad order. Good limestone land.						
62	Esh, Jacob A58 B42 D58 E42 I- II-	Spanhuth, Henry J.	House Barn House is in bad order. Barn in bad order. Ground is oak land.	36 x 20 34 x 18	log rd. log	1	2A 38A	150 266	187.50 319.10
63	Etman, John Ettman, John A57 B41 D57 E41 I- II-	Nole, Leon Noll, Leonard	House Barn Smith shop Buildings in midling order. Ground oak land. Midling order.	26 x 23 30 x 18 20 x 18	hewn log hewn log rd. log	1	2A 13A	105 91	187.50 109.20
64	Fehler, John A64 B47 D64 E47 I- II-	Leitner, Peter Leitner, Peter	House Barn House in bad order and old. Half barn in midling order. Poor ground oak land.	24 x 20 28 x 20	hewn log hewn log	1	2A 30A	150 150	187.50 180
65	Fertig, _____ Sweitzer, John A66 D66 I-	Sheferstown	House House in midling order.	22 x 18		1	100P	105	

Direct Tax of 1798 - Heidelberg Township

No.	Owner/Occupant/Ref.	Adjoining	Building	Dimen.	Matls.	Stories	Acres Perch.	Assmt.	Valuation
66	Fidler, Widow Fudler, Widow	Sheferstown	House House is in bad order.	18 x 16	hewn log	1	1A 100P	105	131.25
67	Filson, Widow Shultz, John A65 D65 I-	Newmanstown	House Stable (small) Buildings in good order.	30 x 30	hewn log log	2	1A	300	375
68	Fisher, George B44 E44 II-	Dierwechter, Ehrhart	Land Good limestone land.				50A	900	1080
69	Fogt, George Foght, George A62 B45 D62 E45 I- II-	Hipshman, Henry	House Wash house Barn House in good order. Wash house in midling order. Barn in good order. Land dry limestone bottom.	42 x 22 14 x 11 60 x 28	stone/wd. log stone/log	2 1	2A 150A	550 2550	687.50 3080
70	Fogt, Mathias Foght, Mathias A63 B46 D63 E46 I- II-	Steiner, Fredk. Steiner, Frederick Weaver, John	House Barn Land Buildings in bad order and old. Barn new and finished. Good limestone land. Land (25 acres) is dry limestone land.	36 x 22 70 x 30	hewn log stone/log	1	2A 142A 25A	175 2556 450	218.75 3067.20 540
71	Fortiney, Henry A59 D59 I-	Myerstown	House Stable Stable is small and old; in bad order.	26 x 20	hewn log	2		150	187.50
72	Fremdling, Widow A280 I-	Newmanstown	House House is in midling order.	20 x 15	hewn log	1	80P	105	
73	Fried, Adam Grumbine, Leonard A60 D60 I-	Sheferstown	House Stable (small) House is on 2 lots; bad order and old.	36 x 20	hewn log	1	1A 40P	200	250
74	Fuhrman, Andw. A61 D61 I-	Sheferstown	House Stable Buildings in bad order and old.	22 x 20	hewn log log	1	100P	110	137.50

75	Gassert, Jacob
	    Shriner, John
	    Krug, Philip
	A77 D77 I-
		Myerstown	House
			Shop
			Shop
			Stable
			All buildings in midling order.
				30 x 20
				18 x 12
				32 x 20
				18 x 16
					limestone
					limestone
					hewn log
					hewn log
						1
						1
						2
								200
								
								200
									250
									
									250

76	Gast, Mathias Gristman, Jacob A78 B57 D78 E57 I- II-	Myerstown Moyer, John	House Stable (small) House - good order; stable - midling good order. House House - old rotten and bad order; smith shop, good order. Smith shop Land Good limestone land.	35 x 22 25 x 20 20 x 18	stone/log log hewn log limestone	2 1 2 1	 2A	300 150 40	375 187.50 48
77	Gehret, Fred	Sheferstown	House	22 x 20	hewn log	1	100P	150	187.50

Direct Tax of 1798 - Heidelberg Township

No.	Owner/Occupant/Ref.	Adjoining	Building	Dimen.	Matls.	Stories	Acres Perch.	Assmt.	Valuation
	Gehret, Christ. A79 D79 I-		Stable (small) House in good order; stable in bad order.		hewn log				
78	Gehret, George Gerret, George A69 B50 D69 E50 I- II-	Zimmerman, George	House Barn House is old and in bad order. Bad barn. Dry limestone land.	30 x 18 45 x 25	hewn log rd. log	1	2A 148A	200 2220	250 2664
79	Gehret, Jacob Gerret, Jacob Gehret, Jacob Gerret, John A67 B48 D67 E48 I- II-	Kapp, Anthony	House Barn Still house (small) House is old and in bad order. Barn in good order. Land is clay and gravel. Two stills.	25 x 35 50 x 25	hewn log stone/log	1 1	2A 146A	300 1606	375 1927.20
80	Gerber, David Gerver, David A72 B53 D72 E53 I- II-	Lantz, John	House Barn House is in midling order. Barn in midling good order. Dry limestone land.	28 x 22 26 x 26	hewn log stone/log	2	2A 81A	300 1296	375 1555.20
81	German, Henry A73 B54 D73 E54 I- II-	Wolff, Michael	House Barn House is old and in bad order. Barn in poor order. Ground oak land.	20 x 18 50 x 20	hewn log log	1	2A 193A	105 1351	131.25 1621.20
82	German, Michl. A75 B55 D75 E55 I- II-	Moyer, John	House Stable (small) House is new, but half finished only. Stable in midling order. Ground oak land.	22 x 18	hewn log	1	2A 30A	105 210	131.25 252
83	Gilbert, Henry A76 D76 I-	Myerstown	House Stable (small) House is in bad order.	40 x 20	hewn log rd. log	1		150	187.50
84	Gips, Negro A202 I-	Myerstown	House House is in bad order.	22 x 18	hewn log	1	36P	102	
85	Gleim, Jacob Gline, Jacob A71 B52 D71 E52 I- II-	Miller, Valentine	House Barn House is half finished - new house. Good barn; poor gravel land.	20 x 25 16 x 14	hewn log rd. log	2	2A 8A	200 40	250 48
86	Grall, Henry A74 B56 D74 E56 I- II-	Mace, George	House Outhouse Outhouse is empty. Barn House is old, midling order. Barn midling. Limestone land, no meadows.	28 x 24 18 x 16 60 x 28	hewn log hewn log hewn log	1 1	2A 178A	250 3026	312.50 3631.20
87	Groff, Andrew Grove, Andrew A68 B49 D68 E49 I- II-	Seibert, Christian	House Barn House is well finished, in good order. Barn in good order. Good limestone land, dry meadows.	30 x 20 70 x 30	hewn log	2	2A 278A	400 5560	500 6672

Direct Tax of 1798 - Heidelberg Township

No.	Owner/Occupant/Ref.	Adjoining	Building	Dimen.	Matls.	Stories	Acres Perch.	Assmt.	Valuation
88	Groh, Widow A80 B58 D80 E58 I- II-	Diel, Abm.	House Barn	24 x 20 28 x 15	hewn log log	1	2A 2A	175 90	218.75 108
	House in good order. *Barn in bad order. Ground oak land.*								
89	Gromer, David A70 B51 D70 E51 I- II-	Bobb, Daniel	House Barn	20 x 18 20 x 15	log rd. log	1	2A 30A	101 150	126.25 180
	House is old and in bad order. Barn is in bad order. *Poor gravel land.*								
90	Grumbine, Widow A81 D81 I-	Sheferstown	House	22 x 18	hewn log	2	1A 36P	150	187.50
	House is in midling order, not finished.								
	Hackman, Henry A87 B64 D87 E64 I- II-	Feler, John	House Barn	30 x 24 55 x 20	hewn log log	1	2A 59A	175 360	218.75 424.80
	House is in midling order. *Barn midling. Ground oak land.*								
91	Haffa, Phillip Mace, Michael A94 D94 I-	Sheferstown	House Hatters shop Stable (small)	24 x 18 20 x 18	hewn log rd. log rd. log	1 1	1A 40P	150	187.50
	Hatters shop is old. *Buildings in bad order.*								
92	Hassinger, Herman A92 D92 I-	Myerstown	House	26 x 20	hewn log	1		150	187.50
	House is in bad order.								
93	Hauter, Samuel Howter, Saml. A86 B63 D86 E63 I- II-	Miller, Samuel	House Barn Land	26 x 24 30 x 20	hewn log log	2	2A 21A 60A	200 126 350	250 151.20 432
	House is in midling order. *Barn is midling. Ground oak land.*								
94	Hawk, Henry A85 B62 D85 E62 I- II-	Hawk, Michael Noaker, Christian	House Kitchen Stable	22 x 30 15 x 15	limestone limestone hewn log	2 1	2A 5A	550 90	687.50 108
	Buildings in good order and well finished. *Limestone land.*								
95	Hawk, Michael A84 B61 D84 E61 I- II-	Hawk, Nicholas	House Barn Saw mill, new	34 x 32 70 x 33	limestone stone/log	2	2A 224A	600 4928 150	750 5913.60 180
	House is old but in midling order. Barn in good order. *Saw mill is new - in good order. Limestone land.*								
96	Hawk, Nicholas Spengler, Martin A83 B60 D83 E60 I- II-	Walburn, Christn.	House Outhouse Smith shop House Barn Barn	36 x 20 20 x 18 20 x 18 28 x 20 70 x 30 20 x 15	limestone hewn log limestone hewn log hewn log hewn log	2 1 1 1	2A 2A 50A 200A	700 150 1200 4000	875 187.50 1440 4800
	House - newly repaired and in good order. Outhouse is in *midling order. Smith shop in good order. Barn in bad order.*								

Direct Tax of 1798 - Heidelberg Township

No.	Owner/Occupant/Ref.	Adjoining	Building	Dimen.	Matls.	Stories	Acres Perch.	Assmt.	Valuation
			Barn (70 x 30) is good. Limestone land - good.						
			Barn (20 x 15) is bad; limestone land - midling good.						
97	Heffelfinger, John A91 D91 I-	Myerstown	House Kitchen	30 x 18 18 x 16	hewn log hewn log	2 1		125	156.25
			House and kitchen are old and in bad order.						
98	Hillyer, Henry Hillger, Henry A93 D93 I-	Myerstown	House Stable (small)	30 x 25	hewn log	2		250	312.50
			Buildings in good order.						
99	Hippert, George A89 D89 I-	Newmanstown	House Stable (small)	30 x 25	hewn log	1	1A 80P	175	218.75
			House is in good order.						
100	Hipshman, Henry A88 B66 D88 E66 I- II-	Achy, Henry	House House Barn	26 x 22 20 x 18 60 x 30	hewn log hewn log stone/log	2 1	2A 250A	300 4250	375 5100
			First house is in bad order and old. Second house is old.						
			Good barn, midling new. Limestone land.						
101	Hoffman, Jacob Lautermilch, John A97 B67 D97 I-	Royer, John	House Outhouse	32 x 30 25 x 15	hewn log sandstone	2 1	2A	450	562.50
			House is in good order. Outhouse is old, in bad order.						
			House Barn	23 x 20 70 x 26	 log	1	 230A	40 5060	48 6072
			House (23 x 20) is of logs, old and much decayed.						
			Barn is old and in bad order.						
102	Hofman, Jacob Hoffman, Jacob Lautermilch, Jacob E67 II-	Royer, John	House Barn	23 x 20 70 x 26	log log		 230A	40 5060	48 6072
			House is old and in bad order.						
			Barn is in bad order. Land pt. gravel, pt. limestone.						
103	Holseid, Peter A275 I-	Newmanstown	House	20 x 18	hewn log	1	1A	200	
			House is in midling order.						
104	Holstein, George Miller, George A82 B59 D82 E59 I- II-	Meisser, Geo.	House Springhouse Springhouse Barn	40 x 34 18 x 12 26 x 22 80 x 36	limestone hewn log hewn log stone	2 1 2A	2A 2A 358A	1000 200 7160	1250 250 8592
			House in very good order, springhouse and barn in midling order.						
			Barn in good order. Good limestone land, good meadows.						
105	Houser, Peter A95 D95 I-	Sheferstown	House Stable (small)	24 x 18	hewn log	1	1A 40P	150	187.50
			Buildings in bad order.						
106	Houston, James Huston, James B65 E65 II-	Sheferstown Kolb, Peter	Land (5 contiguous lots) Land				3A 20P 6A	50 96	60 115.20
			Five lots containing each 100 Perches. In Sheferstown						
			adjoining to Geo. Dissinger.						
			Six acres are near Sheferstown adjoining Peter Kolb.						

Direct Tax of 1798 - Heidelberg Township

No.	Owner/Occupant/Ref.	Adjoining	Building	Dimen.	Matls.	Stories	Acres Perch.	Assmt.	Valuation
107	Howard, Widow A98 B68 D98 E68 I- II-	Wolfersberger, George	House Barn	30 x 16 40 x 18	hewn log log	1	2A 75A	200 1245	250 1494
			House is old and in bad order. Very bad barn. Land midling.						
108	Huber, George A90 D90 I-	Myerstown	House Stable (small)	30 x 24	hewn log	2		175	218.75
			House is in midling order.						
109	Huston, James A96 D96 I-	Sheferstown	House Barn	34 x 15 20 x 12	stone/log log	1	1A 100P	200	250
			Buildings are in midling order.						
110	Iba, Henry A100 B70 D100 E70 I- II-	Sheferstown Miller, Valentine	House Stable Land	30 x 24 18 x 15	hewn log	2	100P 10A	175 160	218.75 192
			House is old, in midling order. Stable in bad order. Limestone land.						
111	Iba, William A101 D101 I-	Sheferstown	House Stable	27 x 20 18 x 12	hewn log	1	100P	250	312.50
			House in good order. Stable in midling order.						
112	Illig, Leonard Newman, _____ A102 B71 D102 E71 I- II-	Miller, Michl. Strack, Henry Strickler, Andw.	House House Barn Barn Land Land Land	30 x 28 18 x 16 80 x 30 70 x 30	hewn log hewn log stone/log limestone	2 1	2A 2A 138A 230A 90A 25A 50A	400 150 3036 3910 360 100 200	500 187.50 3643.20 4692 432 120 240
			House (30 x 28) in good order. 18 x 16 house is old, in bad repair. Barn (80 x 30) is good, new. Good land, watered meadow. Land is mountain land.						
113	Immel, Leonard Beam, George A99 B69 D99 E69 I- II-	Spengler, George Steimer, Frederick Spengler, Peter	House House Barn Barn (old, decayed) Land	32 x 28 24 x 20 96 x 32	limestone hewn log limestone	2 1	2A 2A 144A 95A 104A	700 105 3600 1710 1664	875 131.25 4320 2052 1996.80
			Limestone house is in good order. Log house is in bad order. Barn (96 x 32) is new, good order, limestone land, quality first. Dry limestone land.						
114	Kalbach, Adam A121 D121 I-	Newmanstown	House Kitchen Barn (small)	32 x 24 16 x 13 30 x 15	hewn log hewn log hewn log	2 1	120P	350	437.50
			House and kitchen in good order. Barn indifferent.						
115	Kapp, Anthony A103 B72 D103 E72 I- II-	Gerret, Jacob	House Barn Still house	30 x 28 70 x 28 25 x 18	hewn log stone/log hewn log	1 2	2A 126A	350 1386	437.50 1663.20
			House is in good order. Good barn, poor gravel land. Still house is in midling order.						

Direct Tax of 1798 - Heidelberg Township

No.	Owner/Occupant/Ref.	Adjoining	Building	Dimen.	Matls.	Stories	Acres Perch.	Assmt.	Valuation
116	**Kapp, Frederic** Steiner, Fredk. A122 B90 D122 E90 I- II-		House House Smith shop Barn	30 x 25 26 x 18 20 x 20 50 x 25	hewn log hewn log hewn log stone/log	2 1 1	1A	600	750
			Boring Mill Land Land	20 x 20	log		100A 100A	120 400 40	144 480
			House (30 x 25) in good order. House (26 x 18) in midling order. Smith shop and Barn in good order. Land (400 acres) is mountain land. Land (40 acres) is in midling order.						
117	**Kapp, George** A116 B85 D116 E85 I- II-		House Barn Half	30 x 25	frame/brk hewn log	1	80P	300	375
		Moore, Jacob Shaefer, Henry Esq. Moore, Peter Moore, Adam	Land Land Land Land				2A 80P 2A 80P 2A 80P 2A 80P	35 35 35 35	42 42 42 42
			House is in Sheferstown, adjoining Market Square. House and barn in midling order.						
118	**Kapp, John** Kapp, George A115 B84 D115 E84 I- II-	Sheferstown	House House Barn Shed for 2 teams	40 x 24 13 x 24 40 x 20	frame/brk hewn log hewn log frame	1 2	60P	450	562.50
		Moore, Adam Shaefer, Henry Esq. Weiman, George	Land Land Land				2 1/2A 7 1/2A 1A	35 105 16	42 126 19.20
			House (40 x 24) is in midling order. Tavern house. House (13 x 24) in midling order. Store kept therein. Barn and shed are in midling order. Two lots in Shaeferstown.						
119	**Kapp, John** **Kapp, Jacob** Haupt, Fredk. A118 B87 D116 E87 I- II-	Becker, George	House Weaver shop Barn	27 x 25 18 x 16 45 x 24	hewn log hewn log log	2	2A 145A	250 1595	312.50 1914
			House and weaver shop are old and in midling order. Barn midling; poor gravel land.						
120	**Kenior, Jacob** E93						27A	108	129.60
121	**Kiener, Godfry** A123 B91 D123 E91 I- II-	Myerstown	House Kitchen Shed for 3 teams Land	40 x 20 20 x 18	log/bd. log/bd. frame	2 1	54P	450 10	562.50 12
			House is in good order. Tavern. Shed in bad order.						
122	**Kinsly, Rudy** Kinsly, Gottlieb A124 B92 D124 E92 I- II-	Myerstown Spengler, Peter	House Joiner shop Barn House Stable (small)	32 x 27 27 x 18 40 x 32 30 x 25	hewn log hewn log limestone hewn log rd. log	2 1 2		350 300	437.50 375

Direct Tax of 1798 - Heidelberg Township

No.	Owner/Occupant/Ref.	Adjoining	Building	Dimen.	Matls.	Stories	Acres Perch.	Assmt.	Valu-ation
			Land				26A	460	552
			House, joiner shop are in good order. Barns are new. Stable is indifferent. Good limestone land.						
123	**Kintzer, Jacob** B93 II-	Kapp, Frederick	Mountain land.				27 Sq.Ft.	108	
124	**Klick, Leonard** A112 B81 D112 E81 I- II-	Hackman, Henry	House Stable	20 x 22 18 x 16	hewn log log	1	2A 4A	105 20	131.25 24
			House is in bad order. Ground oak land.						
125	**Kline, John** A114 B83 D114 E83 I- II-	Sheferstown	House Barn	27 x 22 40 x 18	log/bd.	2	100P	300	375
		Sheferstown	Tanhouse	30 x 18	log		3A 96P	245	294
		Moore, Peter	Land				2A 80P	35	42
		Ditman, John	Land				6A	96	115.20
			Land				4A	64	76.80
		Moore, Peter	Land				3A 80P	56	67.20
		Grum, John	Land				3A 80P	56	67.20
			House (27 x 22) in good order, not well finished. House (40 x 18) in midling order. Good land, subject to ground oak.						
126	**Koch, Christian** A111 B80 D111 E80 I- II-	Diel, Abram	House Barn	22 x 20 30 x 20	hewn log rd. log	1	2A 148A	110 888	137.50 1065.60
			House is in bad order, quite old. Poor barn. Ground oak land.						
127	**Kochenderfer, Geo.** A120 B89 D120 E89 I- II-	Gerret, Jacob	House Barn Still house	28 x 20 40 x 20 20 x 18	hewn log log log (old)	1	2A 100A	250 1000	312.50 1200
			House is in bad order. Barn in midling order. White clay and gravel land.						
128	**Koenig, David** A104 B73 D104 E73 I- II-	Hawk, Nicholas	House Barn	22 x 20 45 x 28	hewn log log	1	2A 98A	175 1568	218.75 1881.60
			House is old and bad. Barn is in midling order. Dry limestone land.						
129	**Kolp, Peter** A117 B86 D117 E86 I- II-		House	28 x 20	hewn log	1	100P	150	187.50
		Kapp, John	Land (3 out lots)				7A 80P	105	126
		Ditman, John	Land (free land)				5A 120P	92	110.40
		Ream, Peter	Land (gravel land)				3A	30	36
			House is old and in bad order.						
130	**Koppenheffer, Henry** A110 B79 D110 E79 I- II-	Noaker, Christian	House Barn	33 x 26 65 x 28	hewn log stone	2	2A 142A	400 3308	500 3969.60
			House in midling order, an old springhouse near it. Good barn. Good limestone land.						
131	**Kreutzer, Michl.** A108 B77 D108 E77 I- II-	Hawk, Michl.	House Barn	32 x 28 100 x 32	limestone hewn log	2	2A 168A	500 4200	625 5040
			House is old, the wall cracked, in midling order.						

Direct Tax of 1798 - Heidelberg Township

No.	Owner/Occupant/Ref.	Adjoining	Building	Dimen.	Matls.	Stories	Acres Perch	Assmt.	Valuation
			Good limestone land, good meadows.						
132	Krill, John A106 B75 D106 E75 I- II-	Beiler, John	House Barn	30 x 24 50 x 24	hewn log log	1	2A 140A	200 2100	250 2520
			House is old and in bad order. Barn in midling order. Dry broken limestone land.						
133	Krum, John A119 B88 D119 E88 I- II-	Miller, Valentine	House Weaver shop Barn	35 x 28 18 x 16 60 x 22	hewn log hewn log log	2	2A 160A	550 2560	687.50 3072
			House and weaver shop in good order, old. Barn in poor order. Limestone land.						
134	Kumler, Henry A113 B82 D113 E82 I- II-	Strack, Henry	House Barn Still house	30 x 24 60 x 25 22 x 18	hewn log stone/log log	2	2A 117A	300 1638	375 1965.60
			House is in bad order. Barn midling. Limestone land - dry. Still house is in bad order.						
135	Kuntz, Nichl. Eichholtz, Jacob A124 D125	Myerstown	House	18 x 20	hewn log	1	1A 40P	200	250
136	Kurtz, John A105 B74 D105 E74 I- II-	Koenig, David	House Barn	24 x 20 68 x 18	hewn log log	1	2A 140A	225 2240	281.25 2688
			House is old and in bad order. Barn is in midling order. Dry limestone land.						
137	Kurtz, Stephen Weiss, John A109 B78 D109 E78 I- II-	Lower, Benjm.	House House Barn	40 x 22 22 x 16 61 x 30	hewn log limestone stone/log	1 1	2A 200A	450 4800	562.50 5760
			House is in midling order. Springhouse below and dwelling house above all in midling order. Barn in good order. Good limestone land.						
138	Kuster, John A107 B76 D107 E76 I- II-	Miller, Valentine Simmon, George	House Springhouse Barn Land Land	30 x 20 15 x 12 75 x 30	stone/log	2 1	2A 96A 50A 50A	400 2208 1150 350	500 2649.60 1380 420
			House is in good order; springhouse is in indifferent order. Barn in good order. Good limestone land. First 50 acre lot is good limestone land. Other lot is ground oak land.						
139	Lantz, John Lantz, John Jr. A125 B94 D125 E94 I- II-	Kurtz, John	House	32 x 30	hewn log	2	2A	500	625
			House is of hewn pine log. Fine, good, well finished house.						
			House Stable (small) Barn Still house	24 x 20 70 x 32 30 x 20	hewn log rd. log stone/log log	1	2A 200A	110 3400	137.50 4080
			House (24 x 20) is midling order; Stable - bad order. Good new barn. Dry limestone land. Still house in bad order.						

Direct Tax of 1798 - Heidelberg Township

No.	Owner/Occupant/Ref.	Adjoining	Building	Dimen.	Matls.	Stories	Acres Perch.	Assmt.	Valuation
140	Lehman, Christn. Lehmy, Christian A131 B100 D130 E100 I- II-	Eckert, Jonas	House Kitchen Outhouse Barn	40 x 34 20 x 18 18 x 16 70 x 28	limestone limestone hewn log hewn log	2 1 1	2A 148A	1100 3700	1375 4440
				House and kitchen are new, well finished. Outhouse in midling order. Barn in midling order. Land of the first quality limestone.					
141	Lehn, Jacob A132 B101 D132 E101 I- II-	Ramler, Leonard	House Barn	28 x 24 20 x 12	hewn log log	1	2A 3A	300 75	375 90
				House is in good order. Good order barn. Good limestone land.					
142	Lein, John Line, John David, Daniel A126 B95 D126 E95 I- II-	Shitz, Jacob	House Kitchen House Barn Land	27 x 30 16 x 16 18 x 20 84 x 30 	hewn log limestone stone/log 	2 1 	2A 176A 155A	500 3872 1085	625 4640.40 1302
		Shertel, Bernard	Stable	18 x 15	log			70	84
				House (27 x 30) is in good order. Kitchen goodly - new. Barn in good order. Good limestone land. Land is ground oak. Stable is old and indifferent.					
143	Leiss, Peter Lice, Peter Mattee, Fredk. A134 B103 D134 E103 I- II-	Newmanstown Seibert, Frantz	House Kitchen House Kitchen Barn Shed for 2 teams Land	28 x 22 15 x 15 44 x 20 12 x 10 50 x 25 	brick stone frame/brk stone hewn log frame 	2 1 2 1 	80P 1A 50A	550 500 900	687.50 625 1080
				House (28 x 22) and kitchen are well finished and new. House (44 x 20) is in midling order, Tavern. Kitchen, barn, and shed are in bad order. Land (50 Acres) is good gravel land.					
144	Lentz, George A129 B98 D129 E98 I- II-	Walburn, John	House Barn	30 x 24 45 x 20	hewn log log	1	2A 48A	200 288	250 345.60
				House in midling order. Barn in midling order. Ground oak land.					
145	Ley, Christian Coppenheffer, Widow Xander, George Jungst, _____ A133 B102 D133 E102 I- II-	Spengler, George	House Kitchen Springhouse	40 x 32 18 x 16 40 x 22	limestone limestone limestone	2 1 2	2A	1500	1875
				Well finished, fine, large, good spring. Springhouse and wash house below, grainery above.					
		Deckert, Jacob	House Springhouse	37 x 31 30 x 22	limestone limestone	2 2	2A	800	1000
				House is in midling, good order. Good spring and wash house below, dwelling above.					
		Mase, George Moyer, John	House House Barn Barn Barn	30 x 24 22 x 18 90 x 36 60 x 35 55 x 25	hewn log hewn log stone stone log	1 2 	2A 2A 230A 238A 148A	200 200 5750 4560 2516	250 250 6900 5472 3019.20

Direct Tax of 1798 - Heidelberg Township

No.	Owner/Occupant/Ref.	Adjoining	Building	Dimen.	Matls.	Stories	Acres Perch.	Assmt.	Valuation
			Stable	18 x 12	log		44A	352	422.40
			House (40 x 22) and kitchen are well finished and in good order. House (30 x 24) is in midling order.						
			House (22 x 18) in good order.						
			Barn (90 x 36) in good order. Limestone land first quality.						
			Barn (60 x 35) midling order. Good gravel land.						
			Barn (55 x 25) in poor order. Dry limestone land.						
			Stable - ground oakland, well timbered.						
146	**Lightner, Peter** A128 B97 D128 E97 I- II-	Hackman, John Henry	House Wash house Barn Buildings in good order. Barn in midling order. Ground oak land.	26 x 25 18 x 16 50 x 25	hewn log hewn log log	1 1	2A 65A	200 455	250 546
147	**Long, Henry** A130 B99 D131 E99 I- II-	Urich, John	House Barn House in midling order. Barn in bad order. Ground oak land.	30 x 20 60 x 20	hewn log log	2	2A 100A	200 600	250 720
148	**Louser, John** A136 D136 I-	Sheferstown	House House is in poor order.	24 x 22	stone/brk.	1	1A 40P	150	187.50
149	**Lower, Christian** Lower, Benj. Weiss, George A127 B96 D127 E96 I- II-	Walburn, John	House House Stable (small) Barn Buildings in midling order. Good barn. Good limestone land, first quality.	28 x 22 23 x 20 60 x 30	hewn log hewn log hewn log stone/log	2 1	2A 2A 146A	300 150 3650	375 187.50 4380
150	**Lydig, Peter** Line, Peter Lidig, Peter A135 D135 B104 E104 I- II-	Myerstown Sheferstown	House Stable Land (good gravel land) House and stable are in midling order.	28 x 20 20 x 18	hewn log hewn log	1	 1A	200 16	250 19.20
151	**Mace, George** Mease, George A158 B127 D158 E127 I- II-	Mace, Jacob Mock, Henry	House Barn Land House is in midling order. Barn in good order. Limestone land, dry. Land (60 Acres) is good limestone land.	40 x 25 60 x 30	hewn log stone/log	1	2A 100A 60A	300 1700 960	375 2040 1152
152	**Mace, Jacob** Mease, Jacob A159 B128 D159 E128 I- II-	Mace, George Denius, Jacob	House Barn House is in midling order. Barn in bad order. Dry limestone land.	26 x 24 50 x 22	hewn log hewn log	1	2A 60A	175 900	218.75 1080
153	**Mace, Nicholas** Mease, Nicholas A154 B123 D154 E123 I- II-	Ream, Peter	House Barn House is in bad repair. Barn in midling order. Sand bottom land.	30 x 20 60 x 25	hewn log	1	2A 204A	200 1632	250 1958.40
154	**Mace, Valentine** Mease, Valentine	Sheferstown	House Springhouse	27 x 23	hewn log	1	2A	300	375

Direct Tax of 1798 - Heidelberg Township

No.	Owner/Occupant/Ref.	Adjoining	Building	Dimen.	Matls.	Stories	Acres Perch.	Assmt.	Valuation
	Bricker, Jacob A139 B107 D139 E107 I- II-	Kapp, Anthony	Barn Land	40 x 20	rd. log		15A	165	198
			Buildings are in bad order. Midling good gravel bottom land.						
155	**Marky, John** Markey, John (Berks County) B119 E119 II-	Diffenbach, Benjm.	Land				18A	324	388.80
			Good limestone land.						
156	**Meisser, Benjm.** A151 B120 D151 E120 I- II-	Zeller, Peter Zeller, Andw.	House Barn Land	34 x 24 40 x 18	hewn log log	2	2A 16A 60A	400 256 300	500 307.40 360
			House is in good order. Barn in midling order. Limestone land. Land (60 Acres) is mountain land.						
157	**Meisser, George** A170 B139 D170 E139 I-	Holstein, Geo. Mountain land	House Outhouse Barn Saw mill Land (mountain land)	30 x 26 20 x 18 75 x 30 40 x 12	hewn log	2 1	2A 126A 14A	400 4024 200 56	500 4828.80 240 67.20
			House and outhouse are in midling order. Good barn; good limestone land; good watered meadow. Saw mill in good order; flutter wheel.						
158	**Meisser, John** A161 B130 D161 E130 I- II-	Newmanstown Seibert, Frantz	House Kitchen Shed (small) Barn Land	32 x 25 15 x 15 40 x 20	hewn log hewn log frame log	2 1	1A 80P 12A	500 228	625 273.60
			House and kitchen are in midling order. A Tavern. Shed and barn are in bad order. Good limestone land.						
159	**Miller, Daniel** A156 B125 D156 E125 I- II-	Ditzler, Christn. Miller, David	House Stable	20 x 18 22 x 18	rd. log log	2	2A 28A	105 168	131.25 201.60
			House is in bad order. Poor stable. Gravel land.						
160	**Miller, David** Saltzer, John A160 B129 D160 E129 I- II-	Rudy, Ronimus Ditzler, Christian	House Barn	26 x 24 56 x 26	hewn log log	1	2A 142A	150 852	187.50 1022.40
			House is in midling order. Barn in very bad order. Gravel, ground oak land.						
161	**Miller, Frederick** A140 B108 D140 E108 I- II-	Moyer, Henry	House Barn	30 x 25 65 x 28	hewn log stone/log	2	2A 163A	350 2771	437.50 3325.20
			House is in midling order. Barn in midling order. Part limestone and part gravel land.						
162	**Miller, George** Miller, Frederick A168 B137 D168 E137 I- II-	Miller, Michael	House House Barn	26 x 25 20 x 18 60 x 25	hewn log hewn log log	2 1	2A 2A 130A	400 200 2600	500 250 3120
			House (26 x 25) is in good order.						

Direct Tax of 1798 - Heidelberg Township

No.	Owner/Occupant/Ref.	Adjoining	Building	Dimen.	Matls.	Stories	Acres Perch.	Assmt.	Valuation
			House (20 x 18) is in midling order. Barn in midling order. Good land.						
163	Miller, Henry A146 B114 D146 E114 I- II-	Miller, Valentine Troutman, Jonas	House Barn	32 x 28 60 x 26	hewn log log	2	2A 125A	350 2000	437.50 2400
			House is in midling order. Barn in midling order. Limestone land, dry.						
164	Miller, John Miller, John A155 D155 I-	Moyer, John	House	34 x 26	hewn log	2	2A	450	502.50
			House is in good repair.						
165	Miller, Michael (Amisher) A157 B124 D157 E124 I- II-	Lantz, George	House Barn	28 x 24 60 x 20	hewn log	1	2A 145A	250 1160	312.50
			House is in midling order. Bad barn. Gravel land.						
166	Miller, Michael A169 B138 D169 E138 I- II-	Zimmerman, Geo.	House Barn	32 x 18 18 x 12	hewn log log	1	2A 7A	250 70	312.50 84
			House is in good order. Good barn. Gravel land.						
167	Miller, Michl. (Nichls.' son) A148 B116 D148 E116 I- II-	Strickler, George	House Barn	32 x 30 80 x 30	limestone log	2	2A 200A	550 3600	687.50 4320
			House is in midling order. Barn in bad order. Dry limestone land.						
168	Miller, Nicholas Shreiner, William A141 B109 D141 E109 I- II-	Miller, Fredk.	House House Barn Still house	30 x 24 20 x 18 65 x 25 25 x 20	hewn log log	2	2A 165A	350 60 2445	437.50 72 2934
			House is in good order, not quite finished. Barn in midling order. Land part limestone, greater part gravel. Stillhouse is of old logs. Three stills. House (20 x 18) is in poor order. Has small stable.						
169	Miller, Nicholas (Milbach) Hoover, Andrew A167 B136 D166 E136 I- II-	Becker, George	House House Stable (small) Barn Grist mill Still house Saw mill	40 x 30 28 x 22 100 x 28 50 x 20 30 x 20 40 x 12	limestone hewn log log stone log	2 1	2A 2A 140A 100A 200	1000 200 3500 1000	1250 250 4200 1200 1440
		Mountain land	Land (mountain land)				100A	1000	1200
			House (40 x 30) is in good order. House (28 x 22) and stable are in midling order. Barn in midling order. Land of first quality. Grist mill in good order, new. Stillhouse in good order. Saw mill in very good order.						
170	Miller, Samuel A152 B121 D152 E121 I- II-	Hauter, Samuel	House Barn	36 x 22 55 x 22	hewn log stone/log	1	2A 89A	250 623	312.50 747.60
			House is in bad order.						

Direct Tax of 1798 - Heidelberg Township

No.	Owner/Occupant/Ref.	Adjoining	Building	Dimen.	Matls.	Stories	Acres Perch.	Assmt.	Valuation
			Barn in good order. Gravel, ground oak land.						
171	Miller, Samuel Sr. B126 E126 II-	Miller, Michael	House Stable Buildings in bad order. Ground oak land.	22 x 18 15 X 20	log		16A	80	
172	Miller, Valentine A143 B113 D143 E113 I- II-	Grum, John	House Barn House is in midling order. Good barn - most new. Part gravel, part limestone.	30 x 20 64 x 30	limestone stone/log	1	2A 119A	450 1904	562.50 2284.80
173	Miller, Valentine (Tulpehocken) A150 B118 D150 E118 I- II-	Kuster, John	House Barn House is old and in bad order. Barn in bad order. Good limestone land.	36 x 20 60 x 30	stone/log log	1	2A 150A	250 3450	312.50 4140
174	Mock, Adam A166 B135 D167 E135 I- II-	Swanger, Nicholas	House Barn House in good order. Barn in good order. Good dry limestone land.	30 x 28 60 x 30	limestone stone/log	2	2A 192A	500 3456	625 4147.20
175	Mock, Henry A165 B134 D165 E134 I- II-	Stoler, John	House Barn Buildings are old and in bad order. Barn midling. Good dry limestone land.	30 x 30 60 x 30	hewn log log	1	2A 60A	250 1080	312.50 1296
176	Moore, Adam A162 B131 D162 E131 I- II-	Sheferstown Kapp, John Kolp, Peter	House Barn Land Land Buildings are in midling order and partly occupied as a Cooper Shop. Land (5 Acres) in Sheferstown. Subject to 10% ground rent. Land (8 Acres) free land.	35 x 18 30 x 20	log/bark log/bark	1	100P 5A 8A	200 70 128	250 84 153.60
177	Moore, Jacob A164 B133 D164 E133 I- II-	Sheferstown Kolp, Peter	House Stable Land Buildings are in midling order. Gravel land.	30 x 20 28 x 19	frame	1	100P 3A	200 30	250 36
178	Moore, John A145 B112 D145 E112 I- II-	Bullman, John Royer, John	House Kitchen Outhouse House Outhouse Barn Barn House (30 x 28) and kitchen are in good order. Outhouse (16 x 14) and House (45 x 40) are in midling order. Outhouse (18 x 16) is in bad order. Barn (75 x 28) in bad order. Good limestone land. Good meadow. Barn (70 x 25) is bad; gravel land, watered	30 x 28 16 x 16 16 x 14 45 x 30 18 x 15 75 x 28 70 x 25	limestone limestone hewn log sandstone log log log	2 1 1 2 2	2A 2A 220A A	750 700 4400 3000	937.50 875 5280 3600

Direct Tax of 1798 - Heidelberg Township

No.	Owner/Occupant/Ref.	Adjoining	Building	Dimen.	Matls.	Stories	Acres Perch.	Assmt.	Valuation
			meadow. An excellent spring.						
179	Moore, Peter A163 B132 D163 E132 I- II-	Sheferstown	House Barn	28 x 24 30 x 20	hewn log	2	100P	400	500
		Moore, Adam	Land				5A	80	96
		Kolp, Peter	Land				12A	192	230.40
		Burky, Henry	Land				7A 80P	120	144
		Rex, Samuel	Land				5A	70	84
		Ream, Peter	Land				2A	32	38.40
			Buildings are in midling order. 5 Acres, 12 Acres, 2 Acres all free land. 120 Acres and 70 Acres subject to 5% ground rent.						
180	Mosser, Michl. Lutz, John A153 B122 D153 E122 I- II-	Braun, Michael Shell, Peter	House Barn	40 x 18 65 x 26	hewn log hewn log	1	2A 200A	200 1600	250 1920
			House is in bad repair. Midling barn. Ground oak land.						
181	Mosser, Nicholas Glass, Martin A138 B106 D138 E106 I- II-	Coppenheffer, Henry	House Kitchen Springhouse	44 x 32 18 x 19 25 x 15	limestone limestone stone/wd.	2 1 1	2A	1100	1375
		Lehmy, Christian	House Barn	30 x 20 80 x 30	hewn log stone	1	2A 226A	200 5650	250 6780
		Simmon, George	Land				40A	640	768
			House (44 x 32) and kitchen are in good order. Springhouse and house (30 x 20) are midling. Good barn. Limestone land first quality. Land (40 Acres) is good gravel land.						
182	Moyer, Henry A142 B110 D142 E110 I- II-	Moyer, John	House Barn	32 x 24 75 x 30	hewn log hewn log	1	2A 170A	300 3400	375 4080
			House is in midling order. Good barn. Good limestone land.						
183	Moyer, John A137 B105 D137 E105 I- II-	Leiss, Christian	House Barn	20 x 18 30 x 18	hewn log log	1	2A 7A	105 35	131.25 42
			House is in midling order. Barn in bad order. Ground oak land.						
184	Moyer, John (Isaac's son) A147 B115 D147 E115 I- II-	Baasler, Simon	House Kitchen Barn	40 x 30 22 x 20 95 x 36	limestone limestone stone	2 1	2A 244A	1000 5612	1250 6734.40
			House and kitchen are in good order. Good barn; limestone land of first quality.						
185	Moyer, John in Milbach A144 D144 E111 I- II-	Bullman, John Milbach	House Weaver shop Barn	24 x 26 15 x 12 70 x 28	hewn log hewn log hewn log	2 1	2A 200A	350 4000	437.50 4800
			House and weaver shop are in midling order. Good barn. Good limestone land.						
186	Moyer, Martin A149 B117 D149 E117 I- II-	Miller, Valentine	House Barn	38 x 26 24 x 24	hewn log log	2	2A 3A	350 60	437.50 72

Direct Tax of 1798 - Heidelberg Township

No.	Owner/Occupant/Ref.	Adjoining	Building	Dimen.	Matls.	Stories	Acres Perch.	Assmt.	Valuation
			House is new, not quite finished. Barn midling. Dry limestone land.						
187	**Neff, George** A178 B145 D178 E145 I- II-	Sheferstown Moore, Peter	House Barn Land Buildings are in midling order. Limestone land.	24 x 20 38 x 20	hewn log	1	100P 7A	125 112	156.25 134.40
188	**Neff, Jacob** B146 E146 II-	Fogt, Mathias	Land Good limestone land.				34A	578	693.60
189	**Neff, John** A177 D177 I-	Sheferstown	House Cooper shop Barn Buildings are in midling good order.	30 x 20 15 x 18 40 x 20	hewn log hewn log hewn log	1 1	1A 40P	200	250
190	**Neff, Widow** A179 D179 I-	Sheferstown	House House is in midling order.	22 x 20	hewn log	1	80P	150	187.50
191	**Neil, John** A176 D176 I-	Sheferstown	House Stable House and stable are old, in bad order.	30 x 20 20 x 15	hewn log	1	100P	125	156.25
192	**Newman, Susan** A277 I-	Newmanstown	House House is in midling order.	20 x 18	hewn log	1	40P	105	
193	**Noaker, Christian** A171 B140 D171 E140 I- II-	Coppenheffer, Henry	House Barn Midling old house. Good barn and good land.	36 x 20 60 x 28	stone/log stone/log	2	2A 89A	400 2047	500 2456.40
194	**Noll, John** A175 B144 D175 E144 I- II-	Zeller, George	House House Barn House (32 x 22) is in midling order. House (22 x 18) is in good order. Good barn. Good, broken limestone land.	32 x 22 22 x 18 46 x 22	limestone limestone stone	2 2	2A 2A 146A	500 400 3504	625 500 4204.80
195	**Noll, Leonard** A172 B141 D172 E141 I- II-	Noll, Nicholas	House Barn House in midling order. Barn midling order. Poor gravel land.	29 x 24 56 x 26	hewn log log	2	2A 138A	250 828	312.50 993.60
196	**Noll, Nicholas** A173 B142 D173 E142 I- II-	Noll, Leonard	House Barn House in bad order. Barn midling order. Poor gravel land.	30 x 24 36 x 22	hewn log log	2	2A 128A	250 896	312.50 1075.20
197	**Noll, Phillip** A174 B143 D174 E143 I- II-	Newmanstown Meisser, Benjm.	House House Land Houses are in midling order. Limestone land.	36 x 16 30 x 20	hewn log hewn log	1	1A 10A	200 160	250 192

Direct Tax of 1798 - Heidelberg Township

No.	Owner/Occupant/Ref.	Adjoining	Building	Dimen.	Matls.	Stories	Acres Perch.	Assmt.	Valuation
198	Odenwalt, George A180 D180 I-	Newmanstown	House Stable (small) Buildings in good order.	24 x 20	hewn log	1	1A	200	250
199	Person, George A182 B147 D182 E147 I- II-	Newmanstown Seiss, Peter	House Stable (small) Land Buildings are in good order. Good gravel land.	30 x 18	hewn log log	1	80P 22A	175 396	218.75 475.20
200	Phillipi, Jacob Phillipe, Jacob A183 B148 D183 E148 I- II-	Sheferstown Troutman, Jonas	House Brewhouse Barn Land Land - lot in Sheferstown Buildings are in good order. Good limestone land.	26 x 20 36 x 20 45 x 22	hewn log limestone hewn log	1 1	1A 120 P 20A 100P	450 300 16	562.50 379.20
201	Phillipi, Jacob Jr. Philipe, Jacob A186 B151 D186 E151 I- II-	Miller, Michl.	House Barn House is in midling order. Barn midling. Good dry limestone land.	24 x 22 60 x 22	hewn log log	1	2A 130A	250 2210	312.50 2652
202	Phillipi, John Phillipe, John A185 B150 D185 E150 I- II-	Shefer, Henry Esq.	House Turner shop Barn House is in good order. Turner shop is midling order. Barn in good order. Good, dry limestone land.	32 x 26 24 x 20 64 x 28	boarded hewn log stone/log	2 1	2A 169A	350 2873	437.50 3447.60
203	Pleasant, Philip Toebler, David Gerloff, Godfried A181 D181 I-	Myerstown	House kitchen House House Stable (small) House Stable (small) House and kitchen are in good order. Other buildings are in midling order.	36 x 27 18 x 16 22 x 20 24 x 20 28 x 20 20 x 12	log/bd. limestone log/bd. hewn log log hewn log hewn log	2 1 2 1 2 1		600 110 175	750 137.50 218.75
204	Pollem, John A184 B149 D184 E149 I- II-	Shefer, John	House Barn House is old, in bad order. Good improved mountain land.	30 x 25 60 x 24	hewn log rd. log	1	2A 168A	200 1680	250 2016
205	Ramler, Leonard Ramler, Peter Rambler, Peter A192 B157 D193 E157 I- II-	Ramler, Michael	House Barn House is in bad order. Barn midling. Good limestone land.	32 x 30 60 x 30	stone stone/log	1	2A 145A	500 3190	625 3828
206	Ramler, Michael Rambler, Michl. Maurer, George A191 B156 D192 E156 I- II-	Immel, Leond.	House Outhouse Barn House is in bad order. Outhouse in midling order. Good new barn. Good limestone land.	32 x 24 15 x 20 65 x 30	stone hewn log stone	1 2	2A 145A	450 3335	562.50 4002

Direct Tax of 1798 - Heidelberg Township

No.	Owner/Occupant/Ref.	Adjoining	Building	Dimen.	Matls.	Stories	Acres Perch.	Assmt.	Valuation
207	Rapp, Frederick Est. E228 II-	Zeller, _____	House Land Midling order.	20 x 15	log		42A	50 260	312
208	Ream, Peter, Sr. I-	Kapp, Anthony	House Weaver shop Buildings are in midling order.	22 x 28 18 x 12	hewn log hewn log	1 1	2A	350	
209	Reed, Jacob Conrad, Christ. Joiner, Rich B163 E163 II-	Weich, Christ	House House 120 Acres is mountain land. House (18 x 15) is in bad order.	22 x 18 18 x 15			120A	600 60	792
210	Reidle, John A200 D200 I-		House House in midling order.	24 x 18	hewn log	2	50P	150	187.50
211	Reily, John A202 D202 I-	Myerstown	House House in midling order. Claims himself exempted from paying tax by reason of a wound received during the American Revolution.	20 x 24	hewn log	1	36P	150	187.50
212	Remer, Fredk. A195 D196 I-	Newmanstown	House Stable (small) House is in bad order.	20 x 18	hewn log	1	80P	105	131.25
213	Rex, Samuel Gap, Jacob Kelly, John Seyfort, Anthony Gerret, Christian Rex, Saml. Michael, Valentine A199 B162 D199 E162 I- II-	Sheferstown Reeser, Christian Moore, Jacob Shefer, H. Esq. Krum, John Moore, Peter Shefer, Henry Esq.	House Stables (2) House Shed for 4 teams Barn Hatters shop Land Land Land Land Land Land	36 x 22 30 x 24 40 x 24 11 x 15	frame/brk. log frame/brk. frame log frame/brk.	1 2 1	80P 100P 2A 1A 1A 4A 80P 7A 80P 8A 80P	300 500 32 13 16 63 105 119	375 625 38.40 15.60 19.20 75.60 126 142.80
			House (36 x 22) is in bad order. Two stables in midling order. House (30 x 24) is tavern, but indifferent order. Front part is frame filled with brick and back part of stone. Barn in bad order. Hatter's shop midling for the purpose.						
214	Riem, Christian A189 B154 D190 E154 I- II-	Phillipi, Jacob	House Barn House is in midling order. Barn poor order. Land dry limestone.	22 x 20 30 x 18	hewn log log	1	2A 38A	175 646	218.75 775.20
215	Riem, Peter Jr. Ream, Peter A197 B160 D197 E160 I- II-	Sheferstown Kapp, Anthony Rex, Samuel	House Wagoner shop Barn Land House and shop are in good order. Barn good. Gravel land, poor Land (10 Acres) is good limestone land.	24 x 28 18 x 24 60 x 28	 stone/log	2 1	1A 40P 100A 10A	400 900 160	500 1080 192

Direct Tax of 1798 - Heidelberg Township

No.	Owner/Occupant/Ref.	Adjoining	Building	Dimen.	Matls.	Stories	Acres Perch.	Assmt.	Valuation
216	**Ries, Stophel** Rice, Stophel A196 B159 D196 E159 I- II-	Myerstown	House Barn	32 x 30 45 x 20	hewn log log	1	1A 5A	250 90	312.50 108
			House is in good order. Barn in good order. Good limestone land.						
217	**Risser, Christian** Reesor, Christian A198 B161 D198 E161 I- II-	Kochederfer, Geo.	House Barn	32 x 30 70 x 30	hewn log log	2	2A 160A	450 1920	562.50 2304
			House is in midling order. Barn midling. Gravel land.						
218	**Rist, John** Smith, Catharine A201 D201 I-		House House	20 x 16 18 x 16	hewn log hewn log	1 1	1A 40P 100P	200	250
			House (20 x 16) in bad order. House (18 x 16) decayed. Has been exempted from tax these 5 years past, on account of his age and infirmity.						
219	**Ritter, George** A194 D195 I-	Newmanstown	House Stable (small)	20 x 18	hewn log	1	80P	105	131.25
			House is in bad order.						
220	**Ritter, Henry** A193 B158 D194 E158 I- II-	Immel, Leonard	House Barn	30 x 25 40 x 24	stone log	2	2A 148A	450 2072	572.50 2480.40
			House is in bad order. Old barn, ready to fall. Good limestone land.						
221	**Royer, George** A188 B153 D189 E153 I- II-	Troutman, Jonas	House Barn	24 x 20 50 x 22	hewn log hewn log	1	2A 138A	200 1932	250 2318.40
			House is in midling order. Barn midling. Land midling.						
222	**Royer, John** Lebenstein, Widow A187 B152 D187 D188 E152 I- II-	Hoffman, Jacob Moore, John Diel, _____	House House House Stable (small) Barn	40 x 31 28 x 24 24 x 20 80 x 32	stone hewn log hewn log log stone/log	2 1 1 1	2A 2A 2A 198A	1000 250 150 4772	1250 312.50 187.50 5726.40
			House (40 x 31) is new and well finished. Other houses are in midling order. Barn new and well finished. Good limestone land.						
223	**Rudy, Ronimus** Loser, Stophel Young, John A190 B155 D191 E155 I- II-	Ditzler, Christian	House House Barn	28 x 24 18 x 20 60 x 20	hewn log hewn log stone/log	1 1	2A 2A 111A	200 105 888	250 131.25 1065.60
			Houses are in midling order. Barn in good order. Ground oak, gravel land.						
224	**Saltzgeber, John** Hippert, _____ A222 B177 D222 E177 I- II-	Zeller, Peter Zimmerman, H. J.	House House (old dwelling) Barn Fulling Mill (old) Land	30 x 24 70 x 28	hewn log stone/log	2 1	2A 70A 80A	400 1470 1600	500 1764 1920
			House is in midling order. Barn in good order. Good limestone land. Old house and fulling mill ready to fall. Land (80 Acres) is clay land.						

Direct Tax of 1798 - Heidelberg Township

No.	Owner/Occupant/Ref.	Adjoining	Building	Dimen.	Matls.	Stories	Acres Perch.	Assmt.	Valuation
225	**Schmidt, George**	Strickler, George	limestone	38 x 32		2	2A	700	875
	Smith, George		Kitchen	16 x 16		1			
	A225 B181 D225 E181 I- II-		Outhouse	30 x 18		1	2A	200	250
			Barn	93 x 30	stone		258A	5676	6811.20
		Zimmerman, Henry	Land				223A	4683	5619.60
			House and kitchen are in good order. Outhouse is in bad order. Good barn, finished. Good limestone land. 223 Acres is good limestone land.						
226	**Schmidt, Jacob's widow**		House	30 x 24	hewn log	2	2A	400	500
	Flowers, John Jr.		Potter shop	28 x 20	hewn log	1			
	A232 B187 D232 E187 I- II-		Springhouse	20 x 15	stone/log	2			
		Simmon, George	Barn	40 x 20	log		43A	688	825.60
			House is in good order. Potter's shop and springhouse are in bad order. Barn in bad order. Slate bottom land.						
227	**Seibert, Christn. Sr.**	Groff, Andrew	House	30 x 28	stone	2	2A	600	750
	A211 B171 D211 E171 I- II-		Kitchen	16 x 18	stone	1			
			Barn	80 x 30	stone/log		238A	5236	6283.20
			Boring Mill	24 x 22	frame				
		Mountain land	Land				25A	200	240
			House is in midling order. Kitchen new, good order. Barn in good order. Good limestone land, much meadow. Boring Mill is new. Land is mountain land.						
228	**Seibert, Frantz**	Newmanstown	House	26 x 20	hewn log	2	1A	400	500
	A205 B166 D205 E166 I- II-		Storehouse	20 x 10	hewn log	1			
			Barn	50 x 20	hewn log				
		Newman, Henry	Land				68A	1360	1632
		Seibert, Christn.	Land				25A	100	120
			Buildings in good order. 68 Acres of good limestone land. 100 acres mountain land.						
229	**Seiler, Christian**	Sheferstown	House	32 x 18	hewn log	1	100 P	105	131.25
	Sailor, Christian		Smith shop	12 x 13	hewn log	1			
	A246 B201 D246 E201 I- II-		Stable (small)						
		Valentine, Michl.	Land				2A 80P	35	42
			Buildings old and in bad order. Hitherto exempted from paying tax, on account of having an idiot child. An out lot of Sheferstown; subject to ground rent.						
230	**Shaefer, Henry Esq.**	Shitz, Peter	House	40 x 27	limestone	2	2A	800	1000
	Valentine/Rex		Springhouse	20 x 18	stone/wd.	2			
	Rex/Valentine	Sheferstown	House	40 x 36	limestone	2	80P	1200	1500
	Miller, Jacob		Kitchen	22 x 15	limestone	1			
	Marshall, Wm		Barn/stables	50 x 20	hewn log				
	A214 B175 D214 E175 I- II-		Sheds for 2 teams		frame				
			House	30 x 24	hewn log	2	100P	300	375
			Stable	15 x 12	hewn log				
			House	30 x 18	stone/log	1	100P	110	137.50
			Stable (small, old)		log				
		Shitz, Peter	Barn	90 x 30			100A	2500	3000
		Mock, Adam	Land				100A	1600	1920

Direct Tax of 1798 - Heidelberg Township

No.	Owner/Occupant/Ref.	Adjoining	Building	Dimen.	Matls.	Stories	Acres Perch.	Assmt.	Valuation
			House (40 x 27) in good order. Springhouse is in bad order. House (40 x 36) is in good order - Tavern and Store. Kitchen and Barn/stables are in midling order. Shed is in good order. House (30 x 24) and Stable (15 x 12) are in midling order. Small, old Stable and Barn are in bad order. Barn (90 x 30) is good; land of the first quality. 100 Acres of land is dry limestone land.						
231	**Shaefer, John** B202 E202 II-	Pollem, John	Land Mountain land - stoney.				100A	500	600
232	**Sharf, John** Badorff, Peter A228 B183 D228 E183 I- II-	Dierwechter, Ehrha	House Barn House	28 x 24 60 x 30 20 x 18	hewn log stone/log log	1 1	2A 190A	300 3420 80	375 4104 96
			House (28 x 24) is old, in bad order. Barn in good order. Good limestone land. House (20 x 18) is in midling order.						
233	**Shell, Peter** Shell, ____ Sr. Hostetler, Michl. A233 B188 D233 E188 I- II-	Shitz, Jacob Shitz, Jacob Mosser, Michael	House House House Barn Barn	20 x 16 20 x 18 30 x 18 55 x 25 30 x 20	hewn log hewn log hewn log log log	1 1 1	2A 2A 2A 148A 107A	150 110 105 1776 535	187.50 137.50 131.25 2131.20 642
			House (20 x 16) is old and in bad order. House (20 x 18) is in midling order (and has stable). House (30 x 20) is in bad order. and old. Barn (55 x 25) in midling order. Land is slate bottom. Barn (30 x 20) in poor order. Ground oak land.						
234	**Shenk, John** Flower, John Sr. A224 B179 D224 E179 I- II-	Weiss, Henry	House House House Barn Barn Barn	27 x 29 30 x 29 30 x 24 60 x 30 25 x 36 80 x 34	limestone limestone hewn log stone log stone	2 1 1	2A 2A 138A 255A	900 200 2760 5175	1125 250 3312 6210
			House (27 x 29 is new and well finished; a good spring is in the cellar. House (30 x 29) is old, but in good order. House (30 x 24) is in bad order. Barn (138 Acres) is good. Barn (255 Acres) is new, not quite finished. Good limestone land, good meadows.						
235	**Shertel, Bernard** A229 B185 D229 E185 I- II-	Shlessman, Peter	House Barn	28 x 22 40 x 18	hewn log log	1	2A 68A	150 340	187.50 408
			House is in bad order. Poor barn. Land of the worst ground oak.						
236	**Shiffler, John** A218 D218 I-	Myerstown	House Outhouse Stable (small) Buildings in midling order.	28 x 24 23 x 20	hewn log hewn log	1 1	54P	150	187.50
237	**Shitz, Jacob** Shell, Peter A230 B184 D230 E184 I- II-	Coppenheffer, H.	House House Barn Barn	24 x 22 33 x 30 65 x 30 60 x 22	hewn log hewn log log log	1 1	2A 2A 160A 150A	300 350 3680 2550	375 437.50 4416 3060

Direct Tax of 1798 - Heidelberg Township

No.	Owner/Occupant/Ref.	Adjoining	Building	Dimen.	Matls.	Stories	Acres Perch.	Assmt.	Valuation
			House (24 x 22) is in bad order. House (33 x 30) is in good order. Barn (65 x 30) in midling order; good limestone land. Barn (60 x 22) is midling; part limestone and part gravel land.						
238	**Shitz, Peter** Neip, John A212 B173 D212 E173 I- II-		House	38 x 30	stone	2	2A	800	1000
			Springhouse	20 x 18	stone	2			
			House	20 x 17	hewn log	1	2A	200	250
			Smith shop	20 x 15	log (old)	1			
		Shefer, Henry Esq.	Barn	104 x 40	stone		350A	8750	10500
		Phillipi, John	Land				94A	752	902.40
			House (38 x 30) is in good order, cedar roof. Springhouse is midling. House (20 x 17) is in bad order. Smithshop is in bad order - made of rotten logs. Good barn. Good limestone land, first quality. Land (94 acres) is gravel land.						
239	**Shitz, Widow** A220 D220 I-	Sheferstown	House	22 x 18	hewn log	1	100P	150	187.50
			Stable (small)						
			Buildings are in bad order.						
240	**Shlessman, Peter** A231 B186 D231 E186 I- II-	Sherlet, Bernard	House	24 x 20	hewn log	1	2A	150	187.50
			Barn	40 x 20	log		60A	360	432
			House is in bad order. Barn in poor order. Ground - oak land.						
241	**Sholl, Adam** A203 B164 D203 E164 I- II-	Royer, John	House	30 x 28	hewn log	2	2A	350	437.50
			Still house	28 x 20					
			Barn	65 x 30	log		128A	2560	3072
			House in good order. Barn and still house in midling order. Good gravel land.						
242	**Sholl, John** A206 B167 D206 E167 I- II-	Zeller, Peter	House	24 x 18	hewn log	1	2A	275	343.75
			Outhouse	14 x 12	hewn log	1			
			Barn	60 x 28			88A	1760	2112
			House in bad order. Outhouse in good order, new. Barn in midling order. Good limestone land.						
243	**Sholl, Simon** Lannert, Henry A208 B169 D208 E169 I- II-	Holstein, George	House	27 x 29	hewn log	1	2A	150	187.50
			House	20 x 24	hewn log	2	2A	150	187.50
			Kitchen	15 x 14	hewn log	1			
			Barn	60 x 25	log		188A	3196	3835.20
			House (27 x 29 in bad order. House (20 x 24) only under roof. Kitchen finished. Barn midling. Good land - limestone and gravel. Good meadows.						
244	**Shriver, Widow** Mordock, James A219 D219 I-	Sheferstown	House	24 x 18	boards	1	1A 40P	150	187.50
			Stable (small)						
			Buildings are in good order.						
245	**Shultz, Christn.** **Shetz, Christian** A204 B165 D204 E165 I- II-	Ulrich, Frantz	House	30 x 24	hewn log	2	2A	300	375
			Barn	65 x 28	stone/log		98A	784	940.80
			House in bad order, not finished. Barn in good order. Improved mountain land.						

Direct Tax of 1798 - Heidelberg Township

No.	Owner/Occupant/Ref.	Adjoining	Building	Dimen.	Matls.	Stories	Acres Perch.	Assmt.	Valuation
246	**Shultz, Widow** A276 I-	Newmanstown	House House is in midling order.	28 x 20	hewn log	2	1A 80P	250	
247	**Simmon, George** **Simon, George** A235 B190 D235 E190 I- II-	Mosser, Michael Mosser, Nichls.	House Springhouse (small) Barn Land Buildings in good order. Excellent water. Barn in good order. Limestone land, first quality. Good gravel land.	32 x 28 80 x 30	log/bd. stone	2 	2A 98A 100A	500 2450 1800	625 2940 2160
248	**Sinkel, John Negro** A283 I-	Myerstown	House House is in midling order.	22 x 18	hewn log	2	36P	150	
249	**Slichter, Nicholas** A227 D227 I-	Newmanstown	House House is in good order.	32 x 18	hewn log	1	1A	200	250
250	**Smith, John** A215 D215 I-	Sheferstown	House House is in bad order, never been finished.	28 x 24	hewn log	2	100P	150	187.50
251	**Spanhuth, Henry** A242 B197 D242 E197 I- II-	Esh, Jacob	House Barn House is old and in very bad order. Barn in good order. Ground oak land.	26 x 22 32 x 18	rd. log stone/log	1	2A 38A	105 228	131.25 273.60
252	**Spengler, George** A238 B193 D238 E193 I- II-	Ley, Christian	House Springhouse Barn House is in midling order. Springhouse is in good order, dwelling above. Good barn. Land of the first quality.	36 x 28 38 x 24 70 x 30	limestone limestone stone	2 2	2A 135A	850 3375	1012.50 4050
253	**Spengler, Peter** A226 B182 D226 E182 I- II-	Achy, Henry	House Barn House is in good order. Barn is old and indifferent. Dry limestone land.	36 x 32 45 x 20	limestone rd. log	2	2A 198A	600 3168	750 3801.60
254	**Spengler, Widow** A245 B200 D245 E200 II-	Achy, Henry	House Barn Barn in bad order. Dry rocky limestone land.	30 x 24 60 x 28	hewn log stone/log	2	2A 200A	200 2400	250 2880
255	**Stein, Fredk.** **Stine, Frederick** A209 B170 D209 E170 I- II-	Seibert, Christian	House Barn House in bad order. Barn midling. Dry limestone land.	20 x 18 60 x 30	stone/wd. log	1	2A 160A	300 2880	375 3456
256	**Stein, Peter** **Stine, Peter** A210 B172 D210 E172 I- II-	Seibert, Christian	House Barn House in good order. Barn in good order. Dry limestone land.	20 x 20 40 x 20	hewn log log	1	2A 50A	150 850	187.50 1020
257	**Steiner, August** Steiner, August A243 D243 I-	Newmanstown	House Stable (small) House is in midling order.	32 x 24	hewn log	2	1A	350	437.50

Direct Tax of 1798 - Heidelberg Township

No.	Owner/Occupant/Ref.	Adjoining	Building	Dimen.	Matls.	Stories	Acres Perch.	Assmt.	Valuation
258	Steiner, Frederick Steiner, Michael Steiner, Fredk. Jr. A237 B192 D237 E192 I- II-	Fogt, Mathias Beiler, John Kuster, John	House kitchen House House Barn Barn Stable	40 x 29 12 x 72 30 x 24 24 x 18 58 x 26 60 x 24 18 x 12	 stone/log log log	2 1 2 1	2A 2A 2A 177A 148A 4A	600 350 150 3186 2515 68	750 437.50 187.50 3823.20 3018 81.60
			House (40 x 29) is in good order. Kitchen is in midling order. House (30 x 24) is in good order and well finished. House (24 x 18) is in midling order. Barn (58 x 26) midling; dry limestone land. Barn (60 x 24) is midling; good land. Stable is midling, good land.						
259	Stever, Tobias A241 B196 D241 E196 I- II-	Rudy, Ronimus	House Barn	26 x 24 60 x 22	hewn log log	1	2A 149A	200 894	250 1072.80
			House is in midling order. Barn midling; ground oak land.						
260	Stiegel, Widow A247 D247 I-	Sheferstown	House Stable (small)	32 x 20	hewn log	1	100P	105	131.25
			House is in midling order.						
261	Stoler, Henry Stohler, Henry A217 D217 I-	Sheferstown	House Kitchen Oak house Barn	30 x 26 18 x 16 30 x 20 40 x 20	limestone limestone hewn log hewn log	2 1 1	100P	450	562.50
			House and kitchen are in midling order. Oak house is intended for a Still house. Barn is in good order.						
262	Stoler, John B180 E180 II-	Mock, Henry	Barn	30 x 24	rd. log		122A	2196	2635.20
			Good land.						
263	Strack, Henry A213 B174 D213 E174 I- II-	Achy, Samuel Bobb, Daniel	House Kitchen Barn Land	40 x 30 18 x 15 80 x 27	limestone limestone log	1 1	2A 140A 15A	450 2240 198	562 2688 237.60
			House is in good order. Kitchen in in bad order - ready to fall. Barn is midling. Dry limestone land. 15 Acres is gravel land.						
264	Strickler, Andrew B199 E199 I- II-	Miller, George	House Barn	30 x 24 80 x 20	log log		150A	1200 80	1440 96
			House is old and in bad order. Poor barn. Gravel land, stoney, bad order. Barn is old and has very much decay.						
265	Strickler, George Barr, George A216 D216 I-	Sheferstown	House Barn (small) House Stable (small)	28 x 28 40 x 18 20 x 18	hewn log hewn log hewn log hewn log	2 1	1A 140P 100P	200 105	250 131.25
			Buildings are in midling order.						
266	Strickler, George	Miller, Michael	House	28 x 22		2	2A	350	437.50

Direct Tax of 1798 - Heidelberg Township

No.	Owner/Occupant/Ref.	Adjoining	Building	Dimen.	Matls.	Stories	Acres Perch.	Assmt.	Valuation
	A234 B189 D234 E189 I- II-		Barn	60 x 20	log		144A	2304	2764.80
	House is in midling order. Barn in midling order.								
	Dry limestone land.								
267	**Strickler, George** (Newmanstown) A244 B198 D244 E198 I- II-	Newmanstown Seibert, Frantz	House Stable (small)	26 x 18	hewn log	1	1A 2A	150 40	187.50 48
	House is in bad order. Good land.								
268	**Strickler, Leonard** A223 B178 D223 E178 I- II-	Holstein, George	House Outhouse Barn	30 x 24 18 x 15 54 x 30	stone/log	2 1	2A 150A	350 3000	437.50 3600
	Buildings are in midling order. Good barn.								
	Good limestone land, good meadow.								
269	**Stump, Leonard** Shreck, Geo. A207 B168 D207 E168 I- II-	Bullman, John	House Outhouse House Barn Stable (small)	30 x 24 20 x 15 24 x 20 70 x 30	limestone hewn log hewn log stone	2 1 1	2A 2A 298A	600 200 5960	750 250 7152
	Buildings in midling order. Barn in good order.								
	Good limestone land, good meadow.								
270	**Swan, Joshua** A240 B195 D240 E195 I- II-	Boeshore, Abm.	House Stable	22 x 15 18 x 12	rd. log	1	2A 18A	105 90	131.25 108
	House is old and in bad order.								
	Ground oak land, poor stable.								
271	**Swanger, Nicholas** A239 B194 D239 E194 I- II-	Unbehend, Jacob	House Barn	30 x 26 70 x 28	hewn log log	1	2A 134A	350 2412	437.50 2894.40
	House is in midling order. Barn in good order.								
	Dry limestone land.								
272	**Swarm, Adam** A236 B191 D236 E191 I- II-	Uhrich, John	House Barn	22 x 20 30 x 18	hewn log log	1	2A 18A	105 108	131.25 129.60
	House is in bad order. Barn but midling.								
	Ground oak land.								
273	**Sweitzer, Gertraut Widow** A221 B176 D221 E176 I- II-	Sheferstown Witemoyer Ludwig	House Barn Land Land	34 x 20 40 x 20		1	100P 1A 140P 6A	350 20 96	437.50 24 105.20
	House is in midling good order. Barn is old, in bad order.								
	20 Acres is in good order. Six acres is gravel land.								
274	**Trion, Michl. Doct.** A248 B203 D248 E203 I- II-	Zeller, Peter	House House Stable (2 small)	28 x 26 26 x 10	hewn log hewn log	2 1	2A 6A	400 120	500 144
	Buildings are in midling good order.								
	Stable land is all meadow.								
275	**Troutman, Jonas** A249 B204 D249 E204 I- II-	Oitner, Mathias	House Barn	30 x 22 70 x 30	hewn log stone/log	2	2A 275A	350 4675	437.50 5610
	House is in midling good order. Barn is good.								

Direct Tax of 1798 - Heidelberg Township

No.	Owner/Occupant/Ref.	Adjoining	Building	Dimen.	Matls.	Stories	Acres Perch	Assmt.	Valuation
			Land is limestone and gravel - good.						
276	Uhrich, Valentine A251 B206 D251 E206 I- II-	Eckert, Jonas	House Springhouse Barn	36 x 28 15 x 20 75 x 27	hewn log stone/log	1	2A 170A	350 2720	437.50 3264
			House is in bad order. Springhouse is in midling order. Barn in good order. Good gravel land.						
277	Ulrich, Frantz A250 B205 D250 E205 I- II-	Shultz, Christian	House Barn	30 x 24 50 x 25	hewn log log	1	2A 198A	200 1584	250 1900.80
			House is in bad order. Barn in bad order. Good mountain land.						
278	Ulrich, John A252 B207 D252 E207 I- II-	Uhrich, Valentine	House Barn	28 x 23 50 x 20	hewn log log	2	2A 80A	300 880	375 1050
			House is in good order. Barn is in bad order. Poor gravel land.						
279	Unbehend, Jacob A253 B208 D253 E208 I- II-	Swanger, Nicholas	House Barn	30 x 24 60 x 30	hewn log stone/log	2	2A 143A	350 2717	437.50 3260.40
			House is in midling order. Barn in good order. Good limestone land.						
280	Waggoner, Geo. A260 B215 D260 E215 I- II-	Phillipi, Jacob	House Barn	35 x 30 35 x 20	limestone log	2	2A 300A	550 4200	687.50 5040
			House is in midling order. Barn very bad. Dry, broken limestone land.						
281	Walburn, Christr. Walborn, Christr. A256 B211 D256 E211 I- II-	Kreutzer, Michael	House Barn	36 x 24 60 x 30	limestone stone	2	2A 40A	700 3080	875 3696
			House is new and well finished. Good barn; good land.						
282	Walburn, Herman Walborn, Herman A261 B216 D261 E216 I- II-	German, Henry	House Barn	27 x 24 50 x 25	hewn log log	2	2A 148A	200 1036	250 1243.20
			House is in bad order. Barn in bad order. Ground oak land						
283	Walburn, John (Nichls. son) A257 B212 D257 E212 I- II-	Lower, Benjm.	House Springhouse Barn	32 x 20 18 x 14 50 x 30	hewn log hewn log stone/log	1 2	2A 126A	350 2772	437.50 3326.40
			House is in bad order. Springhouse is new, in good order. Barn in good order. Good limestone land.						
284	Walburn, Martin A258 B213 D258 E213 I- II-	Kurtz, Stephen	House Barn	35 x 30 100 x 30	limestone stone	2	2A 168A	600 3696	750 4435.20
			House is in midling order. Barn in good order. Good land, good meadows.						
285	Weaver, John Weaver, Widow A259 B214 D259 E214 I- II-	Miller, Frederick	House House Barn	32 x 20 18 x 14 52 x 22	hewn log hewn log log	1 1	2A 140A	250 2240	312.50 2688
			House (32 x 20) is in bad order. House (18 x 14) is in midling order.						

Direct Tax of 1798 - Heidelberg Township

No.	Owner/Occupant/Ref.	Adjoining	Building	Dimen.	Matls.	Stories	Acres Perch.	Assmt.	Valuation
			Barn in bad order. Dry limestone land.						
286	Weick, Christian Weick, Adam B223 E223 II-	Kapp, Frederick	House House Barn	26 x 22 20 x 18 30 x 20	log log log		 120A	40 480	48 576
			Bad barn. Mountain land. Poor order.						
287	Weick, Gehret A279 I-	Newmanstown	House	20 x 18	hewn log	1	80P	105	
			House is in midling order.						
288	Weiman, George A254 B209 D254 E209 I- II-	Sheferstown	House Barn Land	30 x 28 40 x 20	hewn log hewn log	1	100P 1A	200 16	250 19.20
			Buildings are old, in bad order.						
289	Weiss, Christn. Weiss, Jacob A264 B219 D264 E219 I- II-	Weiss, Henry Kratzer, Jacob Coleman, Robt, Esq.	House House Barn Land Land	28 x 30 33 x 19 70 x 25	hewn log limestone stone/log	2 2	2A 2A 112A 14A 19A	300 200 2128 140 57	375 250 2553.60 168 68.40
			House (28 x 30) is in bad order. House (33 x 19) is in good order; fine spring and springhouse below and springhouse above. Barn in good order; good limestone land. Lots are mountain land.						
290	Weiss, Henry A262 B217 D262 E217 I- II-	Shenk, John Coleman, Robt.	House Kitchen Barn Land - mountain land	30 x 26 16 x 16 60 x 28	limestone limestone	2 1	2A 110A 14A	500 1980 42	625 2376 50.40
			House is in midling order, not quite finished. Kitchen is in bad order, not finished. Barn in good order. Midling good limestone land.						
291	Whitman, Henry Witman, Henry A267 B222 D267 E222 I- II-	Slessman, Peter	House Barn	22 x 20 40 x 18	hewn log log	1	2A 26A	110 156	137.50 187.20
			House is in bad order. Barn poor order. Ground oak land.						
292	Winter, Widow A268 D268 I-	Sheferstown	House Stable (small)	30 x 18	hewn log	1	1A 40P	150	187.50
			House is in midling order.						
293	Witemoyer, Ludwig A255 B210 D255 E210 I- II-	Troutman, Jonas Sheferstown	House Springhouse Barn Out Lots	30 x 16 10 x 12 35 x 18	hewn log hewn log	1	2A 23A 7 1/2A	200 184 120	250 220.80 144
			House is in bad order. Springhouse in midling order. Barn in poor order. Gravel land.						
294	Wolf, Michael A263 B218 D263 E218 I- II-	German, Henry	House Barn	26 x 24 30 x 18	hewn log log	1	2A 98A	105 686	131.25 823.20
			House is in midling order. Barn in poor order. Ground oak land.						

Direct Tax of 1798 - Heidelberg Township

No.	Owner/Occupant/Ref.	Adjoining	Building	Dimen.	Matls.	Stories	Acres Perch.	Assmt.	Valuation
295	**Wolfersberger, Geo.** A265 B220 D265 E220 I- II-	Shenk, John	House Barn	35 x 30 65 x 28	limestone stone/log	2	2A 148A	650 2812	812.50 3374.40
			New and in good order. Finished. Barn new. Good limestone land.						
296	**Wolfersberger, Peter** Louser, Jacob A266 B221 D266 E221 I- II-	Brubaker, Danl.	House House Barn	28 x 36 20 x 18 65 x 25	hewn log rd. log log	2 1	2A 105A	500 1995	625 2394
			House (28 x 36) is in midling order. House (20 x 18) is old and in poor order. An excellent spring. Barn midling. Good limestone land.						
297	**Zartman, Jacob** A270 D270 I-	Sheferstown	House Stable (small)	24 x 20	hewn log	1	100P	125	156.25
			House is in midling order.						
298	**Zeller, George** A273 B227 D273 E227 I- II-	Zimmerman, Geo. Sr. Meisser, George	House Outhouse Barn Land	24 x 24 20 x 18 70 x 30	limestone hewn log	1 1	2A 100A 60A	550 2000 420	687.50 2400 504
			House is old and in bad order. Outhouse is in midling order. Barn in good order; good limestone land. 60 Acres is mountain land.						
299	**Zeller, Peter** A274 B228 D274 E228 I-	Newmanstown	House Springhouse Barn	33 x 30 20 x 18 65 x 25	stone hewn log log	1 1	2A 148A	550 2664	687.50 3196.80
			House and springhouse are in midling order. Barn is in midling order. Good land.						
300	**Zimmerman, Geo. Jr.** A272 B226 D272 E226 I- II-	Zimmerman, H. J.	House Stable (small) Grist mill Saw mill	25 x 18 40 x 36	hewn log stone	1	2A 12A	175 216 1200 100	218.75 259.20 1440
			Buildings are in midling order. Good gravel land, plenty water. Saw mill in bad order.						
301	**Zimmerman, Geo. S.** A271 B225 D271 E225 I- II-	Saltzgeber, John Mountain. land	House Outhouse Barn Land	24 x 20 30 x 18 65 x 30	hewn log hewn log log	1 1	2A 134A 50A	350 2546 200	437.50 3055.20 240
			Buildings are old and in bad order. Barn in bad order; good gravel land. 50 Acres is mountain land.						
302	**Zimmerman, Henry** Gordon, John A269 B224 D269 E224 I- II-	Smith, George	House House Wash house Barn	40 x 32 30 x 20 10 x 14 75 x 32	limestone hewn log hewn log stone	2 1 1	2A 223A	700 4960	875 5952
			House (40 x 32) is new, not quite finished. House (30 x 20) and wash house are in good order. Barn in good order. Good limestone land, watered meadow.						

Direct Tax of 1798 - Lebanon Township

No.	Owner/Occupant/Ref.	Adjoining	Building	Dimen.	Matls.	Stories	Acres Perch.	Assmt.	Valuation
1	Achenbach, Arnt I- D3	Karsnits, Andw.	House Stable (small) House is indifferent.	20 x 22	hewn log	2	72P	160	200
2	Achenbach, John D4 I-	Bergenhoff, Wm.	House House is old, in bad order.	18 x 15		1	96P	105	131.25
3	Alleman, Leonard Sherer, John Kuntz, Geo. B2 D2 E2 I- II-	Frank, Henry Ney, Peter	House House House Barn Good gravel land. Land Gravel land, poorly timbered. House (25 x 27) - a midling good house. House (20 x 18) - a tenants house.	24 x 27 20 x 18 16 x 15 68 x 29	hewn log hewn log stone	1 1	2A 2A 116A 100A	350 150 1624 1100	437.50 187.50 2030 1375
4	Allwine, Conrad Allwein, Conrad B1 D1 E1 I- II-	Light, Jacob	House Kitchen Barn House - good, midling fine. Pretty good Limestone land. The barn is very good.	40 x 30 20 x 18 80 x 33	limestone limestone limestone	1 1	2A 198A	500 3960	625 4950
5	Alstad, John D5 I-	Embig, Jacob	House 8W 96L Smith shop Stable (small) In Lebanon 8W 96L	27 x 22	hewn log	2	48P	350	437.50
6	Arnold, Herman B4 D7 E4 I- II-	Brandt, Isaac	House Barn	36 x 28 52 x 26	limestone stone/wd.	1	2A 160A	500 2080	625 2600
7	Arnold, John Jr. B6 D9 E6 I- II-	Orendorff, Christian	House Barn House is old. Gravel land.	26 x 21 50 x 26	log	1	2A 143A	230 1573	287.50 1966.25
8	Arnold, John Sr. B5 D8 E5 I- II-	Arnold, Herman	House Barn	28 x 26 60 x 26	hewn log stone/wd.	2	2A 158A	440 2212	550 2765
9	Arnt, Jacob B3 D6 E3 I- II-	Weirich, Jacob Doebler, Abrahm.	House Hatter shop Land (an out lot) House is on Chestnut St. in Lebanon.	23 1/2 x 33 37 x 23 1/2	log stone/wd.	2 2	48P 7A 80P	350 180	437.50 225
10	Bachman, Christn. Huber, Michl. Herr, Henry		House Spring house House	30 x 28 36 x 28 30 x 24	wood wood stone	2 2 1	2A 2A 2A	500 450 430	625 562.50 537.50

Direct Tax of 1798 - Lebanon Township

No.	Owner/Occupant/Ref.	Adjoining	Building	Dimen.	Matls.	Stories	Acres Perch.	Assmt.	Valuation
	B31 D35 E31 I- II-		House	24 x 18	stone	2	2A	360	450
		Coleman, Robt.	Barn	80 x 30	stone/wd.		248A	5952	7440
		Witmer, Peter	Barn	72 x 30	stone/wd.		205A	4920	6150
		Borkholter, Christn.	Barn	80 x 30	stone/wd.		147A	3381	4226.25
			Grist Mill	30 x 36	stone			1100	1375
			House (30 x 28) and Springhouse (36 x 28) are good.						
			House (30 x 24) and House (24 x 18) are midling good.						
			Good land and barns.						
11	Bachman, Christn. Jr. B20 E20 II-	Marter, John	Land Good land.				30A	660	825
12	Bamberger, John B16 D22 E16 I- II-	Strohm, Geo. Strohm, John	Barn	54 x 19	stone		171A	3249	4061.25
			House	28 x 32	stone	1	2A	400	500
			A midling good house.						
			Good dry limestone land.						
13	Bamberger, Joseph B15 D21 E15 I- II-	Krall, Abraham Coleman, Robt.	House	30 x 27	stone	2	2A	800	1000
			House	20 x 27	stone	1			
			Barn	70 x 29	stone		186A	4278	5347.50
			Land				40A	200	250
			Good houses. Good limestone land. Hilly woodland.						
14	Bard, Adam Jr. B10 D16 E10 I- II-	Zerring, John	House	40 x 18	wood	1	2A	180	225
			Land				16A	192	240
			House is indifferent. Part gravel and part bottom land on "Sweetara" Cr.						
15	Bard, Adam Sr. B52 D65 E52 I- II-	Heilman, Adam	House	27 x 40	wood	1	2A	400	500
			Barn	100 x 30	log		138A	1518	1897.50
			House is in good order. Gravel, midling land.						
16	Bard, John Keener, Widow Hener, Widow B14 D17 E14 I- II-	Dutweiler, John Rickert, Christn.	House (small)	18 x 15	log		8A 157P	161	201.25
			House	24 x 20	wood	2	72P	310	412.50
			In midling good order.						
			Limestone land - good land.						
17	Bauman, George Bowman, Geo. Bauman, Widow B55 D62 E55 I- II-	Shnebely, Geo.	House	32 x 24	stone	1	2A	500	625
			House	32 x 22	stone	1	2A	435	540.75
			Barn	70 x 30	stone		246A	4920	6150
			Barn	75 x 32	stone				
			Good land.						
18	Bauman, John Bowman, John B27 D33 E27 I- II-	Killinger, Michl.	House	40 x 32	stone	2	2A	600	750
			Barn (old)	70 x 21	log		144A	3256	4070
			Good new house. Barn not good. Limestone land.						
19	Beck, Christian B61 E61 II-	Herr, Abraham	Land - woodland				5A	90	112.50
20	Beck, John Philip I- D44	Cumberland St.	House	36 x 28	wood	2	48P	550	687.50
			Smith shop	20 x 18	stone				
			House is in good order.						

Direct Tax of 1798 - Lebanon Township

No.	Owner/Occupant/Ref.	Adjoining	Building	Dimen.	Matls.	Stories	Acres Perch.	Assmt.	Valuation
21	Becker, Jacob Beecher, Jacob Ward, Patrick B25 D31 E25 I- II-	Achenbach, Arnt Millerstown land	House Stable (small) Land	20 x 24	wood	1	48A 5A	160 80	200 100
			House is midling good. Out lot at Millers Town joins town land.						
22	Becker, Philip I- D24	Greyder, John	House Smith shop Stable (small)	22 x 27	wood wood wood		1A 90P	300	375
			House is in midling order.						
23	Beckly, George D52 I-	Beckly, Uhrich	House Stable	30 x 24	stone	1	2A	300	375
			House is in good order.						

24	Beckly, Uhrich
	   Kurtz, Geo.
	   Fisher, Christn.
	B49 D55 E49 I- II-
		Dinius, Philip
		Zimmerman, Fred
			House
			Stable
			Barn
				34 x 29
				28 x 20
				26 x 18
					wood
					stone
					log
						2
						2
							48P
							80P
							2A 80P
								290
								450
								45
									362.50
									562.50
									56.25

			House is old and in bad order. Stable is in good order. Good land.						
25	Beeley, Adam Beekly, Adam Bealy, Adam B34 D39 E34 I- II-	Blouch, Abm.	House Barn	24 x 26	wood	1	2A 97A	200 873	250 1091.25
			House is in midling order. "Old barn Building a New." Poor gravel land.						
26	Beever, Dietrich I- D15	Raiguel, Abram	House Tanyard (new) Stable (small)	15 x 40	stone/wd.	1	14P	250	312.50
			Midling good order.						
27	Benner, Charles B50 D63 E50 I- II-	Reifwein, Jacob	House Barn (old)	25 x 20 25 x 16	wood log	1	2A 78A	180 702	225 877.50
			House indifferent. Good land.						

28	Benner, John
	   Gunderman, Jacob
	   Contrehman, Jacob
	B37 D43 E37 I- II-
		Peiffer, Jacob
		
		Orendorff, Christn.
			House
			House
			Barn
			Barn
				20 x 16
				18 x 14
				25 x 16
				18 x 12
					wood
					wood
					log
					log
						1
						1
							2A
							2A
							78A
							78A
								200
								130
								780
								780
									250
									162.50
									975
									975

			Houses are in bad order. Gravel land.						
29	Bergenhoff, Wm. I- D14	Shaake, John in Millers Town	House Stable Shed Hatter shop	18 x 35 30 x 12	wood stone stone	2	48P	700	875
			A Public House, in good order. Shed indifferent Hatter shop not in use.						
30	Berry, Conrad B9 D12 E9 I- II-	Sechrist, Solomon Ulrich, Tobias	Smith Shop House	 28 x 32	wood wood	 2	2A 120P 96P	44 300	55 375
			House is in midling order. Property adjoins Millers Town and out lots.						

Direct Tax of 1798 - Lebanon Township

No.	Owner/Occupant/Ref.	Adjoining	Building	Dimen.	Matls.	Stories	Acres Perch.	Assmt.	Valuation
31	Berry, Henry B8 D11 D- E8 I- II-	Rickert, Christr. Detweiler, John	House House Land House is in good order. Pretty good limestone land.	35 x 20	stone	1	72P 8A 157P	280 161	1100 350 201.25
32	Berry, Peter I- D13	Imboden, Geo.	House Stable (small) Midling good order.	25 x 30	wood	2	96A	330	412.50
33	Betz, Casper B18 D25 E18 I- II-	Stoever, Fred.	House Land House is old and in bad order. Land is out lot joining Lebanon Borough.	24 x 28	wood	1	2A 2A	110 32	137.50 40
34	Bickel, Rudolph Bechel, Rudolph B46 D60 E46 I- II-	Boltz, Geo.	House Barn House is in midling order. Land gravel - midling.	38 x 26 60 x 20	wood stone/log	1	2A 186A	350 2418	437.50 3022.50
35	Biebel, John Breehbill, John D56 I-	Market St.	House House in midling order.	30 x 27	wood	1	48P	200	250
36	Blauch, John Hershberger, Danl. B26 D32 E26 I- II-	Fernsler, Philip Ramberger, Adam	House House (old) Barn (small) Barn (small) House is midling good. Gravel land. Barn not good.	28 x 26 25 x 18 30 x 16 60 x 18	wood	1	2A 88A 56A	280 880 560	350 1100 700
37	Blecher, John Est. Stone, John I- D74	Sig, Henry	House House is old.	21 x 18	log	1	48P	105	131.25
38	Bleistein, George Bleistone, Geo. Blystone, George B43 D57 E43 I- II-	Zebold, Leonard	Barn House House is in good order. Midling quality land.	25 x 18 24 x 18	log wood	1	3A 2A	54 200	67.50 250
39	Bleistone, Isaac Blystine, Isaac D51 I-	Borkhard, Geo.	House In good order.	27 x 21	wood	1	48P	200	250
40	Blouch, Abm. Blough, Abraham Blauch, Abm. B59 D72 E59 I- II-	Knoll, Christn.	House House (old) Barn (old) House (30 x 20) is old. Gravel land.	30 x 20 12 x 15 60 x 25	wood log	1	2A 126A	280 1134	350 1417.50
41	Boal, Frank I- D53	Bushong, Jacob	House Stable House not well finished.	41 x 18	stone/wd.	2	48P	300	375
42	Boehm, Jacob	Boehm, Rudolph	Barn	70 x 30	stone		193A	4632	5790

Direct Tax of 1798 - Lebanon Township

No.	Owner/Occupant/Ref.	Adjoining	Building	Dimen.	Matls.	Stories	Acres Perch.	Assmt.	Valuation
	B29 E29 II-	Mitchell, Thomas	Good barn and limestone land.						
43	**Boehm, Rudolph** Beem, Rudy B28 D34 E28 I- II-	Boehm, Jacob	House Barn A midling good house. Limestone land.	40 x 30 70 x 28	stone log	1	2A 193A	500 4632	625 5790
44	**Boeshor, Henry** Besore, Henry B56 D69 D69 E56 I- II-	Traxel, John	House Barn Midling good house. Ground - midling gravel land.	28 x 24 64 x 34	wood stone/wd.	1	2A 198A	300 2178	375 2722
45	**Boger, Valentine** B53 D66 E53 I- II-	Brenisen, Jacob	House Springhouse Barn (old) House is in midling order. Midling gravel land.	20 x 40 15 x 18 48 x 25	wood wood log	1 1	2A 148A	320 1628	400 2035
46	**Boltz, George** B45 D59 E45 I- II-	Boltz, Jacob	Barn House House is not finished. Gravel land, poor.	35 x 20 24 x 20	log wood	 1	91A 2A	819 180	1023.75 225
47	**Boltz, Jacob** B47 D61 E47 I- II-	Boltz, Geo.	House Barn (old) An old house. Gravel - poor.	24 x 30 40 x 20	wood log	2	2A 98A	260 980	325 1225
48	**Boltz, Michael** B13 D20 E13 I- II-	Frank, Henry	House Barn House is in bad order. Barn of little value. Land gravely.	32 x 14 42 x 21	wood log	1	2A 69A	200 621	250 776.25
49	**Borkert, George** Borkner, Peter Borgner, Peter B39 D47 E39 I- II-	Ley, Andrew	House Smith shop Barn House is in midling order. Gravel land - poor.	28 x 24 18 x 12 52 x 20	wood wood log	1	2A 94	230 940	287.50 1175
50	**Borkholter, Abrahm.** B21 D28 E21 I- II-	Gingrich, John	House Barn House is midling good. Good land.	28 x 28 73 x 27	wood stone	2	2A 172A	360 3440	450 4300
51	**Borkholter, Christ** B22 D29 E22 I- II-	Gingrich, John Gingrich, Michl. Matter, John	House House Barn, old House (29 x 26) is in good order. House (26 x 22) is new and not finished. Part good and part stony land.	29 x 26 26 x 22 72 x 27	wood wood stone	2 1	2A 172A	500 240 3268	625 300 4085
52	**Borkholter, Christn.** B23 E23 II-	Bachman, Christian	Sawmill Barn Barn and land good.	 70 x 83	 stone		89A	2136	2670
53	**Boyer, Michl. Est.** Beyer, Michl. Est. Beyer, John B60 D73 E60 I- II-	Williams, Fredk.	House Barn (old) Midling good house. Gravel land.	40 x 20 50 x 24	log log	1	2A 153A	250 1500	312.50 1875

Direct Tax of 1798 - Lebanon Township

No.	Owner/Occupant/Ref.	Adjoining	Building	Dimen.	Matls.	Stories	Acres Perch.	Assmt.	Valuation
54	Boyer, Philip Est. Beyer, Philip Est. B24 D30 E24 I- II-	Fernsler, Philip	House Barn	27 x 28 80 x 25	wood log	1	2A 138A	240 1242	300 1552.50
			House is not good. Land bad, barn bad.						
55	Brand, Christian B7 D10 E7 I- II-	Eckert, Philip	House Springhouse Barn	24 x 28 19 x 25 64 x 30	wood stone stone	2 1	2A 158A	500 2376	625 2970
			House is in good order. Barn is good. Good limestone land.						
56	Brand, Henry B41 D49 E41 I- II-	Imhoff, John	House Barn	34 x 28 59 x 29 1/2	wood stone	2	2A 84A	550 1344	687.50 1680
			House is in good order. Midling good gravel land.						
57	Brand, Isaac B48 D62 E48 I- II-	Miller, Danl.	House Barn	32 x 28 52 x 25	wood log	2	2A 178A	440 2314	550 2892.50
			House is in midling good order. Ground - gravel, poorly timbered in the 178A. The 20A lately purchased in Bethel Township of Kriegbaum is included.						
58	Braunewell, Mathias Brownewell, Maths. Braunewell, John B17 D23 E17 I- II-	Uhler, Christr.	House Bldg. (small) Barn	21 x 18 12 x 21 25 x 19	wood stone log	1 1	2A 44A	200 792	250 990
			House in bad order. Dry limestone land.						
59	Breamer, Adam Bremmer, Adam D75 I-	Shindel, Peter	House	21 x 18	log	1	48P	130	162.50
			Midling good house.						
60	Breamer, Conrad Brenner, Conrad B32 D37 E32 I- II-	Dohner, John Toner, John	House Barn	28 x 24 66 x 15	wood log	1	2A 48A	240 720	300 900
			House is in midling order. Midling land.						
61	Brechbiel, Henry B30 D36 E30 I- II-	Bickel, Rudolph	House Still house (old) Barn	29 x 15 55 x 20	wood stone/wd.	1	2A 98A	200 1078	250 1347.50
			House is old and bad. Gravel land.						
62	Brechbiel, Jacob Brechbill, Jacob B40 D48 E40 I- II-	Brand, Christn.	House Barn	28 x 24 24 x 16 55 x 26	wood wood log	1	2A 138A	430 3036	537.50 3795
			House is in good order. Good land.						
63	Brechbiel, Nichls. B33 D38 E33 I- II-	Dohner, John Zinn, Geo.	House Barn	38 x 28 60 x 30	stone stone	2	2A 201A	700 4221	875 5276.25
			House is in good order. Good limestone land.						
64	Breitenbach, John Bridenbach, John Embich, Fred B36 D42 E36 I- II-	Follmer, Jacob Stieb, Jacob Waltz, Christr. Keller, John Krause, David	Kitchen Stable Stable Land Land Land	36 x 27 36 x 30	wood stone log	2 2	96P 96P 5A 5A 10A	1175 1550 75 75 170	1468.75 1937.50 93.75 93.75 212.50

Direct Tax of 1798 - Lebanon Township

No.	Owner/Occupant/Ref.	Adjoining	Building	Dimen.	Matls.	Stories	Acres Perch.	Assmt.	Valuation
			House is in good order. Good land. Out lot joining Lebanon.						
65	Brenisen, Jacob Breneyson, Jacob B51 E51 I- II-	Boger, Valentine	House House Spring house Barn	27 x 21 20 x 22 60 x 22	wood wood log	1 1	2A 143A	300 150 1430	375 187.50 1787.50
			Both houses in midling good order on one Plantation. Gravel land.						
66	Bricker, Christn. B57 D70 E57 I- II-	Keller, John	House Stable	20 x 18 20 x 15	wood	1	2A 3A	200 48	250 60
			House is in not very good order. Out lot near Lebanon.						
67	Bucher, Benedict B54 D67 E54 I- II-	Smith, Henry	House Barn Still house	25 x 26 86 x 35 24 x 18	wood stone/log stone/log	1	2A 198A	350 3960	437.50 4950
			House is in good order. Barn - lower stone, upper wood. Still house - lower stone, upper wood. Good land.						
68	Bucher, George D26 I-	Dubs, Martin	House	27 x 20	wood	2	48P	160	200
			In bad order.						
69	Buchler, Henry Beehlor, Henry Braunewde, Maths. B35 D41 E35 I- II-	On Market St. in Lebanon Hoffman, Conrad Clark, Thomas	House Kitchen Smith shop House Barn Land	26 x 29 26 x 16 40 x 25 60 x 31	wood stone stone wood stone	2 2 1 1	2A 48P 164A 6A	700 340 3280 96	875 425 4100 120
			House (26 x 29) is on Market St. in Lebanon. Buildings in good order. 40 x 25 building in midling order. Good land. Out lot joining Lebanon. Slaves: Whole Number of slaves of all ages: 1 No. of slaves above 12 and under 50 years of age, subject to taxation: 1						
70	Buehler, Christ. D50 I-	Koehler, Leonhd.	House Tanyard	20 x 16	wood	1	1A	300	375 375
			House is in bad order. Tanyard out of order - not in use. Good land.						
71	Buecher, Jacob Beecher, Jacob Brechbill, _____ A42 D54 E42 I- II-	Ginder, Christ Est. Allwein, Conrad Beck, John Ph.	House Potter shop House House (35 x 24) well finished. House (20 x 20) in midling good order. Barn (old) Still house Land	35 x 24 20 x 15 20 x 20 30 x 18	wood wood wood stone stone/wd.	2 1 1	48P 2A 75A 144P	500 200 1350 45	625 200 250 1687.50 56.25
72	Buehler, Geo. Est.	Buehler, Henry	House	13 x 24	wood	2	2A	500	625

Direct Tax of 1798 - Lebanon Township

No.	Owner/Occupant/Ref.	Adjoining	Building	Dimen.	Matls.	Stories	Acres Perch.	Assmt.	Valuation
	Bleistone, Abram Been, Abram B44 D58 E44 I- II-	Buehler, Henry	House (old) Still house Barn	26 x 15 60 x 27	stone		150A	2400	3000
			House (13 x 24) in good order. Gravel land of midling quality.						
73	**Buehler, George** Beck, Christian B58 D71 E58 I- II-	Light, John	House Stable Land	25 x 25	wood	1	48P 96A	200 30	250 37.50
			House is old. Two town lots - Lebanon.						
74	**Buehler, Simon** Beelor, Simon Baylor, Simon Buehler, Francis B11 D18 E11 I- II-	Runkle, John Runkle, John	House House (old) Barn, old	20 x 25 12 x 20 30 x 20	wood log	1	2A 80A	140 792	175 990
			House in bad order. Poor gravel land - badly timbered. A tenants house.						
75	**Burkert, George** D46 I-	Bleystone, Isaac	House Stable	28 x 17	wood wood	2	48P	230	287.50
			House is in bad order.						
76	**Burkholder, Ulrich est** B19 D27 E19 I- II-	Meyer, John Myer, John	House Barn, old	36 x 30 72 x 28	stone wood	1	2A 211A	440 3798	550 4747.50
			House in good order. Land is good but stony.						
77	**Bush, Maria** Bush, Marry D40 I-	Ulrich, Martin	House	18 x 25	wood	1	48P	105	131.25
			House in bad order.						
78	**Bush, Martin** B12 D19 E12 I- II-	Miller, John Boltz, _____	House Land	26 x 22	wood	2	2A 33A	140 330	175 412.50
			House not finished. Land gravel and badly timbered.						
79	**Bushong, Jacob** B38 D45 E38 I- II-	Keller, John Cumberland St.	House Stable Land (out lot)	42 x 38	stone wood	2	48P 5A	800 80	1000 100
			House in midling good order. Limestone land.						
80	**Calender, Cloud** D78 I-	Berry, Henry	House House	24 x 18 17 x 15	wood wood	1 1	48P 48P	120 110	150 137.50
			Houses are midling good.						
81	**Canal Company** Kelker, Jacob Stoever, Philip Kinsly, Martin B65 D81 E65 I- II-	Greenawalt, Philip Kelker, Jacob Kintzel, Martin Light, Felix	House House Barn Mill	50 x 36 25 x 14 46 x 27 54 x 32	stone stone log stone	2 1	2A 2A 171A	800 200 3420 1300	1000 250 4275 1625
			House (50 x 36) - midling good; house (25 x 14) - bad order. Good limestone land.						
82	**Capp, Barbara** D80 I-	Walnut St.	House But indifferent.	18 x 13	wood	1	48P	105	131.25

Direct Tax of 1798 - Lebanon Township

No.	Owner/Occupant/Ref.	Adjoining	Building	Dimen.	Matls.	Stories	Acres Perch.	Assmt.	Valuation
83	Casel, Christn.	Miller, Jacob	House	21 x 27	wood	2	96P	500	625
	Cassel, Christn.		Kitchen	15 x 27	stone	1			
	D77 I-		A Public House.						
84	Ceerer, Conrad	Weis, Henry	House	25 x 20	wood	1	2A	260	325
	Cenner, Conrad		Barn	48 x 24	stone/log		138A 80P	2421	3026.25
	B64 D79 E64 I- II-		Midling good order. Limestone land.						
85	Clark, Thomas	Kelker, Rudy	House	30 x 36	wood	2	24P	650	812.50
		Long, William	House	18 x 30	wood	1	24P	110	137.50
	B62 D76 E62 I- II-		House	33 x 28	wood	1	2A	300	375
		Gingrich, John	Barn	60 x 26	stone/log		148A	1840	2300
			Land				10A 10P	200	250
			Grist Mill	38 x 26				900	1125
			House (30 x 36) - good house. House (18 x 30) - in bad order.						
			House (33 x 29) - midling good. Land - good gravel land.						
86	Coleman, Robert		House						400
	Neil, Shea		House	44 x 23	stone	2	2A	410	410
	Rodgers, MCue	Bauman, Geo.	House	33 x 30	stone	2	2A	635	635
	Reili, Ramsey		Kitchen	15 x 18	stone	1			
	Kelker, Rudolph		House	26 x 22	wood	1	1A	160	160
	B63 I- D- E63 II-		House	23 x 19	wood	1	2A	120	120
		Smith, John	Barn	91 x 27	stone/log		288A	6336	7920
			Stable	50 x 30	stone				
			Stable	74 x 34	stone				
			Office	16 x 43	stone				
			Store house	63 x 19 1/2					
			Cornwall Furnace						
			Grist Mill	28 x 33	stone			5250	6562.50
	Smith, Charles		House	18 x 22					
	Brown, Henry		House	21 x 18					
	Ramsy, Reili		House	23 x 19					
			Coal house (large)				198A	33960	42450
			Coal house (large) (including Ore Banks of Cornwall)						
		Meily, Geo.	Coal house (large)						
			Mountain land				1500A	7500	9375
			House (44 x 23) in bad order. House (33 x 20 in						
			midling good order.						
			Land is of very first rate limestone land. Part hill land, good						
			meadow in the land.						
			Slaves: Whole No. of Slaves: 5						
			No. of Slaves Exempted from Taxation by						
			law or disability: 2						
			No. of slaves above 12 and under 50 years						
			of age, subject to taxation: 3						
87	Cornwall Furnace								
	Kelker, Rudy, Mgr.		House	83 1/2 x 40	stone	2	2A	900	1125
	Sheeler, John		House	28 x 20	stone	1	1A	250	312.50
	Meck, Philip		House	26 x 29	stone	1	1A	240	300
	Conrad, George		House	28 x 17	wood	1	1A	160	200
	Garland, Moses		House	22 x 18	wood	1	1A	180	225
	Kieth, James		House	24 x 29	wood	1	1A	180	225

Direct Tax of 1798 - Lebanon Township

No.	Owner/Occupant/Ref.	Adjoining	Building	Dimen.	Matls.	Stories	Acres Perch.	Assmt.	Valu- ation
	Shaw, Neil		House	44 x 23	stone	2	2A	410	512.50
	Smith, Widow		House	33 x 30	stone	2	2A	635	793.75
			Kitchen	15 x 18	stone	1			
	Ramsey, Reily		House	16 x 22	wood	1	1A	160	200
	McCue, Rodger		House	23 x 19	wood	1	2A	120	150
	D 82 I-		All houses are in good order.						
88	Daub, Dillman	Light, John	House	30 x 25	wood	2	2A	375	468.75
	Daub, Conrad	Beyer, Michl. Est.	House	28 x 26	wood	1	2	250	312.50
	B78 D99 E78 I- II-	Byer, John	Barn	40 x 20	log		88A	968	1210
			Barn	30 x 28	log		8A	110	137.50
			House (30 x 25) - good. House (28 x 26) midling good. Gravel land.						
89	Detweiler, John	Mitchell, Thos.	House	41 x 28	stone	1	2A	500	625
	Dutweiler, John		Barn	55 x 30	stone/log	1	153A	3760	4700
	B66 D83 E66 I- II-		House is in good order. Limestone land.						
90	Dietz, John	Brechbiel, Henry	House	21 x 14	wood	1	2A	180	225
	Martzell, Christn.		House	27 x 24	wood	1	2A	200	250
	B75 D96 E75 I- II-		Barn	42 x 27	log		72A	648	810
			House (21 x 14) in good order. House (27 x 24) in bad order. Poor gravel land.						
91	Dinius, Jacob	Krall, Abraham	House	25 x 20	wood	2	2A	550	687.50
	B77 D98 E77 I- II-		Barn	60 x 30	stone		148A	2664	3330
			House - a good house. Limestone land.						
92	Dinius, Nichls.	Werner, Henry	House	30 x 25	wood	2	2A	400	500
	B76 D97 E76 I- II-		Barn	60 x 28	stone		167A	3006	3757.50
			House - a good house. Limestone land.						
93	Dinius, Philip	Beckly, Ulrich	House	28 x 24	wood	2	2A	475	593.75
	B71 D92 E71 I- II-		House is in good order.						
			Barn	45 x 21	log		40A 80P	873	1091.25
			Limestone land.						
94	Dishong, David	Gasser, John	House	24 x 18	wood	2	48P	130	162.50
	D88 I-		House is in bad order.						
95	Doebler, Abram	Reinoehl, George	House	25 x 19	wood	1	5A 48P	500	625
	B68 D87 E68 I- II-	Cumberland St.	House	22 x 19	wood	2			
			Smith shop	19 x 22 1/.	wood				
			Stable	20 x 18					
			Land				4A 81P	72	90
			House (25 x 19) in midling order. House (22 x 19) is new. Limestone out lot.						
96	Doebler, Anthony	Kelker, Rudy	House	48 x 24	wood	2	36P	665	831.25
	B72 D93 E72 I- II-		Stable						
		Fisher, Philip	Land - town lot - Lebanon				48P	15	18.75
		Stieb, Jacob	Land - out lot - Lebanon				1A	24	30
		Gilbert, Henry	Land - out lot - Lebanon				18A	288	360
			House is a Public House.						

Direct Tax of 1798 - Lebanon Township

No.	Owner/Occupant/Ref.	Adjoining	Building	Dimen.	Matls.	Stories	Acres Perch.	Assmt.	Valuation
97	Dohner, Henry Dooner, Henry B67 D86 E67 I- II-	Gisseman, George	House Barn House is in bad order. Limestone land.	20 x 25 60 x 30	wood log	1	2A 177A	200 3717	250 4646.25
98	Dohner, Jacob Dooner, Jacob Weaber, Henry B73 D94 E73 I- II-	Heisey, Michl.	House House Barn Smith shop Houses are in good order. Limestone land.	30 x 20 18 x 15 40 x 20	wood wood log	1 1	2A 2A 216A	300 105 4104	375 131.25 5130
99	Dohner, John B69 D89 E69 I- II-	Dohner, Joseph	House House is in midling order. Barn Limestone land.	36 x 26 60 x 28	wood stone	2	2A 178A	450 3204	562.50 4005
100	Dohner, Joseph Dooner, Joseph Lauers, Jacob B74 D95 E74 I- II-	Uhrich, Philip	House House (old) Barn House - only midling order. Good Limestone land.	26 x 23 20 x 18 70 x 28	wood log	1	2A 173A	300 3979	375 4973.75
101	Dolen, John D85 I-	Raiguel, Abram	House House is in good order.	25 x 17	stone	1	96P	200	250
102	Dorman, Ludwig D91 I-	Thome, John	House House is in bad order.	20 x 18	wood	1	48P	105	131.25
103	Drion, George Dryon, George D100 I-	Sebot, Nicolus	House House Stable Buildings in midling order.	18 x 18 18 x 18 15 x 19	log stone wood	1 1	144P	300	375
104	Dubs, John Dubs, Henry B79 D101 E79 I- II-	Stoner, Geo. Est. Kreps, ____ Stoever, Fredk. Cumberland St.	House Back Room Barn House Hatter shop Stable Land - out lots near Lebanon Land - meadowland. House (32 x 30) - Publick House	32 x 30 16 x 22 18 x 45 22 x 24 66 x 14	stone stone log stone/log log stone	2 1 2 2	24P 24P 22A 4A 120P	1000 340 352 118.75	1250 425 440 148.43
105	Dubs, Martin Ellinger, Geo. B80 D84 E80 I- II-	Krause, David Peiffer, Jacob	House Land House is old and in bad order. Good Limestone land.	22 x 16	wood	1	48P 10A	125 190	156.25 237.50
106	Durst, Peter Dorst, Peter Dorsh, Peter B70 D90 E70 I- II-	Shaffner, Henry Mefaudien, John	House Stable Land House only midling. Limestone land.	18 x 20	wood	1	48P 3A 6P	180 66	225 82.50
107	Ebright, Jacob D109 I-	Myer, John	House House - a bad old house.	21 x 25	wood	1	72P	105	131.25
108	Eby, George Est.	Fernsler, Philip	House	39 x 20	stone	1	2A	360	450

Direct Tax of 1798 - Lebanon Township

No.	Owner/Occupant/Ref.	Adjoining	Building	Dimen.	Matls.	Stories	Acres Perch.	Assmt.	Valuation
	B94 D116 E94 I- II-		Barn	50 x 30	stone		206A	3914	4892.50
			House - in good order. Limestone land.						
109	Eby, Henry Est.	Allwein, Conrad	House	24 x 30	wood	1	2A	280	350
	B84 D105 E84 I- II-		Barn	55 x 28	stone/wd.		98A	1764	2205
			A midling good house. Limestone land.						
110	Eby, Jacob	Glassbrenner, Peter	House (new)	28 x 30			100A	1800	2250
	B85 E85 II-		House is not finished. Limestone land.						
111	Eckert, Philip	Brand, Christn.	House	27 x 31	wood	2	2A	550	687.50
	B82 D103 E82 I- II-		Wash House	15 x 20	wood				
			Barn	70 x 30	stone		198A	4356	5445
			House - good. Limestone land.						
112	Eichelberner, Godfried		House	48 x 27	stone/wd.	1	48P	300	375
	Richerd, John	Zebold, Leond.	House	24 x 18	wood	1	48P	140	175
	D113 I-		Houses are but midling.						
113	Elder & Kean (Newmarker Forge)	Near the Forge	House	26 x 23	wood	1	2A	320	400
	Elder, John		Kitchen	23 x 23	wood				
	Kean, John		House	28 x 24	wood	1			
	Buchter, John		House	18 x 17	wood	1	2A	210	262.50
			Kitchen	18 x 17	wood				
			House	18 x 20	wood	1	2A	130	162.50
			House	15 x 15				50	
			House	17 x 19				60	
	Downe, Charles		House	17 x 18				60	
	Kreamer, Adam		House	14 x 15				50	
	Quick, Edward		House	14 x 15				50	
	Bartto, Anthony		Grist Mill	36 x 41	stone				
	Holtzberger, Andrew		Sawmill						
	B81 D102 E81 I- II-		Forge/						
		Kieffer, Christian	Smith shop						
		Shalleberger, John	Barn	90 x 26	log		265A	9495	11868.75
			House (26 x 23) - good. House (28 x 24) - not yet finished.						
			Part in Londonderry, part in Lebanon Township.						
			Gravel land.						
114	Elenberger, John	Myer, John	House	30 x 34	stone	1	2A	540	675
	B95 D118 E95 I- II-		Barn	66 x 30	stone		200A	4400	5500
			Spring house						
			Stable (old)						
			House - good. Limestone land.						
115	Ellenberger, Jacob	Ramberger, Adam	House	27 x 23	wood	1	2A	330	412.50
	B87 D106 E87 I- II-		House is midling good.						
			House	18 x 25	wood	1	2A	200	250
			House is badly finished.						
			Barn	70 x 36	stone		236A	2596	3245
			Stables (2)						
			Gravel land.						

Direct Tax of 1798 - Lebanon Township

No.	Owner/Occupant/Ref.	Adjoining	Building	Dimen.	Matls.	Stories	Acres Perch.	Assmt.	Valuation
116	**Ellenberger, Jacob Jr.** B86 D107 E86 I- II-	Alleman, Leonhard	House Barn	24 x 27 66 x 30	wood stone	1	2A 118A	280 1652	350 2065
			House (27 x 23) - midling. House (18 x 25) - badly finished. House is midling good. Good gravel land.						
117	**Embig, Bernard** B91 D114 E91 I- II-	Embig, Jacob Wentling, Peter Wagner, Henry	House Stable Land - out lot Land - meadow lot. House - midling order.	35 x 20	wood	1	48P 8A 5P 140P	280 128 30	350 160 37.50
118	**Embig, Christr.** B93 D117 E93 I- II-	Krause, Andw. Juengst, Henry	House House Land - lots in Lebanon.	23 x 28 16 x 28	wood wood	1 1	48P 96P	280 30	350 37.50
			House (23 x 28) is old and bad - of round wood. House (16 x 28) is new and in good order.						
119	**Embig, Fredk.** **Empich, Fredk.** B92 D115 E92 I- II-	Gilbert, Henry Walnut St.	House Carpenter Shop Land - out lot House in good order.	30 x 16 19 x 26	wood wood		144P 5A	300 80	375 100
120	**Embig, Jacob** **Empich, Jacob** Gerhart, Conrad B90 D112 E90 I- II-	Altstad, John Embig, Barned Steger, Peter Krause, David Shindle, Peter	House House House Tanyard Land	35 x 27 36 x 20 18 x 20 18 x 15	wood wood wood	2 1	48P 48P 96P 10A 5A	450 200 200 160 80	562.50 250 250 200 100
			House (35 x 27) - midling good house. House (36 x 20) indifferent. 96P located in Lebanon. Tanyard and 5A are "out lots."						
121	**Endress, John** B83 D104 E83 I- II-	Werner, Henry	House Barn Land	24 x 28 55 x 30	wood stone	1	2A 118A 40A	300 2144 720	375 2655 900
			A midling good house. Limestone land.						
122	**Ensminger, Danl.** B89 D112 E89 I- II-	Ensminger, Peter	House Barn	32 x 27 46 x 27	stone log	2	2A 120A	500 2280	625 2850
			A new house. Limestone land.						
123	**Ensminger, Peter** B88 D110 E88 I- II-	Reist, Peter	House Barn Smith shop (small)	42 x 22 72 x 26	stone/wd. log	1	2A 120A	300 2400	375 3000
			House - indifferent. Limestone land.						
124	**Esterlein, Christr.** D108 I-	Stroh, John Hessting, Christn.	House House House not quite finished.	24 x 32	wood	2	1A 32P 96P	320	400
125	**Fasnacht, Conrad** D128 I-	Keller, John, dec. Uhler, Christr.	House House	30 x 20 21 x 18	frame wood	1 1	48P 1A	320 200	400 250
			House (30 x 20) - indifferent House (21 x 18) in bad order.						

Direct Tax of 1798 - Lebanon Township

No.	Owner/Occupant/Ref.	Adjoining	Building	Dimen.	Matls.	Stories	Acres Perch.	Assmt.	Valuation
126	Fegan, George D123 I-	Ney, Fredk.	House House - new building.	16 x 30	wood	1	29P	160	200
127	Fernsler, Fredk. B96 D119 E96 I- II-	Elenberger., Jacob Elenberger, John	House In midling order. House (old) Barn Stable (old) Gravel land.	21 x 30 18 x 25 62 x 24 20 x 18	wood log	1	2A 148A	300 1628	375 2035
128	Fernsler, Jacob B99 D122 E99 I- II-	Steel, David	House House - not good. Stable Gravel land.	22 x 25 15 x 18	wood	1	2A 5A	110 30	137.50 37.50
129	Fernsler, Magdalena B100 E100 II-	Wolf, Christn.	House Stable (small) Poor house and gravel land.	12 x 24			1A 80P	80	100
130	Fernsler, Philip Fernsler, Philip Jr. B106 D131 E106 I- II-	 Resley, Rudolph Peter, Henry	House House House House (35 x 25) in good order. Other houses in midling order. Barn Barn 96A is Limestone land. 138A is gravel land.	35 x 25 26 x 20 30 x 20 56 x 30 54 x 24	stone stone wood stone log	2 1 1	2A 2A 2A 96A 138A	600 220 200 1862 1380	750 275 250 2327.50 1725
131	Fetzberger, Danl. B102 D127 E102 I- II-	Peiffer, Jacob	House Shoemaker shop House - in midling good order. Land - meadow out lot - Lebanon.	24 x 18 1/2 18 x 18	wood	2 1	48P 1A	300 24	375 30
132	Fisher, Peter Est. B104 D129 E104 I- II-	Fernsler, Philip	House In midling good order. Barn Limestone land.	48 x 25 66 x 33	stone/wd. stone	1	2A 148A	450 2812	562.50 3515
133	Fisher, Peter Jr. B103 D126 E103 I- II-	Shnee, John Light, John	House Wagoner shop House in good order. Land - 5 out lots in Lebanon.	30 x 27 20 x 25	wood wood	1 1	48P 1A 80P	300 36	375 45
134	Fisher, Philip B105 D130 E105 I- II-	Huber, Michl. Doebler, Anthony McCondel, John	House House House (36 x 30) - a public house in good order. House (26 x 24) - in bad order. Land - 2 in lots in Lebanon. Land - 5 in lots in Lebanon.	36 x 30 26 x 24	wood wood	2 1	48P 96A 1A 60P	650 30 75	812.50 37.50 93.75
135	Follmer, Jacob B101 D125 E101 I- II-	Breitenbach, John	House Kitchen House House (26 x 35) in good order - well finished. House (35 x 16) old and in bad order.	26 x 35 35 x 16	brick stone/wd.	2 1	24P 24A	1100 200	1375 450

Direct Tax of 1798 - Lebanon Township

No.	Owner/Occupant/Ref.	Adjoining	Building	Dimen.	Matls.	Stories	Acres Perch.	Assmt.	Valuation
		Bauman, John	Land - out lot, Lebanon				5A	80	100
		Krause, David	Land - out lot, Lebanon				5A	80	100
		Zuber, Jacob	Land - in lot - Lebanon				48P	15	18.75
136	Forer, Daniel	Gingrich, Michl.	House	26 x 22	sq. log	2	2A	400	500
	Forey, Danl.		House	16 x 13	sq. log	1	2A	105	131.25
	Bunger, Jacob		Houses - midling good.						
	Boomer, Jacob		Barn	28 x 18	log		96A	1824	2280
	B107 D132 E107 I- II-		Limestone land.						
137	Forny, Peter	Long, Herman	House	39 x 31	stone	1	2A	550	687.50
	B108 D133 E108 I- II-		Good house.						
			Barn	60 x 27	stone			150 2700	3375
			Limestone land.						
138	Fortny, David	Loess, Christr.	House	20 x 28	wood	1	48P	200	250
	D124 I-		Wagoner shop	18 x 23	wood				
			House in bad order.						
139	Franck, Henry	Alleman, Leond.	House	26 x 28	wood	1	2A	350	437.50
	B98 D121 E98 I- II-		In midling order.						
			Still house (old)	16 x 18					
		Alleman, Leonhard	Barn	61 x 28	log		190A	2260	2825
			Good gravel land.						
140	Funck, Martin	Gloninger, Geo.	House	26 x 32	stone	1	2A	450	562.50
	Funck, Widow		Kitchen	18 x 20	stone	1			
	B97 D120 E97 I- II-		House	20 x 25	stone	1	2A	360	450
			House (26 x 32) in good order. Kitchen not finished.						
			House (20 x 25) in good order.						
			Barn	100 x 30	stone/log		190A	4370	5462.50
		Umberger, John	Land				50A	350	437.50
			190A is good Limestone land. 50A is gravel wood land.						
141	Gantzer, Christian		House	30 x 28	wood	1	2A	280	350
	Gries, Philip		House	35 x 26	wood	1	2A	300	375
	B135 D158 E135 I- II-		Houses are midling.						
		Sheffer, Isaac	Barn	50 x 26	stone/wd.		80A	800	1000
		Brand, Christian	Barn	48 x 26	log		26A	520	650
			Limestone land.						
142	Garten, Jacob	Dohner, Jacob	House (old)	38 x 26	log	1	2A	160	200
	Gaurden, Jacob		Barn	28 x 28	log		86A	1204	1505
	Gordon, Jacob		Good gravel land.						
	B150 D177 E150 I- II-								
143	Gasser, John	Dishong, David	House	30 x 19	wood	2	48P	280	350
	D159 I-		House is midling good.						
144	Gassert, Christr.	Zuber, Jacob	House	24 x 16			48P	80	100
	B133 E133 II-		In lot - Lebanon.						
145	Gebhart, George	Steckbeck, Michl.	House	24 x 20	wood	1	2A	300	375
	Steger, John	Market St.	House	22 x 25	wood	2	48P	260	325

Direct Tax of 1798 - Lebanon Township

No.	Owner/Occupant/Ref.	Adjoining	Building	Dimen.	Matls.	Stories	Acres Perch.	Assmt.	Valuation
	B124 D148 E124 I- II-		Stable						
			Barn	60 x 27	log		126A	1386	1732.50
			Midling good houses. Gravel land.						
146	Geib, John	Shaak, Philip	House	26 x 22	sq. log	2	2A	375	468.75
	B139 D164 E139 I- II-		House is midling good. Weather boarded.						
			Barn	60 x 25	stone/wd		173A	3114	3892.50
			Limestone land.						
147	Gilbert, Henry	Peifer, Jacob	House	28 x 28	sq. log	2	96P	500	625
	Stegar, Philip		Dyeing shop	16 x 18	sq. log	1			131.25
	B138 D163 E138 I- II-	Weaver, Widow	Stable						
			House	20 x 15	sq. log	1	48P	105	
			House (28 x 28) is midling good. House (20 x 15) is an old building.						
		Weiss, Jacob	Land - out lot, Lebanon				5	120	150
		Doebler, Anthy.	Land - out lot, Lebanon				5	80	100
		Greenawalt, Maths.	Land - out lot, Lebanon				5	120	150
148	Gingrich, Christn Est.		House	37 x 27	sq. log	1	2A	275	343.75
	Gingrich, Widow		Very old house.						
	B140 D165 E140 I- II-	Dohner, Jacob	Barn	60 x 25	log		198A	3762	4702.50
			Smith shop						
			Limestone land.						
149	Gingrich, Christn.	Myer, John	House	32 x 32	stone	2	2A	540	675
	B113 D138 E113 I- II-	Meyer, John	House is old and good.						
			Still House	22 x 25	stone				
			Barn	70 x 30	stone		228A	5472	6840
			Good land, "madow" and barn.						
150	Gingrich, Henry	Heilman, Adam	House	18 x 22	wood	1	2A	180	225
	Gingry, Henry		Building - old						
	B117 D142 E117 I- II-		Barn	25 x 63	stone/wd.		131A	1441	1801.25
			Gravel land.						
151	Gingrich, John	Karmeny, Martin	House	15 x 33	wood	1	2A	200	250
	Gingry, John		House is old and bad.						
	Clockmaker		Barn	40 x 20	log		148A	2516	3145
	B114 D139 E114 I- II-		Limestone land and bad barn.						
152	Gingrich, John	Dietz, John	House	27 x 24	sq. log	1	2A	200	250
	Gingrich, John Sr.		Springhouse	12 x 10	sq. log	1			
	B149 D176 E149 I- II-		House - old building.						
			Weaver shop	12 x 11					
			Barn	63 x 27	log		144A	1584	1980
			Gravel land.						
153	Gingrich, John Jr.	Hochstetter, John	House	30 x 32	stone	2	2A	380	475
	B116 D141 E116 I- II-	Hostater, John	House is old, but midling good.						
			Barn	30 x 60	log		198A	4356	5445
			Good land and "madow". Poor barn.						
154	Gingrich, Michl.	Reist, John	House	20 x 30	wood	1	2A	300	375

Direct Tax of 1798 - Lebanon Township

No.	Owner/Occupant/Ref.	Adjoining	Building	Dimen.	Matls.	Stories	Acres Perch.	Assmt.	Valuation
	B115 D140 E115 I- II-		Old building.						
			Barn	30 x 84	stone		148A	3404	4255
			Good land, "madow" and barn.						
155	**Gingrich, Michl.**	Forry, Danl.	House	24 x 20	sq. log	1	2A	230	287.50
	B141 D166 E141 I- II-		House is midling good.						
			Barn	50 x 30	log		89A 80P	1773	2216.25
			Limestone land.						
156	**Ginter, Christian Est.**	Shingle, Peter	House	24 x 18	sq. log	1	48P	110	137.50
	Ginter, Widow		Old house.						
	D173 I-								
157	**Gisseman, Henry**	Hoke, Geo.	House	28 x 24	wood	1	2A	300	375
	Gisseman, Geo.		House	20 x 16	wood	1	2A	150	187.50
	B127 D152 E127 I- II-		House (28 x 24) - old; house (20 x 16) - bad.						
			Barn	60 x 28	stone/log		146A	3285	4106.25
			Barn	35 x 14	log				
			Limestone land.						
158	**Glassbrenner, Ansted**	Glassbrenner, Geo.	House	25 x 20	sq. log	1	2A	280	350
	B145 D170 E145 I- II-		House	20 x 22	sq. log	1	2A	140	175
			House (25 x 20) - old; house (20 x 22) - good.						
			Barn	25 x 26	stone		216A	3888	4860
			Limestone land.						
159	**Glassbrenner, Geo.**	Glassbrenner, Ansted	House (old)	20 x 25	sq. log	1	2A	110	137.50
	B144 D169 E144 I- II-		Barn		log		38A	684	855
			Log barn worth nothing. Limestone land.						
160	**Glassbrenner, Peter**	Glassbrenner, Geo.	House	24 x 20	sq. log	1	2A	300	375
	B146 D171 E146 I- II-		Good new house						
		Roesly, Rudolph	Barn	40 x 24	log		58A	1044	1305
			Limestone land.						
161	**Gloninger, George**	Funck, Martin	House	30 x 25	stone	2	2A	400	500
	Gloninger, Widow	Umberger, John	House	20 x 22	wood	1	2A	110	137.50
	B128 D153 E128 I- II-		House (30 x 25) midling good; House (20 x 22) indifferent.						
			Barn		log		96A	2112	2640
			Land				28A	168	210
			Barn - an "old log barn with nothing."						
			96A - Limestone land; 28A - gravel wood land.						
162	**Gloninger, Peter**	Hubly, Fredk.	House	42 x 32	brick	2	48P	2000	2500
	George, John		Kitchen	29 x 15	brick	1			
	Yost, Casper		Storehouse	14 x 40	wood	1			
	Moore, Widow	Mark, Jacob	House	28 x 30	wood	2	24P	300	375
	B132 D156 E132 I- II-	Uhler, Christr.	House	25 x 20	wood	1	1A	200	250
			House	14 x 15	wood	1	96P	110	137.50
			House (42 x 32) - a well finished house. House (28 x 30) - indifferent. House (25 x 20) - midling good house. House (14 x 15) - bad house of round wood.						
		Krause, David	Land - Out lot near Lebanon.				5A	120	150

Direct Tax of 1798 - Lebanon Township

No.	Owner/Occupant/Ref.	Adjoining	Building	Dimen.	Matls.	Stories	Acres Perch.	Assmt.	Valu-ation
		Uhler, Christr.	Land - Limestone land.				6A	144	180
163	Gloninger, Philip Eberhard, Thomas D162 I-	Wentz, Peter	House Stable House - middling	30 x 39	frame/brk.	1	48P	350	437.50
164	Goldman, Jacob B118 E118 II-	Myer, John Meyer, John	House	15 x 18	log		48P	50	62.50
165	Graff, Anna Groff, Anna Becker, Christian B142 D167 E142 I- II-	Greenwalt, Philip	House House Both houses - old. Barn Limestone land.	30 x 27 18 x 25 87 x 21	sq. log rd. log log	1 1	2A 2A 96A	250 110 1728	312.50 137.50 2160
166	Graff, Jacob Grof, Jacob B130 E130 II-	Endress, John	Land Limestone land.				40A	720	900
167	Greenawalt, Maths. B151 D178 E151 I- II-	Greenawalt, Ph. Gilbert, Henry Wentz, Peter	House Stable House - good. Land - out lot near Lebanon Land - in Lebanon Town.	24 x 27	log log	2	24P 5A 48P	450 80 15	562.50 100 18.75
168	Greenawalt, Philip B152 D179 E152 I- II-	Greenawalt, Maths. Light, Felix Kean, Charles Stoever, Fredk. Rohland, Jacob Greenawalt, Ph.	House Stable & shed House - only midling. Barn Land - out lots near Lebanon. Land - out lots near Lebanon. Land - an in lot near Lebanon.	40 x 24	log log	2	24P 118A 80P 9A 120P 4A 72P	1500 2360 140 80 27	1875 2950 175 100 33.75
169	Greenawalt, Philip Sr. Greenewalt, John B137 D161 E137 I- II-	Krebbs, Michl. Dohner, Henry Gisseman, Geo. Reinhard, Bernhd. Steger, Peter	House House House House (30 x 27) - midling good. House (24 x 27) - good. House (25 x 26) - not finished. Barn Land Land 185A is limestone land. 8A is out lot in Lebanon. 49P is in lot in Lebanon.	30 x 27 24 x 27 25 x 26 60 x 30	frame stone stone stone	2 2 2	48P 2A 185A 8A 48P	800 400 3885 128 15	1000 500 4856.25 160 18.75
170	Greider, George B122 D146 E122 I- II-	Greyder, Tobias Greider, Tobias	House House Midling good house. Barn Limestone land.	19 x 21 24 x 21 60 x 27	stone wood stone	1 1	2A 102	300 2346	375 2932.50
171	Greider, Jacob Sr. Grider, Jacob Sr. B111 D136 E111 I- II-	 Reinoehl, George	House House Barn	27 x 53 27 x 30 30 x 75	stone/wd. stone	1 1	2A 2A 168A	135 200 3696	168.75 250 4620

Direct Tax of 1798 - Lebanon Township

No.	Owner/Occupant/Ref.	Adjoining	Building	Dimen.	Matls.	Stories	Acres Perch.	Assmt.	Valu- ation
		Reichert, John	Land Limestone land.				90A	1710	2137.50
172	Greider, John (son of Jacob) Grider, John Haberstich, Geo. B143 D168 E143 I- II-	Shaak, Nicholas	House (old) House (old) Barn Limestone land.	28 x 22 16 x 12 50 x 28	sq. log stone/log	1	2A 148A	260 2664	325 3330
173	Greybiel, Peter Graybill, Peter B112 D137 E112 I- II-	Herr, Abraham Herr, Abram	House Kitchen House - not finished. Barn Limestone and gravel land.	22 x 25 12 x 12 20 x 45	wood wood log	2 1	2A 125A	300 1750	375 2187.50
174	Greyder, Christn. Greider, Christn. Greyder, Tobias B120 D144 E120 I- II-	Greyder, Jacob Greenawalt, Philip	House Kitchen House House (32 x 40) - good House (25 x 30) - midling, not finished. Barn Barn Stable (old) Limestone land.	32 x 40 14 x 18 25 x 30 60 x 30 50 x 20	stone stone wood stone log	2 1 2	2A 2A 108A 108A	600 380 2484 2160	750 475 3105 2700
175	Greyder, Henry Grider, Henry D151 I-	Greyder, Martin	House House - not finished.	28 x 24	wood	1	1A	200	250
176	Greyder, Jacob Grider, Jacob B119 D143 E119 I- II-	Greyder, Christn. Greider, Christn.	House House - in good order. Barn Good land, "madow" bad.	30 x 35 66 x 30	stone log	1	2A 98A	435 2156	543.75 2695
177	Greyder, John Greider, John B125 D149 E125 I- II-	Greyder, Tobias	House An old house. House (old) Barn Land good, barn bad.	28 x 29 20 x 24 66 x 28	wood stone stone/log	1	2A 171A	265 3847	331.25 4808.75
178	Greyder, John Greider, John B129 D154 E129 I- II-	Walter, John	House Midling good house. Barn Gravel land.	24 x 22 62 x 26	wood stone/log	1	2A 121A	280 1331	350 1663.75
179	Greyder, Martin Greider, Martin B121 D145 E121 I- II-	Greyder, Geo.	House Midling good house. Barn Barn Stable (old) Limestone land.	25 x 28 30 x 38 30 x 30	wood stone wood	2	2A 158A	400 3634	500 4542.50
180	Greyder, Michl.	Stoever, Adam	House	29 x 30	wood	2	2A	500	625

Direct Tax of 1798 - Lebanon Township

No.	Owner/Occupant/Ref.	Adjoining	Building	Dimen.	Matls.	Stories	Acres Perch.	Assmt.	Valuation
	Greider, Michl.		Kitchen	12 x 15	stone	1			
	Grider, Michael		House	20 x 25	wood	1	2A	280	350
	B109 D134 E109 I- II-		House (29 x 30) - good. House (20 x 25) - new.						
			Barn	66 x 30	stone		296A	6512	8140
			"Goot" Limestone and gravel land.						
181	Greyder, Tobias	Greyder, Geo.	House	28 x 30	wood	1	2A	310	387.50
	Greider, Tobias	Greider, George	An old house.						
	B126 D150 E126 I- II-		Barn	64 x 30	stone		147A	3381	4226.25
			Stable (old)	27 x 18					
182	Groh, Abraham	Teiss, Michl.	House	31 1/2 x 29	wood	1	2A	400	500
	B136 D160 E136 I- II-	Brand, Christn.	Springhouse	10 x 15	stone	1			
		Miller, Michl.	House is midling good.						
			Barn	50 x 28	log		93A	2232	2790
			Land				35A	335	443.75
			93A - Limestone land. 35A is gravel woodland.						
183	Groh, Mathias	Ridle, Henry	House	42 x 20	wood	1	2A	300	375
	Camred, Ludwig		House - midling good.						
	B134 D157 E134 I- II-		House	17 x 15					
			Barn	56 x 24	stone/wd.		186	1860	2325
			Gravel land.						
184	Grove, Jacob Est.	Boal, Frances	House	27 x 14	stone	1	48P	230	287.50
	Graff, Jacob Est.		House	21 x 18	sq. log	1			
	Grove, Widow		House (27 x 14) - midling good; House (21 x 18) - old.						
	D174 I-								
185	Groy, Jacob	Yordy, Henry	House	25 x 30	wood	2	2A	300	375
	Grey, Jacob	Greider, Jacob	House - not finished.						
	B123 D147 E123 I- II-		Barn	48 x 28	log		98A	2058	2572.50
			Land				12A	252	315
			Limestone land.						
186	Grubensy, George	Stear, John	House	24 x 20	log	2	48P	325	406.25
	Krause, Joseph		Stable						
	Grouse, Joseph		House	16 x 20	log	1	48P	105	131.25
	D175 I-		House (24 x 20) - good; house (16 x 20) - not good in order.						
187	Gruber, Christian	Seechrist,	House	26 x 24	wood	2	2A	200	250
	B131 D155 E131 I- II-	Lawrence	House - indifferent.						
		Segrist, Lorentz	Barn	55 x 25	stone		98A	1764	2205
			Limestone land.						
188	Gundrum, Fredk. Est.		House	27 x 24	sq. log	1	2A	320	400
	Gundrum, Widow		Good house.						
	B148 D172 E148 I- II-	Ney, Peter	Barn	55 x 30	stone/log		138A	1518	1897.50
			Gravel land.						
189	Guntrum, John	Huber, Geo.	House	20 x 20	wood	1	2A	170	212.50
	Gunterum, John		House	12 x 14	wood	1			
	B110 D135 E110 I- II-		House (12 x 14) is described as a "pice of a House."						

Direct Tax of 1798 - Lebanon Township

No.	Owner/Occupant/Ref.	Adjoining	Building	Dimen.	Matls.	Stories	Acres Perch.	Assmt.	Valuation
			Barn	20 x 40	log				
			Stable	14 x 30	log		48A	336	1120
			Gravel land.						
190	Gussy, Frances B147 E147 II-	Uhler, Martin	House (old) Gravel land.	15 x 18			5A	65	81.25
191	Hamilton, Robt. D195 I-	Waltz, Christr.	House Nailor Shop Stable Midling good house.	30 x 24 13 x 10	sq. log frame/bd.	1 1	48P	170	212.50
192	Hasting, Christn. Hepting, Christn. B173 D184 E173 I- II-	Herr, Abraham	House Old bad house. Land - out lot near Millers Town.	20 x 18	sq. log	1	48P 10A	120 160	150 200
193	Heagey, Jacob Heagy, Jacob Hagey, Jacob Hege, Jacob B161 D189 E161 I- II-	Heisy, Henry	House (old) Barn Limestone land.	26 x 18 45 x 20	sq. log log	1	2A 111A	200 1887	250 2358.75
194	Heilman, Adam Hileman, Adam Heilman, John B171 D202 E171 I- II-	Bard, Adam Heilman, John	House (good) House (new) House (old) Oyl Mill Land Paper Mill Barn Barn Gravel land.	30 x 19 27 x 23 25 x 20 20 x 25 27 x 30 62 x 28 74 x 29	sq. log sq. log sq. log log log/stone log/stone	1 1 1 2	2A 2A 2A 254A 87A 74A	300 320 210 4064 1218 962	375 400 262.50 5080 1522.50 1202.50
195	Heilman, Ansted Heilman, Anastasius B167 D194 E167 I- II-	Heilman, John	House House House (29 x 18) - good; House 25 x 20 - good new house. Barn Stable Gravel land.	29 x 18 25 x 20 50 x 20 18 x 20	sq. log stone log log	1 2	2A 2A 96A	250 400 1056	312.50 500 1320
196	Heilman, John B172 D203 E172 I- II-	Heilman, Adam	House Midling good house. Barn Gravel land.	25 x 21 81 x 30	sq. log stone/wd.	1	2A 288A	250 4032	312.50 5040
197	Heise, Henry Heisy, Henry Hisey, Henry B174 D205 E174 I- II-	Heise, Daniel Heisy, Daniel	House Midling order. House (old) Smith shop Barn Limestone land.	26 x 24 16 x 20 20 x 22 60 x 30	log log stone stone	1	2A 100A	260 1800	325 2250
198	Heisey, Daniel Hisey, Danl. B163 D191 E163 I- II-	Heisy, Henry Uhrich, Michl.	House (good) Barn Limestone land.	30 x 30 57 x 30	stone log	1	2A 98A	430 1764	537.50 2205

Direct Tax of 1798 - Lebanon Township

No.	Owner/Occupant/Ref.	Adjoining	Building	Dimen.	Matls.	Stories	Acres Perch.	Assmt.	Valuation
199	Heisey, Michael B164 D192 E164 I- II-	Steel, David Stiel, David	House House is unfinished. Land - poor gravel land.	20 x 16	sq. log	1	2A 2A	105 14	131.25 17.50
200	Heisey, Michael Hisey, Michael B170 D201 E170 I- II-	Horst, Peter	House Springhouse House - good. Barn Good limestone land.	25 x 20 24 x 20 70 x 28	sq. log stone log	1	2A 198A	450 3762	562.50 4702.50
201	Heisey, Peter Hisey, Peter B162 D190 E162 I- II-	Holtz, George	House (old) Barn Stony land.	39 x 25 57 x 19	sq. log log	1	2A 98A	240 1078	300 1347.50
202	Henning, Danl. B154 D181 E154 I- II-	Rickert, Christr. Ulrich, Martin	House Back bldg. Hatters shop Stable House (28 x 24) midling good. and weather boarded. Part stone & part wood. Land - out lot Millers Town.	28 x 24 22 x 10 36 x 16	sq. log stone sq. log log	2 1 1	144P 2A 28P	700 34.60	875 43.25
203	Herr, Abraham B160 D188 E160 I- II-	Segrist, Solomon Martin, Henry Shenk, Joseph	House (good) Wash house House (good) Grist/Sawmill Still house Barn Stable Limestone land.	52 x 29 20 x 13 40 x 24 40 x 45 25 x 22 77 x 29 18 x 25	stone wood, sq. sq. log stone stone	2 2	2A 1A 248A 10A	1000 430 2500 5952 220	1250 537.50 3125 7440 275
204	Hersberger, Christn. Hershberger, Saml. B158 D186 E158 I- II-	Miller, John	House (old) House (new) Barn Gravel and "Swetara botom" land.	29 x 21 25 x 19 66 x 22	sq. log sq. log log	1 1	2A 2A 136A	280 130 1904	350 162.50 2380
205	Herty, Tobias D204 I-	Feger, Christn.	House (old)	30 x 45	log	1	48P	180	225
206	Hock, George Hoke, George Huber, Jacob Hoover, Jacob B155 D182 E155 I- II-	Zinn, George	House (good) House (new) Barn Limestone land. Good barn.	34 x 30 24 x 21 70 x 28	stone sq. log stone	2 1	2A 2A 176A	600 120 3960	750 150 4950
207	Hoffman, Conrad Urich, Christian Burkhart, ____ B153 D180 E153 I- II-	Lesher, Michael Uhler, Christr. Arnold, John	House Kitchen House (old) House (old) House (34 x 19) and kitchen (16 x 14) - good. Smith shop Barn Stable (small) Land	34 x 19 16 x 14 21 x 14 20 x 13 30 x 56	sq. log sq. log sq. log sq. log log	2 1 1 1	2A 2A 2A 103A 117A 14A	475 130 110 2266 2106 112	593.75 162.50 137.50 2832.50 2632.50 140

Direct Tax of 1798 - Lebanon Township

No.	Owner/Occupant/Ref.	Adjoining	Building	Dimen.	Matls.	Stories	Acres Perch.	Assmt.	Valu- ation
			103A - good limestone land. 117A - limestone land. 14A - gravel land.						
208	Holtz, George B156 E156 II-	Bachman, Christn.	House (old) Barn (old) Barn worth nothing. Stony land.	16 x 18	log		50A	620	775
209	Horst, Peter Bayly, William B169 D200 E169 I- II-	Heisy, Michael	House Middling good house. House (old) Still house Barn Limestone land.	28 x 28 15 x 18 15 x 12 71 x 30	sq. log stone/log	2	2A 298A	500 6556	625 8195
210	Hostater, John Hochstetter, John Alleman, John B159 D187 E159 I- II-	Gingrich, John Coleman, Robt.	House House House (28 x 22) - old building. House (18 x 15) - middling old Still house Barn Land 191A - Limestone land. 49A - stone hills, wood land.	28 x 22 18 x 15 26 x 22 80 x 34	sq. log sq. log stone stone	1 1	2A 2A 191A 49A	300 160 4202 245	375 200 5252.50 306.25
211	Howerter, Christn. D183 I-	Raiguel, Abram	House Smith shop Middling good house.	35 x 20 18 x 25	sq. log stone	2 1	144P	300	375
212	Huber, Andw. Hoober, Andw. Ellinger, Caspar B168 D198 E168 I- II-	Zimmerman, Fred Eby, George	House House House (30 x 22) - weather boarded. House (24 x 20) - old. House (old) Barn Limestone land.	30 x 22 24 x 20 15 x 20 35 x 20	sq. log sq. log log	2 1	48P 2A 126A 80P	280 130 2150.50	350 162.50 2688.12
213	Huber, George Hoover, George B157 D185 E157 I- II-	Ziegler, Jacob Seegely, Jacob	House (old) Barn Part gravel land. Part Swatara bottom land.	27 x 24 70 x 21	sq. log log	1	2A 113A	270 1469	337.50 1836.25
214	Huber, John Hoober, John B166 D197 E166 I- II-	Krause, David Kean, Charles	House Kitchen House (33 x 27) - good; Kitchen (20 x 13) - new. Land - out lot near Lebanon.	33 x 27 20 x 13	sq. log sq. log	2 1	48P 2A 80P	360 40	450 50
215	Huber, Michl. Hoober, Michl. D199 I-	Baylor, Harvey	House Joiner shop Stable House - old, weather boarded.	27 x 23 20 x 20	sq. log stone	2 2	48P	400	500
216	Huber, Philip Est. Hoover, Philip Kapp, Susanna D196 I-	Thome, John	House Stable House (24 x 19) - old. Stable - old.	24 x 19	sq. log sq. log	1	48P	250	312.50
217	Hubley, Fredk.	Gloninger, Peter	House	49 x 40	stone	2	48P	1600	2000

Direct Tax of 1798 - Lebanon Township

No.	Owner/Occupant/Ref.	Adjoining	Building	Dimen.	Matls.	Stories	Acres Perch.	Assmt.	Valuation
	B165 D193 E165 I- II-		Coppersmith Shp.	24 x 17	brick	1			
			Stable		stone				
			Good house.						
		Light, John	Land - out lot - Lebanon Town.				40A 93P	109.50	136.87
		Kreps, Michl.	Land - one lot in Lebanon.				96P	32	40
218	**Imboden, Adam**	Miller, Rudolph	House (old)	26 x 22	sq. log	1	2A	280	350
	B180 D215 E180 I- II-		Barn	70 x 24	stone		188A	3948	4935
			Limestone land.						
219	**Imboden, George**	Berry, Peter	House	26 x 22	sq. log	2	48P	400	500
	D216 I-		Good order, and a good house.						
220	**Imboden, John**	Siegrist, Lorentz	House (good)	36 x 30	stone	2	2A	600	750
	B178 D213 E178 I- II-		Oyl Mill	22 x 26					
			Barn	70 x 30	stone		188A	4324	5405
			Limestone land.						
221	**Imboden, Philip**	Imboden, John	House (good)	24 x 21	sq. log	2	2A	400	500
	B179 D214 E179 I- II-		Barn	50 x 28	stone/log		188A	3384	4230
			Limestone land.						
222	**Imhoff, Martin**	Teiss, Michl.	House	38 x 28	brick	2	2A	1000	1250
	B176 D207 E176 I- II-		Kitchen		brick	1			
			House - new, good.						
			Barn	45 x 27	log		39A 138P	957	1196.25
			Limestone land.						
223	**Ishler, George**	Straw, George	House	27 x 27	log	1	48P	250	312.50
	D212 I-		Stable						
			House - midling good.						
224	**Jacobey, Adam**	Laber, Baltzer	House	26 x 20	sq. log	1	2A	240	300
	Jacoby, Adam		House	18 x 16	sq. log	1	2A	160	200
	B177 D211 E177 I- II-		House (26 x 20) - midling good; house (18 x 16) - almost new.						
			Barn	45 x 27	log		98A	1764	2205
			Limestone land.						
225	**Jager, Christn.**	Hirte, Tobias	House (old)	22 x 21	sq. log	1	48P	160	200
	D222 I-								
226	**Jager, John**	Spyker, Benj.	House	25 x 18	stone/wd.	1	48P	210	262.50
	D210 I-		Stable						
			Midling good.						
227	**Jengst, Henry**	Souder, Jacob	House (old)	23 x 18	sq. log	1	48P	105	131.25
	D209 I-		Stable						
228	**Jensel, Martin**	Snotterly, Barbara	House	30 x 25	sq. log	1	48P	150	187.50
	D208 I-		Stable						
			Midling old house.						
229	**Jordy, Jacob Est.**	Heise, Danl.	House	22 x 18	sq. log	1	2A	120	150
	Est. of Dr. Franer	Gingerich, Michl.	House	26 x 17	sq. log	1	2A	120	150

Direct Tax of 1798 - Lebanon Township

No.	Owner/Occupant/Ref.	Adjoining	Building	Dimen.	Matls.	Stories	Acres Perch.	Assmt.	Valuation
	B185 D221 E185 I- II-		Two old tenements.						
			Barn	27 x 55	stone/wd.		46A	864	1080
230	Jordy, John B184 D220 E184 I- II-	Jordy, Henry	House House is good and well finished.	40 x 30	Limestone	2	2A	675	843.75
			House (old)	22 x 24	log				
			Barn Limestone land.	60 x 30	stone/log		253A	5566	6957.50
231	Jorty, Henry B175 D206 E175 I-	Groy, Jacob	House House old and weatherboarded.	30 x 28	sq. log	2	2A	350	437.50
			Barn Limestone land.	60 x 27	log		198A	4158	5197.50
232	Jung, Abm. B183 D219 E183 I- II-	Bachman, Christn.	House House - part old.	30 x 22	sq. log	1	2A	200	250
			Barn Gravel land.	51 x 24	log		68A	544	680
233	Jung, Felix Joung, Felix B181 D217 E181 I- II-	Bachman, Christn.	House House is old, of little value.	22 x 16	sq. log	1	2A	110	137.50
			Barn Gravel "hille" land.	38 x 28	log		78A	546	682.50
234	Jung, Michael B182 D218 E182 I- II-	Jung, Felix	House Old and poor house.	26 x 20	sq. log	1	2A	150	187.50
			Barn Gravel land.	25 x 18	log		30A	210	262.50
235	Karch, George Kurtz, George B211 D251 E211 I-	Rehr, John	House Stable (old) House is in bad order and old.	18 x 24	log log	1	24P	150	187.50
		Weirich, Jacob	Land - an out lot near Lebanon.				3A 80P	84	105
236	Karch, Jacob D253 I-	Stoy, Wm.	House Stable An old frame house.	27 x 31	log	2	48P	425	531.25
237	Karmany, John B193 D231 E192 I- II-	Karmany, Philip	House Good finished house.	30 x 38	stone	2	2A	630	787.50
			Barn Limestone land.	60 x 20	log		148A	2664	3330
238	Karmany, Martin B189 D227 E189 I- II-	Gingry, John Gingrich, John	House House in good order.	16 x 20	log	1	2A	300	375
			Barn Limestone land.	60 x 28	stone		148A	2812	3575
239	Karmany, Philip B194 D232 E194 I- II-	Karmany, John	House Good house.	30 x 36	stone	1	2A	435	543.75
			Barn Limestone land.	55 x 28	stone		126A	2394	2992.50
240	Kaufman, Abraham	Elenberger, Jacob	House	24 x 27	sq. log	2	2A	360	450

Direct Tax of 1798 - Lebanon Township

No.	Owner/Occupant/Ref.	Adjoining	Building	Dimen.	Matls.	Stories	Acres Perch.	Assmt.	Valuation
	B192 D230 E192 I- II-		House	22 x 18	log	1	2A	160	200
			Springhouse	12 x 15	log	1			
			House (24 x 27) - good order.						
			Springhouse - out of repair.						
			Smith shop	15 x 12					
			Barn	66 x 29	stone/log		116A	1276	1595
			Gravel land.						
241	Kaufman, Christ B191 D229 E191 I- II-	Breneison, Jacob	House	20 x 24	log	2	2A	300	375
			House is in good order.						
			Fulling Mill		log				
			Barn	36 x 16	log		38A	530	662.50
			Gravel land.						
242	Kealer, Leonart D240 I-	Licht, Abram	House	24 x 19	log	2	1A	500	625
			Kitchen	15 x 12	log	1			
			Wagoner shop	20 x 20					
			Good house.						
243	Kean, Charles Keen, Charles B198 D236 E198 I- II-	Westman, John	House	24 x 26	log	1	48P	260	325
			Stable						
			House - midling order.						
		Huber, John	Land - out lot near Lebanon.				2A 80P	40	50
244	Kelcker, Anthony Kelker, Anthy. B202 D242 E202 I- II-		House	30 x 24	log	2	96P	300	375
			Barn	40 x 20	log				
			Old buildings.						
		Shantz, George	Land - out lot Lebanon.				11A 69P	182.92	228.65
		Weber, Widow	Land - Town lot.				48P	20	25
245	Kelcker, Henry D241 I-	Kress, Michael	House	28 x 18	brick/wd.	1	48P	450	562.50
			Hatter shop			2			
			House - middling						
246	Kelcker, Rudolph Peters, John B188 D226 E188 I- II-	Clark, Thomas	House	42 x 27	sq. log	2	36P	600	750
			House	16 x 20	sq. log	1	24P	105	131.25
			Barn	30 x 22	sq. log				
			Buildings in good order.						
			Land - Limestone land.				4A	96	120
			Land - out lot to Lebanon.				10A 80P	168	210
			Land - out lot to Lebanon.				3A	60	75
			Land - out lot to Lebanon.				3A	60	75
247	Keller, George B199 D237 E199 I- II-	Keller, Jacob	House (good)	30 x 26	sq. log	1	2A	300	375
			Smith shop	18 x 15	log				
			Barn	60 x 26	stone/log		98A	1078	1347.50
			Gravel land.						
248	Keller, Jacob B201 D238 E201 I- II-	Keller, George	House	23 x 10	sq. log	1	2A	250	437.50
			House in midling order.						
			Smith shop	18 x 15	log				
			Barn	50 x 25	stone/log		68A	748	935
			Has made a fraudulent return. He acknowledges to have 14 acres more. Gravel land.						

Direct Tax of 1798 - Lebanon Township

No.	Owner/Occupant/Ref.	Adjoining	Building	Dimen.	Matls.	Stories	Acres Perch.	Assmt.	Valuation
249	**Keller, John Est.**	Fasnacht, Conrad	House	41 x 22	log/stone	2	48P	800	1000
	Gloninger, John	Bricker, Christn.	Stable (small)	20 x 17	log	1	2A	120	150
	Shott, George		House - good; Stable - midling order.						
	B209 D249 E209 I- II-		Barn	45 x 22	log		114A	2166	2707.50
			Limestone land.						
250	**Kerning, Geo**	Rieguel, Abraham	House	35 x 20	log	2	144P	200	250
	Karmany, George		House in good order.						
	D223 I-								
251	**Killian, Henry**	Reinohl, George	House	18 x 16	log	1	2A	110	107.50
	B204 D244 E204 I- II-		House is in midling order.						
			Stable (small)				6A 80P	104	130
			Out lot near Lebanon.						
252	**Killian, Jacob**	Shaak, Philip	House (good)	24 x 20	sq. log	1	2A	200	250
	B203 D243 E203 I- II-		Stable (small)				14A 95P	233.50	291.87
			Sand and Limestone land.						
253	**Killinger, Michael**	Elenberger, John	House (good)	28 x 26	log	1	2A	600	750
	B208 D248 E208 I- II-		House	16 x 26	stone	1			
			Smith shop	18 x 10					
			Barn	55 x 30	stone		110A	2420	3025
			Limestone land.						
254	**Kitzmiller, Jacob**	Miller, John	House (old)	18 x 24	log	1	2A	120	150
	B197 D235 E197 I- II-		Barn (old)	24 x 44	log		45A	405	506.25
			Gravel land.						
255	**Klein, Dietrich**	Fernsler, Philip	House	24 x 16	log	1	2A	110	137.50
	Kline, Dietrich		House is not good in repair.						
	B196 D234 E196 I- II-		Barn	26 x 16	log		6A	60	75
			Gravel land.						
256	**Kleiser, Ignazius**	Karch, Jacob	House	18 x 27	log	1	48P	280	350
	Kliser, Nasarus		Butcher shop	18 x 20	stone	1			
	D252 I-		Stable (old)		log				
			A midling good house.						
257	**Knoll, Christr.**	Meyer, John	House	30 x 28	sq. log	2	2A	500	625
	Knoll, Widow (mother)		House	26 x 24	log	1	1A	120	150
	Knol, Jacob		House (30 x 28) - new, good. House (26 x 24) - in bad order.						
	B190 D228 E190 I- II-		House (old)	16 x 18					
			Barn	50 x 27	log		176A	1750	2187.50
			Gravel land.						
258	**Kochenderfer, John**	Ley, Andrew	House	25 x 18	log	1	2A	360	450
	B205 D245 E205 I- II-		Springhouse	10 x 18					
			Buildings - old and not in good order.						
			Barn	45 x 20	log		148A	1628	2035
			Gravel land.						
259	**Kope, Valentine**	Lang, William	House (old)	20 x 13	log	1	2A	120	150
	Kobe, Valentine		Stable (small)	16 x 14			5A 14P	40.70	50.87

Direct Tax of 1798 - Lebanon Township

No.	Owner/Occupant/Ref.	Adjoining	Building	Dimen.	Matls.	Stories	Acres Perch.	Assmt.	Valuation
	B207 D247 E207 I- II-		Gravel land.						
260	Kornman, George	Gebhart, George	House (old)	16 x 20	log	1	2A	160	200
	B187 D225 E187 I- II-		Barn	38 x 15	log		88A	616	770
			Stable	15 x 15					
			Gravel land.						
261	Kraemer, Martin	Witmer, Peter	House	20 x 18	log	1	1A	120	150
	Kremer, Martin		Midling order.						
	B195 D233 E195 I- II-		Stable (small)				2A	20	25
			Gravel land.						
262	Krall, Abraham	Bomberger, Joseph	House	40 x 31	stone	2	2A	500	625
	B206 D246 E206 I- II-	Dinius, Jacob	House	28 x 27	log	1	2A	350	437.50
			House (40 x 31) - new not yet finished.						
			House (28 x 27) - in midling order.						
			Barn	80 x 35	stone/log		198A	4356	5445
			Barn	55 x 30	stone		196A	3724	4655
			198A - good land. 196A - Limestone land.						
263	Krause, Andrew	Melfadian, John	House	21 x 18	log	1	144P	110	137.50
	Linemacher, Daniel		House is in bad order.						
	B210 D250 E210 I- II-	Embig, Christr.	Land - town lots - Lebanon.				144P	45	50.25
264	Krause, David	Greenawalt, Philip	House	53 x 20	stone	2	48P	1000	1250
	Fulmer, John	Stover, Fredrick	House	32 x 27	sq. log	2	48P	500	625
	B186 D224 E186 I- II-		Kitchen	27 x 17	log	1			
			Stable	66 x 20					
			Buildings in good order.						
		Uhler, Christopher	Land - good Limestone land.				145A	2755	3443.75
		Funck, Martin	Land - out lot near Lebanon.				12A	324	405
		Imhoff, Martin	Land - good "madow" land.				12A 114P	304.50	380.62
265	Kross, Michael	Greenawald, Philip	House (good)	24 x 28	brick/wd.	2	48P	575	718.75
	Kreps, Michl.		House has wooden trim filled with bricks.						
	Krebs, Michl.		Kitchen	19 x 12	brick	1			
	B200 D239 E200 I- II-		Hatter shop						
		Dubs, John	Land - out lots to Lebanon.				10A	160	200
		Hubely, Fredk.	Land - Town lot - Lebanon.				48P	15	18.75
266	Laber, Balser	Weise, Henry	House (old)	30 x 26	log	1	2A	280	350
	Lauber, Baltzer		Smith shop	15 x 18					
	B230 D273 E230 I- II-		Barn	51 x 26	log		98A	1566	1957.50
			Limestone land.						
267	Landis, Christn.	Hostater, John	House	24 x 27	log	1	2A	200	250
	B232 D275 E232 I- II-	Hochstetter, John	House is old and out of repair.						
			Barn (old)	38 x 24	log		98A	1274	1592.50
			Stony land.						
268	Lang, Abraham	Long, Christian	House	32 x 25	stone	1	2A	440	550
	Long, Abm.		House	24 x 20		1	2A	300	375
	Long, Christ.		Good houses.						

Direct Tax of 1798 - Lebanon Township

No.	Owner/Occupant/Ref.	Adjoining	Building	Dimen.	Matls.	Stories	Acres Perch.	Assmt.	Valuation
	Herry, William B216 D258 E216 I- II-		House (old) Hemp Mill Barn Limestone land, good "madow."	15 x 20 70 x 28	 stone		 148A	 3552	 4440
269	Lang, Christian Long, Christian B217 D259 E217 I- II-	Long, Abraham	House Good house. Barn Good limestone land.	38 x 29 75 x 30	stone stone	2	2A 158A	675 3476	843.75 4345
270	Lang, Herman Long, Herman B215 D257 E215 I- II-	Long, Abraham	House Good house. Barn Limestone land.	28 x 30 60 x 30	stone stone	2	2A 198A	500 3762	625 4702.50
271	Lang, William Long, William B231 D274 E231 I- II-	Kope, George	House (old) Barn Gravel land.	26 x 32 35 x 19	log stone/wd.	1	2A 23A	160 207	200 258.75
272	Laudermilch, John B212 D254 E212 I- II-	Reinohl, George	House Springhouse House in midling order. Barn Good barn; limestone land.	36 x 27 23 x 19 70 x 30	stone/log stone stone	1 1	2A 138A	500 3105	625 3881.25
273	Laurey, John Lowrey, John Ellinger, Caspar B227 D270 E227 I- II-	Meily, Jacob	House Good land. Land Good land.	24 x 18	log	1	2A 138A	200 1794	250 2242.50
274	Leob, Christ. Est. B222 D265 E222 I- II-	Fordny, Daniel Light, Abraham Teis, Jacob	House Midling good order. Barn Land Limestone land.	30 x 22 51 x 30	log stone	1	48P 21A 48P 24A	200 511.20 432	250 639 540
275	Lesher, Michael B228 D271 E228 I- II-	Hoffman, Conrad	House Midling order. Barn Limestone land.	18 x 15 30 x 20	log log	1	2A 168A	270 3696	337.50 4620
276	Ley, Andrew B229 D272 E229 I- II-	Swope, Jacob	House House is old. Still house Barn Gravel land.	40 x 19 50 x 25	log log	1	2A 98A	200 1078	250 1347.50
277	Licht, Abraham Brough, Daniel B219 D261 E219 I- II-	Lebanon town Groe, Mattias	House Springhouse House House (28 x 32) is old but good order.	28 x 32 25 x 20 28 x 32	stone stone log	1 1 1	2A 2A	500 130	625 162.50

Direct Tax of 1798 - Lebanon Township

No.	Owner/Occupant/Ref.	Adjoining	Building	Dimen.	Matls.	Stories	Acres Perch.	Assmt.	Valuation
			House (28 x 32) is old - out of repair.						
		Light, Felix	Barn	98 x 25	log		148A	3552	4440
		Groh, Maths.	Barn	25 x 12	log		82A	820	1025
			Barn	38 x 25	log				
			148A - good limestone land. 82A - gravel land.						
278	**Licht, Fred.**	Light, Abraham	House	34 x 26	stone	1	2A	500	625
	Light, Felix		Kitchen	18 x 12	stone	1			
	Licht, John (his father)		Springhouse	24 x 12	stone				
	B225 D268 E225 I- II-		House is in good order.						
			House (old)	18 x 14					
			Barn	75 x 28	stone		148A	3552	4440
			Limestone land.						
279	**Licht, Henry**	Uhler, Martin	House	40 x 30	stone	2	2A	500	625
	Light, Henry		Old strong house. Limestone land						
	D264 I- II-								
280	**Licht, Jacob**	Alwine, Conrad	House	20 x 25	log	1	2A	330	412.50
	B214 D256 E214 I- II-	Allwein, Conrad	House is in midling order.						
			Barn	70 x 28	log		138A	2622	3277.50
			Limestone land.						
281	**Licht, Jacob**	Stear, Adam	House	28 x 24	stone	2	48P	450	562.50
	Light, Jacob		House	22 x 20	log	1			
	B221 D263 E221 I-		House in midling order.						
		Uhler, Martin	Barn	90 x 26	log		153A 80P	3377	4221.25
282	**Licht, Jacob Jr.**	Licht, Martin	House	36 x 30	stone	2	2A	600	750
	Hany, Hugh	Gingry, John	House	40 x 20	log	1	2A	105	131.25
	B220 D262 E220 I- II-		House (36 x 30) - good. House (40 x 20) - out of repair.						
			Barn	60 x 26	stone		136A	2720	3400
			Barn	30 x 20	log				
			Limestone land.						
283	**Licht, John**	Uhler, Martin	House	36 x 30	stone	1	2A	435	543.75
	Light, John	Snee, John	House	43 x 18	stone/log	1	144P	200	250
	Lear, John	Mill dam	House (36 x 30) in good order.						
	B223 D266 E223 I- II-		House (43 x 18) is out of repair.						
			Barn	76 x 30	log		148A	2368	2960
			Most all gravel land; no good.						
284	**Licht, John Jr.**	Licht, Henry	House	28 x 30	log	1	1A	300	375
	Light, John	Bueler, Henry	House	18 x 21	log	1	1A	205	256.25
	Ruder, Peter		House	28 x 30	log	2	2A	500	625
	Geiger, Jacob		House (28 x 30) is old but midling. House (18 x 21) is good.						
	B224 D267 E224 I- II-		House (28 x 30) is old and midling.						
			Barn	66 x 28	log		113A	2486	3107.50
			Barn	40 x 20	log		63A	1134	1417.50
		Uhler, Martin	Land				117A	702	877.50
			113A and 63A - Limestone land.						

Direct Tax of 1798 - Lebanon Township

No.	Owner/Occupant/Ref.	Adjoining	Building	Dimen.	Matls.	Stories	Acres Perch.	Assmt.	Valuation
			117A is "hille" stony wood land.						
285	Licht, John Sr. Light, John Sr. Leydig, Martin B226 D269 E226 I- II-	Orendorf, John Ohrendorff, John	House (old) Barn Gravel land.	27 x 24 39 x 19	log log	1	2A 78A	300 858	375 1072.50
286	Licht, Martin Light, Martin Ott, Emanuel D276 I-	Fisher, Peter	House Stable (old) House is midling good.	18 x 19	log	1	144P	200	250
287	Licht, Martin Jr. B213 D255 E213 I- II-	Lang, Herman	House (old) Barn Limestone land.	48 x 32 66 x 30	stone/wd. stone	1	2A 148A	400 2960	500 3700
288	Lochman, George E-		Land				1A		24
289	Loeb, Casper D277 I-	Huber, John	House House is midling good	22 x 24	log	1	48P	105	131.25
290	Long, Henry B218 D260 E218 I- II-	Ensminger, Peter Gingry, Christn. Gingrich, Christn.	House House House House (31 x 28) is "goot" as is House (22 x 18). House (20 x 15) is old and midling good. Saw mill Barn Stable 248A - Limestone land. 211A - most all mountain land.	31 x 28 22 x 18 20 x 15 83 x 33	log log log stone	2 1 1	2A 2A 2A 248A 211A	400 230 120 4464 1266	500 287.50 150 5580 1582.50
291	Mark, Jacob Merck, Jacob B236 D283 E236 I- II-	Gloninger, Peter Teis, Henry	House (good) Stable Land	36 x 27 25 x 12	log log	2	48P 8A	480 144	600 180
292	Marshal, David Dr. D303 I-	Shertzer, John	House Good house.	30 x 40	sq. log	2	96P	500	625
293	Marter, George Matter, George B256 D310 E256 I- II-	Marter, John	House (old) Stable (old) Limestone land.	22 x 18 15 x 18	log	1	2A 18A	110 306	137.50 382.50
294	Marter, John Matter, John B248 D300 E248 I- II-	Reist, John	House House is old and in bad order. Barn Limestone land.	40 x 24 50 x 28	log log	1	2A 198A	300 3366	375 4207.50
295	Martin, Alexander B245 D293 E245 I- II-	Traxel, John	House (old) Barn Stable (old)	20 x 19 30 x 17 20 x 17	log log	1	2A 235A	230 2885	287.50 3606.25

Direct Tax of 1798 - Lebanon Township

No.	Owner/Occupant/Ref.	Adjoining	Building	Dimen.	Matls.	Stories	Acres Perch.	Assmt.	Valu- ation
			Gravel land.						
296	Martin, Henry D304 I-	Herr, Abram	House Midling good repair.	21 x 18	stone	1	84P	130	162.50
297	Maulfer, Michael B257 D311 E257 I- II-	Franck, Henry	House (good) Barn Good gravel land.	30 x 20 46 x 24	log log	2	2A 107A	400 1177	500 1471.25
298	Mayer, Martin Moyer, Martin Meyer, Martin B240 D288 E240 I- II-	Snavly, Peter	House (old) Barn Part good land, others not good.	30 x 28 60 x 30	log log	2	2A 98A	250 1274	312.50 1592.50
299	McMullin, Daniel B262 D316 E262 I- II-	Meyer, Martin	House (old) House (old) Stable (old) Gravel and "hille" land.	24 x 17 18 x 16	log log	1 1	2A 2A 36A	130 105 288	162.50 131.25 360
300	Mecondel, Georg McConnel, George D296 I-	Wentling, Peter	House House is mitling good.	24 x 30	sq. log	2	48P	250	312.50
301	Mecondel, John McCohnel, John D295 I-	Shantz, Henry	House (old) Stable	30 x 17 15 x 20	log	1	48P	260	325
302	Meily, Jacob Miley, Jacob B241 D289 E241 E- I- II-	Snevly, Peter	House (old) Joiner shop Barn Land Some good land, some not.	25 x 20 15 x 15 55 x 26	log	1	2A 198A 67A	270 2772	337.50 3465 1172
303	Meily, Philip Miley, Philip B244 D292 E244 I- II-	Snevly, Peter	House Midling good house. Barn Midling good land.	28 x 24 64 x 24	log stone/log	2	2A 136A	380 1904	475 2380
304	Meily, Samuel Miley, Saml. B234 D281 E234 I- II-	Tratten, Sarah Kelker, Rudolph	House Smith shop Stable Midling house. Land - out lot Lebanon.	34 x 25	log	2	96P 6A 90P	340 105.60	425 132
305	Melfadinn, John Mefaudien, John McFadgen, John B259 D313 E259 I- II-	Wagner, Henry Reinoehl, George Shnee, John Dubs, John	House Stable House is old and bad. Land Land Land 12A and 3A - Limestone land. 2A 100P - "madow" land.	20 x 18	log	1	48P 12A 3A 2A 100P	140 288 72 82.50	175 360 90 103.12

Direct Tax of 1798 - Lebanon Township

No.	Owner/Occupant/Ref.	Adjoining	Building	Dimen.	Matls.	Stories	Acres Perch.	Assmt.	Valuation
306	Mellinger, Jacob D279 I-	Smith, Jacob	House (old)	25 x 20	log	1	48P	105	131.25
307	Mensinger, Conrad Hershberger, Abram B246 D294 E246 I- II-	Breneisen, Jacob	House House House (24 x 16) - of little value. House (25 x 12) - midling order. Barn Gravel land.	24 x 16 25 x 12 42 x 19	log log log	1 1	2A 2A 76A	110 140 684	137.50 175 855
308	Mentzer, George Mentser, George B258 D312 E258 I- II-	Roeser, John	House (old) Stable (small) Gravel land.	21 x 18	log	1	2A 3A	105 21	131.25 26.25
309	Mentzer, Jacob Menser, Jacob B247 D298 E247 I- II-	Zehrung, John Zerring, John	House House is old and of little value. Stables (2) (small) Gravel land.	22 x 20	log	1	1A 2A 80P	105 22.50	131.25 28.12
310	Merck, Conrad Mark, Conrad B233 D278 E233 I- II-	Shantz, George Shnee, John Weitman, John	House Good house. Tanyard Barn Land - town out lot. Land - town out lot. Tanyard is in good order.	30 x 28 30 x 20	log log	2	48P 48P 4A 110P 2A 80P	350 300 75 40	437.50 375 93.75 50
311	Meyer, Abram Moyer, Abm. Peffer, George Trump, George B235 D282 E235 I- II-	Steger, Fredrich Keen, Charles Sne, John	House House House Stable House (23 x 17) not finished; house (18 x 15) - old; House (25 x 28) midling. Barn Limestone land.	23 x 17 18 x 15 25 x 28 18 x 25	stone/log log log log	2 1 2	2A 48P 48P 18A	240 250 105 324	300 312.50 131.25 405
312	Meyer, Christr. Moyer, Christophr. B253 D307 E253 I- II-	Rigart, Mathis Richert, Maths.	House Good house. Barn Limestone land.	30 x 28 70 x 30	stone stone/log	2	2A 198A	550 4158	687.50 5197.50
313	Meyer, Henry Moyer, Henry A237 B237 D284 D285 E237 I- II- Rauch, John Juengst, John	Gloninger, John Rupp, John Mensinger, Conrad Kofman, Abraham Rupp, John Mensinger, Conrad Kaffman, Abraham	House (old) Stable Still house House (good) House (old) House (old) Barn Barn Barn 118A - good land. Other barns - gravel land.	22 x 17 15 x 18 20 x 21 38 x 32 22 x 15 1/2 22 x 19 95 x 25 30 x 18 35 x 20	log log stone log log log/stone log log	1 2 1 1	96P 2A 2A 2A 118A 148A 148A	290 500 160 200 2360 1184 1628	362.50 625 200 250 2950 1480 2035

Direct Tax of 1798 - Lebanon Township

No.	Owner/Occupant/Ref.	Adjoining	Building	Dimen.	Matls.	Stories	Acres Perch.	Assmt.	Valuation
314	Meyer, John Moyer, John B254 D308 E254 I- II-	Borckholder, Ulrich	House House Buildings midling good. Barn Good land.	28 x 24 22 x 48 50 x 25	log stone log	1 1	2A 2A 196A	280 240 4116	350 300 5145
315	Meyer, John Moyer, John B250 D302 E250 I- II-	Herr, Abram Herr, Abraham	House House House House not finished. Saw mill Grist mill Still house Barn (old) Barn Stable (small) Limestone land.	30 x 36 28 x 26 36 x 30 36 x 36 20 x 22 50 x 27 68 x 30	stone log stone stone log log stone	1 1 2	2A 2A 2A 200A	430 300 450 3800 2000	537.50 375 562.50 4750 2500
316	Meyer, Martin Moyer, Martin B249 D301 E249 I- II-	Myer, Henry	House (good) Barn Part gravel land, part good.	27 x 22 60 x 26	log stone/log	2	2A 92A 80P	400 1850	500 2312.50
317	Miller, Daniel B243 D291 E243 I- II-	Swope, Jacob	House (old) Barn Gravel land.	30 x 20 30 x 20	log log	1	2A 98A	250 980	312.50 1225
318	Miller, Jacob D299 I-	Casel, Christn.	House Stable House not finished.	52 x 20	sq. log	2	96P	300	375
319	Miller, John Miller, John (father) Sheller, _____ Kiffer, _____ Keller, _____ B239 E239 I- II-	Heilman, Adam Gingry, Henry	House (good) House (good) House (old) Barn Barn 174A - Good gravel land. 100A - gravel land.	32 x 26 22 x 26 22 x 24 69 x 27 61 x 22	log log log stone/log log	2 1 1	2A 2A 2A 174A 100A	460 300 200 2610 1100	575 375 250 3262.50 1375
320	Miller, John B242 D290 E242 I- II-	Shaak, Phillip	House (old) Barn Old barn, sandstone land.	20 x 20 50 x 18	log log	1	2A 115A	230 1955	287.50 2443.75
321	Miller, John B260 D314 E260 I- II-	Hershberger, Christl Kitzmiller, Jacob	House House Houses are midling order. Gravel land. Barn Barn 140A - good barn and good gravel land. 130A - gravel land.	29 x 24 22 x 18	log log stone log	1 1	2A 2A 140A 130A	300 110 1960 1430	375 137.50 2450 1787.50
322	Miller, Peter Est. Miller, Peter Jr. B261 D315 E261 I- II-	Krause, David	House Still house Stable/barn	22 x 27 15 x 22 30 x 20	log log log	2 1	48P	440	550

Direct Tax of 1798 - Lebanon Township

No.	Owner/Occupant/Ref.	Adjoining	Building	Dimen.	Matls.	Stories	Acres Perch.	Assmt.	Valuation
		Ebright, Jacob	House	21 x 17	log	1	144P	240	300
			Stable/barn		log				
			House (22 x 27) - good; House (21 x 17) - midling good.						
		Weirich, Jacob	Land - In lots - all "madow" ground.				3A	72	90
323	Miller, Rudolph	Imboden, John	House	44 x 27	stone/log	2	2A	530	662.50
	B251 D305 E251 I- II-		Barn	70 x 30	log		149A	3129	3911.25
			Good house. Limestone land.						
324	Mitchel, Thomas	Boehm, Jacob	House	26 x 20	log	2	2A	360	450
	B252 D306 E252 I- II-		House	16 x 22	stone	1			
			Midling good.						
			Barn	30 x 75	log		187A	3553	4441.25
			Limestone land.						
325	Moore, Saml. Est.	Keller, John Est.	House (good)	39 x 36	stone	2	40P	2000	2500
	Buchler, George		Kitchen	20 x 36	stone	1			
	D280 I-		Kitchen	13 x 36	brick	1			
			Storehouse	24 x 16	log	1			
			Stable						
326	Morret, Mathis Est.	Imhof, Martin	House (old)	27 x 21	log	1	2A	300	375
	Light, Martin		Springhouse	18 x 20	stone				
	B238 D286 E238 I- II-		House (old)	22 x 20					
			Barn	58 x 30	stone/log		98A	2058	2572.50
			Limestone land.						
327	Moyer, John	Goltman, Jacob	House (old)	24 x 21	log	1	36P	110	137.50
	D297 I-								
328	Muma, John	Burckholder, Ulrich	House	50 x 20	stone	2	2A	500	625
	Mumma, John		Good house.						
	B255 D309 E255 I- II-		Barn	40 x 22	log		171A	3078	4716.25
			Part good land.						
329	Nagel, Fredrich	Sne, John	House	30 x 24	log	1	48P	200	250
	Naugel, Fredk.	Shome, Joseph	Preach room	16 x 10	log				
	B263 D317 E263 I- II-		Midling good order.						
			Land - 2 in lots in Lebanon.				96P	30	37.50
330	Neff, Jacob	Beckly, Ulrich	House	25 x 25	stone	2	1A	700	875
	Neaff, Jacob	Uhler, Christr.	House	24 x 20	log	2			
	B264 D318 E264 I- II-		Good house.						
			Barn	42 x 22	log		3A	54	67.50
			Land				86P	8	10
			Good land.						
331	Ney, John	Blough, John	House	20 x 18	log	1	2A	180	225
	Neigh, John	Blauch, John	Gravel land.						
	B268 D322 E268 I- II-		Barn	45 x 16	log		60A	600	750
			Gravel land.						

Direct Tax of 1798 - Lebanon Township

No.	Owner/Occupant/Ref.	Adjoining	Building	Dimen.	Matls.	Stories	Acres Perch.	Assmt.	Valuation
332	Ney, Michael Neight, Michael B267 D321 E267 I- II-	Blough, John Blauch, John	House House is midling good. Stable (small) Gravel land.	21 x 20	log	1	2A 8A	130 80	162.50 100
333	Ney, Petter Nigh, Peter B265 D319 E265 I- II-	Guntrum, Fredrich	House (old) Barn Gravel land.	35 x 33 55 x 21	log log	1	2A 78A	300 780	875 975
334	Nickelson, John Hoffman, Conrad B266 D320 E266 I- II-	Hofman, Conrad	House House is old and bad. Barn Limestone land.	26 x 30 60 x 26	log	1	2A 138A	220 3036	275 3795
335	Orndorf, Christn. Orendorf, Christn. B272 D326 E272 I- II-	Orndorf, John Ohrendorff, John	House Midling good house. Still house Barn Gravel land.	28 x 26 18 x 20 54 x 24	log log stone/log	1	2A 134A	350 1474	437.50 1842.50
336	Orndorf, John Orendorff, John B271 D325 E271 I- II-	Orndorf, Christn.	House Good house. Still house Barn Gravel land.	30 x 25 12 x 18 60 x 26	log stone/log	2	2A 133A 120P	400 1605	500 2006.25
337	Orth, Gotlieb B269 D323 E269 I- II-	Orth, Joseph Sheirer, John	House Kitchen Good house and kitchen. House is of sandstone and limestone. House (old) Barn Barn 227A - good land, some stony. 100A - "hille and stone" wood land.	36 x 27 33 x 18 16 x 18 55 x 25 35 x 20	stone stone stone/log log	2 1	2A 227A 100A	1000 4540 600	1250 5675 750
338	Orth, Joseph Stoufer, Daniel B270 D324 E270 I- II-	Orth, Gotlib	House Springhouse House House (34 x 20) - good building House - (22 x 18) - midling order. Barn Good land, some stony.	34 x 20 20 x 18 22 x 18 66 x 30	sq. log log stone/log	2 1	2A 2A 288A	600 110 5760	750 137.50 7200
339	Peiffer, Jacob Fertig, Christopher Jager, John Kuntz, Lawrentz B273 D327 E273 I- II-	Reinhart, Bernard Gilbert, Henry Fetzberg. Daniel Lesher, Michael	House Tanner Shop House House House (old) House (34 x 18) mitling good. Barn	34 x 18 24 x 20 20 x 24 28 x 24 24 x 20	log log log log log log	2 2 1 2 1	1A 80P 144P 24P 2A 103A	800 200 260 230 1957	1000 250 325 287.50 2446.25

Direct Tax of 1798 - Lebanon Township

No.	Owner/Occupant/Ref.	Adjoining	Building	Dimen.	Matls.	Stories	Acres Perch.	Assmt.	Valuation
			Land				7A 80P	120	150
			Some good, some gravel land. 7A 80P - out lot near Lebanon.						
340	**Peter, Henry**	Alleman, Leonhart	House	25 x 22	log	1	2A	260	325
	Bile, Fredrick		Springhouse	14 x 16					
	B274 D328 E274 I- II-		House	42 x 26	stone/log	2			
			House (25 x 22) - out of repair. House (42 x 26) is not nearly finished.						
			House (old)	18 x 20					
			Barn	72 x 25	stone/log		218A	1534	1917.50
			Gravel land.						
341	**Raiguel, Abraham**		House	35 x 26	log	1	2A	350	437.50
	Reagle, Abram		House	20 x 18	stone	1	2A	120	150
	Achey, Peter		House	36 x 22	log	2	48P	480	600
	Weitzel, Elias		*House (35 x 26) - old; House (20 x 18) - midling order.*						
	B292 D349 E292 I- II-		Saw mill						
			Grist Mill	50 x 46	stone			2500	3125
		Imboden, Adam	Barn	60 x 26	log		72A	1440	1800
			Good limestone land.						
342	**Ramberger, Adam**	Elenberger, Jacob	House	24 x 27	log	1	2A	370	462.50
	B291 D348 E291 I- II-		Springhouse	15 x 24	stone	1			
			House - midling order.						
			Barn	65 x 24	log		148A	1624	2030
			Gravel land.						
343	**Ramler, Michl.**		House	30 x 22	log	2	48P	500	625
	Rambler, Michl.		Kitchen	12 x 22	log	1			
	D356 I-		Stables (2)						
			A well finished house.						
344	**Reifwine, Jacob**	Miller, Daniel	House (old)	18 x 10	log	1	2A	170	212.50
	B282 D337 E282 I- II-		Barn	30 x 30	log		78A	702	877.50
			Gravel land.						
345	**Reinhart, Bernard**	Bucher, Conrad	House	40 x 20	log	1	48P	380	475
	Georg, Peter	Grenewald, Philip	House	35 x 18	log	1	2A	150	187.50
	B287 D343 E287 I- II-		Stable	26 x 18	log				
			House (40 x 20) - good; House 35 x 18 - old, out of repair.						
			Land - out lot near Lebanon.				8A	128	160
		Peiffer, Jacob	Land - lot in Lebanon.				48P	20	25
346	**Reinoehl, Conrad**	Shindel, Peter	House	23 x 18	log	1	48P	300	375
	Rinale, Conrad		Smith shop	23 x 19	log				
	B277 D331 E277 I- II-		Stable	24 x 18	log				
			Midling order.						
		Teis, Jacob	Land				25A 80P	450	562.50
			Limestone land.						

Direct Tax of 1798 - Lebanon Township

No.	Owner/Occupant/Ref.	Adjoining	Building	Dimen.	Matls.	Stories	Acres Perch.	Assmt.	Valuation
347	Reinoehl, Henry Rineale, Henry B284 D340 E284 I- II-	Xander, Jacob	House (old) Smith shop Barn Limestone land.	20 x 18 20 x 14 30 x 20	log log	1	2A 22A	240 374	300 467.50
348	Reinohl, Georg Rinale, George Reinohl, George his son. B275 D329 E275 I- II-	Greider, Jacob Bibel, John Uhler, Christr. Buehler, Henry Karch, Jacob	House (good) House (good) Smith shop Stable House (32 x 24) in Lebanon. Smith shop Barn Land Land Land 126A - Limestone land. 41A - good land but stony. 10A and 5A - out lots near Lebanon.	36 x 32 32 x 24 60 x 30	stone log log stone	2 2	2A 48P 126A 41A 10A 5A	500 400 2835 697 244 120	625 500 3543.75 871.25 305 150
349	Reist, John B296 D353 E296 I- II-	Gingry, Michael Gingrich, Michl.	House Good house. Barn Limestone land.	38 x 38 80 x 30	stone stone	2	2A 168A	560 3948	700 4935
350	Reist, Peter B295 D352 E295 I- II-	Reist, John	House Good house. Still house Barn Good land.	40 x 30 20 x 24 82 x 30	stone stone	2	2A 186A	560 3906	700 4882.50
351	Reser, Daniel Roeser, Danl. Reesor, Daniel B297 D355 E297 I- II-	Umberger, John	House House is old, out of repair. Barn Gravel land.	39 x 21 60 x 21	log log	1	2A 120A	290 1320	362.50 1650
352	Resly, Rudolph B280 D335 E280 I- II-	Fernsler, Philip	House Good house. Barn Limestone land.	39 x 27 60 x 28	stone stone	1	2A 88A	435 1584	543.75 1980
353	Rewalt, John Raywalt, John D357 I-	Ritcher, Adam	House (old) Stable	23 x 21	log	1	24P	200	250
354	Richert, Jacob Riegar, Jacob B294 D351 E294 I- II-	Miller, Rudolph	House (old) Barn Good land, old barn.	20 x 25 48 x 26	log log	1	2A 98A	160 1666	200 2082.50
355	Richert, Mathes Est. Righart, Maths. Est. B285 D341 E285 I- II-	Dutweiler, John	House (old) Barn Limestone land.	32 x 18 40 x 26	log/stone log	1	2A 100A	260 1900	325 2375

Direct Tax of 1798 - Lebanon Township

No.	Owner/Occupant/Ref.	Adjoining	Building	Dimen.	Matls.	Stories	Acres Perch.	Assmt.	Valuation
356	Ricker, Michael Ritter, Michael Krause, David D354 I-	Folmer, Jacob	House (old) Stable	21 x 16 24 x 17	log log	1	144P	250	312.50
357	Rickert, Christ. Ritter, Christopher D339 I-	Hening, Daniel	House Midling good order.	28 x 24	log	2	72P	300	375
358	Ridel, Henry Riddle, Henry Ridle, Widow B283 D338 E283 I- II-	Groh, Mathes	House House House (22 x 20) - midling good; house (18 x 25) - good. Barn Gravel land.	22 x 30 18 x 25 40 x 20	stone/log stone log	1 2	2A 2A 76A	200 300 760	250 375 950
359	Rigart, John Est. Richert, John Riegar, John Est. B293 D350 E293 I- II-	Licht, Jacob Light, Jacob Lang, Herman	House Back Room Midling good order. Barn Land Good barn and land. Good limestone land.	26 x 28 12 x 28 73 x 33	log stone stone	1	2A 250A 55A	300 5000 990	375 6250 1237.50
360	Riser, Christian Reesor, Christn. Tise, Jacob B279 D334 E279 I- II-	Eby, George	House New house, not finished. Stable Limestone land.	34 x 25	log	2	2A 98A	340 1666	425 2082.50
361	Riser, John Roeser, John Rieser, John B289 D346 E289 I- II-	Snog, John Snoke, John	House (old) Oyl Mill Barn Gravel land.	20 x 18 20 x 30 20 x 80	log log	1	2A 112A	220 1232	275 1540
362	Ritsher, Adam Richard, Adam D332 I-	Reinohl, John	House Hatter shop Midling order.	30 x 27 22 x 16	sq. log frame	2 1	48P	400	500
363	Ritsherd, Peter Richard, Peter B276 D330 E276 I- II-	Romer Graveyard Uhler, Christr.	House House Good house in Lebanon. Land - out lot to Lebanon. Land - out lot to Lebanon.	30 x 24 30 x 18	log log	2	48P 5A 55P 6A 73P	580 85.50 103.30	725 106.87 129.12
364	Rohrer, John Rohr, John B286 D342 E286 I- II-	Sherer, John Doebler, Abraham	House Smith shop House is midling good. Land - out lot near Lebanon.	22 x 19 12 x 16	log	2	36P 4A 120P	250 76	312.50 95
365	Roland, Jacob Rowland, Jacob B298 D358 E298 I- II-	Greenawald, Philip	House (old) Barn Out lot.	30 x 18 24 x 18	log log	1	1A 80P 2A	280 32	350 40

Direct Tax of 1798 - Lebanon Township

No.	Owner/Occupant/Ref.	Adjoining	Building	Dimen.	Matls.	Stories	Acres Perch.	Assmt.	Valuation
366	**Ronckel, John** Runkle, John Runcle, John B288 D344 E288 I- II-	Miller, John	House Springhouse Barn Gravel land.	27 x 30 15 x 18 60 x 27	log log stone/log	2	2A 178A	400 1780	500 2225
367	**Rudy, Henry** B281 D336 E281 I- II-	Laber, Baltzer	House Good house. Barn Limestone land.	27 x 26 45 x 25	log log	1	2A 131A	300 2358	375 2947.50
368	**Ruhl, Peter** Rule, Peter B278 D333 E278 I- II-	Huber, Andrew	House House not finished. Joiner shop Barn Lime and sandstone land.	25 x 29 21 x 19 40 x 20	log log	2	2A 48A	330 816	412.50 1020
369	**Rup, Jacob** Rubb, Jacob D345 I-	Rup, John	House Wagoner shop Stable Midling good house.	30 x 25 18 x 20	log log log	1	1A 80P	280	350
370	**Rup, John** Rubb, John B290 D347 E290 I- II-	Meyer, Henry	House (old) Barn Part good, part gravel land.	16 x 35 59 x 27	log stone/log	1	2A 128A	260 2304	325 2880
371	**Sauder, Jacob** Souder, Jacob B326 D395 E326 I- II-	Jengst, Henry Shaffner, Henry	House (poor) Joiner shop Stable (old) Land - out lot near Lebanon.	20 x 19 20 x 18	log log	1 1	48P 2A 80P	205 40	256.25 50
372	**Segrist, Lorentz** Seechrist, Lawrence B311 D380 E311 I- II-	Imboden, John	House House Houses - good; good order. Barn Good Limestone land.	26 x 33 26 x 18 86 x 30	log log stone	2 1	2A 2A 246A	450 220 5166	562.50 275 6457.50
373	**Segrist, Salomon** Seechrist, Salomon B310 D379 E310 I- II-	Herr, Abram Shenk, Joseph	House Midling good house. Barn Land 160A - Limestone land. 70A - some part good, some gravel.	24 x 27 70 x 26	log log	2	2A 160A 70A	350 2720 1190	437.50 3400 1487.50
374	**Sergant, Joseph** D372 I-	Achenbach, Arnt	House (old) Stable (small)	20 x 17 18 x 14	log rd. log	1	96P	105	131.25
375	**Seyly, Jacob** Seegely, Jacob Sickele, Jacob Sigle, Jacob B301 D367 E301 I- II-	Wolf, Christian Huber, George	House House is in midling order. Grist mill Barn Stable (small) Gravel land.	28 x 20 33 x 30 82 x 28	log log	1	2A 125A 90A	280 1375 1700	350 1718.75 2125

Direct Tax of 1798 - Lebanon Township

No.	Owner/Occupant/Ref.	Adjoining	Building	Dimen.	Matls.	Stories	Acres Perch.	Assmt.	Valu- ation
376	**Shaack, Philip** **Shaake, Philip** **Shawk, Philip** B330 D400 E330 I- II-	Shaak, Nicolus	House (old) House (old) Barn Limestone land.	24 x 20 15 x 12 50 x 26	log log	1	2A 148A	265 2664	331.25 3330
377	**Shaake, Nicolas** **Shawk, Nicholas** B323 D391 E323 I- II-	Shaak, Philip	House Good house. Barn Limestone land.	26 x 20 50 x 60	log log	1	2A 138A	300 2484	375 3105
378	**Shaffner, Henry** B322 D390 E322 I- II-	Huble, Fredrich	House Barn (small) House is midling good.	28 x 26 30 x 18	log log	2	48P	500	625
		Miller, Peter	Land - out lot near Lebanon.				5A	85	106.25
		Kreps, Michl.	Land - out lot near Lebanon.				2A 80P	40	50
		Daub, Dillman	Land - gravel land.				5A 80P	44	55
		Durst, Peter	Land - in lot near Lebanon.				120P	26.25	32.52
379	**Shallenberger, John** Bayley, William B313 D382 E313 I- II-	Elder, John	House (old) House (old) House (old) Saw mill Barn Gravel land.	26 x 20 20 x 15 18 x 15 70 x 25	log log log log	1 1 1	2A 2A 2A 169A	200 180 140 1859	250 225 175 2323.75
380	**Shally, Baltzer** B333 D403 E333 I- II-	Arnold, John	House House House Good house. Gravel land.	28 x 30 20 x 16 60 x 30	log stone/log		2A 178A	360 2314	450 2892.50
381	**Shally, Lucas** Stream, John B307 D376 E307 I- II-	Breneisen, Jacob	House House House (26 x 25) - old and of little value. House (26 x 24) - midling order. Barn Gravel land.	26 x 25 26 x 24 36 x 18	log log log	1 1	2A 2A 116A	105 110 928	131.25 137.50 1160
382	**Shantz, George** B317 D386 E317 I- II-	Alstat, John	House Dorner? Shop Barn (small) Midling good house.	22 x 20 21 x 10 25 x 17	log log log	2 1	48P	350	437.50
		Mark, Conrad	Land - out lot near Lebanon.				9A	144	180
		Sander, Jacob	Land - out lot near Lebanon.				8A	128	160
383	**Shantz, Henry** B300 D363 E300 I- II-	Mecondel, John	House Tanner shop Wash house Stable/Barn House is in midling order.	28 x 24 24 x 12 20 x 14 25 x 16	log log frame log	1 1 1	96P	400	500
		Greider, George	Land - out lot near Lebanon. Land - Limestone land.				13A 128P 7A	212.80 126	266 157.50

Direct Tax of 1798 - Lebanon Township

No.	Owner/Occupant/Ref.	Adjoining	Building	Dimen.	Matls.	Stories	Acres Perch.	Assmt.	Valuation
384	Shawk, John Shay, John D361	Bergenhof, Wilm.	House Smith shop House - midling order.	30 x 16 15 x 20	log	2	96P	250	312.50
385	Sheffer, Isaac Shaeffer, Isaac B321 D389 E321 I- II-	Tice, Michael	House (good) Barn Good land.	40 x 31 94 x 30	brick stone/log	2	2A 288A	800 6336	1000 7920
386	Shenk, Joseph B304 D373 E304 I- II-	Meyer, John	House Wash House Good house. Barn Good land.	30 x 27 18 x 15 85 x 25	stone stone	2 1	2A 210A	600 4200	750 5250
387	Sherer, John Shearer, John B348 D421 E348 I- II-	Rorer, John Bucher, Jacob	House Land 50 Lights. Limestone land.	26 x 22	log	2	48P 29A 120P	250 535	312.50 668.75
388	Sherg, Samuel Sherck, Saml. Sherk, Saml. B341 E341 I- II-	Kantz, Christn. Kantzer, Christn.	House Barn Good house. Gravel land.	30 x 26 45 x 20	log	1	2A 145A	300 1450	375 1812.50
389	Shertzer, John D370 I-	Marshal, David	House Stable House - good.	40 x 32 15 x 10	stone log	2	48P	825	1031.25

390	Shindel, Peter
	Shendle, Peter
	  Hess, Geo.
	B327 D396 E327 I- II-
		Beck, John
		
		Reinohl, Conrad
		Embig, Jacob
		Miller, Peter
			House (good)
			Blue deyer ?
			  shop
			Stable
			House (good)
			Stable
			Land - out lot near Lebanon
			Land - out lot near Lebanon.
				36 x 30
				
				20 x 16
				
				28 x 24
					stone
					
					log
					
					log
						2
						
						2
						
						2
							48P
							
							24P
							
							10A
							2A 12P
								1000
								
								350
								
								150
								62.30
									1250
									
									437.50
									
									187.50
									77.87

391	Shnee, John
	Sne, John
	  Grigauf, Widow
	  Griegdoff, Widow
	B328 D397 E328 I- II-
		Nagel, Fredrich
		
		Merck, Conrad
		Mark, Conrad
		
		Fisher, Peter
		Mefaudien, John
		Kelker, Rudolph
		Clark, Thomas
			House
			Kitchen
			House
			House (24 x 33) - good order.
			House (18 x 12) - good
			Grist mill
			Barn
			Land - "madow" lot, out lot.
			Land - Limestone land.
			Land - out lot near Lebanon.
			Land - out lot near Lebanon.
				24 x 33
				15 x 16
				18 x 12
				
				24 x 33
				26 x 18
					stone
					stone
					log
					
					stone
					log
						2
						1
						1
							24P
							
							48P
							
							1A 80P
							3A 35P
							2A 54P
							3A 110P
							3A 132P
								560
								
								105
								
								1000
								111
								60
								88.50
								51.20
									700
									
									131.25
									
									1250
									138.75
									75
									110.62
									64

392	Shomo, Joseph Est. B347 E347 II-	Weiny, Jacob	House (old)		log		48P	60	75

Direct Tax of 1798 - Lebanon Township

No.	Owner/Occupant/Ref.	Adjoining	Building	Dimen.	Matls.	Stories	Acres Perch.	Assmt.	Valuation
393	**Shott, Lotwig**	Bowman, George	House	25 x 17	stone	1	2A	375	468.75
	Shirk, Jacob	Bauman, Geo.	House	22 x 18	log	1	2A	150	187.50
	B320 D388 E320 l- ll-		Midling good.						
			Barn	70 x 30	stone		246A	4674	5842.50
			Limestone land.						
394	**Sig, Henry**	Strow, Elisabeth	House	32 x 28	log	2	24P	300	375
	Seck, Henry		Stable		log				
	D365 l-		Good order.						
395	**Singer, Michael**	Ulrich, Tobias	House (good)	28 x 24	log	2	48P	400	500
	Wagner, Daniel		Kitchen	18 x 14	log	1		280	350
	B316 D385 E316 l- ll-		Stable	24 x 10	log				
		Boger, Valentine	House (old)	26 x 24	log	1	2A	280	350
			Barn	61 x 26			148A	1480	1850
			Gravel land.						
396	**Six, Jacob**	Tice, Jacob	House	30 x 27	log	1	2A	300	375
	Faber, Michael	Greider, Christn.	House	25 x 20	log	1	2A	120	150
	Stough, Conrad		House	35 x 30	stone	1	2A	400	500
	Stouch, Conrad		House (30 x 27) - midling good house.						
	B308 D377 E308 l- ll-		House (25 x 30) - not good.						
			House (35 x 30) - midling good repair.						
			Barn	68 x 30	stone/log		121A	2420	3025
			Barn	50 x 20	log		125A	2125	2656.25
			Limestone land.						
397	**Sloterbeck, John**	Fisher, Peter	House	25 x 20	log	1	48P	240	300
	Slotterbech, John		Stable						
	B329 D398 E329 l- ll-		House is in midling good order.						
		Mark, Conrad	Land - out lot near Lebanon.				5A	85	106.25
398	**Smith, Henry**	Smith, John	House	33 x 27	stone	2	2A	600	750
	B342 D412 E342 l- ll-		Still house	21 x 16					
			Barn	70 x 30	stone		182A	4004	5005
			Good house. Good land.						
399	**Smith, Jacob**	Mellinger, Jacob	House (old)	16 x 18			48P	70	87.50
	B319 E319 ll-								
400	**Smith, Jacob**	Geib, John	House	28 x 30	log	2	2A	400	500
	Smith, Peter		Barn	40 x 20	log		168A	2856	3570
	Stoever, George		Good house. Limestone land.						
	B343 D413 E343 l- ll-								
401	**Smith, John**	Smith, Henry	House (good)	24 x 22	log	2	2A	350	437.50
	German, Adam		House	21 x 22	log	1	2A	240	300
	B344 D360 D414		House (old)	20 x 18			96P	105	131.25
	D360 E344 l- ll-		Barn	60 x 33	stone		196A	4312	5390
			Limestone land.						

Direct Tax of 1798 - Lebanon Township

No.	Owner/Occupant/Ref.	Adjoining	Building	Dimen.	Matls.	Stories	Acres Perch.	Assmt.	Valu- ation
402	Sneider, Michael Snyder, Michl. Snider, Michl. B338 D408 E338 I- II-	Strome, John Strohm, John	House Barn Good house. Limestone land.	20 x 16 25 x 20	log log	1	2A 148A	260 2664	325 3330
403	Snevly, George Shnebely, Geo. Kinsey, John B331 D401 E331 I- II-	Bowman, George Bauman, Geo.	House Springhouse Smith shop Barn Good house. Limestone land.	40 x 35 20 x 16 15 x 15 70 x 30	stone log stone/log	1 1	2A 2A 156A	585 150 3276	731.25 187.50 4095
404	Snevly, Henry Shnebely, Henry Snevely, Henry B306 D375 E306 I- II-	Stoever, Adam	House (good) Barn Good land - part gravel.	30 x 36 66 x 30	log stone	2	2A 168A	400 3024	500 3780
405	Snevly, Jacob B334 D404 E334 I- II-	Snevly, Henry Shnebly, Henry	House Barn Good house. Gravel land.	25 x 25 56 x 30	log stone/log	2	2A 173A	300 2422	375 3027.50
406	Snevly, John Shnebely, John Snevely, John B305 D374 E305 I- II-	Stoever, John	House (good) Barn Limestone land.	40 x 22 60 x 30	log stone/log	1	2A 153A	270 2754	337.50 3442.50
407	Snevly, Peter Shnebely, Peter Snevely, Peter B332 D402 E332 I- II-	Snevly, George Shnebely, Geo.	House Barn Good house. Limestone land.	36 x 31 75 x 30	log stone	2	2A 148A	515 3108	642.75 3885
408	Snoderle, Barbara Snatterly, Barbara D394 I-	Jensee, Martin	House Stable House is in midling order.	30 x 20 25 x 17	log log	2	48P	350	437.50
409	Snog, John Snoke, John Snoak, John B314 D383 E314 I- II-	Zering, John	House (old) Smith shop Barn	45 x 27 108 x 21	log	1	2A 168A	300 1680	375 2100
410	Spengler, John B324 D392 E324 I- II-	Brechbil, Jacob	House Midling good house. Smith shop Barn Limestone land.	20 x 24 15 x 15 20 x 15	log log	1	2A 3A	270 54	337.50 67.50
411	Sprecher, Frederick B346 D417 E346 I- II-	Stoever, Adam	House House - old building. Barn Limestone land	21 x 21 30 x 26	log log	1	2A 138A	120 2622	150 3277.50
412	Stear, Adam	Light, Jacob	House	27 x 24	log	2	48P	280	350

Direct Tax of 1798 - Lebanon Township

No.	Owner/Occupant/Ref.	Adjoining	Building	Dimen.	Matls.	Stories	Acres Perch.	Assmt.	Valuation
	Stehr, Adam D420 I-		House - midling good order..						
413	Stear, John Stehr, John D399 I-	Kaufman, George	House (old) Stable	25 x 20	log	1	48P	110	137.50
414	Steckbeck, Michael Steckbeck, Frany (his mother). Fox, Jacob B302 D368 E302 I- II-	Gebhart, George Licht, John Light, John	House House House House (36 x 30) - good; House (22 x 24) - midling order; house (40 x 24) - old, in no repair. Still house Barn Land 277A - gravel and part stony hills. 55A 80P - gravel land.	36 x 30 22 x 24 40 x 24 115 x 30	log log log stone/log	2 1 1	2A 2A 2A 277A 55A 80P	460 140 210 4155 555	575 175 262.50 5193.75 693.75
415	Steel, David B312 D381 E312 I- II-	Shalenberger, John	House Barn A poor house. Poor gravel land.	30 x 26 40 x 20	log log	1	2A 38A	120 266	150 332.50
416	Steger, Fredrick B339 D409 E339 I- II-	Uhler, Christr.	House Barn Good house. Limestone land.	36 x 16 60 x 30	log stone	1	2A 193A	350 3474	437.50 4342.50
417	Steger, Peter D415 I-	Embigh, Jacob	House Stable (small) House - not good.	26 x 18	frame	1	48P	120	150
418	Stieb, Jacob Steeb, Jacob B318 D387 E318 I- II-	Bowman, John Lochman, Geo.	House (old) Stable (old) Land - "Madow" lot near Lebanon.	33 x 28	log	1	48P 1A 40P	325 30	406.25 37.50
419	Stoever, Adam Stoever, Adam Jr. B345 D416 E345 I- II-	Stoever, John Greider, Michael Stoever, John	House Kitchen House House (31 x 40) - good new house. House (36 x 29) - midling good. Grist/sawmill Barn Barn Barn Good limestone land.	31 x 40 19 x 10 36 x 29 60 x 38 62 x 27 60 x 30 46 x 26	limestone limestone limestone stone stone stone	2 1 1	2A 2A 200A 136A	1000 450 1800 4400 2992	1250 562.50 2250 5500 3740
420	Stoever, Fredrich Stoy, Gustavus B325 D393 E325 I- II-	Krause, David Mark, Conrad	House Kitchen Stable House Barn Houses are good. Land - out lots.	46 x 42 19 x 24 36 x 30 30 x 20	brick brick log log	3 2 2	24P 24P 47A	3000 800 846	3750 1000 1057.50

Direct Tax of 1798 - Lebanon Township

No.	Owner/Occupant/Ref.	Adjoining	Building	Dimen.	Matls.	Stories	Acres Perch.	Assmt.	Valuation
		Sholly, Baltzer	Land - "stone hille wood land."				32A	160	200
421	**Stoever, John** B315 D384 E315 I- II-	Gloninger, George	House Good Publick House. Grist/saw mill Barn Note: has not made a return of all his lands - fraudulent. Good Limestone land.	40 x 30 45 x 30 60 x 30	stone stone	2	2A 150A	1000 1800 3300	1250 2250 4125
422	**Stoever, Tobias** B299 D362 E299 I- II-	Stoever, Adam	House Good house. Barn Limestone land.	48 x 22 75 x 30	log stone/wd.	1	2A 200A	400 4200	500 5250
423	**Stone, Geo. Est.** Shaffner, Peter D418 I-	Dubs, John	House Hatter, shop Stable/Barn Midling good	36 x 26 20 x 16	log log log	2 1	48P	350	437.50
424	**Stoufer, John** **Stauffer, John** B303 D369 E303 I- II-	Reser, John Roeser, John Steel, David	House (good) Grist/sawmill Stable (small) Land - part "madow." 55A - poor gravel land.	32 x 26 40 x 48 18 x 20	log stone	1	1A 5 5A 80P	300 1500 30 88	375 1875 37.50 110
425	**Stoy, William Sr.** Stoy, Wm. Jr. D419 I-	Karete?, Jacob	House Kitchen House Stable House (42 x 40) not finished.	42 x 40 40 x 16 30 x 19	stone stone log	2 1 2	24P 24P	950 240	1187.50 300
426	**Strear, John** **Stroeher, John** **Stehr, John** B340 D410 E340 I- II-	Breneison, Jacob	House Barn Old house. Gravel land.	28 x 26 61 x 25	log log	1	2A 113A	225 791	281.25 988.75
427	**Stroh, Daniel** D371 I-	Marshal, David	House Wagoner shop Stable (small) House is midling good.	20 x 24 14 x 20	log log	1	120P	280	350
428	**Strome, George** **Strohm, George** B336 D406 E336 I- II-	Strome, Henry Strohm, Henry	House Barn Good house. Limestone land.	30 x 27 60 x 30	log stone/log	1	2A 198A	360 3564	450 4455
429	**Strome, Henry** **Strohm, Henry** B335 D405 E335 I- II-	Snider, Michael Snyder, Michl.	House Barn Good house. Limestone land.	30 x 26 60 x 27	stone stone/log	1	2A 198A	400 3564	500 4455
430	**Strome, John** **Strohm, John**	Fitzberger, Daniel	House Stable	22 x 16	log log	2	48P	150	187.50

Direct Tax of 1798 - Lebanon Township

No.	Owner/Occupant/Ref.	Adjoining	Building	Dimen.	Matls.	Stories	Acres Perch.	Assmt.	Valuation
	D366 I-		House - old, not in repair.						
431	Strome, John Strohm, John B337 D407 E337 I- II-	Snider, Michael Snyder, Michl.	House Barn Old house. Limestone land.	30 x 27 60 x 27	log stone/log	1	2A 184A	240 3312	300 4140
432	Strow, Elisabeth D364 I-	Sig, Henry	House Stable House is in midling order.	24 x 24	log	1	24P	105	131.25
433	Strow, John D359 I-	Bergenhof, Wilm. Esterlein, Christian	House Smith Shop Wagoner Shop Midling order.	30 x 16 15 x 20	log	2 1	48P	200	250
434	Swope, Jacob Swop, Jacob B309 D378 E309 I- II-	Brand, Isaac	House (good) Still house Barn Gravel land.	28 x 26 20 x 18 55 x 25	log log	2	2A 148A	 2072	 2590
435	Thoma, Jacob D424 I-	Meyer, John	House House is old and in bad order.	24 x 20	log	1	1A 80P	120	150
436	Thoma, John Est. B353 D429 E353 I- II-	Bomberger, Josh	House Barn House is old. Limestone land.	25 x 20 63 x 30	log stone/log	1	2A 181A	150 3439	187.50 4298.75
437	Thomas, Eberhart D427 I-	Weise, Jacob	House Doctor Shop House is midling good.	18 x 24 15 x 15	stone wood	1 1	48P	200	250
438	Thome, John Esq. B351 D425 E351 I- II-	Kapp, Susana Clark, Thomas	House House in midling order. Land	27 x 33	frame/brk.	2	48P 3A	500 60	625 75
439	Tice, David Teis, David B352 D426 E352 I- II-	Shaffer, Isaac	House Barn Good house. Good land, some gravel.	30 x 24 70 x 30	log stone/log	2	2A 98A	300 1764	375 2205
440	Tice, Henry Teis, Henry B354 D430 E354 I- II-	Imhof, Martin	House Barn Good house. Good limestone land.	16 x 25 30 x 20	log log	1	2A 88A	230 1760	287.50 2200
441	Tice, Jacob Teis, Jacob B350 D423 E350 I- II-	Six, Jacob	House Barn House - old, out of repair. Good limestone land.	56 x 19 70 x 24	log log	1	2A 178A	300 3560	375 4450
442	Tice, Michael Teis, Michl. B349 D422 E349 I- II-	Shaffer, Isaac Sheffer, Isaac	House House Good old houses. Barn	40 x 30 27 x 23 80 x 30	stone stone log	2 1	2A 2A 196A	550 250 4704	687.50 312.50 5880

Direct Tax of 1798 - Lebanon Township

No.	Owner/Occupant/Ref.	Adjoining	Building	Dimen.	Matls.	Stories	Acres Perch.	Assmt.	Valuation
			Good limestone land.						
443	Tratter, Sarah Trotter, Sarah D428 I-	Meily, Saml.	House Stable (small) House is good, but old.	25 x 20	log	1	48P	220	275
444	Traxel, Abraham B356 D432 E356 I- II-	Traxel, John	House Stable House - not finished. Gravel land.	24 x 22 15 x 12	log	1	2A 18A	160 198	200 247.50
445	Traxel, John B355 D431 E355 I- II-	Roeser, Daniel	House Barn Good house. Gravel land.	26 x 20 60 x 30	log stone/log	2	2A 188A	360 2256	450 2820
446	Uhler, Christo'r. B357 D433 E357 I- II-	Kap, Susana	House Kitchen Joiner shop Barn	38 x 29 18 x 21 20 x 29 32 x 17	stone stone stone log	2 1 1	48P	800	1000
	Moor, Benjamin Gibbony, Hugh Goldman, Christn. Moyer, William Martin, _____	Peiffer, Jacob Six, Jacob Hofman, Conrad Peifer, Jacob Werner, Henry Shally, Baltzer	House House House House House House (38 x 29) - not finished. House (28 x 26) - old house, not in repair. House (32 x 16) - old. House (24 x 22) - new, not finished. House (20 x 22) is an old building. House (20 x 47) is an old building.	28 x 26 32 x 16 24 x 22 20 x 22 20 x 47	log stone/wd. frame log log	2 1 2 1 1	2A 2A 2A 2A 2A	260 130 200 105 105	325 162.50 250 131.25 131.25
			Barn Barn Barn Land - stony "hille" wood land. 22A - good land and "madow." 90A - midling good land, some stony. 116A - Limestone land.	50 x 25 44 x 26 43 x 26	stone stone frame		22A 90A 116A 28A	528 1620 2088 140	660 2025 2610 175
447	Uhler, Martin B367 D444 E367 I- II-	Light, Henry	House House - midling good. Weaver shop Still house	26 x 30 18 x 22 22 x 25	log	2	2A	400	500
		Uhler, Michl.	Barn Land Gravel land, midling good.	25 x 56			130A 21A	1820 147	2275 183.75
448	Uhler, Michael B358 D434 E358 I- II-	Umberger, John	House Barn House is midling good. Gravel land.	26 x 20 75 x 25	log stone/log	1	2A 113A	300 1469	375 1836.25
449	Uhrich, Christn. B359 D435 E359 I- II-	Buehler, Henry	House Barn Good house. Gravel land.	19 x 24 30 x 20	log log	1	2A 45A	300 675	375 843.75

Direct Tax of 1798 - Lebanon Township

No.	Owner/Occupant/Ref.	Adjoining	Building	Dimen.	Matls.	Stories	Acres Perch.	Assmt.	Valuation
450	Uhrich, George B364 D441 E364 I- II-	Xander, Jacob	House Barn	25 x 22 46 x 19	log log	1	2A 128A	280 2304	350 2880
			House in midling good order. Limestone land.						
451	Uhrich, Michael B365 D442 E365 I- II-	Bachman, Christn. Xander, Jacob Miller, Rudolph	House (good) House (old) Barn Barn Land	30 x 35 30 x 28 55 x 26 40 x 20	stone log	1 1	2A 2A 138A 98A 20A	450 260 2760 1764 100	542.50 325 3450 2205 125
			138A - good land. 98A - Limestone land. 20A - "hille wood land."						
452	Uhrich, Philip B366 443 E366 I- II-	Dohner, Joseph	House Barn	33 x 27 66 x 28	stone stone/log	2	2A 184A	450 3496	562.50 4370
			House - good but not finished. Limestone land.						
453	Ulrich, Christo'r. Est. Ulrich, Christo'r. B362 D438 E362 I- II-	Meyer, Martin	House House Houses are in midling order. Weaver shop Barn	32 x 28 20 x 16 12 x 18 58 x 27	stone log stone/log	2 2	2A 2A 198A	480 200 3564	600 250 4455
			Part good, part gravel land.						
454	Ulrich, Martin B363 D439 E363 I- II-	Raiguel, Abraham Shenck, Joseph	House Hatter shop Barn Land	26 x 28 20 x 18 50 x 27	log stone/log	2	2A 6A 120P 93A 50A	450 175.50 1674 300	562.50 219.37 2092.50 375

			House is an old building. 93A - Limestone land.
			50A - gravel wood land. 6A 120P - "madow" lot.
			Slaves: Whole Number of slaves of all ages: 1
			    No. of slaves above 12 and under 50 years of
			    age, subject to taxation: 1						

455	Ulrich, Tobias D440 I-	Singer, Michael	House Stable (small) Midling order.	20 x 18	log	1	48P	280	350
456	Umberger, John B361 D437 E361 I- II-	Uhler, Michael	House House (old) Still house Barn	30 x 27 17 x 15 20 x 18 30 x 26	log log log	2	2A 298A	400 5368	500 6710
			House in midling order. Gravel land.						
457	Umberger, Jonas B360 D436 E360 I- II-	Beshore, Henry	House House (old) Barn Gravel land.	24 x 20 18 x 15 70 x 26	log log log	2	2A 98	250 980	312.50 1225
458	Wagoner, Henry D-		House						375

Direct Tax of 1798 - Lebanon Township

No.	Owner/Occupant/Ref.	Adjoining	Building	Dimen.	Matls.	Stories	Acres Perch.	Assmt.	Valuation
459	Walter, Abram B390 D470 E390 I- II-	Stiel, David Steel, David	House Stable House - not good. Gravel land.	20 x 24 15 x 12	log	1	1A 2A	105 14	131.25 17.50
460	Walter, Christr. B380 D459 E380 I- II-	Kornman, George	House Stable House is in midling order. Gravel land.	22 x 20 15 x 20	log	1	2A 7A	150 49	187.50 61.25
461	Walter, Henry B388 D468 E388 I- II-	Blough, John Blauch, John	House House - not good. Land	18 x 16	log	1	2A 3A	105 21	131.25 26.25
462	Walter, John Walter, John Walter, Peter B387 D467 E387 I- II-	Greider, John Snevly, Jacob Roeser, Daniel	House Springhouse House House House (27 x 21) - old and midling. House (24 x 18) is in midling order. House (20 x 15) is old. Barn Stable Gravel land.	27 x 21 24 x 18 20 x 16 80 x 18 16 x 14	log log log log	1 1 1	2A 2A 2A 129A 50A	240 200 105 1419 550	300 250 131.25 1773.75 687.50
463	Waltz, Christor. B371 D449 E371 I- II-	Hamelton, Robert Reinoehl, Conrad Breitenbach, John	House Stable House is in midling good order. Land - Limestone land Land - out lot near Lebanon.	42 x 24	log	2	96P 25A 5A	280 450 80	350 562.50 100
464	Weidman, John Wideman, John B368 D445 E368 I- II-	Gebhard, George Funck, Martin	House Stable House - well finished. Land - out lot near Lebanon.	42 x 36	stone	2	48P 9A 28P	800 146.80	1000 183.50
465	Weirich, Christn. Wirick, Christn. B377 D456 E377 I- II-	Uhler, Martin	House Stable House - not good order. Gravel land.	22 x 18 16 x 14	log	1	2A 7A	140 49	175 61.25
466	Weirich, Jacob Wirick, Jacob B375 D454 E375 I- II-	Weirich, Peter	House (old) Barn Gravel land.	24 x 21 41 x 15	log log	1	2A 17A	140 119	175 148.75
467	Weirich, Jacob Wirick, Jacob Wishter, Anthony Slaterback, Michael Linewever, Peter B382 D460 E382 I- II-	Gloninger, Peter Doebler, Abraham Peiffer, Jacob Stoever, Fredk. Kreps, Michl.	House Kitchen House Stable House House Stable Good houses. Land - "matow" lot near Lebanon. Land - out lot near Lebanon.	36 x 48 15 x 20 25 x 23 15 x 20 18 x 22	stone stone log stone log	2 1 2 1 1	72P 48P 48P 48P 4A 5A	1600 450 300 200 94 75	2000 562.50 375 250 117.50 93.75

Direct Tax of 1798 - Lebanon Township

No.	Owner/Occupant/Ref.	Adjoining	Building	Dimen.	Matls.	Stories	Acres Perch.	Assmt.	Valuation
		Arnt, Jacob	Land - out lot near Lebanon.				2A 80P	45	56.25
		Grubenseh, Geo.	Land - in lots in Lebanon.				144P	45	56.25
		Peiffer, Jacob	Brew House		stone		48P	300	375
468	Weirich, John	Ley, Andrew	House	17 x 19	log	1	1A	105	131.25
	Wirick, John		Stable	14 x 12			2A	16	20
	B378 D457 E378 I- II-		House - new. Gravel land.						
469	Weirich, Peter	Uhler, Martin	House	20 x 15	log	1	2A	140	175
	Wirick, Peter		Stable	18 x 15			14A	98	122.50
	B379 D458 E379 I- II-		House is in midling order. Gravel land.						
470	Weis, Henry	Laber, Balser	House	20 x 18	log	1	2A	260	325
	B372 D450 E372 I- II-		House - Midling good order.						
			House (old)	15 x 12					
			Barn	59 x 30			144A	2592	3240
			Limestone land.						
471	Weis, Jacob	Eberhard, Thomas	House (old)	24 x 18	log	2	144P	280	350
	B370 D448 E370 I- II-		Stable						
		Fetzberger, Danl.	Land - out lot near Lebanon.				2A 80P	40	50
472	Weis, Nicolas	Daub, Dillman	House (old)	20 x 20	log	1	2A	300	375
	Wiss, Nichlos		Barn	40 x 20	log		120A	1320	1650
	B376 D455 E376 I- II-		Gravel land.						
473	Wenner, Henry	Uhler, Christr.	House (good)	30 x 34	stone	1	2A	435	543.75
	Werner, Henry		Barn	49 x 24	stone		88A	1584	1980
	B385 D464 E385 I- II-		Limestone land.						
474	Wentling, Peter	Peifer, Jacob	House (good)	28 x 20	log	2	96P	380	475
	B384 D463 E384 I- II-		Stable/barn						
		Lautermilch, John	Land - out lot - Lebanon.				7A	112	140
475	Wentz, Peter	Grinwold, Mathis	House (old)	27 x 25	log	2	48P	300	375
	B369 D447 E369 I- II-		Stable						
		Stoehr, John	Land - 2 town lots - Lebanon.				96P	30	37.50
476	Wert, Christian Est.	Fernsler, Fredrick	House	36 x 20	log	1	2A	220	275
	B381 D465 E381 I- II-		Barn	45 x 27	stone/log		48P	528	660
			Midling good house. Gravel land.						
477	Wever, Widow	Kelker, Rudolph	House (old)	20 x 16	log	1	144P	140	175
	Welsh, Catrina	Gilbert, Henry	House (old)	24 x 15	log	1	48P	105	131.25
	D472 I-								
478	Wilhelm, Christn.	Blough, John	House	28 x 20	log	1	1A 80P	105	131.25
	B386 D466 E386 I- II-		House - not good.						
			Land - gravel land.				2A	16	20
479	Wilhelm, John	Herr, Abraham	House (old)	18 x 20	log	1	48P	105	131.25

Direct Tax of 1798 - Lebanon Township

No.	Owner/Occupant/Ref.	Adjoining	Building	Dimen.	Matls.	Stories	Acres Perch.	Assmt.	Valuation
	D461 I-								
480	Williams, Fredrick Wheelen, Fredk. B374 D453 E374 I- II-	Boyer, John	House (old) Still house Barn Gravel land.	30 x 22 22 x 20 60 x 25	log log log	1	2A 113A	240 1343	300 1678.75
481	Williams, Henry B383 D462 E383 I- II-	Raiguel, Abraham	House Barn House is midling good. Limestone land.	26 x 24 60 x 28	log stone	1	2A 112A	250 2128	312.50 2660
482	Wime, Jacob Winey, Jacob D446 I-	Shamo, Joseph	House Lots (2) - in Lebanon House is good.	25 x 20	log	2	96P	300	375
483	Witmore, Peter Witmer, Peter B391 D471 E391 I- II-	Orth, Joseph	House House Barn Houses are midling good. Good land.	30 x 28 30 x 12 70 x 28	log stone log	1 1	2A 308A	350 7084	437.50 8855
484	Wolf, Christn. B389 D469 E389 I- II-	Sickle, Jacob Seegely, Jacob	House Barn House is midling good. Gravel land.	30 x 28 42 x 18	log	1	2A 109A	240 1090	300 1362.50
485	Wolfersperger, Lisabeth Wolfesberger, Eliza D451 I-	Melinger, Jacob	House (old) Stable	30 x 18	log	1	48P	105	131.25
486	Woolf, Abram Wolf, Abraham B373 D452 E373 I- II-	Ridle, Henry	House (old) Barn (small) Gravel land.	18 x 15 18 x 15	log log	1	2A 4A 120P	105 33.25	131.25 41.50
487	Xander, Emanuel B393 D474 E393 I- II-	Reinoehl, Henry	House Good house. Smith shop Stable (small)	36 x 24	stone	2	2A 2A	460 34	575 42.50
488	Xanders, Jacob B392 D473 E392 I- II-	Uhrich, Michael	House Grist/sawmill Barn House is in good order. Limestone land.	24 x 22 36 x 25 60 x 26	log stone stone/log	1	2A 146A	250 1000 2592	312.50 1250 3240
489	Zehrung, John Zerring, John B405 D487 E405 I- II-	Snog, John Snoke, John	House Smith shop Barn Stable Midling good house. Gravel land.	24 x 36 66 x 25 22 x 15	log	2	2A 141A	440 1974	550 2467.50
490	Zent, Jacob B404 D486 E404 I- II-	Zimerman, Gotfry	House Barn Good house. Midling good land.	30 x 26 56 x 26	log stone/log	2	2A 158A	480 2528	600 3160

Direct Tax of 1798 - Lebanon Township

No.	Owner/Occupant/Ref.	Adjoining	Building	Dimen.	Matls.	Stories	Acres Perch.	Assmt.	Valuation
491	Zibold, Leonhart Zebolt, Leonhard Ramberger, Adam B399 D481 E399 I- II-	Fernsler, Philip	House House House (30 x 23) - good. Stable Barn Limestone land.	30 x 23 30 x 27 House (30 x 27) 57 x 25	log stone/log - midling order. stone/log	1 1	2A 2A 166A	320 300 2988	400 375 3735
492	Zibold, Nicolas Est. Zebolt, Nichl. Est. Zeabolt, Leonard Fernsler, Fredrick B397 D479 E397 I- II-	Eby, George	House Barn Good house. Limestone land.	41 x 21 49 x 21	log log	1	2A 92A	360 1656	450 2070
493	Zigler, John Ziegler, John B403 D485 E403 I- II-	Buehler, George est.	House Barn Midling good house. Gravel land.	27 x 25 43 x 18	log log	1	2A 53A	260 477	325 596.25
494	Zimerman, Fredrick Est. B395 D476 E395 I- II-	Hauer, Andrew Wentling, Peter	House Stable House - good. Land - out lot near Lebanon.	30 x 22	log	1	48P 7A 14P	300 112.40	375 140.50
495	Zimerman, Gotfry Zimerman, Michael ("father of Gotfry") B402 D484 E402 I- II-	Zent, Jacob	House House House (30 x 35) in bad order. House (18 x 14) - good house. Barn Stable Midling good land.	30 x 35 18 x 14 65 x 28 15 x 16	frame log log	2 1	2A 2A 146A	440 200 2336	550 250 2920
496	Zimerman, Leonhart B401 D483 E401 I- II-	Greider, Martin	House Barn Good house. Limestone land.	28 x 22 50 x 22	stone stone/log	1	2A 98A	440 1764	550 2205
497	Zimmerman, John B396 D477 E396 I- II-	Miller, Peter	House Stable House - not in repair. Limestone land.	47 x 20 22 x 15	stone	1	1A 3A 143P	260 93.45	325 116.81
498	Zimmerman, Michl. Est. B398 D480 E398 I- II-	Breamer, Conrad	House Barn House - good. Limestone land.	30 x 27 40 x 20	log log	1	2A 128A	260 2048	325 2560
499	Zinn, George Killian, John Killinger, John B394 D475 E394 I- II-	Snevly, George Shnebly, Geo.	House Springhouse House Grist/sawmill Barn Houses are in good order. Limestone land.	30 x 24 18 x 24 18 x 16 25 x 24 60 x 22	stone stone stone stone stone/log	1 2 1	2A 2A 196A	550 140 2000 4116	687.50 175 2500 5145
500	Zuber, Jacob D478 I-	Gaser, Christn.	House Stable	23 x 18	log	1	96P	200	250

Direct Tax of 1798 - Lebanon Township

No.	Owner/Occupant/Ref.	Adjoining	Building	Dimen.	Matls.	Stories	Acres Perch.	Assmt.	Valu-ation
			House is in midling order.						
501	Zweyer, George Zweier, George B400 D482 E400 I- II-	Arnold, John	House Tanner shop Stable Good house.	24 x 21 26 x 18 Gravel land.	log	1	2A 20A	300 280	375 350

Direct Tax of 1798 - Londonderry Township

No.	Owner/Occupant/Ref.	Adjoining	Building	Dimen.	Matls.	Stories	Acres Perch	Assmt.	Valuation
1	**Aliman, Hen.** Alleman, Henry A1 B- D1 E1 I- II-	Musser, Nicholas Remer, Abraham Reymer, Abrm.	House 16W 216L - Well finished. Barn Stony and poor land.	37 x 29 53 x 22	stone	2	1A 200A	500 1500	550 1650
2	**Anderson, James** Lynch, John A2 B- D2 E2 I- II-	Staner, Jacob Longnecker, Christn.	House 6W 52L - old logs. Barn Wet land.	40 x 20 67 x 24	wood	1	1A 150A	150 1720	165 1892
3	**Balm, John Dr.** Ballum, John Dr. A10 B8 D10 E10 I- II-	Bowman, Jacob	House 3W 36L - old. Barn Limestone land of a midling quality.	27 x 27 60 x 15	wood	1	1A 100A	150 960	165 1056
4	**Balm, William** Ballum, Wm. Hollingsworth, Levy Bishoff, Jacob A19 B17 D19 E19 I- II-	Welpmer, Abm.	House 12W 132L - old and bad. House 16W 184L - new and good. Stable House Barn Dry land.	40 x 25 34 x 28 18 x 18 50 x 18	wood wood	1 2	1A 1A 27A	600 300 514	660 330 565.40
5	**Beal, John** Boal, John A22 B21 D22 E23 I- II-	Miller, Michl.	House 9W 108L - House is not finished. New. Weaver shop Barn Sandy land.	26 x 24 15 x 12 30 x 15	stone	2	1 149A	400 1065	440 1171.50
6	**Beal, William** A3 B-1 D3 E3 I- II-	Landis, John	House 6W 61L - old. Kitchen Springhouse Barn Limestone land of midling quality.	30 x 28 30 x 10 14 x 12 60 x 22	stone stone stone	1	1A 143A	400 2271	440 2498.10
7	**Belteon, Phlip** Betleem, Philip Ellinger, Jacob A9 B7 D9 E9 I- II-	Karmany, Joseph	House 2W 24L - new. Kitchen 2W 16L - new. House Barn Gravel hilly land.	27 x 23 23 x 13 15 x 12 30 x 22	wood wood	1 1	1A 100A 12A	250 970 138	275 1067 151.80
8	**Bernhard, Herman** A12 B11 D12 E13 I- II-	Noll, Christn. Sheller, Adam	House 9W 86L - new. Out house Out house - 2W 18L. Barn	38 x 25 25 x 21 40 x 14	stone wood	1 1	1A 49A	300 428	330 470.80

142

Direct Tax of 1798 - Londonderry Township

No.	Owner/Occupant/Ref.	Adjoining	Building	Dimen.	Matls.	Stories	Acres Perch	Assmt.	Valuation
			Poor land.						
9	Bernhard, John A11 B10 D11 E12 I- II-	Elder & Kain	House 12W 166L - new. Barn Poor land.	28 x 28 51 x 27	wood	2	1A 67A	200 750	220 825
10	Bowman, Henry A23 B22 D23 E24 I- II-	Bowman, Jacob Kratzer, John Killinger, Michl. Sayer, John Bowman, Jacob	House 6W - ?L - a good house. Barn Land Land Land Land Part limestone and chiefly dry lands.	30 x 28 60 x 25	wood	1	1A 127A 28A 20A 40A 30A	200 2078 196 280 560 360	220 2285.80 215.60 308 616 396
11	Bowman, Jacob Balm, Michl. Betleem, Isaac A20 B9 B18 D20 E20 I- II-	Bowman, Henry Early, John Esq. Balm, Doctor	House 10W 50L - good house. House 2W 18L - old house. House 3W 36L - old house. House 1W 4L - poor land, hilly. Outhouse Still house Barn Limestone land and gravel. Barn All gravel land. Barn Limestone land.	30 x 30 25 x 20 25 x 20 20 x 16 20 x 20 80 x 32 40 x 20 40 x 78	wood wood wood wood	1 1 1 1	1A 1A 1A 2A 249A 124A 99A	400 150 105 80 4325 1786 822	440 165 115.50 4757.50 1964.60 904.20
12	Boyd, Benjamin A5 B3 D5 E5 I- II-	Hershe, Isaac	House 8W 96L - finished. Kitchen 4W 48L - finished. Wash house Barn Limestone land.	33 x 33 32 x 27 80 x 30	stone	2 1	1A 182A	780 4040	858 4444
13	Boyd, Elizabeth (widow) A6 B4 D6 E6 I- II-	Wray, David	House 5W 33L old. Barn Poor land, stone land.	37 x 18 60 x 25	wood	1	1A 222A	140 1976	154 2173.60
14	Boyer, Widow A4 B2 D4 E4 I- II-	Rodger, George Rogers, Geo.	House 2W 18L - new. Barn "Slayty land."	21 x 18 54 x 24	wood	1	1A 138A	120 2200	132 2420
15	Bradley, Widow heirs B19 E21 II-	Bradley, Saml.	Barn Limestone land (good).	60 x 20			100A	3680	4048

Direct Tax of 1798 - Londonderry Township

No.	Owner/Occupant/Ref.	Adjoining	Building	Dimen.	Matls.	Stories	Acres Perch	Assmt.	Valuation
16	**Bradly, Samuel** Beadley, Samuel A18 B23 D18 E25 I- II-	Craig, John	House 10W 120L - new house. Outhouse 2W 10L - new. Outhouse 4W 36L. Limestone land - midling. Land	32 x 30 18 x 15 26 x 24	stone wood wood	2 1 1	1A 120A	650 2190	715 2409
17	**Brand, David** A17 B16 D17 E18 I- II-	Logan, Wm. Brubacker, Benj.	House 5W 45L - Poor old house. Kitchen Kitchen not built on 1 of October. Barn Poor land, stone land, hilly.	27 x 15 15 x 13 20 x 15	wood	1	1A 130A	105 1570	115.50 1727
18	**Brand, Joseph** Carver, Jacob Cober, Jacob A16 B15 D16 E17 I- II-	Layman, Jacob Stauffer, Henry	House 3W 33L - new, not finished. Barn	36 x 21 51 x 22	wood	1	1A 126A 42P	180 1572	198 1724.20
19	**Brand, Saml.** A15 B13 D15 E15 I- II-	Cook, John	House 8W 71L - good. Wash house Barn Poor land, stone.	30 x 24 20 x 12 60 x 25	wood wood	1 1	1A 221A	300 2531	330 2784.10
20	**Branstator, Andw.** Beanstetter, Andw. A8 B6 D8 E8 I- II-	MaClay, John	House 3W 25L - old. Springhouse - new. Springhouse Barn Very poor land, stone land.	30 x 28 16 x 11 38 x 24	wood	1 1	1A 64A	220 571	242 628.10
21	**Brown, Philip** A21 B20 D21 E22 I- II-	Coleman, Robt. land Herkelroth, ____ Karmany, Anthony	House 11W 118L - old logs. House 3W 19L - old logs. Barn Barn Stony and poor land.	28 x 25 20 x 15 45 x 18 30 x 15	wood wood	2 1	2A 1A 117A 59A	200 105 1240 494	220 115.50 1364 543.40
22	**Brubacker, Henry** A14 B12 D14 E14 I- II-	Ober, Christr. Hoffart, John	House 7W 75L - good. Out house 1W 6L Barn Poor land.	30 x 30 21 x 20 60 x 26	wood	1 1	1A 221A	300 2510	330 2761
23	**Brubecker, Benj.** Bixler, Joseph Pixler, John A13 B14 D13 E16 I- II-	Logan, William	House 3W 17L - old house. Barn Poor land.	36 x 18 63 x 26	stone/wd.	1	1A 123A	200 1546	220 1700.60

Direct Tax of 1798 - Londonderry Township

No.	Owner/Occupant/Ref.	Adjoining	Building	Dimen.	Matls.	Stories	Acres Perch	Assmt.	Valuation
24	**Buck, Christian** A7 B5 D7 E7 I- II-	Shank, Michl.	House 5W 48L - old.	30 x 28	wood	1	1A	280	308
			Wash house 3W 18L - new.	20 x 18	wood	1			
			Barn Poor land, stone land.	70 x 30			159A	1781	1959.10
25	**Campbell, Ellenor** Campbell, John Campbell, Robt. A25 B25 D25 E27 I- II-	Landis, John	House 4W 20L - old.	30 x 27	wood	1	1A	165	171.50
			Kitchen 2W 8L.	16 x 14	wood	1			
			Barn Part limestone and gravel land.	60 x 30			336A	5406	5946.60
26	**Carsnetts, Peter** A26 B26 D26 E28 I- II-	Forney, John Forney, Joseph	House 2W 15L - old.	27 x 22	wood	1	1A	120	132
			Barn Poor gravel lands.	40 x 14			35A	345	379.50
27	**Clark, Walter** A24 B24 D24 E26 I- II-	Kettering, Valentine	House 10W 120L - finished.	35 x 29	stone	2	1A	600	660
			Barn Good limestone land.	77 x 30			249A	5380	5918
28	**Coble, Jacob** A29 B28 D29 E30 I- II-	Reesor, Peter	House 8W 47L - good log house.	27 x 27	wood	2	1A	605	661.50
			Wash house 2W 18L.	28 x 22	stone	1			
			Barn Good meadow uplands. Midling.	117 x 30			150A	2100	2310
29	**Coleman, Robt. Esq.** A31 B31 D31 D- E33 I- II-								
	Ramstead, Henry	Colebrook Furnace	House	24 x 20	wood	1	2A	120	132
	Bryan, Edward	Colebrook Furnace	House	24 x 20	wood	1	2A	105	115.50
	Points, Saml.	Colebrook Furnace	House	24 x 20	wood	1	2A	105	115.50
	Hennington, Thos.	Colebrook Furnace	House	24 x 20	wood	1	2A	105	115.50
	Henry, Philip	Colebrook Furnace	House	24 x 20	wood	1	2A	105	115.50
	Ritter, Fred	Colebrook Furnace	House	24 x 20	wood	1	2A	105	115.50
	Sink, Henry	Colebrook Furnace	House	24 x 20	wood	1	2A	105	115.50
	Dorsht, Abm.	Colebrook Furnace	House	24 x 20	wood	1	2A	105	115.50
	Kennedy, John	Colebrook Furnace	House	24 x 20	wood	1	2A	105	115.50
	Kinney, John	Colebrook Furnace	House	24 x 20	wood	1	2A	105	115.50
	Montford, John	Colebrook Furnace	House	24 x 20	wood	1	2A	140	154
	Montford, John						200A	1600	1760
	Crawford, Saml.	Colebrook Furnace	House	24 x 20	wood	1	2A	105	115.50
	Baggs, James	Colebrook Furnace	House	24 x 20	wood	1	2A	105	115.50
	Baggs, James						116A 25P	580	638
	Moore, Richard	Colebrook Furnace	House	24 x 20	wood	1	2A	105	115.50
	Bartram, James	Colebrook Furnace	House	24 x 20	wood	1	2A	105	115.50
	Bartram, James						32A	160	176
	Bigham, James	Colebrook Furnace	House	24 x 20	wood	1	2A	105	115.50
	Sheadle, John	Colebrook Furnace	House	24 x 20	wood	1	2A	105	115.50
	McGlade, John	Colebrook Furnace	House	24 x 20	wood	1	2A	105	115.50

Direct Tax of 1798 - Londonderry Township

No.	Owner/Occupant/Ref.	Adjoining	Building	Dimen.	Matls.	Stories	Acres Perch	Assmt.	Valuation
	McKinnet, Adm.	Colebrook Furnace	House	24 x 20	wood	1	2A	105	115.50
	McKinnet, Adm.						75A	375	412.50
	Tollebach, _____								51.50
	Tollebach, _____						51A 50P	257	282.70
	Bingham, Jas.								198
	Bingham, Jas.						198A	1782	1960.20
	Jacobs, Saml.		Furnace					2000	2200
			Grist mill					1500	1650
			Saw mill					200	220
			Small houses - built for the use of the workmen.						
			Meadows good; the lands poor. The wood chiefly cut off.						
30	Cooke, John Esq.	Brand, Saml.	House	35 x 30	wood	1	1A	250	275
	Plough, Christn.		10W 111L - old logs.						
	Blough, Christ.		Barn	60 x 20			263A	2990	3289
	A28 B27 D28 E29 I- II-		Poor land (part).						
31	Coyar, Casper	Coleman, Robt. Esq.	House	14 x 16			28A	235	258.50
	B30 E32 II-		Very poor.						
32	Craig, John	Bradley, Widow	House	30 x 26	wood	2	1A	340	364
	A30 B29 D30 E31 I- II-		9W 80L - good log house.						
			Outhouse	14 x 12	wood	1		20	
			Tan house	46 x 24		1			
			Out house			1	61A	1175	1292.50
			Barn	50 x 26					
			Good land, part stony.						
33	Cratzer, John	Betleem, Philip	House (old)	20 x 18	wood	1	2A	105	105.50
	A27 D27 I-								
34	Dasher, Alexr.	Henry, Andw.	House	22 x 26	wood	1		290	319
	A36 B36 D36 E38 I- II-		9W 108L - good log house.						
			Kitchen	16 x 15	wood				
			1W 12L						
			Barn	24 x 18			6A	125	137.50
			Good (dry) land.						
35	Dearman, Joseph	Henry, Andw.	House	36 x 38	stone	2	1A	1000	1100
	Deyermond, Joseph		36 x 33 - good, not finished.						
	A35 B35 D35 E37 I- II-		Kitchen	26 x 17		1			
			5W 66L.						
		Balm, Wm.	Barn	30 x 28			19A	395	434.50
			Dry land but good.						
36	Deninger, Michl.	Carmany, Joseph	House	30 x 20	stone	2	1A	650	715
	Burnett, Widow		12W 186L - good house.						
	A37 B37 D37 E39 I- II-		Kitchen	18 x 12	stone	1			
			5W 60L.						
			House	28 x 26	wood	1	1A	110	121
		Balm, Doctor	6W 54L - old log house.						
			House	24 x 24	wood	1	1A	105	115.50
			2W 24L - old log house.						
		Deninger, Adm.	Stable	16 x 14			4A	52	57.20

Direct Tax of 1798 - Londonderry Township

No.	Owner/Occupant/Ref.	Adjoining	Building	Dimen.	Matls.	Stories	Acres Perch	Assmt.	Valuation
			Barn	70 x 30			149A	2735	3008.50
			Part good and part bad land.						
37	Dininger, Adam A38 B38 D38 E40 I- II-	Welpmer, Abm.	House 12W 136L - very good log house.	28 x 26	wood	2	1A	230	253
		Fernsler, Peter	House 3W 36L.	24 x 20	wood	1	1A	180	198
		Deninger, Michl.	Barn	80 x 30			174A	3285	3613.50
		Fernsler, Peter	Land				4A	64	70.40
			Part good and part bad land.						
38	Dolebach, Peter Dellebach, Peter Tolleback, Peter Talebach, Peter	Maclay, John	House 11W 110L - a good stone house.	20 x 26	stone	1	1A	425	407.50
			Springhouse 12W 18L.	20 x 16	stone	1			
	A39 B177 D39- E179 I- II-	Maclay, Michael	Barn	57 x 27			99A	1050	1155
			Midling land - good meadow.						
39	Doll, Leonard Dull, Leonard	Hemperly, Eleanor Hemperly, George	House 3W 32L - old.	28 x 24	wood	1	2A	160	176
	A33 B33 D33 E35 I- II-		Land				3A	27	29.70
			Hilly poor land.						
40	Duglass, John Douglass, John	Hershey, Isaac Hershe, Isaac	House 25W 304L - new house on the Public Road.	37 x 32	stone	2	1A	800	880
	A32 B32 D32 E34 I- II-		Smith shop	30 x 20					
			Barn	54 x 20			59A 80P	1200	1320
			Good dry land.						
41	Duncan, James A34 B34 D34 E36 I- II-	Coleman, Robt.	House 2W 9L - old log house.	22 x 20	wood	1	2A	105	115.50
			Stable	12 x 12			23A	170	187
			Poor land.						
42	Early, John Esq. Todd, John	Miller, Thos. Bowman, Jacob	House 18W 308L - good stone house.	40 x 30	stone	2	1A	800	880
	A42 B40 D42 E42 I- II-	McAllen, Thos.	House 3W 32L - old stone house.	30 x 28	stone	1	1A	130	143
			Barn	60 x 28			183A	2945	3239.50
			Land (late purchase)				115A	1610	1771
			Good dry land.						
43	Early, Thomas A45 B43 D45 E45 I- II-		House 7W 78L - midling log house.	30 x 28	wood	1	1A	160	176
			Still house	25 x 20					
			Barn	60 x 20			148A	1645	1809.50
			Thin and poor land.						
44	Eather, Saml. Etter, Saml.	Sayer, John Sayer, Mrs.	House 8W 92L - good house.	34 x 28	stone	1	1A	500	550
	A44 B42 D44 E44 I- II-		Barn	60 x 30			199A	3960	4350
			Very good land.						
45	Elder & Kain	Bernhard, John	House	30 x 36	wood	1	1A	140	154

Direct Tax of 1798 - Londonderry Township

No.	Owner/Occupant/Ref.	Adjoining	Building	Dimen.	Matls.	Stories	Acres Perch	Assmt.	Valuation
	Schroff, Nichlous A40 D40 I-		6W 64L - old logs.						
46	Elleberger, Christr. Umberger, John A43 B41 D43 E43 I- II-	Bowman, John Killinger, Michael	House 14W 168L - new good house. House 2W 24L - new log house. Still house Barn Good land.	35 x 25 22 x 18 42 x 18	stone wood	2 1	1A 59A	500 105 975	550 115.50 1072.50
47	Eshelman, Henry A41 B39 D41 E41 I- II-	Coleman, Robt. Esq.	House 3W 27L - old logs. Smith shop Barn Poor land.	24 x 18 14 x 14 45 x 15	wood	1	2A 28A	105 265	115.50 291.50
48	Farmer, John A53 B50 D53 E52 I- II-	Shaeffer, Geo. Coleman, Robt. Esq.	House 3W 36L - good log house. Stable Very poor land.	25 x 16	wood	1	2A 5A	115 35A	126.50 38.50
49	Fernsler, Peter A55 B52 D55 E54 I- II-	Longnecker, Danl. Longnecker, John	House 10W 117L - poor house. Barn Good land (dry).	20 x 18 20 x 18	wood	2	1A 13A	350 238	385 261.80
50	Finney, John B56 E58 II-		Land Midling land.				40A	480	528
51	Fishburn, Ludwig Camp, Jacob Grimm, Widow A46 B44 D46 E46 I- II-	Stoner, Christn.	House 4W 48L - of old logs. House 4W 30L - new house. House 4W 30L - new house. Stable Stable Barn Good land - limestone.	30 x 26 25 x 20 25 x 20 14 x 12 14 x 12 60 x 30	wood wood wood	1 1 1	1A 2A 2A 195A	250 120 120 3810	275 132 132 4191
52	Fleagar, John Fliegar, John A47 A45 D47 E47 I- II-	Campbell, Elenor	House 2W 13L - old house. Barn Very poor land.	20 x 18 50 x 20	wood	1	2A 144A	100 735	110 808.50
53	Folgate, James A54 B51 D54 E53 I- II-	Miller, Danl.	House 1W 12L - poor log house. Barn Very poor land.	15 x 15 29 x 16	wood	1	2A 12A	105 125	115.50 137.50
54	Forney, John A48 B46 D48 E48 I- II-	Shrobaker, Joseph Nasecker, Joseph	House 5W 60L - finished. Barn	25 x 20 60 x 28	wood	1	1A 150A	250 1800	275 1980

Direct Tax of 1798 - Londonderry Township

No.	Owner/Occupant/Ref.	Adjoining	Building	Dimen.	Matls.	Stories	Acres Perch	Assmt.	Valuation
			Gravel land, good meadows.				149A	1340	1474
55	Foster, Andrew A51 B57 D51 E59 I- II-	Foster, David	House 1W 12L - midling good house. Barn Tolerable land.	18 x 18 40 x 20	wood	1	2A 78A	110 737	121 810.70
56	Foster, Barbara B55 E57 II-	Foster, Mary	Stable Midling land.	18 x 18			80A	980	1078
57	Foster, David A50 B48 D50 E50 I- II-	Foster, Andw.	House 3W 27L - old log house. Barn Very good land.	40 x 23 52 x 22	wood	1	2A 139A	150 1290	165 1419
58	Foster, James A52 B49 D52 E51 I- II-	Coleman, Robt. land	House 4W 36L - old house. Barn Tolerable good land.	28 x 22 58 x 20	wood	1	1A 245A	200 3020	220 2222
59	Foster, Joseph A49 B47 D49 E49 I- II-	Foster, Andw. Reeser, John	House 2W 18L - old poor house. Barn Tolerable land.	38 x 18 32 x 14	wood	1	2A 182A	120 1830	133 2013
60	Foster, Maria Foster, Mary A57 B54 D57 E56 I- II-	Foster, Jas.	House 10W 76L - good wood house. Barn Midling land.	34 x 19 52 x 20	wood	1	1A 75A	200 950	220 1045
61	Frazier, William A56 B53 D56 E55 I- II-	Groe, Abram Morrison, Jas. Alliman, Henry	House 6W 63L - good house. House Barn Good meadows - the upland stony.	30 x 25 12 x 12 64 x 20	wood	2	1A 200A 148A 80P	360 2080 1055	396 2288 1160.50
62	Gates, Henry A61 B61 D61 E62 I- II-	Casper, John	House 7W 84L - good house. Kitchen Stable Good dry limestone land.	21 x 18 20 x 9 20 x 20	wood wood	2 1	1A 14A	350 200	385 220
63	Gillman, Christr. B63 E64 II-	Crotzer, John	House Poor land.	20 x 18			6A	108	118.80
64	Graybill, Geo. A60 B60 D60 E61 I- II-	Pile, Jacob Phile, Jacob	House 4W 26L - poor old house. Barn Poor land.	42 x 16 40 x 14	wood	1	2A 80A	105 590	115.50 649
65	Grove, Abraham A62 B62 D62 E63 I- II-	Alliman, Henry Reymore, Abm.	House 3W 36L - old house. Barn	24 x 22 60 x 30		1	1A 160A	130 1295	143 1424.50

Direct Tax of 1798 - Londonderry Township

No.	Owner/Occupant/Ref.	Adjoining	Building	Dimen.	Matls.	Stories	Acres Perch	Assmt.	Valuation
			Poor thin land.						
66	Grubb, B. Henry Porter, John A59 B59 D59 E61 I- II-	Coleman, Robt. Esq.	House 2W 13L - old log house. Land Poor thin land.	18 x 15	wood	1	2A 148A	105 1036	115.50 1139.60
67	Grubb, John A58 B58 D58 E60 I- II-	Macley, John	House 3W 28L - old house. Barn Good meadow land, hilly and stony.	27 x 22 50 x 28	wood	1	1A 196A	150 1825	165 2007.50
68	Hamilton, Wm. A67 B68 D67 E69 I- II-	Hoober, Michl.	House 23W 350L - all fine but the upper story. Barn Good limestone land.	40 x 32 62 x 29	stone	2	1A 185A	800 3755	880 4130.50
69	Hay, Wm. Esq. A74 B76 D74 E77 I- II-	Nicholson, John	House 4W 39L - old logs. Kitchen Stable Land Midling good lands (in dispute).	25 x 23 20 x 12 24 x 24	wood	1 1	2A 133A 100A	160 2825 600	176 3107.50 660
70	Hays, David McKissock, John Snyder, George Sider, Geo. A63 B64 D63 E65 I- II-	Hays, Patrick Clark, Walter Shank, Adm. Longnecker, Abm.	House 10W 120L - house about 20 yrs. standing - in good repair. Wash house House 8W 96L - new house in good repair. House 3W 18L - old logs, little value. Stable Limestone land (dry). Barn Part limestone, part sand and gravel land. Barn Stony land. Land Dry poor land.	49 x 27 25 x 12 24 x 18 26 x 20 20 x 20 65 x 33 64 x 20	stone/wd. stone wood	1 2 1	1A 1A 2A 99A 96A 118A 47A	450 300 110 1785 2120 975 330	495 330 121 1963.50 2332 1072 363
71	Hays, Patrick A64 B65 D64 E66 I- II-	Hays, David Longnecker, Abm.	House 13W 241L - well finished. Kitchen 4W 32L - not finished. Barn Poor dry land. Land Limestone land - good. Slaves: Whole No. of slaves: 3 No. of slaves above 12 and under 50 years of age, subject to taxation: 3	40 x 30 20 x 18 81 x 30	stone stone	2 1	1A 99A 47A	890 325 2380	979 357.50 2618
72	Hays, Robert	Hays, Patrick	House	35 x 28	stone	1	1A	700	770

Direct Tax of 1798 - Londonderry Township

No.	Owner/Occupant/Ref.	Adjoining	Building	Dimen.	Matls.	Stories	Acres Perch	Assmt.	Valu-ation
	A65 B66 D65 E67 I- II-		6W 66L - well finished.						
			Kitchen	28 x 20	stone	1			
			5W 60L - well finished.						
			Barn	60 x 30			154A	3400	3740
			Land				19A	385	423.50
			Limestone land - good.						
			Slaves: Whole No. of Slaves: 1						
			No. of slaves exempted from taxation by law or disability: 1						
73	Hemperly, George A73 B75 D73 E76 I- II-	Parsonage, Peter Cassenett, Peter	House	28 x 26	wood	1	1A	400	440
			3W 36L - new logs.						
			Barn	60 x 28			140A	1460	1606
			Gravel land.						
74	Henning, Danl. Contreman, Danl. A77 B79 D77 E80 I- II-	Early, Thos.	House	24 x 30	wood	1	1A	160	176
			2W 24L - old log house.						
			Barn	60 x 30			198A	1962	2158.20
			Poor hilly land.						
75	Henry, Andrew B72 E73 II-	Henry, Vendl.	Land				60A	900	990
			Good land (dry).						
76	Henry, George A69 B70 D69 E71 I- II-	Kettering, Valentine Ketrin, Felty	House	35 x 30	stone	2	1A	650	715
			16W 192L - all finished but the upper story.						
			Barn	60 x 30			200A	2990	3289
			Good limestone land.						
77	Henry, Vendel A70 B71 D70 E72 I- II-	Kettering, Val.	House	40 x 33	stone	2	1A	850	935
			16W 256L - finished in the common way.						
			Barn	60 x 33			200A	3670	4037
			Good limestone land.						
78	Herkelroth, Henry Herkelroth, John A76 B78 D76 E79 I- II-	Wolfersberger, Philip	House	26 x 23	wood	1	1A	180	190
			4W 44L - midling good repair.						
			House (old)	22 x 18	wood	1	1A		
			4W 32L - old house.						
			Still house	22 x 22			276A	2745	3019
			Hilly poor lands.						
79	Hershey, Benjm. Hershe, Benjm. A72 B74 D72 E75 I- II-	Hershey, Martin	House	36 x 26	wood	2	1A	270	297
			13W 139L - old square logs.						
			Wash house	20 x 16	wood	1			
			Barn	70 x 30			200A	3230	3553
			Midling lands.						
80	Hershey, Isaac Hirshe, Isaac A68 B69 D68 E70 I- II-	Clark, Walter	House	40 x 30	stone	2	1A	890	979
			9W 123L - a very good house and well finished.						
			Kitchen	20 x 17	stone	1			
			1W 12L - good and well finished.						
			Barn	84 x 32			310A	6750	7425
			Good limestone land.						
81	Hershey, Martin	Hershey, Benjm.	House	30 x 28	wood	1	1A	120	132

Direct Tax of 1798 - Londonderry Township

No.	Owner/Occupant/Ref.	Adjoining	Building	Dimen.	Matls.	Stories	Acres Perch	Assmt.	Valuation
	A71 B73 D71 E74 I- II-		5W 60L - old house out of repair.						
			Barn	35 x 25			200A	3070	3377
			Midling lands.						
82	Hoover, Michael Hoober, Michael A66 B67 D66 E68 I- II-	Landis, John	House	40 x 30	stone	2	1A	980	1078
			22W 287L - new house.						
			Kitchen	20 x 17	stone	1			
			4W 54L - of old logs.						
			Outhouse	26 x 24					
			Smith shop	20 x 14					
			Hemp mill						
			Barn	53 x 27			169A	3410	3751
			Good limestone land.						
83	Hostetter, John Rule, Jacob A75 B77 D75 E78 I- II-	Coleman, Robt. land	House	15 x 15	wood	1	2A	105	115.50
			2W 6L - poor house.						
			House	20 x 18	wood	1	1A	105	115.50
			2W 8L - poor house.						
			Barn	26 x 16			39A	305	335.50
			Barn	20 x 15			144A	830	913
			Poor lands - stony.						
84	Isenhawer, Peter A80 B82 D80 E83 I- II-	Fernsler, Peter	House	23 x 22	wood	1	1A	180	198
			5W 33L - good log house.						
			Stable	23 x 22			4A	85	93.50
			Good land.						
85	Johns, Peter A79 B81 D79 E82 I- II-	Wolfersberger, Philip Bradly, Widow	House	30 x 22	wood	2	1A	600	660
			14W 168L - good repair.						
			House	22 x 15	wood	1	1A	200	220
			3W 20L.						
			Barn	50 x 18			129A	3425	3767.50
			Stable	27 x 22					
			Midling good land.						
86	Johnston, David Johnson, David A78 B80 D78 E82 I- II-	Grubb, John	House	24 x 20	wood	1	2A	105	115.50
			3W 9L - little value.						
			Saw mill						
			Barn	67 x 30			108A	2145	2359.50
			Stony land.						
87	Judy, Christn. A81 B83 D81 E84 I- II-	Miller, Michl. Wolfelsberger, Philip	House	23 x 21	wood	1	1A	200	132
			5W 48L - good repair and new.						
			Stable	26 x 16			3A	60	66
			Poor hilly land.						
88	Karmany, Anthony Jr. A89 B91 D89 E92 I- II-	Shaeffer, Geo.	House	20 x 20	wood	1	2A	140	154
			4W 40L - good order.						
			Stable	14 x 14			2A	55	60.50
			Midling land.						
89	Karmany, Anthony Sr. A90 B92 D90 E93 I- II-	Shaeffer, Geo.	House	26 x 24	wood	2	1A	250	275
			8W 72L - good repair.						

Direct Tax of 1798 - Londonderry Township

No.	Owner/Occupant/Ref.	Adjoining	Building	Dimen.	Matls.	Stories	Acres Perch	Assmt.	Valuation
			Barn	55 x 25			149A	1435	1578.50
			Midling land.						
90	Karmany, Joseph Jr. A91 B93 D91 E94 I- II-	Balm, Wm.	House	24 x 22	wood	2	1A	280	308
			13W 150L - good repair.						
			Kitchen	19 x 23		1			
			Stable	24 x 22			6A 80P	125	137.50
			Part limestone land (dry).						
91	Karmany, Joseph Sr. A92 B94 D92 E95 I- II-	Dininger, Michl.	House	35 x 29	stone	1	1A	450	495
			5W 60L - good old house.						
			Weaver shop	15 x 15					
		Shellinger, Michl.	Barn	50 x 28			70A	1380	1518
			Land				29A	320	352
			Part limestone and gravel - good land (dry).						
92	Karper, John A84 B86 D84 E87 I- II-	McAllan, Robt. McCallan, Robt.	House	31 x 27	stone	1	1A	450	495
			6W 66L - finished.						
			Kitchen	23 x 14	stone	1			
			3W 14L - finished.						
			Barn	73 x 29			225A	4565	5021
			Good land.						
93	Kelly, James Wallace, Wm. Shell, Michl. A95 A97 B95 D97 E98 I- II-	Brubacher, Benjm.	House	25 x 22	wood	1	1A	160	176
			5W 45L - midling good.						
		Morrison, Jas.	House	25 x 22	wood	1	2A	110	121
			1W						
		Kelly, Patrick	House	40 x 30	stone	2	1A	890	979
			23W 299L - not finished. Good order.						
			Kitchen	21 x 15		1			
			Spring house	22 x 15		1			
		Nichelson, John	Barn	60 x 30			93A	1465	1611.50
		Reesor, John	Barn	55 x 20			174A	1920	2112
			Barn	50 x 18			155A	1965	2161.50
			Midling upland - good meadow land.						
			Land (poor land - good meadow)				102A	918	1009.80
			Land (poor land - dry)				50A	350	385
			Land (poor stony land)				44A	352	387.20
			Slaves: Whole No. of Slaves: 1						
			No. of slaves exempted from taxation by law or disability: 1						
94	Kelly, Patrick A94 B96 D94 E97 I- II-	Shelly, Jas. Morrison, Pat	House	25 x 20	wood	2	1A	170	187
			5W 45L - midling good.						
			Stable	14 x 14			46A	470	517
			Midling land.						
95	Kelly, Patt Kelly & Orth Orth & Kelly A96 B145 D96- E146 I- II-	Coleman, Robt. land	House	22 x 18	wood	1	2A	105	115.50
			2W 12L - out of repair.						
		Brown, _____	Land				100A	700	770
			Poor land.						
96	Kennedy, John Kinaday, John	Foster, David Coleman, Robt.	House	18 x 16	wood	1	2A	105	115.50
			1W 4L - bad house.						

153

Direct Tax of 1798 - Londonderry Township

No.	Owner/Occupant/Ref.	Adjoining	Building	Dimen.	Matls.	Stories	Acres Perch	Assmt.	Valuation
	A88 B90 D88 E91 I- II-		Barn Very poor land.	45 x 15			45A	340	374
97	Kettering, Val Kittering, Valentine Ketrin, Felty A82 B84 D82 E85 I- II-	Clark, Walter	House 16W 192L - old building. Barn Very good land.	40 x 30 70 x 30	stone	2	1A 500A	600 9070	660 9977
98	Kiefer, Christn. A85 B87 D85 E88 I- II-	Masher, Jos. Knopsker, Joseph	House 2W 16L - new. Kitchen House 2W 12L - midling. Stable Barn Midling land - good meadow.	26 x 22 20 x 16 20 x 15 16 x 14 75 x 24	wood wood wood	1 1 1	1A 1A 124A	250 105 1540	275 115.50 1694
99	Kile, Robert B98 E99 II-	Coleman, Robt.	House Poor land.	20 x 16			30A	250	275
100	Killinger, John A87 B89 D87 E90 I- II-	Over, Peter	House 2W 24L - old House Adjoining house above. Built since 1 October. Barn Part limestone and part gravel.	21 x 18 30 x 26 50 x 25	wood wood	1 1	1A 150A	105 2310	115.50 300 2541
101	Killinger, Michl. B95 E96 II-	Elleberger, Chrisn.	Barn Very good (dry) land.	34 x 28			200A	3400	3740
102	Killinger, Peter A86 B88 D86 E89 I- II-	Knopsker, Christr.	House 15W 160L - good house. Barn Land Part limestone and part gravel.	30 x 24 54 x 18	wood	2	1A 124A 35A	365 1550 280	401.50 1705 308
103	Kisler, Jacob Kisnor, Jacob A83 B85 D83 E86 I- II-	Sharp, _____ Miller, Danl.	House 2W 24L - new house. Barn Poor land.	24 x 21 30 x 16	wood	1	1A 19A	130 175	143 192.50
104	Knobsker, Chrisn. Knofsker, Christn. A98 B99 D98 E100 I- II-	Bowman, Jacob	House 4W 36L - good order. Out house Land Part good, part gravel land.	30 x 28	wood	1	1A 124A 35A	260 2150 280	286 2365 308
105	Knofsker, Joseph Knopsker, Joseph A100 B101 D100 E102 I- II-	Cooper, Christ.	House 4W 40L - midling order. Barn Smith shop Weaver shop Land	24 x 24 70 x 29	wood	1	1A 130A 20A	200 1650 280	220 1815 308

Direct Tax of 1798 - Londonderry Township

No.	Owner/Occupant/Ref.	Adjoining	Building	Dimen.	Matls.	Stories	Acres Perch	Assmt.	Valuation
			Gravel land - good meadows.						
106	**Kratzger, John** A93 B102 D93 E103 I- II-	Betleem, Philip	House House - 2W 16L - old. Tan yard Barn Poor land.	20 x 18 40 x 13	wood	1	2A 35A	105 370	115.50 407
107	**Krider, John** A99 B100 D99 E101 I- II-	Knofsker, Christr.	House 15W 164L - new house, not finished 1 October. Barn Part good, part gravel land.	30 x 28 28 x 15	wood	2	1A 100A	105 1420	115.50 1562
108	**Landis, Christn.** A102 B104 D102 E105 I- II-	Landis, John	House 7W 84L - in good repair - old. Kitchen 2W 24L - good. Barn Good land.	40 x 30 30 x 12 60 x 30	stone stone	1 1	1A 149A	500 2752	550 3027.20
109	**Landis, Henry** Fry, George A106 B108 D106 E109 I- II-	Weltmer, Ulrich	House 16W 192L - upper at present for a Meeting House - good. Kitchen 2W 8L. House 2W 18L - old. Barn Good upland and meadow.	34 x 30 18 x 12 20 x 18 90 x 30	stone stone wood	2 1 1	1A 2A 299A	480 105 4935	528 115.50 5428
110	**Landis, John Jr.** A101 B105 D101 E106 I- II-	Hoober, Michl. Landis, John	House 15W 180L - old house. Kitchen 1W 12L - old. Spring house 3W 36L - old. Grist/saw mill Barn Barn Good limestone land.	36 x 30 15 x 12 14 x 12 60 x 26 30 x 20	stone stone stone	2 1 1	1A 177A	590 4155	649 4570.50
111	**Landis, John Sr.** Dey, Abm. A103 B103 D103 I- II-	Landis, Christn. Hoober, Michael	House 4W 48L - old House 4W 48L - new. House 3W 12L - good repair. Stable Grist mill Good land.	30 x 28 26 x 18 17 x 16 30 x 20	stone stone stone	1 1 1	1A 2A 39A	260 150 250 2245	286 165 275 2469.50
112	**Lantz, Jacob** A109 B111 D109 E112 I- II-	Doll, Leonard Hemperly, Geo.	House 6W 44L - new and good order. Barn	32 x 26 60 x 15	wood	1	1A 120A	200 1140	220 1254

Direct Tax of 1798 - Londonderry Township

No.	Owner/Occupant/Ref.	Adjoining	Building	Dimen.	Matls.	Stories	Acres Perch	Assmt.	Valuation
			Poor land.						
113	Layman, Abm. Leaman, Abraham B119 E120 I- II-		Land Poor, dry land.				42A	294	323.40
114	Layman, Danl. Leaman, Danl. A104 B106 D104 E107 I- II-	Layman, Peter Landis, Peter	House 4W 48L - Built since 1st of October. Land Poor dry land.	24 x 22	wood		1A 49A	1 345	200 379.50
115	Layman, Jacob Leaman, Jacob A112 B114 D112 E115 I- II-	Logan, Wm.	House 5W 60L - good order. Barn Smith shop Poor dry stony land.	30 x 27 50 x 2? 18 x 18	stone	1	1A 49A	270 465	297 511.50
116	Layman, Peter Leaman, Peter A105 B107 D105 E108 I- II-	Hays, David	House 4W 37L - old house. Outhouse 3W 28L - new. Barn Poor upland, good meadow.	27 x 27 16 x 14 60 x 27	wood wood	1 1	1A 169A	180 1590	198 1749
117	Lineawever, Peter A116 B116 D116 E117 I- II-	Early, John Esq.	House 6W 65L - good house. Barn Poor lands (dry)	30 x 25 45 x 18		1	1A 164A	300 2385	330 2623.50
118	Logan, William Logan, Widow A111 B113 D111 E114 I- II-	Reesor, Peter	House 18W 392L - upper story not finished in Oct. last. Kitchen House 2W 8L - bad repair. Barn Stable Barn Midling land - good meadow.	36 x 30 27 x 16 33 x 15 45 x 26 25 x 15 51 x 18	stone wood wood	2 1 1	1A 1A 212A 108A	820 105 2640 1325	902 115.50 2904 1457.50
119	Long, Martin A108 B110 D108 E111 I- II-	Hershey, Benjm.	House 2W 20L - midling order. Barn Poor dry land.	20 x 18 35 x 15	wood	1	2A 5A	105 80	115.50 88
120	Longnecker, Abm. A113 B115 D113 E116 I- II-	Hays, David	House 17W 352L - not finished first of October last. Barn Poor land - good meadow.	40 x 33 70 x 30	stone	2	1A 350A	600 3900	660 4290
121	Longnecker, Christ. Henry, Andw. A110 B112 D110 E113 I- II-	Brand, Saml.	House 8W 60L - old. House Smith shop	27 x 20 16 x 12	wood	2	1A	150	165

Direct Tax of 1798 - Londonderry Township

No.	Owner/Occupant/Ref.	Adjoining	Building	Dimen.	Matls.	Stories	Acres Perch	Assmt.	Valu- ation
			Barn	60 x 20			149A	1898	2087.80
			Midling land - good meadow.						
122	**Longnecker, Danl.** Jordan, Geo. A107 B109 D107 E110 I- II-	Landis, Henry Early, John Esq.	House	28 x 24	wood	1	1A	160	176
			4W 30L - old.						
			House	20 x 18	wood	1	1A	110	121
			4W 24L - good repair.						
			Barn	70 x 30			100A	970	1067
			Poor gravel land - good meadows.						
			Barn	40 x 18			115A	1640	1804
			Dry lands (good).						
123	**Longnecker, Jacob** Longnecker, Jacob A115 B117 D115 E118 I- II-	Hays, David	House	30 x 28	stone	2	1A	700	770
			17W 190L - compleat order.						
			House	36 x 32	wood	1		140	154
			8W 60L.						
			Barn	67 x 20			200A	1860	2046
			Poor land - good meadow.						
124	**Loyter, Joseph** B118 E119 II-	Alliman, Henry	House	18 x 14			20A	170	187
			Poor land.						
125	**Lutz, Isaac** A114 D114 I-	Sibert, Henry	House	30 x 28	wood	2	1	380	418
			12W 144L - good repair.						
126	**Macklay, John Jr.** Maclay, John Jr. B129 E130 II-	Maclay, Melchor	Barn	45 x 20			99A	850	935
			Lands poor.						
127	**Mackley, Melchor** A124 B127 D124 E128 I- II-	Maclay, John	House	23 x 22	wood	1	1A	130	143
			4W 32L - old.						
			Outhouse						
			Barn	54 x 20			99A	872	959.20
			Poor land.						
128	**Maclay, John** Macklay, John Jr. A125 B128 D125 E129 I- II-	Maclay, Melchor	House	30 x 20	wood	1	1A	130	143
			5W 34L - old.						
			House	24 x 20	wood	1	1A	140	154
			3W 23L - good order.						
		Maclay, John Jr.	Barn	60 x 20			99A	1090	1199
			Poor land, good meadow.						
129	**McAllister, Alex.** A130 B134 D130 E135 I- II-	Coleman, Robt. Esq.	House	20 x 18	wood	1	1A		150
			4W 36L - Not finished - Built since 1st of October last.						
			Land				5A	35	38.50
			Poor land.						
130	**McAllister, Archbd.** Forney, Chris. A120 B123 D120 E124 I- II-	Hays, Patrick	House	37 x 24	stone	2	1	500	550
			8W 40L - good.						
			Barn	60 x 33			290A	7190	7909
			Good limestone land.						
131	**McCallan, Robt.** A123 B125 D123 E126 I- II-	McCallan, Thos.	House	35 x 20	wood	1	1	150	165
			9W 70L - part old and new.						

Direct Tax of 1798 - Londonderry Township

No.	Owner/Occupant/Ref.	Adjoining	Building	Dimen.	Matls.	Stories	Acres Perch	Assmt.	Valuation
			Barn	104 x 20			202	3320	3652
			Tolerable good land.						
132	McCallan, Thos. A119 B122 D119 E123 I- II-	McCallan, Robt.	House	37 x 25	wood	1	1A	260	286
			7W 110L - good repair.						
			Barn	34 x 20			160A	2590	2849
			Good limestone land (dry).						
133	McDonald, John A133 B137 D133 E138 I- II-	Sayer, John	House	24 x 21	wood	1	1A	150	165
			8W 88L - new and good.						
			Stable	17 x 15			9A	167	183.70
			Weaver Shop						
			Good land (dry).						
134	McRath, Thos. McElrath, Thos. Shaeffer, Jost. A131 B135 D131 E136 I- II-	Coleman, Robt. Esq. Frazier, Wm.	House	18 x 15	wood	1	1A	105	115.50
			2W 12L - a poor house.						
			House	20 x 18	wood	1	1A	120	132
			5W 45L - not good.						
			Barn	40 x 12			66A	550	605
			Barn	40 x 16			100A	830	913
			Weaver shop						
			Poor lands.						
135	Mentzger, James Minsker, James A134 B138 D134 E139 I- II-	Morrison, Jas.	House	40 x 16	wood	1	2A	102	112.20
			5W 22L - poor house.						
			Barn	36 x 14			73A	540	594
			Very poor land.						
136	Mertzell, Christn. A128 B132 D128 E133 I- II-	Coleman, Robt.	House	24 x 22	wood	1	2A	140	154
			3W 32L - midling order.						
			Stable				23A	180	198
			Very poor land.						
137	Miller, Danl. A117 B120 D117 E121 I- II-	Campbell, Elnr. Rogers, George	House	20 x 18	wood	1	2A	120	132
			4W 28L - old.						
			Barn	40 x 20			90A	775	852.50
			Weaver shop						
			Gravel land (poor).						
138	Miller, Michael A129 B133 D129 E134 I- II-	Boal, John	House	22 x 18	wood	1	1A	125	137.50
			3W 24L - poor.						
			Kitchen	14 x 12		1			
			Barn	40 x 18			119A	855	940.50
			Midling (poor, sandy) land.						
139	Miller, Rudolph B139 E140 II-	Coleman, Robt.	Land				30A	210	231
			Poor land.						
140	Mitchell, David A132 B136 D132 E137 I- II-	Mitchell, Thos.	House	25 x 20	stone	1	1A	200	220
			3W 36L - bad house.						
			Barn	58 x 18			178A	3235	3558.50
			Good limestone land.						

Direct Tax of 1798 - Londonderry Township

No.	Owner/Occupant/Ref.	Adjoining	Building	Dimen.	Matls.	Stories	Acres Perch	Assmt.	Valuation
141	Morrison, James A127 B131 D127 E132 I- II-	Kelly, Patrick	House 4W 16L - old. Barn Poor land (good meadow)	21 x 20 50 x 16	wood	1	1A 160A	105 1135	115.50 1248.50
142	Mortwell, Christn. Mertel, Christr. A126 B130 D126 E131 I- II-	Brubaker, Henry Hoffart, John	House 5W 60L - good house. Stable Poor land.	30 x 21 14 x 12	wood	1	1A 2A	130 35	143 38.50
143	Musser, Nichls. A122 B124 D122 E125 I- II-	Alliman, Henry Stickley, Abm.	House 5W 16L - Built since 1st of October. Barn Poor dry land.	27 x 24 26 x 18	wood	1	1A 62A	 340	140 374
144	Myer, John Forney, Vendel A118 D118 E127 I-	Reeser, John	House House on very poor land.	14 x 12			15A	150	165
145	Myers, John Hoover, Danl. B121 E122 II-	Weltmer, Ulrich	House 3W 40L - old Barn Part gravel and limestone land (good).	27 x 24 72 x 22	wood	1	1A 300A	170 4560	187 5016
146	Ney, William A136 B141 D136 E142 I- II-	Cooper, Christ.	House 6W 72L - good house. Barn Hemp mill Gravel land - good meadow.	30 x 20 50 x 20 20 x 12	wood	1	1A 130A	200 1260	220 1386
147	Nicholson, John Little, John Little, James A135 B140 D135 E141 I- II-	Hay, Wm. Esq.	House 3W 30L - poor house. Barn Midling land - good meadow.	30 x 28 36 x 30	wood	1	1A 300A	200 4540	220 4994
148	Noll, Christn. A137 B142 D137 E143 I- II-	Brand, David	House 8W 72L - poor house. Barn Stable Poor land.	28 x 25 50 x 18 14 x 14	wood	1	1A 149A	200 1185	220 1303.50
149	Over, Christn. A139 B144 D139 E146 I- II-	Brubacher, Henry	House 7W 79L - good order. Barn Smith shop Poor land.	33 x 38 40 x 15	wood	1	1A 33A	300 395	330 434.50
150	Over, Peter A138 B143 D138 E144 I- II-	Weltmer, Abm. Killinger, John	House 2W 24L - very poor. Barn Gravel and limestone land.	28 x 27 70 x 20	wood	1	1A 160A	120 2650	132 2915
151	Peelor, Jacob	Coleman, Robt.	House	20 x 16			100A	740	814

Direct Tax of 1798 - Londonderry Township

No.	Owner/Occupant/Ref.	Adjoining	Building	Dimen.	Matls.	Stories	Acres Perch	Assmt.	Valuation
	B149 E150 ll-								
152	Peugh, Brian A140 B146 D140 E147 l- ll-	Crotzer, John Kratzer, John	House 2W 12L - old poor house. Barn Poor land.	20 x 18 30 x 15	wood	1	2A 1A	105 28	115.50 30.8
153	Pewly, William Puly, William Twigg, Edwn. A141 B147 D141 E148 l- ll-	Bernhard, John	House 3W 38L - old poor house. Land Poor land.	24 x 18	wood	1	2 8A	105 80	115.50 88
154	Pile, Jacob A142 B148 D142 E149 l- ll-	Frazier, Wm.	House 3W 44L - good house. Barn Stony land, good meadow.	35 x 28 50 x 16	wood	1	1A 200A	200 1660	220 1826
155	Quigley, William A143 B150 D143 E151 l- ll-	Stoner, Jacob	House 3W 15L - indifferent building. Barn Midling land.	30 x 18 45 x 16	wood	1	1A 99A	110 1120	121 1232
156	Rayman, Abm. Reemor, Abraham A145 B152 D145 E153 l- ll-	Alleman, Henry Grove, Abraham	House 12W 192L - well finished. Barn Poor land, stony.	36 x 22 32 x 18	stone	1	1A 126A	400 895	440 984.50
157	Reesor, John A147 B154 D147 E155 l- ll-	Kelly, James	House 10W 120L - good well finished. Barn Poor land - good meadow.	36 x 30 70 x 26	stone	2	1A 120A	500 1130	550 1243
158	Reesor, Peter Forry, _____ A146 B153 D146 E154 l- ll-	Cole, Jacob Koble, Jacob	House 13W 186L - good house, well finished. House 2W 18L - very poor house. Barn Stable Grist mill Saw mill Midling land - good meadow.	33 x 33 16 x 16 75 x 30 14 x 12 45 x 33	stone wood	2 1	1A 2A 300A	660 5570	726 6127
159	Riegart, Adam Shuntz, Peter A150 B157 D150 E158 l- ll-	Kratzer, John	House 4W 40L - midling house. House Stable Stable Poor land - dry.	26 x 24 20 x 16 25 x 18 15 x 12	wood wood	1 1	1 2 138A 2A	115 105 985 24	126.50 115.50 1083.50 26.40
160	Riegart, John Ney, Nichls. A148 B155 D148 E156 l- ll-	Hershey, Benjm. Boyer, Mrs.	House 7W 40L - not very good. Barn	30 x 20 50 x 78	wood	1	1A 24A	105 515	115.50 566.50

Direct Tax of 1798 - Londonderry Township

No.	Owner/Occupant/Ref.	Adjoining	Building	Dimen.	Matls.	Stories	Acres Perch	Assmt.	Valuation
			Thin poor land.						
161	**Rodgers, George** A144 B151 D144 E152 I- II-	Miller, Danl.	House 4W 30L - poor building. Barn Midling land - good meadow.	26 x 22 70 x 16	wood	1	2A 148A	150 1530	165 1573
162	**Rugar, Jacob** **Reegar, Jacob** Dousenberger, Jacob Doubenberger, ___ A149 B156 D149 E157 I- II-	Witmyer, David Hays, David	House 5W 60L - decay situation. House 9W 105L - midling good. Wash house 2W 6L. Barn Good land - dry. Barn Thin land - good meadow. Outhouse Smith shop	28 x 24 30 x 20 16 x 12 60 x 20 60 x 26	wood wood wood	2 2 1	1A 1A 1A 84A 209A	500 350 1610 1800	550 385 1771 1980
163	**Sayer, John Jr.** **Sawyer, John** Stewart, John A164 B171 D164 E173 I- II-	Bowman, Jacob Mitchell, David	House 6W 59L - good and old house. House 3W 27L Barn Stable Good land - dry.	45 x 20 20 x 18 90 x 30 20 x 18	wood wood	1 1	1A 1A 220A	260 105 3695	280 115.50 4064.50
164	**Sayer, Joseph** **Sawyer, Joseph** A163 B172 D163 E174 I- II-	Sayer, John Sawyer, John	House 7W 70L - midling good. Barn Good land (dry).	32 x 16 60 x 24	wood	1	1A 200A	180 3380	198 3718
165	**Sayer, Widow** **Sawyer, Widow** Orr, John A165 B178 D165 E175 I- II-	Luther?, Saml. Wolfelsberger, Philip	House 12W 251L - excellent and in good repair. House 3W 27L - ancient house. Kitchen 3W 33L. Barn Barn Good land.	32 x 28 40 x 18 26 x 16 60 x 28 22 x 14	stone wood stone	2 1 1	1A 1A 224A	700 105 4590	770 115.50 5049
166	**Sayer, Willm. Est.** McClarey, Alex. A161 B168 D161 E170 I- II-	Sayers, Widow Bradly, Widow	House 6W 72L - tolerable repair. Barn Good land.	30 x 27 48 x 27	wood	1	1A 224A	300 4115	330 4526.50
167	**Shaeffer, George** **Shaffer, George** A166 B174 D166 E176 I- II-	Karmany, Anthy.	House 2W 24L - poor house. Barn Gravel thin land.	21 x 15 40 x 18	wood	1	2A 147A	105 1385	115.50 1523.50

Direct Tax of 1798 - Londonderry Township

No.	Owner/Occupant/Ref.	Adjoining	Building	Dimen.	Matls.	Stories	Acres Perch	Assmt.	Valuation
168	**Shank, Adam** A154 B161 D154 E162 I- II-	Shank, Michael	House 10W 120L - well finished. Barn Stony land - mid. meadow.	33 x 28 64 x 26	stone	1	1A 139A	350 1330	385 1463
169	**Shank, Michael** A153 B160 D153 E161 I- II-	Shank, Adam	House 7W 84L - good and well finished. Barn Stony land - good meadow.	36 x 33 87 x 25	stone	1	1A 149A	500 1445	550 1589.50
170	**Sharp,** _____ Thompson, Saml. A152 B159 D152 E160 I- II-	Boger, Mrs. Swatara Creek	House 5W 35L - old and of little value. Barn Poor land.	34 x 26 55 x 22	wood	1	2A 230A	150 2770	165 3047
171	**Sheller, Adam** A158 B165 D158 E167 I- II-	Merkley, John McClay, John	House 16W 154L - the whole not finished. Barn Poor land, good meadow.	49 x 30 49 x 25	stone	2	1A 179A	450 1545	495 1699.50
172	**Shire, George** A168 B176 D168 E178 I- II-	Coleman, Robt. Esq.	House 2W 28L - very bad. Barn Poor land.	28 x 24 35 x 20	wood	1	1A 100A	130 780	143 858
173	**Shire, Jacob** A167 B175 D167 E177 I- II-	Coleman, Robt. land	House 4W 36L - good house. Barn Poor land.	26 x 24 45 x 17	wood	1	1A 69A	160 545	176 599.50
174	**Shitz, Maths.** Shutz, Mathias B169 E171 II-	Bradley, Widow	House Poor land.	18 x 14			2A	80	88
175	**Sower, Henry** Server, Henry Shriver, Henry A162 B170 D162 E172 I- II-	Lutz, Isaac Dearmon, Joseph	House 6W 72L - unfinished. Stable Smith shop Good land (dry).	34 x 21 26 x 18	stone/wd.	2	1 25A	200 465	220 511.50
176	**Stevick, Charles** Stevcek, Christn. A156 B163 D156 E164 I- II-	Stevick, John	House 3W 9L - old and of little value. Stable Poor land - mid. meadow.	28 x 24 22 x 20	wood	1	2A 108A	102 1205	112.20 1325.50
177	**Stevick, John** A155 B162 D155 E163 I- II-	Johnston, David	House 3W 18L - old. Barn Poor land, stony.	25 x 23 48 x 18	wood	1	2A 86A	105 655	115.50 720.50
178	**Stickley, Abm.** A157 B164 D157 E165 I- II-	Bransteller, Andw.	House 4W 13L - new, good, and well built. Barn	27 x 20 60 x 20	wood	1	1A 106A	150 910	165 1001

Direct Tax of 1798 - Londonderry Township

No.	Owner/Occupant/Ref.	Adjoining	Building	Dimen.	Matls.	Stories	Acres Perch	Assmt.	Valu-ation
			Poor land - mid. meadow.						
179	**Stoner, Christr.** A151 B158 D151 E159 I- II-	Hays, Robt.	House	30 x 30 13W 176L - old and unfinished.	stone	2	1A	620	682
			Kitchen	25 x 15 4W 48L.	stone	2			
			Barn Good land - limestone.	60 x 30			239A	502	572
180	**Stoner, Jacob** A159 B166 D159 E168 I- II-	Anderson, James Hay, Wm. Esq.	House	30 x 21 5W 60L - indifferent building.	wood	1	1A	150	165
			Barn Poor land.	73 x 30			130A	1830	2013
			Land Mid. land.				100A	1100	1210
181	**Stoufer, Henry** **Staufer, Henry** A160 B167 D160 E169 I- II-	Coble, Jacob	House	50 x 18 4W 22L - little value.	wood	1	1A	160	176
			Barn Poor land - out of order.	50 x 20			126A 42P	1425	1567.50
182	**Thoma, Martin** A169 B178 D169 E180 I- II-	Wolfersberger, Philip	Kitchen	30 x 27 12W 144L - old, good.	stone	2	1A	480	528
			Wash house	16 x 12 2W 8L	stone	1			
			Barn Out house Midling land - good meadow.	65 x 25			371A	5875	6462.50
183	**Ulrich, Michael** B179 E181 II-	Coleman, Robt. Esq.	Land Poor land.				20A	140	154
184	**Weltmer, Abm.** A173 B184 D173 E186 I- II-	Brown, David Dininger, Adm.	House	27 x 18 8W 72L - midling.	wood	1	1A	130	143
			Barn Gravel and limestone land.	58 x 27			205A	2920	3212
185	**Weltmer, Ulrich** A171 B182 D171 E184 I- II-	Landis, Henry	House	35 x 32 17W 231L - new building, unfinished but occupied.	stone	2	1	610	671
			Kitchen	14 x 14 1W 12L	stone	1			
		Myers, John	House Barn Good land.	20 x 14 52 x 32			237A	4575	5032.50
186	**White, Thos.** A175 B186 D175 E187 I- II-	Boyer, Widow	House	26 x 20 5W 32L - poor house.	wood	1	1A	120	132
			Barn Poor hilly land.	50 x 18			24A	198	217.80
187	**Witmyer, David** **Wittemyer, David** A170 B180 D170 E182 I- II-	Landis, John	House	20 x 15 3W 25L - old and bad.	stone	1	1A	216	237.60
			Kitchen	12 x 6	stone	1			

Direct Tax of 1798 - Londonderry Township

No.	Owner/Occupant/Ref.	Adjoining	Building	Dimen.	Matls.	Stories	Acres Perch	Assmt.	Valuation
			4W 40L Barn	70 x 20			126A 80P	2205	2425.50
			Land midling - dry.						
188	**Wolf, Barbara** B181 E183 II-	Plugar, John	House Stable	20 x 14 12 x 10			2A	60	66
			Poor land.						
189	**Wolfelsberger, Fred.** A176 B187 D176 E188 I- II-	Wolfersberger, Philip	House 14W 168L	32 x 28	wood	2	1A	600	660
			Stable	18 x 16			2A	75	82.50
			Good land.						
190	**Wolfelsberger, Philip** Shidenhawer, John A177 B188 D177 E189 I- II-	Wolfelsberger, Fred Thoma, Martin	House 8W 84L	33 x 25	wood	2	1A	200	220
			House 4W 24L - of little value.	20 x 18	wood	1	1A	105	115.50
			Barn	96 x 34			450A	7810	8591
			Good land - a small part gravel.						
191	**Wolfersberger, John** A174 B185 D174 I- II-	Wolfersberger, Philip	House 5W 45L - poor house.	20 X 22	wood	1	1A	200	220
			Barn	40 x 22					
192	**Wray, David** A172 B183 D172 E185 I- II-	Hay, Patrick	House 9W 93L - "compleatly finished."	32 x 25	wood	1 1/2	1A	340	374
			Barn	49 x 17			196A	1865	2051.50
			House Stable	20 x 18					
			Poor land.						

INDEX

The Index includes all variations of spelling used by the assessors. If a name with the same spelling appears more than one time on a specific page, a parenthetical number appears by the name indicating the number of times the name is listed on the page.

A separate column lists the township where the specific name appears. Abbreviations for the townships are:

Bethel Township	BE
East Hanover Township	EH
Heidelberg Township	HD
Lebanon Township	LE
Londonderry Township	LO

INDEX

Name	Page	Code	Name	Page	Code	Name	Page	Code
Ache, John	11	BE	Arnold, John	128	LE	Baylor, Simon	95	LE
Achenbach, Anthony	54	HD	Arnold, John	141	LE	Bayly, William	110	LE
Achenbach, Arnt	88	LE	Arnold, John Jr.	88	LE	Beadley, Samuel	144	LO
Achenbach, Arnt	90	LE	Arnold, John Sr.	88	LE	Beal, John	142	LO
Achenbach, Arnt	127	LE	Arnt, Jacob	88	LE	Beal, William	142	LO
Achenbach, John	88	LE	Arnt, Jacob	138	LE	Bealy, Adam	90	LE
Achey, John	24	BE	Artz, Christn.	54	HD	Beam, George	65	HD
Achey, John	38	BE	Artz, John	11	BE	Bean?, Jacob	27	BE
Achey, Peter	124	LE	Baasler, Adam	54	HD	Beanstetter, Andw.	144	LO
Achy, Henry	54	HD	Baasler, Simon	74	HD	Beany, Melchor	16	BE
Achy, Henry	64	HD	Baasler, Simon (2)	54	HD	Beany, Melchor	17	BE
Achy, Henry (2)	82	HD	Baasler, Simon, Exr.	55	HD	Beany, Melchor	35	BE
Achy, Samuel	54	HD	Bacastose, Henry	11	BE	Beashore, George	40	EH
Achy, Samuel	83	HD	Bacastose, Jacob (2)	11	BE	Beashore, Mathias	40	EH
Ainsworth, John	39	EH	Bachman, Christian	92	LE	Bechel, Rudolph	91	LE
Ainsworth, John	43	EH	Bachman, Christn.	88	LE	Beck, Christian	89	LE
Ainsworth, John	47	EH	Bachman, Christn.	110	LE	Beck, Christian	95	LE
Ainsworth, John	48	EH	Bachman, Christn.	136	LE	Beck, John	129	LE
Ainsworth, John	50	EH	Bachman, Christn. (2)	112	LE	Beck, John Ph.	94	LE
Ainsworth, Widow	39	EH	Bachman, Christn. Jr.	89	LE	Beck, John Philip	89	LE
Alberdal, Francis	39	EH	Backenstose, Henry	30	BE	Beck, Michael	11	BE
Alberdal, John	39	EH	Backenstose, Henry	34	BE	Beck, Philip	14	BE
Alberdal, Nichlos	39	EH	Backenstose, Jacob	35	BE	Beck, Philip	26	BE
Alberdal, Nicholas	39	EH	Backenstose, Jacob	39	EH	Becker, Christian	105	LE
Alberdall, Nichlos	51	EH	Backenstose, John Sr.	39	EH	Becker, Frederick	55	HD
Albert, Nicholas	11	BE	Bader, Geo.	16	BE	Becker, George	66	HD
Albertall, Frances	41	EH	Badorff, John	55	HD	Becker, George	72	HD
Albertall, Francis	51	EH	Badorff, Peter	80	HD	Becker, George Jr.	55	HD
Albrecht, Martin	54	HD	Badorff, Peter (2)	55	HD	Becker, George Sr.	55	HD
Albrecht, Widow	54	HD	Baggs, James (2)	145	LO	Becker, Jacob	12	BE
Albright, John	46	EH	Ballum, John Dr.	142	LO	Becker, Jacob	90	LE
Albright, John (2)	39	EH	Ballum, Wm.	142	LO	Becker, John	12	BE
Albright, John (2)	52	EH	Balm, Doctor	143	LO	Becker, John	31	BE
Aliman, Hen.	142	LO	Balm, Doctor	146	LO	Becker, John	55	HD
Alleman, Henry	142	LO	Balm, John Dr.	142	LO	Becker, John	58	HD
Alleman, Henry	160	LO	Balm, Michl.	143	LO	Becker, Nichls.	55	HD
Alleman, John	110	LE	Balm, William	142	LO	Becker, Philip	90	LE
Alleman, Leonard	88	LE	Balm, Wm.	146	LO	Beckly, Frederick	55	HD
Alleman, Leond.	102	LE	Balm, Wm.	153	LO	Beckly, George	90	LE
Alleman, Leonhard	100	LE	Bamberger, John	89	LE	Beckly, Uhrich (2)	90	LE
Alleman, Leonhard	102	LE	Bamberger, Joseph	89	LE	Beckly, Ulrich	97	LE
Alleman, Leonhart	124	LE	Bamgartner, Philip	39	EH	Beckly, Ulrich	122	LE
Alliman, Henry	157	LO	Bard, Adam	108	LE	Bee, John	55	HD
Alliman, Henry	159	LO	Bard, Adam Jr.	89	LE	Beecher, Jacob	90	LE
Alliman, Henry (2)	149	LO	Bard, Adam Sr.	89	LE	Beecher, Jacob	94	LE
Allwein, Conrad	88	LE	Bard, John	89	LE	Beehlor, Henry	94	LE
Allwein, Conrad	94	LE	Barr, George	83	HD	Beekly, Adam	90	LE
Allwein, Conrad	99	LE	Barthmay, Adam	40	EH	Beeley, Adam	90	LE
Allwein, Conrad	117	LE	Bartlemy, Vendle	40	EH	Beelor, Simon	95	LE
Allwine, Conrad	88	LE	Bartram, James (2)	145	LO	Beem, Rudy	92	LE
Alstad, John	88	LE	Bartto, Anthony	99	LE	Been, Abram	95	LE
Alstat, John	128	LE	Basler, Simon	54	HD	Been, Henry	12	BE
Altstad, John	100	LE	Batteicher, Casper	11	BE	Beever. Dietrich	90	LE
Alwine, Conrad	117	LE	Batteicher, Saml.	11	BE	Beiler, Christian	56	HD
Alwine, Werner	31	BE	Batteigor, Casper	11	BE	Beiler, John	56	HD
Anderson, James	11	BE	Bauman, Geo.	96	LE	Beiler, John	68	HD
Anderson, James	142	LO	Bauman, Geo.	130	LE	Beiler, John	83	HD
Anderson, James	163	LO	Bauman, Geo.	131	LE	Bell, Robert	40	EH
Andrews, Hugh (2)	39	EH	Bauman, George	89	LE	Bell, Robert	43	EH
Angst, Nichls.	52	EH	Bauman, John	89	LE	Bell, Robt.	51	EH
Ardtz, John	25	BE	Bauman, John	102	LE	Belteon, Phlip	142	LO
Armeshan, Mathias	54	HD	Bauman, Widow	89	LE	Ben, Henry	12	BE
Arnold, Herman (2)	88	LE	Bayley, William	128	LE	Ben, Jacob	12	BE
Arnold, John	109	LE	Baylor, Harvey	110	LE	Bender, Adam	12	BE

INDEX

Name	Page	Code
Bene, Henry	12	BE
Bene, Jacob	12	BE
Bennage, Henry	56	HD
Benner, Charles	90	LE
Benner, John	90	LE
Benner, Martin	56	HD
Beny, John	12	BE
Beny, Melchior	12	BE
Beny, Melchor	15	BE
Beny, Melchr.	11	BE
Bergenhof, Wilm.	129	LE
Bergenhof, Wilm.	134	LE
Bergenhoff, Wm.	88	LE
Bergenhoff, Wm.	90	LE
Bernhard, Herman	142	LO
Bernhard, John	143	LO
Bernhard, John	147	LO
Bernhard, John	160	LO
Berry, Conrad	90	LE
Berry, Henry	91	LE
Berry, Henry	95	LE
Berry, Peter	91	LE
Berry, Peter	111	LE
Beshor, Elisabh.	12	BE
Beshor, John	15	BE
Beshor, John (2)	13	BE
Beshor, John (3)	12	BE
Beshor, Peter	13	BE
Beshor, Peter	15	BE
Beshore, George	45	EH
Beshore, Henry	136	LE
Besore, George	40	EH
Besore, George	46	EH
Besore, George	53	EH
Besore, George (2)	45	EH
Besore, Henry	92	LE
Besore, Isaac	40	EH
Besore, Isaac	45	EH
Besore, Isaac	51	EH
Besore, John	30	BE
Besore, John	33	BE
Besore, Mathias	40	EH
Besore, Mathias	41	EH
Besore, Peter	17	BE
Besore, Widow	30	BE
Betleem, Isaac	143	LO
Betleem, Philip	142	LO
Betleem, Philip	146	LO
Betleem, Philip	155	LO
Bettz, Samuel	56	HD
Betz, Casper	91	LE
Beyer, John	92	LE
Beyer, Michl. Est.	92	LE
Beyer, Michl. Est.	97	LE
Beyer, Philip Est.	93	LE
Bibel, John	125	LE
Bickel, John	21	BE
Bickel, John	28	BE
Bickel, John	33	BE
Bickel, John	38	BE
Bickel, John Esq.	13	BE
Bickel, John Esq.	40	EH
Bickel, Rudolph	91	LE
Bickel, Rudolph	93	LE
Bickle, John	13	BE
Bickle, John Jr.	13	BE
Biebel, John	91	LE
Bigham, James	145	LO
Bigham, Joseph	43	EH
Bile, Fredrick	124	LE
Bingham, Jas. (2)	146	LO
Bishoff, Jacob	142	LO
Bitner, Mathias (2)	56	HD
Bixler, Joseph	13	BE
Bixler, Joseph	21	BE
Bixler, Joseph	144	LO
Blauch, Abm.	91	LE
Blauch, John	91	LE
Blauch, John	122	LE
Blauch, John	123	LE
Blauch, John	137	LE
Blecher, Jacob	56	HD
Blecher, John Est.	91	LE
Blecher, Widow	56	HD
Blecker, George	58	HD
Bleistein, George	91	LE
Bleistone, Abram	95	LE
Bleistone, Geo.	91	LE
Bleistone, Isaac	91	LE
Bleystone, Isaac	95	LE
Blouch, Abm.	90	LE
Blouch, Abm.	91	LE
Blough, Abraham	91	LE
Blough, Christ.	146	LO
Blough, John	122	LE
Blough, John	123	LE
Blough, John	137	LE
Blough, John	138	LE
Blystine, Isaac	91	LE
Blystone, George	91	LE
Boal, Frances	107	LE
Boal, Frank	91	LE
Boal, John	142	LO
Boal, John	158	LO
Boal, Robert	40	EH
Boal, Robt.	40	EH
Boal, Robt.	43	EH
Boal, Robt.	51	EH
Boal, Robt.	53	EH
Bob, Daniel	56	HD
Bobb, Daniel	63	HD
Bobb, Daniel	83	HD
Boehm, Jacob	91	LE
Boehm, Jacob	92	LE
Boehm, Rudolph	91	LE
Boehm, Rudolph	92	LE
Boeshor, Henry	92	LE
Boeshore, Abm.	84	HD
Boeshore, Adam	56	HD
Boger, Mrs.	162	LO
Boger, Valentine	92	LE
Boger, Valentine	94	LE
Boger, Valentine	130	LE
Bolton, Felty	51	EH
Bolton, Valtn.	51	EH
Boltz, _____	95	LE
Boltz, Geo.	91	LE
Boltz, Geo.	92	LE
Boltz, George	92	LE
Boltz, Jacob (2)	92	LE
Boltz, Michael	92	LE
Bombartner, Philip	45	EH
Bomberger, Christly	45	EH
Bomberger, Joseph	115	LE
Bomberger, Josh	134	LE
Boomer, Jacob	102	LE
Borckholder, Ulrich	121	LE
Borgner, Peter	92	LE
Borkert, George	92	LE
Borkhard, Geo.	91	LE
Borkholter, Abrahm.	92	LE
Borkholter, Christ	92	LE
Borkholter, Christn.	89	LE
Borkholter, Christn.	92	LE
Borkner, Peter	92	LE
Boticher, Casper	35	BE
Botiger, Casper	27	BE
Botiger, Casper	35	BE
Botiger, Caspr.	27	BE
Botiger, Saml.	19	BE
Bowan, James	40	EH
Bowen, James	53	EH
Bowen, James (2)	52	EH
Bowen, Jas.	52	EH
Bowman, Geo.	89	LE
Bowman, George	130	LE
Bowman, George	131	LE
Bowman, Henry (2)	143	LO
Bowman, Jacob	142	LO
Bowman, Jacob	147	LO
Bowman, Jacob	154	LO
Bowman, Jacob	161	LO
Bowman, Jacob (3)	143	LO
Bowman, John	89	LE
Bowman, John	132	LE
Bowman, John	148	LO
Boyd, Benjamin	143	LO
Boyd, Elizabeth	143	LO
Boyer, John	13	BE
Boyer, John	139	LE
Boyer, Michl. Est.	92	LE
Boyer, Mrs.	160	LO
Boyer, Philip Est.	93	LE
Boyer, Phillip	57	HD
Boyer, Widow (2)	143	LO
Bradley, Danl. Esq.	40	EH
Bradley, Saml.	143	LO
Bradley, Widow	146	LO
Bradley, Widow	162	LO
Bradley, Widow heirs	143	LO
Bradly, Danl.	40	EH
Bradly, Danl. Esq.	52	EH
Bradly, Samuel	144	LO
Bradly, Widow	152	LO
Bradly, Widow	161	LO
Brado, Kitty	13	BE
Brand, Adam	13	BE
Brand, Christian	93	LE
Brand, Christian	102	LE
Brand, Christn.	93	LE
Brand, Christn.	99	LE
Brand, Christn.	107	LE

INDEX

Name	Page	Code	Name	Page	Code	Name	Page	Code
Brand, David	144	LO	Brightbill, Peter	43	EH	Burkholder, Ulrich est.	95	LE
Brand, David	159	LO	Brost, George	40	EH	Burky, Henry	58	HD
Brand, Henry	93	LE	Brough, Daniel	116	LE	Burky, Henry	74	HD
Brand, Isaac	93	LE	Brown, ____	153	LO	Burnett, Widow	146	LO
Brand, Isaac	134	LE	Brown, Adam	59	HD	Bush, Maria	95	LE
Brand, Joseph	144	LO	Brown, Andrew	25	BE	Bush, Marry	95	LE
Brand, Saml.	144	LO	Brown, David	163	LO	Bush, Martin	95	LE
Brand, Saml.	146	LO	Brown, David (2)	14	BE	Bushong, Jacob	91	LE
Brand, Saml.	156	LO	Brown, Henry	96	LE	Bushong, Jacob	95	LE
Brandt, Isaac	88	LE	Brown, Jacob (2)	14	BE	Byer, John	97	LE
Branstator, Andw.	144	LO	Brown, John	28	BE	Calender, Cloud	95	LE
Bransteller, Andw.	162	LO	Brown, Philip	15	BE	Camp, Jacob	148	LO
Braun, George (heirs)	57	HD	Brown, Philip	144	LO	Camp, John	24	BE
Braun, Michael	56	HD	Brown, Phillip	57	HD	Camp, John	27	BE
Braun, Michael	57	HD	Brown, Widow	57	HD	Camp, John	38	BE
Braun, Michael	74	HD	Brownewell, Maths.	93	LE	Camp, Mathias	28	BE
Braun, Phillip	57	HD	Brubacher, Benjm.	153	LO	Campbell, Elenor	148	LO
Braunewde, Maths.	94	LE	Brubacher, Henry	159	LO	Campbell, Ellenor	145	LO
Braunewell, John	93	LE	Brubacker, Benj.	144	LO	Campbell, Elnr.	158	LO
Braunewell, Mathias	93	LE	Brubacker, Henry	144	LO	Campbell, John	14	BE
Breamer, Adam	93	LE	Brubaker, Daniel	57	HD	Campbell, John	41	EH
Breamer, Conrad	93	LE	Brubaker, Danl.	87	HD	Campbell, John	145	LO
Breamer, Conrad	140	LE	Brubaker, Henry	159	LO	Campbell, Margt.	41	EH
Brechbiel, Henry	93	LE	Brubecker, Benj.	144	LO	Campbell, Robt.	145	LO
Brechbiel, Henry	97	LE	Bruner, Daniel	14	BE	Campbell, William	41	EH
Brechbiel, Jacob	93	LE	Bruner, Henry	44	EH	Campbell, Wm.	39	EH
Brechbiel, Nichls.	93	LE	Bryan, Edward	145	LO	Campbell, Wm.	41	EH
Brechbil, Jacob	131	LE	Bucher, Benedict	94	LE	Camred, Ludwig	107	LE
Brechbill,	94	LE	Bucher, Conrad	124	LE	Canal Company	58	HD
Brechbill, Jacob	93	LE	Bucher, George	94	LE	Canal Company	95	LE
Brecht, John	13	BE	Bucher, Jacob	129	LE	Capp, Barbara	95	LE
Brecht, John	32	BE	Bucher, Peter	14	BE	Capp, Christian	14	BE
Brecht, Phillip	57	HD	Bucher, Peter	28	BE	Capp, Christn.	14	BE
Brecht, Widow	57	HD	Buchler, George	122	LE	Capp, Christoph	30	BE
Breckbill, Henry	41	EH	Buchler, Henry	94	LE	Capp, Christopher	14	BE
Breckbill, John	41	EH	BuchMeier, John	14	BE	Capp, Jacob	12	BE
Breehbill, John	91	LE	Buchmyer, John	14	BE	Capp, Jacob	13	BE
Breidenbach, Phillip	57	HD	Buchter, John	99	LE	Capp, Jacob	14	BE
Breitenbach, John	93	LE	Buck, Christrian	145	LO	Capp, Jacob	36	BE
Breitenbach, John	101	LE	Buecher, Jacob	94	LE	Carmany, Joseph	146	LO
Breitenbach, John	137	LE	Buehler, Christ.	94	LE	Carsnetts, Peter	145	LO
Brekbill, John	41	EH	Buehler, Francis	95	LE	Carver, Jacob	144	LO
Brekbill, John Jr.	41	EH	Buehler, Geo. Est.	94	LE	Casel, Christn.	96	LE
Brekbill, Peter	41	EH	Buehler, George	95	LE	Casel, Christn.	121	LE
Brekbill, Peter	43	EH	Buehler, George est.	140	LE	Casper, John	149	LO
Bremmer, Adam	93	LE	Buehler, Henry	94	LE	Cassart, John	47	EH
Breneisen, Jacob	120	LE	Buehler, Henry	95	LE	Cassel, Christn.	96	LE
Breneisen, Jacob	128	LE	Buehler, Henry	125	LE	Cassenett, Peter	151	LO
Breneison, Jacob	113	LE	Buehler, Henry	135	LE	Ceerer, Conrad	96	LE
Breneison, Jacob	133	LE	Buehler, Simon	95	LE	Cenner, Conrad	96	LE
Breneyson, Jacob	94	LE	Bueler, Henry	117	LE	Clark, Benjamin	45	EH
Brenisen, Jacob	92	LE	Bullman, Fredk.	58	HD	Clark, Benjamin	51	EH
Brenisen, Jacob	94	LE	Bullman, John	58	HD	Clark, Benjamin Jr.	41	EH
Brenner, Conrad	93	LE	Bullman, John	73	HD	Clark, Thomas	15	BE
Brensencober, Casp.	14	BE	Bullman, John	74	HD	Clark, Thomas	44	EH
Brensenkobr, Casp.	14	BE	Bullman, John	84	HD	Clark, Thomas	53	EH
Brichbill, John	14	BE	Bumgartner, Henry	46	EH	Clark, Thomas	94	LE
Bricker, Christn.	94	LE	Bun, Henry (2)	14	BE	Clark, Thomas	96	LE
Bricker, Christn.	114	LE	Bun, Jacob	14	BE	Clark, Thomas	113	LE
Bricker, Jacob	71	HD	Bunger, Jacob	102	LE	Clark, Thomas	129	LE
Bridenbach, John	93	LE	Bunner, Henry Esq.	58	HD	Clark, Thomas	134	LE
Bright, John (2)	19	BE	Burckholder, Ulrich	122	LE	Clark, Thomas Esq.	41	EH
Brightbill, John	41	EH	Burkert, George	95	LE	Clark, Thomas Esq.	45	EH
Brightbill, Peter	41	EH	Burkhart, ____	109	LE	Clark, Walter	145	LO

INDEX

Name	Page	Code	Name	Page	Code	Name	Page	Code
Clark, Walter	150	LO	Crawford, Saml.	145	LO	Dinius, Nichls.	97	LE
Clark, Walter	151	LO	Crill, John	56	HD	Dinius, Philip	90	LE
Clark, Walter	154	LO	Crotzer, John	149	LO	Dinius, Philip	97	LE
Clinefelter, Abm.	18	BE	Crotzer, John	160	LO	Dinninger, John	50	EH
Cober, Jacob	144	LO	Cumberland St.	98	LE	Dishong, David	97	LE
Coble, Jacob	145	LO	Darkis, John	42	EH	Dishong, David	102	LE
Coble, Jacob	163	LO	Darkis, Michael	42	EH	Dissinger, Geo.	59	HD
Colb, Philip	30	BE	Dasher, Alexr.	146	LO	Dissinger, Geo.	64	HD
Cole, Jacob	160	LO	Daub, Conrad	97	LE	Dissinger, John	59	HD
Colebrook Furnace	145	LO	Daub, Dillman	97	LE	Ditman, John	59	HD
Colebrook Furnace	146	LO	Daub, Dillman	128	LE	Ditman, John (2)	67	HD
Coleman, Robert	96	LE	Daub, Dillman	138	LE	Ditzler, Casper	15	BE
Coleman, Robert Esq.	58	HD	Daub, John	15	BE	Ditzler, Casper	16	BE
Coleman, Robt. land	152	LO	David, Daniel	69	HD	Ditzler, Casper	20	BE
Coleman, Robt.	86	HD	Dearman, Joseph	146	LO	Ditzler, Casper (2)	28	BE
Coleman, Robt.	110	LE	Dearmon, Joseph	162	LO	Ditzler, Christ.	59	HD
Coleman, Robt.	147	LO	Deckert, Jacob	69	HD	Ditzler, Christian	71	HD
Coleman, Robt.	154	LO	Deckert, Jacob (2)	58	HD	Ditzler, Christian	78	HD
Coleman, Robt.	153	LO	Deiss, David	15	BE	Ditzler, Christian (2)	59	HD
Coleman, Robt.	159	LO	Deiss, John	16	BE	Ditzler, Christn.	71	HD
Coleman, Robt. (2)	89	LE	Dellebach, Peter	147	LO	Dixler, Abraham	15	BE
Coleman, Robt. (2)	158	LO	Dengler, John	58	HD	Dixler, Casper	16	BE
Coleman, Robt. Esq.	86	HD	Deninger, Adm.	146	LO	Doebler, Abraham	126	LE
Coleman, Robt. Esq.	145	LO	Deninger, John	42	EH	Doebler, Abraham	137	LE
Coleman, Robt. Esq.	146	LO	Deninger, Michl.	146	LO	Doebler, Abrahm.	88	LE
Coleman, Robt. Esq.	150	LO	Deninger, Michl.	147	LO	Doebler, Abram	97	LE
Coleman, Robt. Esq.	157	LO	Denius, Jacob	70	HD	Doebler, Anthony	97	LE
Coleman, Robt. Esq.	158	LO	Derr, Rudolph	15	BE	Doebler, Anthony	101	LE
Coleman, Robt. Esq.	163	LO	Derr, Rudolph	22	BE	Doebler, Anthy.	103	LE
Coleman, Robt. Esq. (2)	148	LO	Desh, John	37	BE	Dohner, Henry	98	LE
Coleman, Robt. Esq. (2)	162	LO	Desh, John (2)	15	BE	Dohner, Henry	105	LE
Coleman, Robt. land	42	EH	Desh, Margaret	15	BE	Dohner, Jacob	98	LE
Coleman, Robt. land	144	LO	Desh, Margaret	34	BE	Dohner, Jacob	102	LE
Coleman, Robt. land	149	LO	Detweiler, John	91	LE	Dohner, Jacob	103	LE
Coleman, Robt. land	153	LO	Detweiler, John	97	LE	Dohner, John	98	LE
Conrad, Christ.	77	HD	Dewees, David	24	BE	Dohner, John (2)	93	LE
Conrad, George	96	LE	Dey, Abm.	155	LO	Dohner, Joseph	136	LE
Conrad, Jacob	15	BE	Deyermond, Joseph	146	LO	Dohner, Joseph (2)	98	LE
Conrad, Jacob	20	BE	Dice, David	15	BE	Dolebach, Peter	147	LO
Contrehman, Jacob	90	LE	Dice, David	21	BE	Doll, Leonard	147	LO
Contreman, Danl.	151	LO	Dice, David	26	BE	Doll, Leonard	155	LO
Cook, John	144	LO	Dice, David (2)	22	BE	Dollinger, Geo.	31	BE
Cooke, John Esq.	146	LO	Dice, John	16	BE	Dollinger, Georg	20	BE
Cooper, Christ.	154	LO	Diel, _____	78	HD	Dooner, Henry	98	LE
Cooper, Christ.	159	LO	Diel, Abm.	63	HD	Dooner, Jacob	98	LE
Copenhaver, Thos.	41	EH	Diel, Abram	59	HD	Dooner, Joseph	98	LE
Copenhever, Thos.	40	EH	Diel, Abram	67	HD	Dorman, Ludwig	98	LE
Copinhaffer, Thos.	41	EH	Dierwechter, Ehrhart	59	HD	Dorsh, Peter	98	LE
Coppenheffer, H.	80	HD	Dierwechter, Ehrhart	61	HD	Dorsht, Abm.	145	LO
Coppenheffer, Henry	74	HD	Dierwechter, Ehrhart	80	HD	Dorst, Peter	98	LE
Coppenheffer, Henry	75	HD	Dietz, John	97	LE	Doubenberger, _____	161	LO
Coppenheffer, Widow	69	HD	Dietz, John	103	LE	Douglass, John	147	LO
Core, Christian	40	EH	Diffebach, Benj.	59	HD	Dousenberger, Jacob	161	LO
Core, John	37	BE	Diffebach, Peter	59	HD	Downe, Charles	99	LE
Core, Michl.	27	BE	Diffebach, Widow	59	HD	Drion, George	98	LE
Cornwall Furnace	96	LE	Diffenbach, Benjm.	59	HD	Dryon, George	98	LE
Cossart, Jacob	41	EH	Diffenbach, Benjm.	71	HD	Dubbs, Henry	16	BE
Cossart, John	41	EH	Dininger, Adam	147	LO	Dubbs, John	16	BE
Cossart, John	42	EH	Dininger, Adm.	163	LO	Dubbs, John	29	BE
Cossart, John	49	EH	Dininger, John	39	EH	Dubler, Morris	60	HD
Cossert, John	45	EH	Dininger, John	42	EH	Dubler, Widow	60	HD
Coyar, Casper	146	LO	Dininger, Michl.	153	LO	Dubs, Henry	26	BE
Craig, John	146	LO	Dinius, Jacob	97	LE	Dubs, Henry	38	BE
Cratzer, John	146	LO	Dinius, Jacob	115	LE	Dubs, Henry	98	LE

INDEX

Name	Page	Code
Dubs, Henry (2)	37	BE
Dubs, Jacob	42	EH
Dubs, Jacob	53	EH
Dubs, John	31	BE
Dubs, John	32	BE
Dubs, John	98	LE
Dubs, John	115	LE
Dubs, John	119	LE
Dubs, John	133	LE
Dubs, Martin	94	LE
Dubs, Martin	98	LE
Duglass, John	147	LO
Dull, Leonard	147	LO
Duncan, James	147	LO
Duncan, Ph.	60	HD
Dups, John	16	BE
Durst, Peter	98	LE
Durst, Peter	128	LE
Dutweiler, John	89	LE
Dutweiler, John	97	LE
Dutweiler, John	125	LE
Early, John Esq.	143	LO
Early, John Esq.	147	LO
Early, John Esq.	156	LO
Early, John Esq.	157	LO
Early, Thomas	147	LO
Early, Thos.	151	LO
Eather, Saml.	147	LO
Eberhard, Thomas	105	LE
Eberhard, Thomas	138	LE
Ebright, Jacob	98	LE
Ebright, Jacob	122	LE
Eby, George	110	LE
Eby, George	126	LE
Eby, George	140	LE
Eby, George Est.	98	LE
Eby, Henry Est.	99	LE
Eby, Jacob	99	LE
Eckert, Jonas	58	HD
Eckert, Jonas	60	HD
Eckert, Jonas	69	HD
Eckert, Jonas	85	HD
Eckert, Philip	93	LE
Eckert, Philip	99	LE
Eckhart, Jonas	60	HD
Ege, George Esq.	60	HD
Egler, Jacob	16	BE
Eichelberner, Godfried	99	LE
Eichholtz, Jacob	60	HD
Eichholtz, Jacob	68	HD
Eisseman, Widow	60	HD
Elder & Kain	143	LO
Elder & Kain	147	LO
Elder & Kain Co.	42	EH
Elder & Kean	99	LE
Elder, John	99	LE
Elder, John	128	LE
Elenberger, Jacob	112	LE
Elenberger, Jacob	124	LE
Elenberger, John	99	LE
Elenberger, John	101	LE
Elenberger, John	114	LE
Elenberger., Jacob	101	LE
Elleberger, Chrisn.	154	LO
Elleberger, Christr.	148	LO
Elleberger, John	58	HD
Ellenberger, Jacob	99	LE
Ellenberger, Jacob Jr.	100	LE
Eller, Michael	16	BE
Eller, Michl.	17	BE
Ellinger, Caspar	110	LE
Ellinger, Caspar	116	LE
Ellinger, Geo.	98	LE
Ellinger, Jacob	142	LO
Embich, Fred	93	LE
Embig, Barned	100	LE
Embig, Bernard	100	LE
Embig, Christr.	100	LE
Embig, Christr.	115	LE
Embig, Fredk.	100	LE
Embig, Jacob	129	LE
Embig, Jacob (2)	100	LE
Embigh, Jacob	132	LE
Emerick, John	50	EH
Empich, Fredk.	100	LE
Empich, Jacob	100	LE
Emrich, John	42	EH
Emrich, Widow	16	BE
Endress, John	100	LE
Endress, John	105	LE
Ensminger, Danl.	100	LE
Ensminger, Peter	118	LE
Ensminger, Peter (2)	100	LE
Erpff, Phillip	60	HD
Esh, Jacob	60	HD
Esh, Jacob	82	HD
Eshelman, Henry	148	LO
Esinhower, John	18	BE
Esinhower, John (2)	16	BE
Esterlein, Christian	134	LE
Esterlein, Christr.	100	LE
Etman, John	60	HD
Etter, Saml.	147	LO
Ettman, John	60	HD
Everhard, John	16	BE
Eyer, John	42	EH
Eysenhouer, John	16	BE
Faber, Adam	42	EH
Faber, Jacob (heirs)	16	BE
Faber, Margaret	17	BE
Faber, Michael	130	LE
Faber, Philip	17	BE
Faber, Philip	36	BE
Farling, George	42	EH
Farmer, John	148	LO
Fasnacht, Conrad	100	LE
Fasnacht, Conrad	114	LE
Faver, Philip	14	BE
Favour, Adam	42	EH
Fechman, Geo.	37	BE
Fecht, Peter	42	EH
Feehman, Leonard	17	BE
Feeman, George	17	BE
Feeser, Peter	31	BE
Feeser, Peter (2)	17	BE
Feesich, George	17	BE
Fegan, George	101	LE
Feger, Christn.	109	LE
Fehler, Jacob	42	EH
Fehler, John	60	HD
Fehman, Leond.	17	BE
Feler, John	63	HD
Felker, Henry	17	BE
Felker, Henry	25	BE
Felty, Sebastian	18	BE
Felty, Sebastian	19	BE
Felty, Sebastian	34	BE
Felty, Ulrich	18	BE
Ferling, George	42	EH
Fernsler, Fredk.	101	LE
Fernsler, Fredrick	138	LE
Fernsler, Fredrick	140	LE
Fernsler, Jacob	101	LE
Fernsler, Magdalena	101	LE
Fernsler, Peter	148	LO
Fernsler, Peter	152	LO
Fernsler, Peter (2)	147	LO
Fernsler, Philip	91	LE
Fernsler, Philip	93	LE
Fernsler, Philip	98	LE
Fernsler, Philip	114	LE
Fernsler, Philip	125	LE
Fernsler, Philip	140	LE
Fernsler, Philip (2)	101	LE
Fernsler, Philip Jr.	101	LE
Fertig, _____	60	HD
Fertig, Christopher	123	LE
Fesich, Geo.	20	BE
Fetterer, Stephen	18	BE
Fetterer, Stephen	19	BE
Fetterer, Stephen	21	BE
Fetterhof, Balzer	18	BE
Fetterhof, Jacob	18	BE
Fetterhoff, Baltzer	16	BE
Fetterhoff, Balzar	14	BE
Fetterrer, Stephen	27	BE
Fettle, Henry	33	BE
Fetzberg. Daniel	123	LE
Fetzberger, Danl.	101	LE
Fetzberger, Danl.	138	LE
Feuks, John	58	HD
Fidler, Ludwig	56	HD
Fidler, Widow	61	HD
Fiegart, William	18	BE
Figart, Hannah	18	BE
Figart, William	18	BE
Figart, William	24	BE
Figart, Wm.	18	BE
Fihman, George	17	BE
Filson, Widow	61	HD
Finkel, Widow	22	BE
Finney, John	148	LO
Firbner, George	40	EH
Firrer, Petter	17	BE
Fishburn, Ludwig	148	LO
Fisher, Christn.	90	LE
Fisher, George	61	HD
Fisher, Jacob	15	BE
Fisher, Jacob	18	BE
Fisher, John	52	EH
Fisher, Michael	17	BE
Fisher, Peter	118	LE

INDEX

Name	Page	Code	Name	Page	Code	Name	Page	Code
Fisher, Peter	129	LE	Frantz, Jacob	44	EH	Gembell, John	19	BE
Fisher, Peter	130	LE	Frazier, William	149	LO	Gembill, John	19	BE
Fisher, Peter Est.	101	LE	Frazier, Wm.	158	LO	Georg, Peter	124	LE
Fisher, Peter Jr.	101	LE	Frazier, Wm.	160	LO	George, Henry	19	BE
Fisher, Philip	97	LE	Frelinghausen, Peter	19	BE	George, Henry	24	BE
Fisher, Philip	101	LE	Fremdling, Widow	61	HD	George, John	104	LE
Fisher, Vendel	18	BE	Fried, Adam	61	HD	Gerber, David	62	HD
Fisher, Wendel	18	BE	Fry, George	155	LO	Gerhart, Conrad	100	LE
Fisher, Wendel	23	BE	Fuchs, Barbara	19	BE	Gerloff, Godfried	76	HD
Fitterrn, Stephen	18	BE	Fuchs, Henry	18	BE	German, Adam	130	LE
Fitzberger, Daniel	133	LE	Fudler, Widow	61	HD	German, Henry	62	HD
Fleagar, John	148	LO	Fuhrman, Andw.	61	HD	German, Henry	85	HD
Fliegar, John	148	LO	Fulck, Christian	19	BE	German, Henry	86	HD
Flower, John Sr.	80	HD	Fulk, Christn.	19	BE	German, Michl.	62	HD
Flowers, John Jr.	79	HD	Fulmer, John	115	LE	Gerret, Christian	77	HD
Focht, George	55	HD	Fulmor, George	40	EH	Gerret, George	59	HD
Foessig, George	17	BE	Funck, Martin	102	LE	Gerret, George	62	HD
Fogel, Andrew	18	BE	Funck, Martin	104	LE	Gerret, Jacob	62	HD
Foght, George	61	HD	Funck, Martin	115	LE	Gerret, Jacob	65	HD
Foght, Mathias	61	HD	Funck, Martin	137	LE	Gerret, John	62	HD
Fogt, George	61	HD	Funck, Widow	102	LE	Gerver, David	62	HD
Fogt, Mathias	61	HD	Gantzer, Christian	102	LE	Gettel, Jacob	19	BE
Fogt, Mathias	75	HD	Gap, Jacob	77	HD	Gettle, Jacob	19	BE
Fogt, Mathias	83	HD	Garbarich, Adam	43	EH	Gibbony, Hugh	135	LE
Folgate, James	148	LO	Garbarich, Phillip	42	EH	Gilbert, Henry	62	HD
Follmer, Jacob	93	LE	Garbarick, Adm.	49	EH	Gilbert, Henry	97	LE
Follmer, Jacob	101	LE	Garbarick, Philip	43	EH	Gilbert, Henry	100	LE
Fordny, Daniel	116	LE	Garberich, Adam	43	EH	Gilbert, Henry	103	LE
Forer, Daniel	102	LE	Garberik, Philip	42	EH	Gilbert, Henry	105	LE
Forey, Danl.	102	LE	Garbrick, Adam	43	EH	Gilbert, Henry	123	LE
Forney, Chris.	157	LO	Garbrick, Adam	43	EH	Gilbert, Henry	138	LE
Forney, John	145	LO	Garbrick, John	43	EH	Gilbert, Saml.	24	BE
Forney, John	148	LO	Gardner, Barnhard	43	EH	Gilbert, Saml.	29	BE
Forney, Joseph	145	LO	Gardner, Bernard	43	EH	Gilbert, Saml.	33	BE
Forney, Vendel	159	LO	Gardner, George	43	EH	Gilbert, Samuel	19	BE
Forny, Peter	102	LE	Gardner, Martin	43	EH	Gillman, Christr.	149	LO
Forry, ____	160	LO	Garland, Moses	96	LE	Ginder, Christ Est.	94	LE
Forry, Danl.	104	LE	Garten, Jacob	102	LE	Gingerich, Michl.	111	LE
Fortiney, Henry	61	HD	Gartner, George	43	EH	Gingrich, Christn Est.	103	LE
Fortny, David	102	LE	Gaser, Christn.	140	LE	Gingrich, Christn.	103	LE
Foster, Andrew (2)	149	LO	Gass, John	31	BE	Gingrich, Christn.	118	LE
Foster, Barbara	149	LO	Gasser, John	97	LE	Gingrich, Henry	103	LE
Foster, David	153	LO	Gasser, John	102	LE	Gingrich, John	96	LE
Foster, David (2)	149	LO	Gassert, Adam	60	HD	Gingrich, John	110	LE
Foster, James	149	LO	Gassert, Christr.	102	LE	Gingrich, John	112	LE
Foster, Jas.	149	LO	Gassert, Jacob	61	HD	Gingrich, John (2)	92	LE
Foster, Joseph	149	LO	Gassert, Jacob Est.	19	BE	Gingrich, John (2)	103	LE
Foster, Maria	149	LO	Gast, Mathias	61	HD	Gingrich, John Jr.	103	LE
Foster, Mary	149	LO	Gates, Henry	149	LO	Gingrich, John Sr.	103	LE
Foster, Mary	149	LO	Gaurden, Jacob	102	LE	Gingrich, Michl.	92	LE
Fox, Anthony	42	EH	Gebhard, George	137	LE	Gingrich, Michl.	102	LE
Fox, Anthony	46	EH	Gebhart, George	102	LE	Gingrich, Michl.	103	LE
Fox, Charles	29	BE	Gebhart, George	115	LE	Gingrich, Michl.	104	LE
Fox, Henry	18	BE	Gebhart, George	132	LE	Gingrich, Michl.	125	LE
Fox, Henry	38	BE	Gebhart, Nicolas	12	BE	Gingrich, Peter	47	EH
Fox, Jacob	132	LE	Geese, Henry	27	BE	Gingrich, Widow	103	LE
Fox, John	43	EH	Geesy, George	19	BE	Gingry, Christn.	118	LE
Franck, Barbara	19	BE	Gehret, Christ.	62	HD	Gingry, Henry	103	LE
Franck, Henry	102	LE	Gehret, Fred	61	HD	Gingry, Henry	121	LE
Franck, Henry	119	LE	Gehret, George	62	HD	Gingry, John	103	LE
Franer, Dr., Est. of	111	LE	Gehret, Jacob (2)	62	HD	Gingry, John	112	LE
Frank, Barbara	19	BE	Geib, John	103	LE	Gingry, John	117	LE
Frank, Henry	88	LE	Geib, John	130	LE	Gingry, Michael	125	LE
Frank, Henry	92	LE	Geiger, Jacob	117	LE	Ginter, Christian Est.	104	LE

INDEX

Name	Page	Code
Ginter, Widow	104	LE
Gips, Negro	62	HD
Gisseman, Geo.	104	LE
Gisseman, Geo.	105	LE
Gisseman, George	98	LE
Gisseman, Henry	104	LE
Gissey, George	35	BE
Glass, Martin	74	HD
Glassbrenner, Ansted (2)	104	LE
Glassbrenner, Geo. (3)	104	LE
Glassbrenner, Peter	99	LE
Glassbrenner, Peter	104	LE
Gleim, Jacob	62	HD
Gleinfelter Albt. Jr.	23	BE
Gleinfelter, Albt. Sr.	23	BE
Glesmer, Abm.	12	BE
Glick, John	37	BE
Glick, Ludwig (2)	44	EH
Gline, Jacob	62	HD
Glinefelter, Abraham	23	BE
Glinfelter, Albert	12	BE
Gloninger, Geo.	102	LE
Gloninger, George	104	LE
Gloninger, George	133	LE
Gloninger, John	114	LE
Gloninger, John	120	LE
Gloninger, Peter	104	LE
Gloninger, Peter	110	LE
Gloninger, Peter	118	LE
Gloninger, Peter	137	LE
Gloninger, Philip	105	LE
Gloninger, Widow	104	LE
Gnaus, Jacob	25	BE
Gneagey, Jacob	20	BE
Gneagy, Jacob	20	BE
Goldman, Christn.	135	LE
Goldman, Jacob	105	LE
Goltman, Jacob	122	LE
Goodman, Adam	41	EH
Gordon, Jacob	102	LE
Gordon, John	87	HD
Graff, Anna	105	LE
Graff, Jacob	105	LE
Graff, Jacob Est.	107	LE
Graham, Henry	43	EH
Graham, Henry Esq.	40	EH
Graham, Henry Esq.	43	EH
Graham, James (heirs)	43	EH
Grall, Henry	62	HD
Graybill, Geo.	149	LO
Graybill, Israel	12	BE
Graybill, Peter	106	LE
Greechbam, Wm.	20	BE
Greenawald, Philip	115	LE
Greenawald, Philip	126	LE
Greenawalt, Maths.	103	LE
Greenawalt, Maths. (2)	105	LE
Greenawalt, Ph. (2)	105	LE
Greenawalt, Philip	95	LE
Greenawalt, Philip	105	LE
Greenawalt, Philip	106	LE
Greenawalt, Philip	115	LE
Greenawalt, Philip Sr.	105	LE
Greenewalt, John	105	LE
Greenwalt, Leond.	26	BE
Greenwalt, Philip	105	LE
Greider, Christn.	130	LE
Greider, Christn. (2)	106	LE
Greider, George	105	LE
Greider, George	107	LE
Greider, George	128	LE
Greider, Jacob	107	LE
Greider, Jacob	125	LE
Greider, Jacob Sr.	105	LE
Greider, John	137	LE
Greider, John (3)	106	LE
Greider, Martin	106	LE
Greider, Martin	140	LE
Greider, Michael	132	LE
Greider, Michl.	107	LE
Greider, Tobias	105	LE
Greider, Tobias	107	LE
Grenewald, Philip	124	LE
Grey, Jacob	107	LE
Greybiel, Peter	106	LE
Greyder, Christn. (2)	106	LE
Greyder, Geo.	106	LE
Greyder, Geo.	107	LE
Greyder, Henry	106	LE
Greyder, Jacob (2)	106	LE
Greyder, John	90	LE
Greyder, John (2)	106	LE
Greyder, Martin (2)	106	LE
Greyder, Michl.	106	LE
Greyder, Tobias	105	LE
Greyder, Tobias	107	LE
Greyder, Tobias (2)	106	LE
Grichbam, Wm.	20	BE
Grider, Henry	106	LE
Grider, Jacob	106	LE
Grider, Jacob Sr.	105	LE
Grider, John	106	LE
Grider, Michael	107	LE
Griegdoff, Widow	129	LE
Gries, Philip	102	LE
Grigauf, Widow	129	LE
Grigbaum, Wilm.	20	BE
Grimm, Widow	148	LO
Grinwold, Mathis	138	LE
Gristman, Jacob	61	HD
Groe, Abram	149	LO
Groe, Mattias	116	LE
Grof, Jacob	105	LE
Groff, Andrew	62	HD
Groff, Andrew	79	HD
Groff, Anna	105	LE
Groff, Peter	20	BE
Groh, Abraham	107	LE
Groh, John	20	BE
Groh, Mathes	126	LE
Groh, Mathias	107	LE
Groh, Maths.	117	LE
Groh, Peter	20	BE
Groh, Peter	23	BE
Groh, Peter	27	BE
Groh, Widow	59	HD
Groh, Widow	63	HD
Gromer, David	63	HD
Grouse, Joseph	107	LE
Grove, Abraham	149	LO
Grove, Abraham	160	LO
Grove, Andrew	62	HD
Grove, Jacob	20	BE
Grove, Jacob Est.	107	LE
Grove, Peter	20	BE
Grove, Peter	32	BE
Grove, Widow	107	LE
Grow, Peter	27	BE
Groy, Jacob	107	LE
Groy, Jacob	112	LE
Grubb, B. Henry	150	LO
Grubb, John	150	LO
Grubb, John	152	LO
Grubenseh, Geo.	138	LE
Grubensy, George	107	LE
Gruber, Christian	107	LE
Grum, John	57	HD
Grum, John	67	HD
Grum, John	73	HD
Grumbine, Jacob	16	BE
Grumbine, Jacob	20	BE
Grumbine, Jacob	38	BE
Grumbine, Leonard	61	HD
Grumbine, Widow	63	HD
Gunderman, Jacob	90	LE
Gundrum, Fredk. Est.	107	LE
Gundrum, Widow	107	LE
Gunterum, John	107	LE
Guntrum, Fredrich	123	LE
Guntrum, John	107	LE
Gussy, Frances	108	LE
Haberstich, Geo.	106	LE
Hackman, Henry	63	HD
Hackman, Henry	67	HD
Hackman, John Henry	70	HD
Haffa, John	14	BE
Haffa, Phillip	63	HD
Haffe, John	21	BE
Hagey, Jacob	108	LE
Haldeman, John	24	BE
Hamelton, Robert	137	LE
Hamer, Peter	50	EH
Hamilton, Robt.	108	LE
Hamilton, Wm.	150	LO
Hammel, Isaac	52	EH
Hany, Hugh	117	LE
Harman, John	13	BE
Harper, John	40	EH
Harper, John	41	EH
Harper, John	43	EH
Harper, Thom.	43	EH
Harper, Widow	43	EH
Harrison, Isaac	43	EH
Harrison, Isaac	46	EH
Harrison, Isaac	47	EH
Hassinger, Herman	63	HD
Hasting, Christn.	108	LE
Hauer, Andrew	140	LE
Haupt, Fredk.	66	HD
Hauter, Samuel	63	HD
Hauter, Samuel	72	HD
Hauty, John	15	BE

INDEX

Name	Page	Code	Name	Page	Code	Name	Page	Code
Hautz, Henry	22	BE	Henning, Mathias	53	EH	Hileman, Geo.	31	BE
Hautz, John	17	BE	Hennington, Thos.	145	LO	Hileman, Geo.	33	BE
Hawk, Henry	63	HD	Henry, Andrew	151	LO	Hileman, George	21	BE
Hawk, Michael (2)	63	HD	Henry, Andw.	156	LO	Hiller, George	18	BE
Hawk, Michl.	67	HD	Henry, Andw. (2)	146	LO	Hiller, George	21	BE
Hawk, Michl.	68	HD	Henry, George	151	LO	Hillger, Henry	64	HD
Hawk, Nicholas	67	HD	Henry, Philip	145	LO	Hillyer, Henry	64	HD
Hawk, Nicholas (2)	63	HD	Henry, Vendel	151	LO	Hinckel, Henry	20	BE
Hawkly, Henry	55	HD	Henry, Vendl.	151	LO	Hinckel, Henry	21	BE
Hay, Patrick	164	LO	Hepting, Christn.	108	LE	Hinckel, Henry	31	BE
Hay, Wm. Esq.	150	LO	Herkelroth, ___	144	LO	Hinkel, Henry	21	BE
Hay, Wm. Esq.	159	LO	Herkelroth, Henry	151	LO	Hinkel, Henry	30	BE
Hay, Wm. Esq.	163	LO	Herkelroth, John	151	LO	Hippert, ___	78	HD
Hays, David	157	LO	Herman, Dan'l.	13	BE	Hippert, George	64	HD
Hays, David	161	LO	Herman, George	13	BE	Hipshman, Henry	61	HD
Hays, David (2)	150	LO	Herner, Michael	15	BE	Hipshman, Henry	64	HD
Hays, David (2)	156	LO	Herner, Michl.	20	BE	Hirner, Michl.	36	BE
Hays, Patrick	157	LO	Herner, Michl.	22	BE	Hirshe, Isaac	151	LO
Hays, Patrick (3)	150	LO	Herner, Unger	22	BE	Hisey, Danl.	108	LE
Hays, Robert	150	LO	Heron, Ned	47	EH	Hisey, Henry	108	LE
Hays, Robt.	163	LO	Herr, Abraham	89	LE	Hisey, Michael	109	LE
Heagey, Jacob	108	LE	Herr, Abraham	106	LE	Hisey, Peter	109	LE
Heagy, Jacob	108	LE	Herr, Abraham	108	LE	Hochlander, Geo.	20	BE
Heckedorn, Albert	33	BE	Herr, Abraham	109	LE	Hochlander, George	21	BE
Heckedorn, Erhart	33	BE	Herr, Abraham	121	LE	Hochstetter, John	103	LE
Heckendorn, Erhart	20	BE	Herr, Abraham	138	LE	Hochstetter, John	110	LE
Hecketsweler, Geo.	20	BE	Herr, Abram	106	LE	Hochstetter, John	115	LE
Hecktorn, Ernst	20	BE	Herr, Abram	119	LE	Hock, George	109	LE
Hedrick, John	43	EH	Herr, Abram	121	LE	Hoeman, Fredk.	21	BE
Hedrick, Peter	41	EH	Herr, Abram	127	LE	Hoffart, John	144	LO
Heffelfinger, John	64	HD	Herr, Henry	88	LE	Hoffart, John	159	LO
Hege, Jacob	108	LE	Herry, William	116	LE	Hoffer, John	21	BE
Heilman, Adam	89	LE	Hersberger, Abm.	21	BE	Hoffman, Conrad	94	LE
Heilman, Adam	103	LE	Hersberger, Abm.	41	EH	Hoffman, Conrad	109	LE
Heilman, Adam	121	LE	Hersberger, Christn.	109	LE	Hoffman, Conrad	116	LE
Heilman, Adam (2)	108	LE	Hershberger, Abm.	22	BE	Hoffman, Conrad	123	LE
Heilman, Anastasius	108	LE	Hershberger, Abm.	44	EH	Hoffman, Jacob	55	HD
Heilman, Ansted	108	LE	Hershberger, Abram	120	LE	Hoffman, Jacob	78	HD
Heilman, George	12	BE	Hershberger, Christn.	121	LE	Hoffman, Jacob (2)	55	HD
Heilman, George	21	BE	Hershberger, Danl.	91	LE	Hoffman, Jacob (2)	64	HD
Heilman, John (4)	108	LE	Hershberger, Saml.	109	LE	Hoffman, Michl.	33	BE
Heise, Daniel	108	LE	Hershe, Benjm.	151	LO	Hofman, Conrad	123	LE
Heise, Danl.	111	LE	Hershe, Isaac	143	LO	Hofman, Conrad	135	LE
Heise, Henry	108	LE	Hershe, Isaac	147	LO	Hofman, Jacob	64	HD
Heisey, Daniel	108	LE	Hershey, Benjm.	151	LO	Hofman, Michl.	21	BE
Heisey, Michael (2)	109	LE	Hershey, Benjm.	151	LO	Hofman, Michl.	28	BE
Heisey, Michl.	98	LE	Hershey, Benjm.	156	LO	Hoke, Geo.	104	LE
Heisey, Peter	109	LE	Hershey, Benjm.	160	LO	Hoke, George	109	LE
Heisy, Daniel	108	LE	Hershey, Isaac	147	LO	Holdeman, John	13	BE
Heisy, Henry (3)	108	LE	Hershey, Isaac	151	LO	Holdeman, John	21	BE
Heisy, Michael	110	LE	Hershey, Martin (2)	151	LO	Holdeman, John	31	BE
Hele, John	20	BE	Herty, Tobias	109	LE	Hollingsworth, Levy	142	LO
Helem, Conrad	44	EH	Hess, Geo.	129	LE	Holsberger, ___	52	EH
Helm, Conrad	44	EH	Hess, Henry	45	EH	Holseid, Peter	64	HD
Hemperly, Eleanor	147	LO	Hess, Henry	47	EH	Holstein, Geo.	71	HD
Hemperly, Geo.	155	LO	Hess, Henry (2)	44	EH	Holstein, George	64	HD
Hemperly, George	147	LO	Hess, John	21	BE	Holstein, George	81	HD
Hemperly, George	151	LO	Hess, John	29	BE	Holstein, George	84	HD
Hener, Widow	89	LE	Hess, John	30	BE	Holtz, George	109	LE
Hening, Daniel (2)	126	LE	Hess, John (2)	24	BE	Holtz, George	110	LE
Henner, Michl.	35	BE	Hess, Mathias	44	EH	Holtzberger, Andrew	99	LE
Henning, Danl.	109	LE	Hessting, Christn.	100	LE	Homan, Fred	18	BE
Henning, Danl.	151	LO	Hickesweller, Geo.	20	BE	Honning, Mathias	44	EH
Henning, Mathias	44	EH	Hileman, Adam	108	LE	Hoober, Andw.	110	LE

INDEX

Name	Page	Code	Name	Page	Code	Name	Page	Code
Hoober, Fredk.	21	BE	Hunsecker, Rudy	12	BE	Kalbach, Adam	65	HD
Hoober, Henry	22	BE	Hunsecker, Rudy	22	BE	Kantz, Christn.	129	LE
Hoober, John	110	LE	Hunsecker, Saml.	20	BE	Kantzer, Christn.	129	LE
Hoober, Michael	152	LO	Hunsecker, Saml.	22	BE	Kap, Susana	135	LE
Hoober, Michael	155	LO	Hunsecker, Saml.	24	BE	Kapp, Anthony	62	HD
Hoober, Michl.	110	LE	Huston, James	64	HD	Kapp, Anthony	65	HD
Hoober, Michl.	150	LO	Huston, James	65	HD	Kapp, Anthony	71	HD
Hoober, Michl.	155	LO	Iba, Henry	65	HD	Kapp, Anthony (2)	77	HD
Hoofnagel, Felty	51	EH	Iba, William	65	HD	Kapp, Frederic	66	HD
Hoofnagel, Valentine	44	EH	Illig, Leonard	65	HD	Kapp, Frederick	67	HD
Hoofnagel, Valn.	51	EH	Imboden, Adam	111	LE	Kapp, Frederick	86	HD
Hoofnagle, Felty	44	EH	Imboden, Adam	124	LE	Kapp, George	66	HD
Hoover, Andrew	72	HD	Imboden, Geo.	91	LE	Kapp, George	66	HD
Hoover, Danl.	159	LO	Imboden, George	111	LE	Kapp, Jacob	66	HD
Hoover, Fredk.	30	BE	Imboden, John	122	LE	Kapp, John	67	HD
Hoover, George	110	LE	Imboden, John	127	LE	Kapp, John	73	HD
Hoover, Jacob	109	LE	Imboden, John (2)	111	LE	Kapp, John (2)	66	HD
Hoover, Michael	152	LO	Imboden, Philip	111	LE	Kapp, Susana	134	LE
Hoover, Philip	110	LE	Imhof, Martin	122	LE	Kapp, Susanna	110	LE
Horst, Peter	109	LE	Imhof, Martin	134	LE	Karch, George	112	LE
Horst, Peter	110	LE	Imhoff, John	93	LE	Karch, Jacob	112	LE
Hostater, John	103	LE	Imhoff, Martin	111	LE	Karch, Jacob	114	LE
Hostater, John	110	LE	Imhoff, Martin	115	LE	Karch, Jacob	125	LE
Hostater, John	115	LE	Immel, Leonard	65	HD	Karete?, Jacob	133	LE
Hostetler, Michl.	80	HD	Immel, Leonard	78	HD	Karmany, Anthony	144	LO
Hostetter, John	152	LO	Immel, Leond.	76	HD	Karmany, Anthony Jr.	152	LO
Houser, Peter	64	HD	Isenhawer, John	16	BE	Karmany, Anthony Sr.	152	LO
Houston, James	64	HD	Isenhawer, John	18	BE	Karmany, Anthy.	161	LO
Houtz, Christian	22	BE	Isenhawer, John	36	BE	Karmany, George	114	LE
Houtz, Henry	22	BE	Isenhawer, Peter	152	LO	Karmany, John (2)	112	LE
Houtz, Henry	28	BE	Ishler, George	111	LE	Karmany, Joseph	142	LO
Houtz, Henry	33	BE	Jackey, Lorentz	17	BE	Karmany, Joseph Jr.	153	LO
Houtz, Jacob	44	EH	Jacobey, Adam	111	LE	Karmany, Joseph Sr.	153	LO
Houtz, John	13	BE	Jacobs, Saml.	146	LO	Karmany, Martin	112	LE
Houtz, John	22	BE	Jacoby, Adam	111	LE	Karmany, Philip (2)	112	LE
Houtz, John (2)	32	BE	Jager, Christn.	111	LE	Karmeny, Martin	103	LE
Howard, Widow	65	HD	Jager, John	111	LE	Karper, John	153	LO
Hower, Fred	16	BE	Jager, John	123	LE	Karsnits, Andw.	88	LE
Hower, Fredk.	22	BE	Jengst, Henry	111	LE	Kaufman, Abraham	112	LE
Hower, John	44	EH	Jengst, Henry	127	LE	Kaufman, Christ	113	LE
Howerter, Christn.	110	LE	Jensee, Martin	131	LE	Kaufman, George	132	LE
Howter, Saml.	63	HD	Jensel, Martin	111	LE	Kavin, Nichs.	46	EH
Hubely, Fredk.	115	LE	Johns, Peter	152	LO	Kealer, Leonart	113	LE
Huber, Andrew	127	LE	Johnson, David	152	LO	Kean, Charles	105	LE
Huber, Andw.	110	LE	Johnston, David	152	LO	Kean, Charles	110	LE
Huber, Geo.	107	LE	Johnston, David	162	LO	Kean, Charles	113	LE
Huber, George	65	HD	Joiner, Rich	77	HD	Kean, John	99	LE
Huber, George	110	LE	Jones, John Est.	24	BE	Keen, Charles	113	LE
Huber, George	127	LE	Jones, William Est.	22	BE	Keen, Charles	120	LE
Huber, Jacob	109	LE	Jordan, Geo.	157	LO	Keener, Widow	89	LE
Huber, John	110	LE	Jordy, Henry (2)	112	LE	Keeny, Peter	23	BE
Huber, John	113	LE	Jordy, Jacob Est.	111	LE	Keeny, Peter	25	BE
Huber, John	118	LE	Jordy, John	112	LE	Keiser, Godfrid	23	BE
Huber, Michl.	88	LE	Jorty, Henry	112	LE	Kelcker, Anthony	113	LE
Huber, Michl.	101	LE	Joung, Felix	112	LE	Kelcker, Henry	113	LE
Huber, Michl.	110	LE	Judy, Christn.	152	LO	Kelcker, Rudolph	113	LE
Huber, Philip Est.	110	LE	Juengst, Henry	100	LE	Kelker, Anthy.	113	LE
Huble, Fredrich	128	LE	Juengst, John	120	LE	Kelker, Jacob (2)	95	LE
Hubley, Fredk.	110	LE	Jung, Abm.	112	LE	Kelker, Rudolph	96	LE
Hubly, Fredk.	104	LE	Jung, Felix (2)	112	LE	Kelker, Rudolph	119	LE
Huby, Fred (2)	13	BE	Jung, Michael	112	LE	Kelker, Rudolph	129	LE
Hunsecker, Christian	22	BE	Jungst, _____	69	HD	Kelker, Rudolph	138	LE
Hunsecker, Christian	37	BE	Kaffman, Abraham	120	LE	Kelker, Rudy	96	LE
Hunsecker, Rud.	21	BE	Kairn, Nicholas	44	EH	Kelker, Rudy	97	LE

INDEX

Name	Page	Code	Name	Page	Code	Name	Page	Code
Kelker, Rudy, Mgr.	96	LE	Kinsey, John	131	LE	Kore, John (2)	23	BE
Keller, _____	121	LE	Kinsly, Gottlieb	66	HD	Kore, Michael	23	BE
Keller, George (2)	113	LE	Kinsly, Martin	95	LE	Kore, Michl.	27	BE
Keller, Jacob	22	BE	Kinsly, Rudy	66	HD	Kornman, George	115	LE
Keller, Jacob	26	BE	Kintzel, Martin	95	LE	Kornman, George	137	LE
Keller, Jacob (2)	113	LE	Kintzer, Jacob	67	HD	Kraemer, Martin	115	LE
Keller, John	93	LE	Kisler, Jacob	154	LO	Krall, Abraham	89	LE
Keller, John	94	LE	Kisnor, Jacob	154	LO	Krall, Abraham	97	LE
Keller, John	95	LE	Kitler, Jacob	11	BE	Krall, Abraham	115	LE
Keller, John Est.	114	LE	Kittering, Valentine	154	LO	Kratzer, Jacob	86	HD
Keller, John Est.	122	LE	Kittle, Jacob	14	BE	Kratzer, John	143	LO
Keller, John, dec.	100	LE	Kitzmiller, Jacob	114	LE	Kratzer, John (2)	160	LO
Kelly & Orth	153	LO	Kitzmiller, Jacob	121	LE	Kratzger, John	155	LO
Kelly, James	153	LO	Kleick, Ludwigh	45	EH	Krause, Andrew	115	LE
Kelly, James	160	LO	Klein, Dietrich	114	LE	Krause, Andw.	100	LE
Kelly, John	77	HD	Kleinfelter, Albt.	18	BE	Krause, David	93	LE
Kelly, Patrick	159	LO	Kleiser, Ignazius	114	LE	Krause, David	98	LE
Kelly, Patrick (2)	153	LO	Klick, John	23	BE	Krause, David	100	LE
Kelly, Patt	153	LO	Klick, Leonard	67	HD	Krause, David	102	LE
Kemp, John	22	BE	Klick, Ludwig	42	EH	Krause, David	104	LE
Kemp, Mathias	23	BE	Klick, Ludwig	44	EH	Krause, David	110	LE
Kemple, Christn.	47	EH	Klick, Ludwig	45	EH	Krause, David	115	LE
Keney, Peter	23	BE	Kline, Dietrich	114	LE	Krause, David	121	LE
Kenior, Jacob	66	HD	Kline, John	59	HD	Krause, David	126	LE
Kennedy, John	145	LO	Kline, John	67	HD	Krause, David	132	LE
Kennedy, John	153	LO	Klinefelter, Albert Jr.	23	BE	Krause, Joseph	107	LE
Kern, Nicholas	44	EH	Klinefelter, Albert Sr.	23	BE	Kreamer, Adam	99	LE
Kern, Nicklos	46	EH	Kliser, Nasarus	114	LE	Kreamer, Andrew	43	EH
Kerning, Geo	114	LE	Kneagey land	27	BE	Krebbs, Michl.	105	LE
Ketrin, Felty	151	LO	Kneagy, Jost	45	EH	Krebs, Michl.	115	LE
Ketrin, Felty	154	LO	Knegey, Jacob	15	BE	Kremer, Martin	115	LE
Kettering, Val	154	LO	Knobsker, Chrisn.	154	LO	Kreps, _____	98	LE
Kettering, Val.	151	LO	Knofsker, Christn.	154	LO	Kreps, Michl.	111	LE
Kettering, Valentine	145	LO	Knofsker, Christr.	155	LO	Kreps, Michl.	115	LE
Kettering, Valentine	151	LO	Knofsker, Joseph	154	LO	Kreps, Michl.	128	LE
Ketz, Nichlos	45	EH	Knol, Jacob	114	LE	Kreps, Michl.	137	LE
Ketz, Nicholas	44	EH	Knoll, Christn.	91	LE	Kress, Michael	113	LE
Kiefer, Christn.	154	LO	Knoll, Christr.	114	LE	Kreutzer, Michael	85	HD
Kieffer, Christian	99	LE	Knoll, Widow	114	LE	Kreutzer, Michl.	67	HD
Kiener, Godfry	66	HD	Knopsker, Christr.	154	LO	Krider, John	155	LO
Kieth, James	96	LE	Knopsker, Joseph	154	LO	Krider, Lewis	13	BE
Kiffer, _____	121	LE	Knopsker, Joseph	154	LO	Krider, Lewis	23	BE
Kile, Robert	154	LO	Kobe, Valentine	114	LE	Krill, John	68	HD
Killian, Henry	114	LE	Koble, Jacob	160	LO	Kriser, Godfried	23	BE
Killian, Jacob	114	LE	Koch, Christian	67	HD	Kross, Michael	115	LE
Killian, John	140	LE	Kochederfer, Geo.	78	HD	Krug, Philip	61	HD
Killinger, John	140	LE	Kochenderfer, Geo.	67	HD	Krum, John	68	HD
Killinger, John	154	LO	Kochenderfer, John	114	LE	Krum, John	77	HD
Killinger, John	159	LO	Koehler, Leonhd. (2)	94	LE	Kumler, Henry	54	HD
Killinger, Michael	114	LE	Koenig, David	67	HD	Kumler, Henry	68	HD
Killinger, Michael	148	LE	Koenig, David	68	HD	Kuntz, Geo.	88	LE
Killinger, Michl.	89	LE	Kofman, Abraham	120	LE	Kuntz, Lawrentz	123	LE
Killinger, Michl.	143	LO	Kohr, Christian	45	EH	Kuntz, Nichl.	68	HD
Killinger, Michl.	154	LO	Kohr, John (2)	23	BE	Kurtz, Geo.	90	LE
Killinger, Peter	154	LO	Kohr, Michl.	23	BE	Kurtz, George	112	LE
Kimp, John	23	BE	Kolb, Peter	64	HD	Kurtz, John (2)	68	HD
Kinaday, John	153	LO	Kolp, Peter	67	HD	Kurtz, Stephen	68	HD
King, Peter	11	BE	Kolp, Peter	74	HD	Kurtz, Stephen	85	HD
King, Peter	23	BE	Kolp, Peter (2)	73	HD	Kurtz, Widow	24	BE
King, Peter	25	BE	Kolp, Philip	45	EH	Kurtz, Widow	30	BE
King, Widow	44	EH	Kope, George	116	LE	Kurtz, Widow	37	BE
Kingrich, Christn.	47	EH	Kope, Valentine	114	LE	Kuster, John	57	HD
Kingrich, Peter	44	EH	Koppenheffer, Henry	67	HD	Kuster, John	68	HD
Kinney, John	145	LO	Kore, Christian	45	EH	Kuster, John	73	HD

INDEX

Name	Page	Code	Name	Page	Code	Name	Page	Code
Kuster, John	83	HD	Leamy, Jacob	24	BE	Light, Henry	27	BE
Laber, Balser	115	LE	Leamy, Tobias	20	BE	Light, Henry	30	BE
Laber, Balser	138	LE	Leamy, Tobias	24	BE	Light, Henry	32	BE
Laber, Baltzer	111	LE	Lear, John	117	LE	Light, Henry	117	LE
Laber, Baltzer	127	LE	Lebenstein, Widow	78	HD	Light, Henry	135	LE
Landis, Christn.	115	LE	Lee, Andrew	39	EH	Light, Henry (2)	50	EH
Landis, Christn. (2)	155	LO	Lee, Andrew	45	EH	Light, Henry (3)	25	BE
Landis, Henry	155	LO	Lehman, Christn.	69	HD	Light, Jacob	88	LE
Landis, Henry	157	LO	Lehmy, Christian	60	HD	Light, Jacob	117	LE
Landis, Henry	163	LO	Lehmy, Christian	69	HD	Light, Jacob	126	LE
Landis, John	142	LO	Lehmy, Christian	74	HD	Light, Jacob	131	LE
Landis, John	145	LO	Lehn, Jacob	69	HD	Light, John	27	BE
Landis, John	152	LO	Leidig, Michl.	45	EH	Light, John	95	LE
Landis, John	163	LO	Leightner, Jacob	25	BE	Light, John	97	LE
Landis, John (2)	155	LO	Lein, John	69	HD	Light, John	101	LE
Landis, John Jr.	155	LO	Leiss, Christian	74	HD	Light, John	111	LE
Landis, John Sr.	155	LO	Leiss, Peter	69	HD	Light, John	132	LE
Landis, Peter	156	LO	Leitner, Peter (2)	60	HD	Light, John	25	BE
Lang, Abraham	115	LE	Lemy, Jacob	24	BE	Light, John (2)	23	BE
Lang, Christian	116	LE	Lentz, Abraham	24	BE	Light, John (2)	25	BE
Lang, Herman	116	LE	Lentz, George	69	HD	Light, John (2)	117	LE
Lang, Herman	118	LE	Lentz, Jacob	24	BE	Light, John Jr.	25	BE
Lang, Herman	126	LE	Lentz, John	24	BE	Light, John Sr.	118	LE
Lang, William	114	LE	Leob, Christ. Est.	116	LE	Light, Martin	118	LE
Lang, William	116	LE	Lerch, Christoph	24	BE	Light, Martin	122	LE
Lannert, Henry	81	HD	Lerch, John	24	BE	Light, Peter	25	BE
Lantz, Abm.	28	BE	Lesher, Michael	109	LE	Light, Peter	26	BE
Lantz, Abraham	19	BE	Lesher, Michael	116	LE	Lightner, Jacob	16	BE
Lantz, George	72	HD	Lesher, Michael	123	LE	Lightner, Jacob	25	BE
Lantz, Henry	24	BE	Ley, Andrew	92	LE	Lightner, Peter	70	HD
Lantz, Henry	25	BE	Ley, Andrew	114	LE	Line, John	69	HD
Lantz, Jacob	24	BE	Ley, Andrew	116	LE	Line, Peter	70	HD
Lantz, Jacob	155	LO	Ley, Andrew	138	LE	Lineawever, Peter	156	LO
Lantz, John	22	BE	Ley, Christian	69	HD	Linemacher, Daniel	115	LE
Lantz, John	56	HD	Ley, Christian	82	HD	Linewever, Peter	137	LE
Lantz, John	62	HD	Leydig, Martin	118	LE	Litener, Jacob	11	BE
Lantz, John	68	HD	Lice, Peter	69	HD	Little, James	159	LO
Lantz, John Jr.	68	HD	Licht, Abraham	116	LE	Little, John	159	LO
Large, Stephen	52	EH	Licht, Abram	113	LE	Littner, Jacob	25	BE
Larick, Christoph	24	BE	Licht, Fred.	117	LE	Lochman, Geo.	132	LE
Larick, John	24	BE	Licht, Henry (2)	117	LE	Lochman, George	118	LE
Larick, John	26	BE	Licht, Jacob	126	LE	Loeb, Casper	118	LE
Lauber, Baltzer	115	LE	Licht, Jacob (2)	117	LE	Loess, Christr.	102	LE
Lauch, John	19	BE	Licht, Jacob Jr.	117	LE	Logan, Widow	156	LO
Laudermilch, John	116	LE	Licht, John	117	LE	Logan, William	144	LO
Lauers, Jacob	98	LE	Licht, John	132	LE	Logan, William	156	LO
Laurey, John	116	LE	Licht, John	117	LE	Logan, Wm.	144	LO
Lautermilch, Jacob	64	HD	Licht, John Jr.	117	LE	Logan, Wm.	156	LO
Lautermilch, John	64	HD	Licht, John Sr.	118	LE	Long, Abm.	25	BE
Lautermilch, John	138	LE	Licht, Martin	117	LE	Long, Abm.	26	BE
Layman, Abm.	156	LO	Licht, Martin	118	LE	Long, Abm.	115	LE
Layman, Danl.	156	LO	Licht, Martin Jr.	118	LE	Long, Abraham (2)	116	LE
Layman, Jacob	35	BE	Lidig, Catherine	24	BE	Long, Christ.	115	LE
Layman, Jacob	144	LO	Lidig, Kitty	18	BE	Long, Christian	115	LE
Layman, Jacob	156	LO	Lidig, Peter	70	HD	Long, Christian	116	LE
Layman, Peter (2)	156	LO	Light, Abraham	116	LE	Long, Christian (2)	25	BE
Leaman, Abraham	156	LO	Light, Abraham	117	LE	Long, Christn.	26	BE
Leaman, Danl.	156	LO	Light, Felix	95	LE	Long, Henry	26	BE
Leaman, Jacob	33	BE	Light, Felix	105	LE	Long, Henry	70	HD
Leaman, Jacob	35	BE	Light, Felix (2)	117	LE	Long, Henry	118	LE
Leaman, Jacob	156	LO	Light, Henry	20	BE	Long, Herman	102	LE
Leaman, Peter	156	LO	Light, Henry	22	BE	Long, Herman	116	LE
Leamy, Christian	16	BE	Light, Henry	23	BE	Long, Israel	25	BE
Leamy, Jacob	12	BE	Light, Henry	24	BE	Long, Israel	26	BE

INDEX

Name	Page	Code	Name	Page	Code	Name	Page	Code
Long, Isral	12	BE	Mark, Conrad	129	LE	McKinney, John	43	EH
Long, Kilian	26	BE	Mark, Conrad	130	LE	McKissock, John	150	LO
Long, Kilian	37	BE	Mark, Conrad	132	LE	McMullin, Daniel	119	LE
Long, Killian	25	BE	Mark, David	45	EH	McRath, Thos.	158	LO
Long, Martin	156	LO	Mark, George	42	EH	Mease, Geo.	52	EH
Long, William	96	LE	Mark, George (2)	46	EH	Mease, George	70	HD
Long, William	116	LE	Mark, Henry	26	BE	Mease, Henry	23	BE
Long, Wm.	25	BE	Mark, Jacob	104	LE	Mease, Henry	26	BE
Longnecker, Abm.	156	LO	Mark, Jacob	118	LE	Mease, Henry	26	BE
Longnecker, Abm. (2)	150	LO	Markey, John	71	HD	Mease, Henry	30	BE
Longnecker, Christ.	156	LO	Marky, John	71	HD	Mease, Jacob	70	HD
Longnecker, Christn.	142	LO	Marshal, David	129	LE	Mease, John	28	BE
Longnecker, Danl.	148	LO	Marshal, David	133	LE	Mease, John (2)	26	BE
Longnecker, Danl.	157	LO	Marshal, David Dr.	118	LE	Mease, Nicholas	70	HD
Longnecker, Jacob (2)	157	LO	Marshall, Wm	79	HD	Mease, Valentine	70	HD
Longnecker, John	148	LO	Marter, George	118	LE	Meck, Philip	96	LE
Loose, Jacob	26	BE	Marter, John	89	LE	Mecklin, Philip	42	EH
Loose, Jacob	27	BE	Marter, John (2)	118	LE	Mecklin, Philip	46	EH
Lose, Jacob	26	BE	Martin,	135	LE	Mecondel, Georg	119	LE
Lose, Jacob	45	EH	Martin, Alexander	118	LE	Mecondel, John	119	LE
Loser, Jacob	26	BE	Martin, Alexr.	32	BE	Mecondel, John	128	LE
Loser, Stophel	78	HD	Martin, George	46	EH	Mefaudien, John	98	LE
Louser, Jacob	87	HD	Martin, Henry	109	LE	Mefaudien, John	119	LE
Louser, John	70	HD	Martin, Henry	119	LE	Mefaudien, John	129	LE
Low, James	43	EH	Martin, John	23	BE	Meily, Geo.	96	LE
Low, James	45	EH	Martin, John	26	BE	Meily, Henry (2)	20	BE
Low, James	46	EH	Martin, John	28	BE	Meily, Jacob	11	BE
Lower, Benj.	70	HD	Martin, John	31	BE	Meily, Jacob	27	BE
Lower, Benjm.	68	HD	Martin, John	37	BE	Meily, Jacob	116	LE
Lower, Benjm.	85	HD	Martin, John	46	EH	Meily, Jacob	119	LE
Lower, Christian	70	HD	Martin, King	13	BE	Meily, Martin	27	BE
Lowmiller, John	45	EH	Martin, Shewey	31	BE	Meily, Martn.	23	BE
Lowrey, John	116	LE	Martzell, Christn.	97	LE	Meily, Martn.	36	BE
Loyter, Joseph	157	LO	Mase, George	69	HD	Meily, Philip	119	LE
Ludwig, Casper	16	BE	Masher, Jos.	154	LO	Meily, Saml.	135	LE
Luther?, Saml.	161	LO	Mattee, Fredk.	69	HD	Meily, Samuel	119	LE
Lutz, Henry	44	EH	Matter, George	118	LE	Meisser, Benjm.	71	HD
Lutz, Henry	45	EH	Matter, John	92	LE	Meisser, Benjm.	75	HD
Lutz, Henry	51	EH	Matter, John	118	LE	Meisser, Geo.	64	HD
Lutz, Isaac	157	LO	Matzenberger, John	60	HD	Meisser, George	71	HD
Lutz, Isaac	162	LO	Maulfer, Michael	119	LE	Meisser, George	87	HD
Lutz, John	74	HD	Maurer, George	76	HD	Meisser, John	71	HD
Lutz, Philip	26	BE	Mayer, Martin	119	LE	Melfadian, John	115	LE
Lydig, Peter	70	HD	McAllan, Robt.	153	LO	Melfadinn, John	119	LE
Lynch, James	11	BE	McAllen, Thos.	147	LO	Melinger, Jacob	139	LE
Lynch, John	142	LO	McAllister, Alex.	157	LO	Mellinger, Jacob	120	LE
Mace, George (2)	70	HD	McAllister, Archbd.	157	LO	Mellinger, Jacob	130	LE
Mace, Jacob (2)	70	HD	McCady, Jeremiah	52	EH	Menser, Jacob	120	LE
Mace, Michael	63	HD	McCallan, Robt.	153	LO	Mensinger, Conrad (3)	120	LE
Mace, Nicholas	70	HD	McCallan, Robt.	157	LO	Mentser, George	120	LE
Mace, Valentine	70	HD	McCallan, Robt.	158	LO	Mentzer, George	120	LE
Macklay, John Jr. (2)	157	LO	McCallan, Thos.	157	LO	Mentzer, Jacob	120	LE
Mackley, Melchor	157	LO	McCallan, Thos.	158	LO	Mentzger, James	158	LO
MaClay, John	144	LO	McClarey, Alex.	161	LO	Merck, Conrad	120	LE
Maclay, John	147	LO	McClay, John	162	LO	Merck, Conrad	129	LE
Maclay, John (2)	157	LO	McCohnel, John	119	LE	Merck, Henry	26	BE
Maclay, John Jr. (2)	157	LO	McCondel, John	101	LE	Merck, Jacob	118	LE
Maclay, Melchor (2)	157	LO	McConnel, George	119	LE	Merkley, John	162	LO
Maclay, Michael	147	LO	McCue, Rodger	97	LE	Mertel, Christr.	159	LO
Macley, John	150	LO	McDonald, John	158	LO	Mertzell, Christn.	158	LO
Mark, Adam	45	EH	McElrath, Thos.	158	LO	Meyer, Abram	120	LE
Mark, Adam	48	EH	McFadgen, John	119	LE	Meyer, Christr.	120	LE
Mark, Conrad	120	LE	McGlade, John	145	LO	Meyer, Henry	120	LE
Mark, Conrad	128	LE	McKinnet, Adm. (2)	146	LO	Meyer, Henry	127	LE

INDEX

Name	Page	Code	Name	Page	Code	Name	Page	Code
Meyer, John	95	LE	Miller, Henry	50	EH	Mock, Henry	83	HD
Meyer, John	103	LE	Miller, Henry	72	HD	Montford, John (2)	145	LO
Meyer, John	105	LE	Miller, Jacob	79	HD	Moor, Benjamin	135	LE
Meyer, John	114	LE	Miller, Jacob	96	LE	Moore, Adam	73	HD
Meyer, John	129	LE	Miller, Jacob	121	LE	Moore, Adam	74	HD
Meyer, John	134	LE	Miller, John	46	EH	Moore, Adam (2)	66	HD
Meyer, John (2)	121	LE	Miller, John	95	LE	Moore, Jacob	66	HD
Meyer, Martin	121	LE	Miller, John	109	LE	Moore, Jacob	73	HD
Meyer, Martin	136	LE	Miller, John	114	LE	Moore, Jacob	77	HD
Meyer, Martin (2)	119	LE	Miller, John	127	LE	Moore, John	58	HD
Michael, Valentine	77	HD	Miller, John (2)	53	EH	Moore, John	73	HD
Mickling, Philip	46	EH	Miller, John (2)	72	HD	Moore, John	78	HD
Mier, Jacob	47	EH	Miller, John (4)	121	LE	Moore, Peter	58	HD
Mier, Jacob	51	EH	Miller, Michael	71	HD	Moore, Peter	66	HD
Miley, Henry	20	BE	Miller, Michael	73	HD	Moore, Peter	74	HD
Miley, Henry	27	BE	Miller, Michael	83	HD	Moore, Peter	75	HD
Miley, Jacob	17	BE	Miller, Michael	158	LO	Moore, Peter	77	HD
Miley, Jacob	27	BE	Miller, Michael (2)	72	HD	Moore, Peter (2)	67	HD
Miley, Jacob	31	BE	Miller, Michl.	65	HD	Moore, Richard	145	LO
Miley, Jacob	35	BE	Miller, Michl.	72	HD	Moore, Saml. Est.	122	LE
Miley, Jacob	37	BE	Miller, Michl.	76	HD	Moore, Widow	104	LE
Miley, Jacob	119	LE	Miller, Michl.	107	LE	Mordock, James	81	HD
Miley, John	27	BE	Miller, Michl.	142	LO	Morret, Mathis Est.	122	LE
Miley, Martin	27	BE	Miller, Michl.	152	LO	Morrison, James	159	LO
Miley, Martin	29	BE	Miller, Nicholas (2)	72	HD	Morrison, Jas.	149	LO
Miley, Martn.	31	BE	Miller, Odelia	47	EH	Morrison, Jas.	153	LO
Miley, Philip	119	LE	Miller, Peter	128	LE	Morrison, Jas.	158	LO
Miley, Saml.	119	LE	Miller, Peter	129	LE	Morrison, Pat	153	LO
Miller, Christian	25	BE	Miller, Peter	140	LE	Mortwell, Christn.	159	LO
Miller, Christian	26	BE	Miller, Peter Est.	121	LE	Moser, Geo.	27	BE
Miller, Christian	27	BE	Miller, Peter Jr.	121	LE	Mosser, Michael	57	HD
Miller, Christian	46	EH	Miller, Rudolph	111	LE	Mosser, Michael	80	HD
Miller, Christian	53	EH	Miller, Rudolph	122	LE	Mosser, Michael (2)	82	HD
Miller, Christn.	21	BE	Miller, Rudolph	125	LE	Mosser, Michl.	74	HD
Miller, Christr.	46	EH	Miller, Rudolph	136	LE	Mosser, Nichls.	82	HD
Miller, Conrad	27	BE	Miller, Rudolph	158	LO	Mosser, Nicholas	74	HD
Miller, Daniel	59	HD	Miller, Samuel	63	HD	Mourer, Michael	46	EH
Miller, Daniel	71	HD	Miller, Samuel	72	HD	Mowra, Michael	46	EH
Miller, Daniel	121	LE	Miller, Samuel Sr.	73	HD	Moyer & Feeser	22	BE
Miller, Daniel	124	LE	Miller, Stophel	46	EH	Moyer, ____	28	BE
Miller, Danl.	93	LE	Miller, Thos.	147	LO	Moyer, Abm.	120	LE
Miller, Danl.	148	LO	Miller, Valentine	62	HD	Moyer, Christian	23	BE
Miller, Danl.	154	LO	Miller, Valentine	65	HD	Moyer, Christian	28	BE
Miller, Danl.	158	LO	Miller, Valentine	72	HD	Moyer, Christn.	28	BE
Miller, Danl.	161	LO	Miller, Valentine	74	HD	Moyer, Christn.	36	BE
Miller, David	22	BE	Miller, Valentine (2)	68	HD	Moyer, Christophr.	120	LE
Miller, David	25	BE	Miller, Valentine (2)	73	HD	Moyer, Fred	35	BE
Miller, David	27	BE	Mily, Jacob (2)	32	BE	Moyer, Frederick	28	BE
Miller, David	37	BE	Mily, Martin	31	BE	Moyer, Henry	71	HD
Miller, David (2)	59	HD	Minnick, John	46	EH	Moyer, Henry	74	HD
Miller, David (2)	71	HD	Minsker, James	158	LO	Moyer, Henry	120	LE
Miller, Frederick	85	HD	Mish, Jacob	28	BE	Moyer, Jacob	22	BE
Miller, Frederick (2)	71	HD	Miss, Henry	26	BE	Moyer, Jacob	28	BE
Miller, Fredk.	72	HD	Miss, John	26	BE	Moyer, Jacob	47	EH
Miller, George	28	BE	Mitchel, Thomas	122	LE	Moyer, John	28	BE
Miller, George	64	HD	Mitchell, David	158	LO	Moyer, John	54	HD
Miller, George	71	HD	Mitchell, David	161	LO	Moyer, John	61	HD
Miller, George	83	HD	Mitchell, Thomas	92	LE	Moyer, John	62	HD
Miller, Henry	18	BE	Mitchell, Thos.	97	LE	Moyer, John	69	HD
Miller, Henry	28	BE	Mitchell, Thos.	158	LO	Moyer, John	72	HD
Miller, Henry	30	BE	Mock, Adam	73	HD	Moyer, John	122	LE
Miller, Henry	31	BE	Mock, Adam	79	HD	Moyer, John (2)	121	LE
Miller, Henry	46	EH	Mock, Henry	70	HD	Moyer, John (4)	74	HD
Miller, Henry	49	EH	Mock, Henry	73	HD	Moyer, Martin	74	HD

INDEX

Name	Page	Code	Name	Page	Code	Name	Page	Code
Moyer, Martin	119	LE	Noaker, Christian	63	HD	Peiffer, Jacob	101	LE
Moyer, Martin	121	LE	Noaker, Christian	67	HD	Peiffer, Jacob	123	LE
Moyer, William	135	LE	Noaker, Christian	75	HD	Peiffer, Jacob	124	LE
Moyers, Jacob	51	EH	Nole, Leon	60	HD	Peiffer, Jacob	135	LE
Muma, John	122	LE	Noll, Christn.	142	LO	Peiffer, Jacob	137	LE
Mumma, John	122	LE	Noll, Christn.	159	LO	Peiffer, Jacob	138	LE
Musser, Henry	46	EH	Noll, George	57	HD	Person, George	76	HD
Musser, Henry	49	EH	Noll, John	28	BE	Peter, Henry	101	LE
Musser, Nichls.	159	LO	Noll, John	75	HD	Peter, Henry	124	LE
Musser, Nicholas	142	LO	Noll, Leonard	60	HD	Peters, John	113	LE
Myer, Henry	121	LE	Noll, Leonard (2)	75	HD	Petrie, John	29	BE
Myer, Jacob	28	BE	Noll, Nicholas (2)	75	HD	Petrie, John	35	BE
Myer, Jacob	44	EH	Noll, Phillip	75	HD	Peugh, Brian	160	LO
Myer, Jacob	47	EH	Nyman, Wm.	26	BE	Pewly, William	160	LO
Myer, Jacob	51	EH	Ober, Christr.	144	LO	Phile, Jacob	149	LO
Myer, John	28	BE	Oberholzer, Christn.	29	BE	Philipe, Jacob	76	HD
Myer, John	95	LE	Odenwalt, George	76	HD	Phillipe, Jacob	76	HD
Myer, John	98	LE	Ohrendorff, John	118	LE	Phillipe, John	76	HD
Myer, John	99	LE	Ohrendorff, John	123	LE	Phillipi, Jacob	76	HD
Myer, John	103	LE	Oitner, Mathias	84	HD	Phillipi, Jacob	77	HD
Myer, John	105	LE	Orendorf, Christian	29	BE	Phillipi, Jacob	85	HD
Myer, John	159	LO	Orendorf, Christn.	123	LE	Phillipi, Jacob Jr.	76	HD
Myers, John	159	LO	Orendorf, John	118	LE	Phillipi, John	76	HD
Myers, John	163	LO	Orendorff, Christian	88	LE	Phillipi, John	81	HD
Nagel, Fredrich	122	LE	Orendorff, Christn.	90	LE	Pickel, John	20	BE
Nagel, Fredrich	129	LE	Orendorff, John	123	LE	Pifer, Peter	27	BE
Nasecker, Joseph	148	LO	Orndorf, Christn. (2)	123	LE	Pile, Jacob	149	LO
Naugel, Fredk.	122	LE	Orndorf, John (2)	123	LE	Pile, Jacob	160	LO
Neaff, Jacob	122	LE	Orr, John	161	LO	Pixler, John	144	LO
Neese, Henry	28	BE	Orth & Kelly	153	LO	Pleasant, Philip	76	HD
Neff, George	75	HD	Orth, Gotlib	123	LE	Plough, Christn.	146	LO
Neff, Jacob	75	HD	Orth, Gotlieb	123	LE	Plugar, John	164	LO
Neff, Jacob	122	LE	Orth, Joseph	139	LE	Pointer, Adam	53	EH
Neff, John	75	HD	Orth, Joseph (2)	123	LE	Points, Saml.	145	LO
Neff, Widow	75	HD	Ott, Emanuel	118	LE	Polk, John	36	BE
Neigh, John	122	LE	Over, Christn.	159	LO	Pollem, John	54	HD
Neight, Michael	123	LE	Over, Peter	154	LO	Pollem, John	76	HD
Neil, John	75	HD	Over, Peter	159	LO	Pollem, John	80	HD
Neil, Shea	96	LE	Overholser, Christ	33	BE	Poor, Nicklos	47	EH
Neip, John	81	HD	Overholser, Christ.	19	BE	Porter, John	150	LO
Neise, Jacob	17	BE	Overholser, Christn.	15	BE	Potts, John	34	BE
Ness, Henry	30	BE	Overholser, Christn. (2)	19	BE	Pross, George	47	EH
Ness, Jacob	17	BE	Overholser, Christn. (3)	29	BE	Pross, George	49	EH
Newcomer, Jacob	28	BE	Overholser, Jacob	20	BE	Pross, Peter	40	EH
Newman, ____	65	HD	Overholser, Jacob Jr.	29	BE	Pross, Peter	47	EH
Newman, Henry	79	HD	Overholser, Jacob Sr.	29	BE	Prost, George	40	EH
Newman, John	58	HD	Oyer, Rudy	23	BE	Pruner, Henry	47	EH
Newman, Susan	75	HD	Painter, Jacob	42	EH	Pruner, Henry Jr.	47	EH
Ney, Fredk.	101	LE	Parsonage, Peter	151	LO	Prunner, Henry	47	EH
Ney, John	122	LE	Peck, Andrew	47	EH	Prunner, Henry Jr.	47	EH
Ney, Michael	123	LE	Peck, Philip	33	BE	Pruss, George	40	EH
Ney, Nichls.	160	LO	Peck, Philip	34	BE	Pruss, George	47	EH
Ney, Peter	88	LE	Peelor, Jacob	159	LO	Pruss, George	49	EH
Ney, Peter	107	LE	Peffer, George	120	LE	Pruss, Peter	47	EH
Ney, Petter	123	LE	Pefley, John	29	BE	Puly, William	160	LO
Ney, William	159	LO	Pefly, David	29	BE	Quick, Edward	99	LE
Neycomer, Jacob	28	BE	Pefly, Jacob	29	BE	Quigley, William	160	LO
Neyman, Wm.	26	BE	Pefly, John	32	BE	Raiguel, Abraham	124	LE
Nichelson, John	153	LO	Peifer, Henry	42	EH	Raiguel, Abraham	136	LE
Nicholson, John	150	LO	Peifer, Jacob	103	LE	Raiguel, Abraham	139	LE
Nicholson, John	159	LO	Peifer, Jacob	135	LE	Raiguel, Abram	90	LE
Nickelson, John	123	LE	Peifer, Jacob	138	LE	Raiguel, Abram	98	LE
Nigh, Peter	123	LE	Peiffer, Jacob	90	LE	Raiguel, Abram	110	LE
Niss, Jacob	17	BE	Peiffer, Jacob	98	LE	Ramberger, Adam	91	LE

INDEX

Name	Page	Code	Name	Page	Code	Name	Page	Code
Ramberger, Adam	99	LE	Regengast, Geo.	31	BE	Ridle, Henry	107	LE
Ramberger, Adam	124	LE	Rehr, John	112	LE	Ridle, Henry	139	LE
Ramberger, Adam	140	LE	Reichert, John	106	LE	Ridle, Widow	126	LE
Rambler, Leond.	47	EH	Reidle, John	77	HD	Riegar, Jacob	125	LE
Rambler, Michl.	76	HD	Reifwein, Jacob	90	LE	Riegar, John Est.	126	LE
Rambler, Michl.	124	LE	Reifwine, Jacob	124	LE	Riegart, Adam	160	LO
Rambler, Peter	76	HD	Reili, Ramsey	96	LE	Riegart, John	160	LO
Ramler, Leonard	69	HD	Reily, John	77	HD	Rieguel, Abraham	114	LE
Ramler, Leonard	76	HD	Reinhard, Bernhd.	105	LE	Riem, Christian	77	HD
Ramler, Leond.	47	EH	Reinhart, Bernard	123	LE	Riem, Peter Jr.	77	HD
Ramler, Michael (2)	76	HD	Reinhart, Bernard	124	LE	Ries, Stophel	78	HD
Ramler, Michl.	124	LE	Reinoehl, Conrad	124	LE	Rieser, John	126	LE
Ramler, Peter	76	HD	Reinoehl, Conrad	137	LE	Rigart, John Est.	126	LE
Ramsey, James	39	EH	Reinoehl, George	97	LE	Rigart, Mathis	120	LE
Ramsey, James	47	EH	Reinoehl, George	105	LE	Righart, Maths. Est.	125	LE
Ramsey, Reily	97	LE	Reinoehl, George	119	LE	Rinale, Conrad	124	LE
Ramstead, Henry	145	LO	Reinoehl, Henry	125	LE	Rinale, George	125	LE
Ramsy, James	39	EH	Reinoehl, Henry	139	LE	Rineale, Henry	125	LE
Ramsy, Reili	96	LE	Reinohl, Conrad	129	LE	Riser, Christian	126	LE
Ranck, John	30	BE	Reinohl, Georg	125	LE	Riser, John	126	LE
Ranck, Peter	16	BE	Reinohl, George	114	LE	Risser, Christian	78	HD
Ranck, Peter	29	BE	Reinohl, George	116	LE	Rist, John	78	HD
Ranck, Peter	30	BE	Reinohl, George	125	LE	Ritcher, Adam	125	LE
Rancke, John	19	BE	Reinohl, John	126	LE	Ritsher, Adam	126	LE
Rank, George	47	EH	Reist, John	103	LE	Ritsherd, Peter	126	LE
Rank, John	21	BE	Reist, John	118	LE	Ritter, Christopher	126	LE
Rank, John	30	BE	Reist, John (2)	125	LE	Ritter, Fred	145	LO
Rank, Peter	21	BE	Reist, Peter	100	LE	Ritter, George	78	HD
Rank, Peter	27	BE	Reist, Peter	125	LE	Ritter, Henry	78	HD
Rank, Peter	29	BE	Remer, Abraham	142	LO	Ritter, Michael	126	LE
Rank, Peter	38	BE	Remer, Fredk.	77	HD	Road, Conrad	49	EH
Rapp, Frederick Est.	77	HD	Reser, Daniel	125	LE	Road, Conrad (2)	48	EH
Rauch, George	47	EH	Reser, John	133	LE	Road, John	51	EH
Rauch, Henry	50	EH	Resley, Rudolph	101	LE	Roads, John	39	EH
Rauch, Jacob	31	BE	Resly, Rudolph	125	LE	Rodger, George	143	LO
Rauch, Jacob	35	BE	Rewalt, John	125	LE	Rodgers, George	161	LO
Rauch, John	120	LE	Rex, Saml.	77	HD	Rodgers, MCue	96	LE
Rauch. Jacob	30	BE	Rex, Samuel	74	HD	Roeser, Daniel	135	LE
Rauck, Henry	48	EH	Rex, Samuel (2)	77	HD	Roeser, Daniel	137	LE
Raumler, Leonard	47	EH	Rex/Valentine	79	HD	Roeser, Danl.	125	LE
Raybock, Peter	27	BE	Reymer, Abrm.	142	LO	Roeser, John	120	LE
Rayman, Abm.	160	LO	Reymore, Abm.	149	LO	Roeser, John	126	LE
Raywalt, John	125	LE	Rhoad, Conrad	49	EH	Roeser, John	133	LE
Reagle, Abram	124	LE	Rhoad, John	48	EH	Roesly, Rudolph	104	LE
Ream, Peter	67	HD	Rhoads, Conrad (2)	48	EH	Rogers, Geo.	143	LO
Ream, Peter	70	HD	Rhoads, John	39	EH	Rogers, George	158	LO
Ream, Peter	74	HD	Rhoads, John	42	EH	Rohland, Jacob	105	LE
Ream, Peter	77	HD	Rhoads, John	51	EH	Rohr, John	126	LE
Ream, Peter Sr.	54	HD	Rice, Stophel	78	HD	Rohrer, John	126	LE
Ream, Peter, Sr.	77	HD	Richard, Adam	126	LE	Roland, Jacob	126	LE
Reed, Jacob	77	HD	Richard, Peter	126	LE	Romer Graveyard	126	LE
Reegar, Jacob	161	LO	Richerd, John	99	LE	Ronckel, John	127	LE
Reemor, Abraham	160	LO	Richert, Jacob	125	LE	Rorer, John	129	LE
Reeser, Christian	77	HD	Richert, John	126	LE	Rouch, Henry	48	EH
Reeser, John	149	LO	Richert, Mathes Est.	125	LE	Roush, Jacob	30	BE
Reeser, John	159	LO	Richert, Maths.	120	LE	Rowan, Hugh	50	EH
Reesor, Christian	78	HD	Ricker, Michael	126	LE	Rowland, Jacob	126	LE
Reesor, Christn.	126	LE	Rickert, Christ.	126	LE	Royer, George	78	HD
Reesor, Daniel	125	LE	Rickert, Christn.	89	LE	Royer, John	73	HD
Reesor, John	153	LO	Rickert, Christr.	91	LE	Royer, John	78	HD
Reesor, John	160	LO	Rickert, Christr.	109	LE	Royer, John	81	HD
Reesor, Peter	145	LO	Riddle, Henry	126	LE	Royer, John	55	HD
Reesor, Peter	156	LO	Riddle, Jacob	30	BE	Royer, John (2)	64	HD
Reesor, Peter	160	LO	Ridel, Henry	126	LE	Royer, Saml. (2)	48	EH

INDEX

Name	Page	Code
Rubb, Jacob	127	LE
Rubb, John	127	LE
Ruder, Peter	117	LE
Rudy, Henry	127	LE
Rudy, Jacob	30	BE
Rudy, Jacob	36	BE
Rudy, Jacob	51	EH
Rudy, Jonas	12	BE
Rudy, Jonas	14	BE
Rudy, Jonas	30	BE
Rudy, Ronimus	71	HD
Rudy, Ronimus	78	HD
Rudy, Ronimus	83	HD
Rudy, Widow	22	BE
Rudy, Widow	30	BE
Rugar, Jacob	161	LO
Ruhl, Peter	127	LE
Ruker, Christophr.	48	EH
Rule, Jacob	152	LO
Rule, Peter	127	LE
Rumberger, George	48	EH
Runcle, John	127	LE
Runker, Christr.	48	EH
Runkle, John	127	LE
Runkle, John (2)	95	LE
Rup, Jacob	127	LE
Rup, John (2)	127	LE
Rupp, John (2)	120	LE
Ryer, Saml.	48	EH
Ryer, Saml.	50	EH
Sagor, Jacob	49	EH
Sailor, Christian	79	HD
Saltzer, John	71	HD
Saltzgeber, ____	58	HD
Saltzgeber, John	78	HD
Saltzgeber, John	87	HD
Sam, Jacob	25	BE
Sander, Jacob	128	LE
Satazan, Adam	23	BE
Satazan, Adam	30	BE
Satazan, Adam Jr.	30	BE
Satazan, Jacob	26	BE
Satazan, Jacob	30	BE
Satezahn, Peter	48	EH
Satizan, Michl.	23	BE
Sauder, Jacob	127	LE
Sawyer, John (2)	161	LO
Sawyer, Joseph	161	LO
Sawyer, Widow	161	LO
Saybold, Abm.	21	BE
Saybold, Abm.	24	BE
Saybold, Abm.	30	BE
Saybolt, Abm.	21	BE
Saybolt, Abm. (2)	28	BE
Sayer, John	143	LO
Sayer, John	147	LO
Sayer, John	158	LO
Sayer, John	161	LO
Sayer, John Jr.	161	LO
Sayer, Joseph	161	LO
Sayer, Mrs.	147	LO
Sayer, Widow	161	LO
Sayer, Willm. Est.	161	LO
Sayers, Widow	161	LO
Saylor, Peter	18	BE
Saylor, Peter	28	BE
Saylor, Peter	30	BE
Schmidt, George	79	HD
Schmidt, Jacob's widow	79	HD
School, Francis	38	BE
Schroff, Nichlous	148	LO
Sebastian, Fred	25	BE
Sebolt, Abm.	24	BE
Sebolt, Abm.	30	BE
Sebolt, Abm.	33	BE
Sebot, Nicolus	98	LE
Sechrist, Solomon	90	LE
Seck, Henry	130	LE
Seechrist, Lawrence	107	LE
Seechrist, Lawrence	127	LE
Seechrist, Salomon	127	LE
Seegely, Jacob	110	LE
Seegely, Jacob	127	LE
Seegely, Jacob	139	LE
Segar, Widow	32	BE
Segrist, Lorentz	107	LE
Segrist, Lorentz	127	LE
Segrist, Salomon	127	LE
Segrist, Solomon	109	LE
Seibert, Christian	62	HD
Seibert, Christian (2)	82	HD
Seibert, Christian Jr.	57	HD
Seibert, Christn.	79	HD
Seibert, Christn. Sr.	79	HD
Seibert, Frantz	69	HD
Seibert, Frantz	71	HD
Seibert, Frantz	79	HD
Seibert, Frantz	84	HD
Seigler, Henry	48	EH
Seigler, Henry (2)	50	EH
Seiler, Christian	79	HD
Seiler, Peter	30	BE
Seiss, Peter	76	HD
Selsir, Christian	48	EH
Seltzer, Christ	26	BE
Seltzer, Christian	31	BE
Seltzer, Christian	34	BE
Seltzer, Christian	36	BE
Seltzer, Christn.	48	EH
Seltzer, Christn.	49	EH
Seltzer, Christn.	52	EH
Seltzer, Henry	31	BE
Seltzer, John	12	BE
Seltzer, John	16	BE
Seltzer, John	31	BE
Seltzer, Michael	45	EH
Seltzer, Michael	48	EH
Seltzer, Michl.	44	EH
Selzer, Christn.	30	BE
Sergant, Joseph	127	LE
Sering, Christian	49	EH
Sering, Henry (heirs)	49	EH
Sering, Ludwig	50	EH
Sering, Ludwig (3)	49	EH
Server, Henry	162	LO
Seybolt, Abm.	30	BE
Seyfort, Anthony	77	HD
Seyly, Jacob	127	LE
Shaack, Philip	128	LE
Shaak, Nicholas	106	LE
Shaak, Nicolus	128	LE
Shaak, Philip	103	LE
Shaak, Philip	114	LE
Shaak, Philip	128	LE
Shaak, Phillip	121	LE
Shaake, John	90	LE
Shaake, Nicolas	128	LE
Shaake, Philip	128	LE
Shaefer, Henry Esq.	79	HD
Shaefer, Henry Esq. (2)	66	HD
Shaefer, John	80	HD
Shaeffer, Geo.	148	LO
Shaeffer, Geo.	152	LO
Shaeffer, Geo.	152	LO
Shaeffer, George	161	LO
Shaeffer, Isaac	129	LE
Shaeffer, Jost.	158	LO
Shaeffer, Michl.	24	BE
Shaeffer, Michl.	31	BE
Shaffer, George	49	EH
Shaffer, George	161	LO
Shaffer, Isaac (2)	134	LE
Shaffner, Henry	98	LE
Shaffner, Henry	127	LE
Shaffner, Henry	128	LE
Shaffner, Peter	133	LE
Shalenberger, John	132	LE
Shalleberger, John	99	LE
Shallenberger, John	128	LE
Shally, Baltzer	128	LE
Shally, Baltzer	135	LE
Shally, John	17	BE
Shally, John	30	BE
Shally, John	31	BE
Shally, Lucas	128	LE
Shamo, Joseph	139	LE
Shank, Adam (2)	162	LO
Shank, Adm.	150	LO
Shank, Michael (2)	162	LO
Shank, Michl.	145	LO
Shantz, George	113	LE
Shantz, George	120	LE
Shantz, George	128	LE
Shantz, Henry	119	LE
Shantz, Henry	128	LE
Sharf, John	80	HD
Shark, Abm.	46	EH
Shark, Abraham	49	EH
Sharp, ____	154	LO
Sharp, ____	162	LO
Shaufler, Christian	49	EH
Shaufler, Christn.	49	EH
Shaufler, Val.	49	EH
Shaufler, Valentine	50	EH
Shaw, Neil	97	LE
Shawk, John	129	LE
Shawk, Nicholas	128	LE
Shawk, Philip	128	LE
Shay, John	129	LE
Shead, Charles	21	BE
Shead, Charles	31	BE
Shead, Charles	37	BE

INDEX

Name	Page	Code	Name	Page	Code	Name	Page	Code
Shead, Charles	49	EH	Shewey, Martin	31	BE	Shuey, Martin	31	BE
Shead, Charles	53	EH	Shewy, Henry	49	EH	Shultz, Christian	85	HD
Shead, Chas.	41	EH	Shewy, Henry	52	EH	Shultz, Christn.	81	HD
Sheade, Charles	47	EH	Shewy, Ludwig	49	EH	Shultz, John	61	HD
Sheade, Chas.	27	BE	Shidenhawer, John	164	LO	Shultz, Widow	82	HD
Sheadle, John	145	LO	Shiffler, John	80	HD	Shuntz, Peter	160	LO
Sheaffer, Geo.	41	EH	Shindel, Peter	93	LE	Shutz, Mathias	162	LO
Sheaffer, George	47	EH	Shindel, Peter	124	LE	Shuy, Martin	11	BE
Sheaffer, George	49	EH	Shindel, Peter	129	LE	Sibert, Henry	157	LO
Sheaffer, Margt.	43	EH	Shindle, Peter	32	BE	Sickele, Jacob	127	LE
Shearer, John	129	LE	Shindle, Peter	100	LE	Sickle, Jacob	139	LE
Shed, Charles	31	BE	Shingle, Peter	104	LE	Sider, Geo.	150	LO
Sheeler, John	96	LE	Shire, George	162	LO	Siderbricker, Philip	48	EH
Shefer, H. Esq.	77	HD	Shire, Jacob	162	LO	Siderbriker, Philip	50	EH
Shefer, Henry Esq.	76	HD	Shirk, Abm.	46	EH	Sidestricker, Philip	50	EH
Shefer, Henry Esq.	77	HD	Shirk, Abraham	49	EH	Sieffert, Peter	27	BE
Shefer, Henry Esq.	81	HD	Shirk, Casper	22	BE	Siegrist, Lorentz	111	LE
Shefer, John	76	HD	Shirk, Casper	28	BE	Sig, Henry	91	LE
Sheffer, Isaac	102	LE	Shirk, Casper	32	BE	Sig, Henry	130	LE
Sheffer, Isaac	129	LE	Shirk, Casper, Jr.	32	BE	Sig, Henry	134	LE
Sheffer, Isaac	134	LE	Shirk, Jacob	130	LE	Siglar, Henry	50	EH
Sheirer, John	123	LE	Shitz, Jacob	55	HD	Sigle, Jacob	127	LE
Shell, ____ Sr.	80	HD	Shitz, Jacob	69	HD	Simmerman, John	50	EH
Shell, Michl.	153	LO	Shitz, Jacob (3)	80	HD	Simmerman, Michl.	50	EH
Shell, Peter	74	HD	Shitz, Maths.	162	LO	Simmon, George	68	HD
Shell, Peter (2)	80	HD	Shitz, Peter	60	HD	Simmon, George	74	HD
Shellen, Jacob	26	BE	Shitz, Peter	81	HD	Simmon, George	79	HD
Sheller,	121	LE	Shitz, Peter (2)	79	HD	Simmon, George	82	HD
Sheller, Adam	142	LO	Shitz, Widow	81	HD	Simon, George	82	HD
Sheller, Adam	162	LO	Shlessman, Peter	80	HD	Simon, John	42	EH
Shellinger, Michl.	153	LO	Shlessman, Peter	81	HD	Simon, John	50	EH
Shelly, Jas.	153	LO	Shnebely, Geo.	89	LE	Singer, Michael	130	LE
Shenck, Joseph	136	LE	Shnebely, Geo. (2)	131	LE	Singer, Michael	136	LE
Shendle, Peter	129	LE	Shnebely, Henry	131	LE	Sink, Henry	145	LO
Shenk, John	57	HD	Shnebely, John	131	LE	Sinkel, John Negro	82	HD
Shenk, John	80	HD	Shnebely, Peter	131	LE	Six, Jacob	130	LE
Shenk, John	86	HD	Shnebly, Geo.	140	LE	Six, Jacob	134	LE
Shenk, John	87	HD	Shnebly, Henry	131	LE	Six, Jacob	135	LE
Shenk, Joseph	109	LE	Shnee, John	101	LE	Slaterback, Michael	137	LE
Shenk, Joseph	127	LE	Shnee, John	119	LE	Slessman, Peter	86	HD
Shenk, Joseph	129	LE	Shnee, John	120	LE	Slichter, Nicholas	82	HD
Sherck, Saml.	129	LE	Shnee, John	129	LE	Sloan, John	50	EH
Sherer, John	88	LE	Sholl, Adam	81	HD	Sloterbeck, John	130	LE
Sherer, John	126	LE	Sholl, John	81	HD	Slotterbech, John	130	LE
Sherer, John	129	LE	Sholl, Simon	81	HD	Smeltzer, Adam	50	EH
Sherg, Samuel	129	LE	Sholly, Baltzer	133	LE	Smith, Catharine	78	HD
Sherk, Casper	24	BE	Shome, Joseph	122	LE	Smith, Charles	96	LE
Sherk, Casper	28	BE	Shomo, Joseph Est.	129	LE	Smith, Felty	49	EH
Sherk, Casper, Jr.	29	BE	Short, David	20	BE	Smith, Felty	53	EH
Sherk, Saml.	129	LE	Shott, George	114	LE	Smith, George	79	HD
Sherlet, Bernard	81	HD	Shott, Lotwig	130	LE	Smith, George	87	HD
Shertel, Bernard	69	HD	Shoufler, Christian	50	EH	Smith, Henry	94	LE
Shertel, Bernard	80	HD	Shoufler, Christn.	49	EH	Smith, Henry (2)	130	LE
Shertzer, John	118	LE	Shoufler, Valentine	50	EH	Smith, Jacob	120	LE
Shertzer, John	129	LE	Shram, Henry	58	HD	Smith, Jacob (2)	130	LE
Shesler, John	52	EH	Shreck, Geo.	84	HD	Smith, John	82	HD
Shetz, Christian	81	HD	Shreiner, William	72	HD	Smith, John	96	LE
Shewey, Christn.	22	BE	Shriner, John	61	HD	Smith, John (2)	130	LE
Shewey, Christn.	31	BE	Shriver, Henry	162	LO	Smith, Peter	22	BE
Shewey, Henry Jr.	49	EH	Shriver, Widow	81	HD	Smith, Peter	29	BE
Shewey, Mart.	17	BE	Shrobaker, Joseph	148	LO	Smith, Peter	31	BE
Shewey, Martin	14	BE	Shuey, Christn.	31	BE	Smith, Peter	36	BE
Shewey, Martin	17	BE	Shuey, Christn.	32	BE	Smith, Peter	130	LE
Shewey, Martin	29	BE	Shuey, Henry	48	EH	Smith, Peter Jr.	32	BE

INDEX

Name	Page	Code	Name	Page	Code	Name	Page	Code
Smith, Peter Sr.	32	BE	Spengler, Peter	82	HD	Stewart, William (2)	50	EH
Smith, Valentine	49	EH	Spengler, Widow	82	HD	Stickley, Abm.	159	LO
Smith, Valentine	50	EH	Spiker, Peter	33	BE	Stickley, Abm.	162	LO
Smith, Widow	97	LE	Spitler, Henry	31	BE	Stieb, Jacob	93	LE
Snatterly, Barbara	131	LE	Spitler, Jacob	19	BE	Stieb, Jacob	97	LE
Snavely, Henry	36	BE	Spitler, John	19	BE	Stieb, Jacob	132	LE
Snavely, Isaac	25	BE	Spitler, John	25	BE	Stiegel, Widow	83	HD
Snavly, Peter	119	LE	Spitler, John	33	BE	Stiel, David	109	LE
Sne, John	120	LE	Spitler, Widow	26	BE	Stiel, David	137	LE
Sne, John	122	LE	Sprecher, Frederick	131	LE	Stine, Abm.	33	BE
Sne, John	129	LE	Spyker, Benj.	111	LE	Stine, Abm.	47	EH
Snebely, Henry	34	BE	Spyker, Peter (3)	33	BE	Stine, Adam	51	EH
Snebely, Henry	35	BE	Staner, Jacob	142	LO	Stine, Adam (2)	41	EH
Snebly, Henry	13	BE	Stanz, Widow	37	BE	Stine, Adam Jr.	51	EH
Snebly, Isaac	32	BE	Statler, Michl.	33	BE	Stine, Elisabeth	33	BE
Snebly, John	32	BE	Staub, Margaret	33	BE	Stine, Frederick	82	HD
Snee, John	117	LE	Staufer, Henry	163	LO	Stine, George	28	BE
Sneider, Michael	131	LE	Stauffer, Henry	144	LO	Stine, George	33	BE
Snevely, Henry	32	BE	Stauffer, John	133	LE	Stine, Henry	33	BE
Snevely, Henry	131	LE	Stear, Adam	117	LE	Stine, Henry	34	BE
Snevely, Isaac	32	BE	Stear, Adam	131	LE	Stine, Henry	38	BE
Snevely, John	31	BE	Stear, John	107	LE	Stine, Peter	82	HD
Snevely, John	32	BE	Stear, John	132	LE	Stine, Philip	40	EH
Snevely, John	33	BE	Steckbeck, Frany	132	LE	Stine, Philip	41	EH
Snevely, John	131	LE	Steckbeck, Michael	132	LE	Stine, Philip	51	EH
Snevely, Peter	131	LE	Steckbeck, Michl.	102	LE	Stineman, Jacob	20	BE
Snevly, George	140	LE	Steckpeck, Michl.	15	BE	Stineman, Jacob	24	BE
Snevly, George (2)	131	LE	Steeb, Jacob	132	LE	Stineman, Jacob	33	BE
Snevly, Henry (2)	131	LE	Steel, David	101	LE	Stoehr, John	138	LE
Snevly, Jacob	131	LE	Steel, David	109	LE	Stoever, Adam	106	LE
Snevly, Jacob	137	LE	Steel, David	132	LE	Stoever, Adam	132	LE
Snevly, John	131	LE	Steel, David	133	LE	Stoever, Adam	133	LE
Snevly, Peter	131	LE	Steel, David	137	LE	Stoever, Adam (2)	131	LE
Snevly, Peter (2)	119	LE	Steever, Adam	50	EH	Stoever, Adam Jr.	132	LE
Snider, Michael	133	LE	Steever, Casper	21	BE	Stoever, Fred.	91	LE
Snider, Michael	134	LE	Stegar, Philip	103	LE	Stoever, Fredk.	98	LE
Snider, Michl.	131	LE	Steger, Fredrich	120	LE	Stoever, Fredk.	105	LE
Snoak, John	131	LE	Steger, Fredrick.	132	LE	Stoever, Fredk.	137	LE
Snoderle, Barbara	131	LE	Steger, Jacob	49	EH	Stoever, Fredrich	132	LE
Snog, John	126	LE	Steger, John	102	LE	Stoever, George	130	LE
Snog, John	131	LE	Steger, Peter	100	LE	Stoever, John	131	LE
Snog, John	139	LE	Steger, Peter	105	LE	Stoever, John	133	LE
Snoke, John	126	LE	Steger, Peter	132	LE	Stoever, John (2)	132	LE
Snoke, John	131	LE	Stehr, Adam	132	LE	Stoever, Philip	95	LE
Snoke, John	139	LE	Stehr, John	132	LE	Stoever, Tobias	133	LE
Snotterly, Barbara	111	LE	Stehr, John	133	LE	Stohler, Henry	83	HD
Snyder, George	150	LO	Steimer, Frederick	65	HD	Stoler, Henry	83	HD
Snyder, Michl.	131	LE	Stein, Fredk.	82	HD	Stoler, John	73	HD
Snyder, Michl.	133	LE	Stein, Peter	82	HD	Stone, Adam	47	EH
Snyder, Michl.	134	LE	Steiner, August (2)	82	HD	Stone, Adam	51	EH
Souder, Jacob	111	LE	Steiner, Frederick	61	HD	Stone, Adam	52	EH
Souder, Jacob	127	LE	Steiner, Frederick	83	HD	Stone, Adam (2)	41	EH
Sower, Henry	162	LO	Steiner, Fredk.	61	HD	Stone, Adm. Jr.	51	EH
Spangler, Michl.	48	EH	Steiner, Fredk.	66	HD	Stone, Geo. Est.	133	LE
Spanhuth, Henry	82	HD	Steiner, Fredk. Jr.	83	HD	Stone, John	91	LE
Spanhuth, Henry J.	60	HD	Steiner, Michael	83	HD	Stoner, Christn.	148	LO
Speeker, Peter	33	BE	Stevcek, Christn.	162	LO	Stoner, Christr.	163	LO
Spengler, George	65	HD	Stever, Adam	50	EH	Stoner, Geo. Est.	98	LE
Spengler, George	69	HD	Stever, Tobias	83	HD	Stoner, Jacob	11	BE
Spengler, George	82	HD	Stevick, Charles	162	LO	Stoner, Jacob	160	LO
Spengler, John	131	LE	Stevick, John (2)	162	LO	Stoner, Jacob	163	LO
Spengler, Martin	63	HD	Stewart, John	161	LO	Stouch, Conrad	130	LE
Spengler, Peter	65	HD	Stewart, John (2)	50	EH	Stoufer, Daniel	123	LE
Spengler, Peter	66	HD	Stewart, William	43	EH	Stoufer, Henry	163	LO

INDEX

Name	Page	Code
Stoufer, John	133	LE
Stough, Conrad	130	LE
Stover, Casper	33	BE
Stover, Fredrick	115	LE
Stower, Adam	51	EH
Stower, Casper	33	BE
Stoy, Gustavus	132	LE
Stoy, William Sr.	133	LE
Stoy, Wm.	112	LE
Stoy, Wm. Jr.	133	LE
Strack, Henry	54	HD
Strack, Henry	65	HD
Strack, Henry	68	HD
Strack, Henry	83	HD
Straw, Daniel	33	BE
Straw, George	111	LE
Straw, Michael	34	BE
Straw, Michael	44	EH
Straw, Michael	45	EH
Straw, Michael	51	EH
Straw, Michl.	14	BE
Straw, Michl.	36	BE
Straw, Michl. Sr.	34	BE
Stream, John	128	LE
Strear, John	133	LE
Strickler, Andrew	83	HD
Strickler, Andw.	65	HD
Strickler, George	79	HD
Strickler, George	84	HD
Strickler, George (2)	83	HD
Strickler, Leonard	84	HD
Strickler, Peter	58	HD
Stroeher, John	133	LE
Stroh, Daniel	34	BE
Stroh, Daniel	133	LE
Stroh, John	100	LE
Stroh, Michael	34	BE
Strohding, Andrew	51	EH
Strohm, Abm.	28	BE
Strohm, Abm.	34	BE
Strohm, Abm.	35	BE
Strohm, Abm.	38	BE
Strohm, Abraham	15	BE
Strohm, Geo.	89	LE
Strohm, George	133	LE
Strohm, Henry (2)	133	LE
Strohm, John	89	LE
Strohm, John	131	LE
Strohm, John	133	LE
Strohm, John	134	LE
Strome, George	133	LE
Strome, Henry	133	LE
Strome, Henry	133	LE
Strome, John	131	LE
Strome, John	133	LE
Strome, John	134	LE
Strow, Elisabeth	130	LE
Strow, Elisabeth	134	LE
Strow, John	134	LE
Stryker, Peter	37	BE
Stump, Adam	28	BE
Stump, Leonard	84	HD
Swan, Joshua	84	HD
Swanger, Nicholas	58	HD
Swanger, Nicholas	73	HD
Swanger, Nicholas	84	HD
Swanger, Nicholas	85	HD
Swarm, Adam	84	HD
Swartz, George	51	EH
Swartz, Henry	46	EH
Swartz, Henry	48	EH
Swartz, Henry	51	EH
Swartz, John	40	EH
Swartz, John	51	EH
Sweitzer, Gertraut	84	HD
Sweitzer, John	60	HD
Swop, Jacob	134	LE
Swope, Jacob	116	LE
Swope, Jacob	121	LE
Swope, Jacob	134	LE
Talebach, Peter	147	LO
Teis, David	134	LE
Teis, Henry	118	LE
Teis, Henry	134	LE
Teis, Jacob	116	LE
Teis, Jacob	124	LE
Teis, Jacob	134	LE
Teis, Michl.	134	LE
Teiss, Michl.	107	LE
Teiss, Michl.	111	LE
Thoma, Jacob	134	LE
Thoma, John Est.	134	LE
Thoma, Martin	163	LO
Thoma, Martin	164	LO
Thomas, Eberhart	134	LE
Thomas, Widow	51	EH
Thome, John	98	LE
Thome, John	110	LE
Thome, John Esq.	134	LE
Thompson, Saml.	162	LO
Tibbins, John	51	EH
Tibbins, John (2)	49	EH
Tibbins, John (2)	50	EH
Tice, David	134	LE
Tice, Henry	134	LE
Tice, Jacob	130	LE
Tice, Jacob	134	LE
Tice, Michael	129	LE
Tice, Michael	134	LE
Tise, Jacob	126	LE
Title, Henry	12	BE
Tittle, Geo.	52	EH
Tittle, George	44	EH
Tittle, George	51	EH
Tittle, Henry	34	BE
Tittle, Jacob	51	EH
Tittle, Jacob	52	EH
Todd, John	147	LO
Toebler, David	76	HD
Tollebach, _____ (2)	146	LO
Tolleback, Peter	147	LO
Toner, John	93	LE
Tratten, Sarah	119	LE
Tratter, Sarah	135	LE
Traxel, Abraham	135	LE
Traxel, John	92	LE
Traxel, John	118	LE
Traxel, John (2)	135	LE
Trion, Michl. Doct.	84	HD
Trotter, Sarah	135	LE
Troutman, Jonas	56	HD
Troutman, Jonas	72	HD
Troutman, Jonas	76	HD
Troutman, Jonas	78	HD
Troutman, Jonas	84	HD
Troutman, Jonas	86	HD
Trump, George	120	LE
Twigg, Edwn.	160	LO
Uhland, George	52	EH
Uhler, Christopher	115	LE
Uhler, Christo'r.	135	LE
Uhler, Christr.	93	LE
Uhler, Christr.	100	LE
Uhler, Christr.	104	LE
Uhler, Christr.	105	LE
Uhler, Christr.	109	LE
Uhler, Christr.	122	LE
Uhler, Christr.	125	LE
Uhler, Christr.	126	LE
Uhler, Christr.	132	LE
Uhler, Christr.	138	LE
Uhler, John	34	BE
Uhler, Martin	31	BE
Uhler, Martin	34	BE
Uhler, Martin	35	BE
Uhler, Martin	108	LE
Uhler, Martin	135	LE
Uhler, Martin	137	LE
Uhler, Martin	138	LE
Uhler, Martin (4)	117	LE
Uhler, Michael	135	LE
Uhler, Michael	136	LE
Uhler, Michl.	135	LE
Uhrich, Christn.	135	LE
Uhrich, George	136	LE
Uhrich, John	56	HD
Uhrich, John	84	HD
Uhrich, Michael	136	LE
Uhrich, Michael	139	LE
Uhrich, Michl.	108	LE
Uhrich, Philip	98	LE
Uhrich, Philip	136	LE
Uhrich, Valentine (2)	85	HD
Ulrich, Christo'r.	136	LE
Ulrich, Christo'r. Est.	136	LE
Ulrich, Frantz	81	HD
Ulrich, Frantz	85	HD
Ulrich, John	85	HD
Ulrich, Martin	95	LE
Ulrich, Martin	109	LE
Ulrich, Martin	136	LE
Ulrich, Michael	163	LO
Ulrich, Tobias	90	LE
Ulrich, Tobias	130	LE
Ulrich, Tobias	136	LE
Umberger, John	102	LE
Umberger, John	104	LE
Umberger, John	125	LE
Umberger, John	135	LE
Umberger, John	136	LE
Umberger, John	148	LO
Umberger, Jonas	136	LE

INDEX

Name	Page	Code	Name	Page	Code	Name	Page	Code
Unbehend, Jacob	84	HD	Waltz, Christor.	137	LE	Weltmer, Abm.	159	LO
Unbehend, Jacob	85	HD	Waltz, Christr.	93	LE	Weltmer, Abm.	163	LO
Unbehind, Jacob	60	HD	Waltz, Christr.	108	LE	Weltmer, Ulrich	155	LO
Unger, Val	23	BE	Ward, Patrick	90	LE	Weltmer, Ulrich	159	LO
Unger, Valentine	34	BE	Ward, Samuel	29	BE	Weltmer, Ulrich	163	LO
Union Forge	52	EH	Weaber, Henry	98	LE	Wenddelblech, Adam	36	BE
Urich, Christian	109	LE	Weaver, Adam	29	BE	Wendelblech, Adam	17	BE
Urich, Henry	34	BE	Weaver, Adam	35	BE	Wendelblech, Adam	36	BE
Urich, John	70	HD	Weaver, George	35	BE	Wendelblech, Geo.	30	BE
Valentine, Michl.	79	HD	Weaver, Henry	30	BE	Wendelblech, Geo.	36	BE
Valentine/Rex	79	HD	Weaver, Henry	35	BE	Wengard. Joseph	30	BE
Vendling, Jacob	52	EH	Weaver, Henry	36	BE	Wengart, Abram.	52	EH
Volever, Peter	27	BE	Weaver, Henry (2)	34	BE	Wengart, John	17	BE
Volkmartz, Fred	19	BE	Weaver, John	61	HD	Wengart, John	36	BE
Waggoner, Conrad	34	BE	Weaver, John	85	HD	Wengart, Joseph	36	BE
Waggoner, Geo.	56	HD	Weaver, Philip	12	BE	Wenger, Jacob	36	BE
Waggoner, Geo.	85	HD	Weaver, Philip	35	BE	Wenger, John	34	BE
Waggoner, George	56	HD	Weaver, Widow	85	HD	Wenger, John	36	BE
Waggoner, Michl.	34	BE	Weaver, Widow	103	LE	Wenger, Joseph	36	BE
Wagner, Daniel	130	LE	Weaver, Wm.	38	BE	Wengert, John	14	BE
Wagner, Henry	100	LE	Webbert, Andrew	35	BE	Wengert, John	22	BE
Wagner, Henry	119	LE	Weber, George	35	BE	Wenner, Henry	138	LE
Wagoner, Conrd.	32	BE	Weber, Henry	35	BE	Wenner, Jacob	36	BE
Wagoner, Conrd.	34	BE	Weber, Widow	113	LE	Wentling, Peter	100	LE
Wagoner, Henry	136	LE	Weich, Christ	77	HD	Wentling, Peter	119	LE
Wagoner, Jacob	52	EH	Weick, Adam	86	HD	Wentling, Peter	138	LE
Wagoner, John	15	BE	Weick, Christian	60	HD	Wentling, Peter	140	LE
Wagoner, John	34	BE	Weick, Christian	86	HD	Wentz, Peter	138	LE
Wagoner, John	44	EH	Weick, Gehret	86	HD	Wentz, Peter (2)	105	LE
Wagoner, Sebastn.	35	BE	Weidman, John	40	EH	Werner, Henry	97	LE
Wagoner, Sebastn. (2)	30	BE	Weidman, John	137	LE	Werner, Henry	100	LE
Walborn, Andrew	24	BE	Weidman, John Esq.	52	EH	Werner, Henry	135	LE
Walborn, Andrew	35	BE	Weidman, John Esq.	53	EH	Werner, Henry	138	LE
Walborn, Andw.	15	BE	Weiman, George	66	HD	Wert, Christian Est.	138	LE
Walborn, Christn. (2)	35	BE	Weiman, George	86	HD	Wert, Conrad	25	BE
Walborn, Christr.	85	HD	Weiny, Jacob	129	LE	Wert, Michael	37	BE
Walborn, George	35	BE	Weirich, Christn.	137	LE	Westman, John	113	LE
Walborn, Herman	85	HD	Weirich, Jacob	88	LE	Wetzel, William	36	BE
Walborn, Jacob	33	BE	Weirich, Jacob	112	LE	Wetzel, Wm.	12	BE
Walborn, Jacob (2)	35	BE	Weirich, Jacob	122	LE	Wever, Adam	35	BE
Walborn, Martin	11	BE	Weirich, Jacob (2)	137	LE	Wever, Widow	138	LE
Walborn, Martin (2)	35	BE	Weirich, John	138	LE	Wheelen, Fredk.	139	LE
Walburn, Christn.	63	HD	Weirich, Peter	137	LE	White, Thos.	163	LO
Walburn, Christr.	85	HD	Weirich, Peter	138	LE	Whitman, Henry	86	HD
Walburn, Herman	85	HD	Weis, Henry	96	LE	Wickart, Francis	48	EH
Walburn, John	69	HD	Weis, Henry	138	LE	Widel, Danl.	36	BE
Walburn, John	70	HD	Weis, Jacob	138	LE	Widele, Danl.	31	BE
Walburn, John	85	HD	Weis, Nicolas	138	LE	Widele, Danl.	31	BE
Walburn, Martin	85	HD	Weise, Henry	115	LE	Wideman, John	137	LE
Waldemartz, F.	19	BE	Weise, Jacob	134	LE	Wideman, John Sr.	52	EH
Waldemartz, Fred	35	BE	Weiss, Christn.	86	HD	Widle, Daniel	37	BE
Waldemartz, Fred	37	BE	Weiss, George	70	HD	Widle, Danl.	36	BE
Wallace, John	52	EH	Weiss, Henry	80	HD	Widman, John	40	EH
Wallace, Wm.	153	LO	Weiss, Henry (2)	86	HD	Wilhelm, Christn.	138	LE
Walmer, John	52	EH	Weiss, Jacob	86	HD	Wilhelm, Henry	14	BE
Walmer, Peter	44	EH	Weiss, Jacob	103	LE	Wilhelm, Henry	28	BE
Walmer, Peter	49	EH	Weiss, John	68	HD	Wilhelm, Henry	33	BE
Walmer, Peter	53	EH	Weitman, John	120	LE	Wilhelm, Henry	36	BE
Walter, Abram	137	LE	Weitzel, Elias	124	LE	Wilhelm, John	138	LE
Walter, Christr.	137	LE	Weller, Philip	36	BE	Williams, Fredk.	92	LE
Walter, Henry	137	LE	Weller, Philip (2)	28	BE	Williams, Fredrick	139	LE
Walter, John	106	LE	Welpmer, Abm.	142	LO	Williams, Henry	139	LE
Walter, John (2)	137	LE	Welpmer, Abm.	147	LO	Willing, August	37	BE
Walter, Peter	137	LE	Welsh, Catrina	138	LE	Willy, August	35	BE

INDEX

Name	Page	Code
Willy, Augustus	37	BE
Wilt, Dewald Est.	37	BE
Wilt, Dewalt	26	BE
Wilt, Jacob	16	BE
Wilt, Jacob	37	BE
Wime, Jacob	139	LE
Winebecker, Henry	40	EH
Winey, Jacob	139	LE
Wingart, Christn.	52	EH
Wingert, Christn.	48	EH
Winter, Christian	42	EH
Winter, Christn.	53	EH
Winter, Christopher	53	EH
Winter, Henry	43	EH
Winter, Henry (2)	53	EH
Winter, Stophel	42	EH
Winter, Widow	86	HD
Wirick, Christn.	137	LE
Wirick, Jacob (2)	137	LE
Wirick, John	138	LE
Wirick, Peter	138	LE
Wirt, Conrad	37	BE
Wirt, Conrat	13	BE
Wirt, Michael	37	BE
Wishter, Anthony	137	LE
Wiss, Nichlos	138	LE
Witemoyer, Ludwig	84	HD
Witemoyer, Ludwig	86	HD
Witman, Henry	86	HD
Witmer, Peter	89	LE
Witmer, Peter	115	LE
Witmer, Peter	139	LE
Witmore, Peter	139	LE
Witmyer, David	161	LO
Witmyer, David	163	LO
Wittemyer, David	163	LO
Wolever, Peter	37	BE
Wolf, Abraham	139	LE
Wolf, Barbara	164	LO
Wolf, Christian	16	BE
Wolf, Christian	23	BE
Wolf, Christian	37	BE
Wolf, Christian	127	LE
Wolf, Christian Jr.	37	BE
Wolf, Christian Sr. (2)	37	BE
Wolf, Christn.	101	LE
Wolf, Christn.	139	LE
Wolf, Jacob	51	EH
Wolf, Michael	86	HD
Wolf, Nicholas	23	BE
Wolf, Nicholas	37	BE
Wolf, Paul	37	BE
Wolf, Peter	37	BE
Wolf, Widow	38	BE
Wolf, Widow	53	EH
Wolfe, John (lots)	37	BE
Wolfelsberger, Fred (2)	164	LO
Wolfelsberger, Philip	152	LO
Wolfelsberger, Philip	161	LO
Wolfelsberger, Philip	164	LO
Wolfersberger, Philip	152	LO
Wolfersberger, Geo.	87	HD
Wolfersberger, George	65	HD
Wolfersberger, John	164	LO
Wolfersberger, Peter	87	HD
Wolfersberger, Philip	151	LO
Wolfersberger, Philip	163	LO
Wolfersberger, Philip (2)	164	LO
Wolfersperger, Lisabeth	139	LE
Wolfesberger, Eliza	139	LE
Wolff, Michael	62	HD
Wolmer, John	49	EH
Wolmer, Peter	53	EH
Woods, James	31	BE
Woods, James	33	BE
Woods, James	38	BE
Woods, James	52	EH
Woods, James (Col.)	47	EH
Woods, James Col.	53	EH
Woolf, Abram	139	LE
Woolf, John	11	BE
Worrel, Joseph	29	BE
Worrel, Joseph	36	BE
Worrel, Joseph	38	BE
Wray, David	143	LO
Wray, David	164	LO
Xander, Emanuel	139	LE
Xander, George	69	HD
Xander, Jacob	125	LE
Xander, Jacob (2)	136	LE
Xanders, Jacob	139	LE
Yeakly, Henry	18	BE
Yeakly, Rudolph	38	BE
Yeakly, Rudy	18	BE
Yechly, Rudy	18	BE
Yong, John	42	EH
Yordy, Henry	107	LE
Yost, Casper	104	LE
Young, Andrew	41	EH
Young, Andrew	53	EH
Young, Andrew (2)	46	EH
Young, Geo.	22	BE
Young, George	38	BE
Young, Jacob	18	BE
Young, Jacob	38	BE
Young, James	53	EH
Young, John	42	EH
Young, John	53	EH
Young, John	78	HD
Young, Widow	53	EH
Zander, Michl.	20	BE
Zartman, Jacob	87	HD
Zeabolt, Leonard	140	LE
Zearing, Jacob	16	BE
Zebold, Leonard	91	LE
Zebold, Leond.	99	LE
Zebolt, Leonhard	140	LE
Zebolt, Nichl. Est.	140	LE
Zehrung, John	120	LE
Zehrung, John	139	LE
Zeller, _____	77	HD
Zeller, Andw.	71	HD
Zeller, George	75	HD
Zeller, George	87	HD
Zeller, Peter	71	HD
Zeller, Peter	78	HD
Zeller, Peter	81	HD
Zeller, Peter	84	HD
Zeller, Peter	87	HD
Zent, Jacob	139	LE
Zent, Jacob	140	LE
Zering, Jacob	16	BE
Zering, Jacob	38	BE
Zering, John	131	LE
Zerring, John	89	LE
Zerring, John	120	LE
Zerring, John	139	LE
Zibold, Leonhart	140	LE
Zibold, Nicolas Est.	140	LE
Ziegler, Jacob	110	LE
Ziegler, John	140	LE
Zigler, John	140	LE
Zimerman, Fredrick Est.	140	LE
Zimerman, Gotfry	139	LE
Zimerman, Gotfry	140	LE
Zimerman, Leonhart	140	LE
Zimerman, Michael	140	LE
Zimmerman, Fred	90	LE
Zimmerman, Fred	110	LE
Zimmerman, Geo.	72	HD
Zimmerman, Geo. Jr.	87	HD
Zimmerman, Geo. S.	87	HD
Zimmerman, Geo. Sr.	87	HD
Zimmerman, George	62	HD
Zimmerman, H. J.	78	HD
Zimmerman, H. J.	87	HD
Zimmerman, Henry	79	HD
Zimmerman, Henry	87	HD
Zimmerman, John	140	LE
Zimmerman, Michl.	42	EH
Zimmerman, Michl. Est.	140	LE
Zinn, Geo.	93	LE
Zinn, George	109	LE
Zinn, George	140	LE
Zuber, Jacob	140	LE
Zuber, Jacob (2)	102	LE
Zweier, George	141	LE
Zweyer, George	141	LE